BUSINESS AND GOVERNMENT IN AMERICA SINCE 1870

A Twelve-Volume Anthology of Scholarly Articles

Series Editor

ROBERT F. HIMMELBERG
Fordham University

A GARLAND SERIES

SERIES CONTENTS

VOLUME

8

ANTITRUST AND BUSINESS REGULATION IN THE POSTWAR ERA 1946–1964

Edited with introductions by

ROBERT F. HIMMELBERG

GARLAND PUBLISHING, Inc.
New York & London
1994

Library of Congress Cataloging-in-Publication Data

Antitrust and business regulation in the postwar era, 1946–1964 /
edited with introductions by Robert F. Himmelberg.
     p.   cm. — (Business and government in America since
1870 ; v. 8)
    Includes bibliographical references.
    ISBN 0–8153–1410–8
    1. Trade regulation—United States—History.   2. Antitrust
law—United States—History.   3. United States—Economic
conditions—1945–   .   I. Himmelberg, Robert F.   II. Series.
HD3616.U46A77   1994
338.8'0973—dc20   93–47509
                                               CIP

Printed on acid-free, 250-year-life paper
Manufactured in the United States of America

CONTENTS

Series Introduction

This compilation of articles provides a very broad and representative selection of the scholarly literature found in learned journals on the subject of government-business relations in the age of industry, the period since 1870. The scope of this collection is wide, covering all the arenas of business-government interaction. Sectorially, the focus is on manufacturing and transportation, upon whose rapid expansion after the Civil War the modern industrial economy was founded.

For the volumes covering the years from 1870 to 1965 (Volumes I through IX) it has been possible, while exercising selectivity, to include a very high proportion of everything published within the past thirty years. This literature is found largely in historical journals. More selectivity had to be employed for Volumes X through XII, which cover the period since 1965. Historians have not yet trodden much on the ground of the very recent past but social scientists and legal scholars have offered abundant materials, so abundant as to require a relatively severe selectivity. By choosing articles that appear to have a long-term analytical value and by excluding those too narrow in scope, too preoccupied with methodological questions or otherwise unsuitable for a non-specialized audience, an extensive and accessible body of writing has, however, been assembled for the post-1965 period, mainly from economics and legal periodicals.

The volumes are designed to contain articles relating to a particular period and to one or more topics within a period. The literature of business-government relations has four logically distinct major topics: antitrust, regulation, promotion, and cooperation. These topics define distinctive aspects of the relationship. Yet, the distinctions sometimes in practice blur, the ostensible, publicly proclaimed purposes of policy sometimes differing from the actually intended purposes or the actual outcomes.

Antitrust policy emerges in Volume I, which covers the era 1870–1900 when big business appeared, and figures prominently throughout the series. Several volumes are devoted entirely to it. Uniquely American, at least until relatively recently, antitrust policy has a complex history and much of what scholars have discovered about its origin and evolution is recorded only in the articles gathered in this collection. The literature reproduced here makes clear that the intent and impact of antitrust policy has varied enormously during its one-hundred-year history, which dates from the Sherman Act of 1890. Tension between competing objectives has existed from the outset. Should the "trusts" be broken up on the grounds that super-corporations inevitably conflict with democratic government and entrepreneurial opportunity? Or should only "bad trusts", those guilty of crushing competitors through unfair methods, suffer dissolution? Is cartelistic behavior always an illegal restraint of trade, or should it sometimes be tolerated if it helps small business to survive? Put most broadly, should the aim of antitrust policy be simply promoting competition, or should other conflicting social and economic values be recognized?

Business regulation also arose during the early stages of industrialization, appearing at the federal level with the enactment of the Interstate Commerce Act in 1887. The term "regulation" is used here to denote government policies intended, not to promote or restore competition, but to require specific behavior from business. The classic justification for regulation was the argument that in some situations the public interest could be served only through governmental prescription, that in some instances a remedy simply could not be obtained through the workings of the marketplace. Theoretically there are two such instances. The first occurs in the case of "natural monopoly," market situations in which competition would be wasteful and competing firms do not and should not exist. Railroads and public utilities were early identified as industries of this sort and were the first targets of government regulation. Would-be regulators early discovered a second justification for applying the regulatory approach, the situation in which competition fails to provide rival firms with incentives to avoid methods that may injure public health or well being. The argument found early expression in regulation of the meat-packing industry and has over the course of the twentieth century created a remarkable body of federal regulatory practices. The history of regulation, however, has not unfolded, any more than the history of antitrust, according to the logic of theory. It has been determined by the interplay between many factors, including the ideas of reformers, the complaints of those who have felt injured, policy rivalries among businessmen themselves, and the capacity or incapacity of government to execute planned reform. A major focus of recent literature on regulation, and to an extent on antitrust also, is the thesis of capture, the notion that regulatory efforts have often fallen captive to the interests they were intended to oppose.

The third theme of relations between government and business, promotion and encouragement, also emerged during the initial stages of the industrial era. Railroad subsidies abounded during the age of building the transcontinentals, of course, and protective tariffs were almost as old as the Republic itself. In the early twentieth century government support of trade expansion abroad enlarged and gradually became a major thread of government policy. Resembling promotion but logically distinct in many respects is the fourth category of business-government interaction, the area of cooperative relationships. Few scholars, even those who believe ongoing conflict has chiefly characterized business-government relations, would deny that cooperation has occurred at certain points, as during American participation in the major wars of the twentieth century. But in recent years many writers who conceive of business-government relations as taking place within a "corporatist" framework have perceived the scope and continuity of cooperative tendencies as very broad.

These four categories describe the subjects or topics around which scholarly investigation of business-government relations has revolved. There is, however, another approach to analyzing the literature of this relationship, one in which we ask about a writer's interpretive perspective, the conceptualizations the writer brings to the subject. All historians and social scientists, including those who created the literature collected here, adopt an interpretive standpoint from which to view society and its workings. An interpretive standpoint is a way of understanding the structure of society and the way those structural elements relate and interact; in other words, it is a "model" of society. Several rival models have competed for acceptance among scholars in recent times. Readers will be better equipped for informed reading of the literature assembled in these volumes if they are knowledgeable about these interpretive standpoints and the aim here therefore is to define the most important of these and give them appropriate labels.

Until the 1950s the prevailing interpretation of business-government relations—indeed, of American history generally—was the progressive viewpoint. The term progressive refers in the first place to the reform ideology and activity of the early twentieth century, the period before World War I. The perspective of the progressive generation continued for many years to dominate historical writing, not only on the period itself but on the whole of American history. According to the progressive perspective, the rise of big business during the late nineteenth and early twentieth centuries created a radical shift in the balance of economic and political power in America in favor of concentrated wealth. The rise of the "trusts", the powerful firms that came to predominate in many industries in the years after 1880, and the creation of cartels and other arrangements for suppressing competition, threatened independent capitalists and consumers with raw economic exploitation. This concentration of economic power threatened to utterly suborn representative political institutions as well and reduce American democracy to a plutocracy. In the progressive view the predominating tone of business-government relations was therefore necessarily antagonistic and conflictual.

The progressive paradigm became deeply embedded in the American consciousness. Reformist politicians have often reverted to it in shaping their ideological and rhetorical appeals. Franklin D. Roosevelt's attack in the campaign of 1936 upon "economic royalists" and John Kennedy's denunciation in 1962 of Big Steel during the controversy over price guidelines as "utterly contemptuous of the public interest" are vivid examples. The progressive outlook is evidently a persistent element in the popular historical consciousness. The power of the progressive conception of American history is in fact readily confirmed by reference to the way twentieth-century history is periodized, in textbooks and popular histories, into epochs of reform (the Progressive, New Deal, Fair Deal and Great Society periods) and of reaction (the Twenties, the Eisenhower and Reagan eras).

But if the progressive interpretation of business government relations retains some force among some historians and in the consciousness of liberal opinion makers and the public, its hold on much of the academic mind has long since weakened. A reaction among historians and other academics against the progressive paradigm emerged soon after the end of the Second World War and gathered force during the 1950s. The reaction was especially sharp among historians writing business history. Writing at a time when a reinvigorated American economy appeared to have overcome the doldrums of the 1930s and to be demonstrating the superiority of capitalism over other systems, energetic business and economic historians completely revised the progressive interpretation of the founders of American big business. The revisionists interpreted the founders not as greedy robber barons but as heroes of the entrepreneurial spirit, the spirit of enterprise and productivity. This revisionist interpretation proved too one-dimensional and celebratory to be maintained without modification. Revisionism, however, did succeed in thoroughly discrediting the progressive point of view. This circumstance, together with the impact of interpretive concepts emanating from post-war social science, moved historians to replace the progressive paradigm with a new and more sophisticated framework for understanding American political economy, the pluralist framework.

Pluralism as the dominant interpretive mode replaced progressivism in the 1950s and 60s. Speaking broadly, the pluralist model understands public policy as the result of struggle between economic and social groups. A major by-product of industrialization is the sharpening of differences between groups playing distinctive economic roles and a heightened articulation of self-interested goals and purposes on the part of such groups. Thus, government-business relations, that is, the shape of government policies towards business, are the result of rivalries among the major interest groups, business, labor, consumers, and so on. But the nature of the struggle is complex because the major groups are themselves divided into more or less rivalrous sub-groups. Business itself is divided; both intra- and inter-industry rivalries exist, sometimes in acute forms. Government policy is not merely the result of nonbusiness groups seeking to shape that policy but also of some business interests seeking to impose their own wishes on others.

During the 1960s pluralist interpretation became more complex. One important source of this heightened complexity was what some commentators have called the "organizational" outlook. Again influenced by currents in American social science, this time sociology, practitioners employing the organizational perspective are struck by the ever-increasing importance of large bureaucratic organizations in American life since the onset of industrialization. Business has continuously evolved in terms of an ever larger role for the large corporation, but other spheres, including government and the professions, also are organized in terms of large hierarchical bureaucracies. Borrowing from Weberian sociological traditions, writers impressed by the organizational perspective have explored the thesis that large bureaucracies wherever situated have similar requirements and tend to develop in those who manage them similar values and expectations. Thus, this brand of pluralism stresses the extent to which group leaders, including the managers and technicians who run the large corporations, developed accommodative as well as merely self-seeking motives. Business leaders, many of them at least, came to share certain values, such as respect for stability in the overall economy, which leads them to seek harmonious and cooperative relationships between interest groups and between them and the government. Government is assigned the role, in this construct, of facilitating and stimulating cooperative modes of behavior and umpiring conflicts. In the literature on business and government, figures who have advocated this kind of polity are often dubbed "corporatists" or "corporate liberals." Broadly defined, corporatism is the practice of cooperation between government and the corporate world to resolve economic issues. The existence and the importance of corporatist relationships has been one of the major emphases of recent scholarship but there is much disagreement as to the intentions of its practitioners and its impact. Some scholars have interpreted corporatism in a more or less positive light, as an ideology and a practice entailing cooperation rather than conflict between government and business, as an alternative to an adversarial relationship, a way of obtaining desirable economic performance from business without resorting to governmental coercion.

But others, especially but not only those writing in the vein of the "New Left", have argued that members of the corporate elite have frequently pursued their own narrow interests under the cover of ostensibly cooperative endeavors. The New Leftists emerged in the 1960s, expounding a more radical criticism of business than the progressive-liberal historians had advanced. The New Leftists doubted or denied outright that the American system was pluralist at all in any meaningful sense. Control of public policy might appear as a contest between social groups, but in fact one group, or rather class, those who controlled big business, enjoyed such lopsided power that the contest was apparently not real. Behind the facade of political infighting over government policy toward business, the masters of the corporate world quietly steered events toward outcomes which cemented in place control of the economy by monopoly capital.

These four conceptualizations, the progressive, the pluralist, the corporatist, and the New Leftist, are essentially theories of the structure and process of American political economy. However, rarely are researchers slavishly devoted to a theoretical perspective. Thus, those who see, in the progressive vein, an ongoing conflictual relationship between the people and business sometimes argue against the reformers and in favor of the businessmen. Even more significant and widespread is the conclusion of many writers using the pluralist or corporatist modes of interpretation, that regulation has not fostered equity and economic progress but rather has hardened the economy's vital arteries. Pluralists initially assumed that policies arising from a political arena to which all organized interests have access will inevitably achieve benign results, that the policy outputs will construct a system of "countervailing power" among organized interest groups. The assumption of acceptable outcomes is still prevalent, but a skeptical version of the results of interest group rivalries became manifest in the late

1960s, holding that both in origin and ongoing impact, business regulation was too often subject to "capture." In this view, regulatory measures and agencies and other policies seeking to guide business behavior toward balanced and generally acceptable outcomes readily fall under the control of the very interests they were intended to regulate.

There has emerged in recent years still another approach to the origin and process of social-economic policy that has been applied to the business-government connection. In this interpretation of the connection, a few examples of which will be found in articles collected here, emphasis is placed on the relative autonomy of government administrators and regulators. Seen by the pluralists as merely the creatures of the organizational struggles that result in public policies, in this new view regulators are seen as possessing substantial room for independent action. Thus the state is not merely to be seen as a passive receptor and executor of outcomes that social forces determine but as having a partially autonomous role which the officers of the state presumably will use to extend their own interests rather than the interests articulated by social groups.

These categories, progressivism, pluralism, corporatism, Leftism and the "autonomous officialdom" viewpoint, represent the major schools of thought and interpretation that readers will discover in the literature reproduced in these volumes. Writers investigating specific historical incidents, trends or problems have, in most cases, written through the framework provided by one or another of these interpretive models. As an alert reader will discover, most writers do have certain assumptions about the structure and dynamics of social relationships, and these assumptions stem from one of the models that have been described.

Interpretation of the relationship between business and government in the age of industry has given rise to a literature that is large and complex. It presents a stimulating intellectual challenge and is certainly relevant for anyone seeking understanding of contemporary business-government relations and endeavoring to predict, or to shape, their future course.

INTRODUCTION

Published in 1956, C. Wright Mills' *The Power Elite* posited that a directorate of business, political and military leaders, interlocked in an unrestrained conspiracy, had usurped authority in America. Whether the scope of government-business cooperation was so extensive and tightly woven in postwar America as to match Mills' conception is taken up in Volume IX, the next volume in this series. The articles collected in this volume do, however, have relevance for testing the validity of the "military-industrial complex" thesis, for they explore the extent of the adversarial element in postwar business-government relations.

This adversarial relationship between government and business continued to find expression in traditional regulatory policies. The scope of regulation expanded during the postwar years, the most significant new field being oversight of the nuclear power industry. Perhaps the most important single episode in the regulatory history of this period was the debate within the Truman administration over how to meet the economic demands posed by the Korean War. Federal policy-makers had to decide whether to rely upon rapid industrial expansion or to adopt the economy-wide rationing and price regulation resorted to during the two world wars. But the most important expression of the adversarial element was the gradual development, begun under Truman and continuing under Eisenhower and Kennedy, of a much stricter antitrust policy, especially, but not only, with respect to mergers.

During the later years of the New Deal era the conviction developed within certain circles of policy-makers that full recovery from the depression required, not more toleration of the price stabilization attempted during the NRA experience, but a revival of competition. This conviction stemmed partly from traditional conceptions about the benefits of price competition, but partly too from newer influences, especially the prescription the English economist, John M. Keynes, was offering for economic revival, large-scale deficit spending. American Keynsians believed spending might be ineffective, or even inflationary, unless price-making was more flexible downward. President Roosevelt was persuaded to enlarge and reinvigorate the Antitrust Division of the Justice

Department. Meanwhile in Congress the advocates of renewed antitrust prosecution successfully proposed creation of the Temporary National Economic Committee to study the incidence and causes of monopoly power within the American industrial-financial system.

Revival of antitrust prosecution of cartel practices was one result of these initiatives. A second result, however, was the reopening of the old debate over big business, over the advisability of allowing big corporations to control large shares of an industry's output. In the context of the developing theory of oligopolitic markets, many economists now put forward the argument that economic concentration (control of the greater part of an industry's production by a few firms) inevitably reduced competition, even in the absence of explicit cartel agreements.

As in 1917–18, the need to secure business cooperation in mobilizing the economy for war production superseded other considerations during World War II. But the economic debates during the late New Deal had revived deeply embedded traditions within the Democratic party hostile to big business and committed to fostering entrepreneurial opportunity for small business. Harry Truman, the new Democratic president, was squarely within this tradition and was, moreover, plagued during the postwar years by recurring and severe inflationary pressures which, according to the new economic thought, were attributable in part to oligopolistic resistance to price competition.

Supported by Truman, Democratic veterans of the prewar drive against big business pushed through Congress the Celler-Kefauver Anti-Merger Act of 1951. The measure enabled the Justice Department and Federal Trade Commission to block horizontal mergers and thereby prevent increasing concentration of control within the nation's industries. During the Eisenhower and Kennedy years, the new law, vigorously enforced, prevented numerous horizontal mergers and, together with continuing prosecution of cartel practices, presumably maintained a more flexible and competitive economy than otherwise would have been the case.

Antitrust and Business Regulation in the Postwar Era 1946–1964

THE EMPEROR'S OLD CLOTHES:
III. THE FOLKLORE OF CAPITALISM
REVISITED

By THURMAN W. ARNOLD

THE *Folklore of Capitalism*, as I originally saw it in 1937, was written to describe the frustrating effects, in times of revolutionary change, of ideals and symbols inherited from a different past. It therefore may be useful to describe what has happened to our folklore in the quarter of a century since that book was published.

Since that time the greatest war in history has been fought. That war pulled us out of the stagnation of the depression. It forced us to utilize our industrial resources to the utmost and to expand them at a rate which would have been considered impossible twenty-five years ago. We came out of the war far richer in terms of real wealth, by which I mean productive capacity, than when we went in. We became the richest nation the world has ever known.

For a short time after that war we were a confident nation, sure of our destiny. We believed that we were at the beginning of a new age of world order based on fundamental principles acceptable to all civilized nations. The symbol of that belief was the United Nations, which represented world unity under a new kind of international law. The first step we took to dramatize the ideal of international law and order was the Nuremberg trials. The purpose of those trials was to establish a great legal precedent which would outlaw forever the kind of aggressive war Germany had forced on the Western world. And so the United States, England, and Russia set up a joint international tribunal to clothe the ideal of international order with a judicial opinion which would be a guide for the indefinite future. The Nuremberg verdict was designed to teach Germany a lesson it would never forget and to be a permanent warning to all future Hitlers that the new world would no longer put up with military aggression.

With the twin symbols—the United Nations, where international disputes were to be resolved, and the Nuremberg trials, establishing a new principle of international morality—we believed we had achieved an enduring foreign policy. The age-old dream of all utopians—that if we can get men to agree on a principle, institutions and social organizations will arise which will adhere to and carry out that principle—was the basis of short-lived optimism and confidence which followed the destruction of the German empire.

In saying this I do not mean to imply that the United Nations has not made a tremendous contribution to world order. It was the first formal recognition in our history that the industrial revolution of the twentieth century had created a world in which even a nation as large as the United States could no longer exist as an isolated economic or political unit. It would have been indeed a tragedy had the United States rejected the ideal of which the United Nations was a symbol. The significance of the United Nations was the fact that it marked the end of a century of isolationist thinking.

Nevertheless we expected too much of it. The apparent agreement between the Soviets and the Western democracies expressed in the Nuremberg trials, that international aggression was abolished as a matter of international law, coupled with a new organization designed to unite every nation in the world in a common humanitarian purpose, lulled us into a sense of false security. And so we cheerfully dismembered Germany into four zones, French, British, Russian, and American, so that all could be partners in eliminating the menace of another Hitler. To have established a corridor giving access to Berlin would have shown distrust of our Russian partner and disturbed that atmosphere of confidence and cooperation which was to remove the threat of future wars.

The disillusionment that followed the collapse of these shining symbols of peace and international morality gave rise to fears and anxieties about the stability of our own institutions at home which grew to a national neurosis. Somebody had to be blamed for our short period of amity with Russia. The idealistic attempt to establish in cooperation with Russia some sort of world order could only have been caused by the infiltration of local Communists into our own government. The idea spread over the entire nation that the American Communist Party, through devious and secret ways, had the potential power to overthrow the government of the United States. The real danger to our institutions was not Russian power abroad but Communist infiltration at home.

We became more afraid of ideas than realities. This fear increased in intensity as the cold war proceeded. It wasn't enough to discharge suspected persons from government service. A public badge of infamy had to be pinned on them. We had to celebrate our achievements in ridding the country of its internal dangers by a public ceremony. And so President Truman established a hierarchy of quasi-judicial institutions clothing the hunt for subversives with the sanctity of judicial process. It was in this atmosphere that Senator McCarthy rose to power and was able to dictate to the President who should be discharged and who should be retained. Any idea which did not conform to the McCarthy pattern was sufficient to destroy the career of a liberal in government if by some accident his name got into the files of a congressional committee.

It soon became apparent that there weren't enough Communists to keep the costly and rapidly expanding bureaucracy of security officers, hearing boards, and congressional committees supplied with victims. Most of the material they had to work on was hearsay and secret reports by professional informers. To use such material as evidence was contrary to every American ideal of a fair trial. Indeed, an American tribunal in Germany had convicted German judges on the ground that the use of secret evidence was an international crime.

But this ideal of a fair trial had to give way in order to keep the vast bureaucracy in business. And so it was determined that accused individuals could be convicted on secret evidence given by faceless informers whose identity was unknown to the accused.

Nor was the accused permitted to see and rebut the secret evidence given against him. This process tremendously enlarged the supply of game which the security system could track down and shoot. The Supreme Court of the United States gave its tacit approval to the use of this sort of evidence by affirming the conviction of Dorothy Bailey on secret evidence in a four-to-four decision. And from then on, for years, the most publicized policy of government was the rooting out of subversives in government and industry.

Our cold war with Russia assumed all of the aspects of the religious wars of the Reformation. Both the Soviets and the United States engaged in worldwide propaganda appealing to the hearts and souls of men to adopt the only true religion. The preaching of each side was as violent as any delivered during the Reformation. The only difference was that in the Reformation hell was in the next world. In the religious war of the twentieth century the respective hells of communism and capitalistic imperialism were in this world, just around the corner. Millions were spent by the United States on the Voice of America, and counter-millions were spent by Russia in jamming its broadcasts. And so for years we believed that our national salvation depended on preaching the glories of capitalism abroad and the rooting out of subversives at home. This is the kind of phenomenon which always occurs when a religious war is being fought.

Today we have fixed our attention on Russian power instead of internal subversion. Yet the essentially religious character of the cold war still continues. Neither Russia nor the United States is pursuing materialistic objectives. It is indeed a battle for the minds and hearts of men in which symbols are still more important than realities. For example, we have planted our flag in Berlin and are prepared to defend it even at the risk of an atomic war. Berlin is a symbol of the reunification of Germany. The ideological conflict could be resolved, at least with respect to that city, if the United States would recognize the legality of the East German government. Few intelligent men believe that as a practical matter reunification of Germany is even a remote possibility. Yet concessions by either side would be a moral victory for the other with far-reaching psychological consequences in Germany and Western Europe. When wars are fought over markets or for trade advantages they can be ended when they appear too costly. When they are fought for the minds and hearts of men, when it is a struggle between the Catholic and the Protestant churches, or between Communism and Capitalism, neither side can risk defeat on the issue of any symbol which dramatizes its faith. This is true even though defense of that symbol might possibly mean the extinction of half the human race. From a rational point of view this may seem like nonsense. From an anthropological point of view, however, we must recognize that such symbols as Berlin are the cement that holds Western society together, that holds the promise of unity, both political and economic, for Western nations. To abandon such a symbol might utterly defeat the brightest promise of the future. The risk must therefore be taken.

Out of this risk there is emerging a new ideal, and a new set of symbols. The European Common Market, which seemed completely utopian only a few years ago, has become a reality. An international court has been set up to adjudicate the trade practices of the citizens of independent sovereignties. An international code of antitrust laws after the American model has been enacted and is being enforced by the European international court. The United States and England are seeking to join that international economic union.

And here in the Western Hemisphere we have accepted the ideal of the economic unity of the United States and Latin America. That ideal has been embodied in an organization called the Alliance for Progress. The basic concept of that organization is expressed in a treaty by which the United States and Latin American nations committed themselves to an acceleration of economic growth, a more equitable distribution of the fruits of economic development, and recognized the need for tax, land, and institutional reform and new investment capital. In the language of the treaty of Punta del Este these nations and the United States agreed "to unite in a common effort to bring our people accelerated economic progress and broader social justice within the framework of personal dignity and political liberty."

These words could not have been written without a storm of outraged protest when *The Folklore of Capitalism* was published in 1937. No such treaty could possibly have been approved by the Senate of the United States at that time.

In those times Henry Wallace was being denounced as a man who wanted to give a bottle of milk to every Hottentot because of ideas which were insignificant in scope compared with the Alliance for Progress. And yet the Alliance for Progress, which goes further in assuming responsibility for the poverty and economic chaos of Latin American nations than anything Henry Wallace ever dreamed of, has become a political reality supported by liberals and conservatives alike.

Another tremendous change in our ideals and symbols that has taken place since that book was written is in our personification of great corporations as individuals. We no longer feel that government control of industry is something that will end in the destruction of individual liberty. My chapters on "The Personification of Corporations" and "The Ritual of Corporate Reorganization" are largely obsolete today. The amount of regulatory interference with business today which is represented by our vast government bureaus would have been unthinkable to a conservative in 1937. Now these tremendous bureaucratic hierarchies have lost their radical tinge. They have obtained an almost invulnerable place in the hierarchy of our institutions. Our courts, which before the great depression were accustomed to review decisions of administrative tribunals with meticulous care, now affirm them if there is the slightest supporting evidence.

The ideological doctrine which supports the immunity of our present administrative tribunals from judicial review is the theory that they are composed of experts in their particular narrow lines. Under the cloak of this doctrine many of the evils and oppressive bureaucratic practices which were protected by conservatives in 1937 have become a part of our administrative machinery. Yet so securely has our system of administrative tribunals become entrenched that there is no effective protest made today against bureaucratic aggression. This is indeed a revolutionary change since 1937 in our ideas of the proper function of government.

The chapter entitled "The Effect of the Antitrust Laws in Encouraging Large Combinations" needs comment in the light of what has happened since the book was published. That chapter was written after ten years of nonenforcement of the Sherman Act when the total appropriation for the Antitrust Division was less than $250,000. Today it is over $5 million. The decisions of the Supreme Court of the United States since 1937 have tremendously broadened the enforcement of antitrust policy. As Milton Handler said in a recent article: "In few areas of the law is a mature jurisprudence reinforced by so powerful an arsenal of investigative powers and remedies."

And even more astonishing from the point of view of one writing in 1937, when the ideal of the antitrust laws was recognized in no other country in the world except the United States, is the fact that the antitrust ideal has spread to Europe. The Treaty of Rome, which was the foundation of the present European Common Market, contains a set of antitrust rules which is now embodied in regulations and enforced by a supernational European court. The system of domestic and international cartels which in 1937 was legitimate in Europe is under heavy attack, though not completely abolished, in the European Common Market—a development no one would have dreamed of in 1937 before the Second World War.

In the field of monetary and fiscal policy, however, nineteenth-century economic symbols still cloud the realities of the twentieth-century industrial revolution and frustrate American economic progress. Just as during the depression we were unable to utilize our full productive capacity because of a lack of consumer purchasing power, so today we are still unable to utilize it for the same reason. Since 1953 our annual economic growth has not been enough to keep up with our tremendously increasing labor force. The top of every curve in the roller coaster of booms and depressions on which we have been riding since 1953 has shown greater unemployment than the top of the last curve. During this period of nearly ten years our economy has been stagnant and sluggish in growth. During the same period France, Germany, and Italy have been advancing, in terms of goods and services produced, more than twice as fast as we have. We are accumulating an increasing number of unemployed. During the same period France, Germany, and Italy have had an actual shortage of labor.

The actual cost in terms of goods and services resulting from our failure to utilize our full industrial capacity has been estimated by Leon Keyserling to amount to the stupendous sum of $387 billion from 1953 to the middle of 1962. This enormous wealth was available to us but we could not use it because there was not enough purchasing power in the United States economy to absorb the products which our industrial plant was able to produce.

And thus under the same economic symbols and rituals that we had during the great depression we are developing today the same symptoms that prolonged that depression. The only time we were free from the tyranny of these nineteenth-century economic images was during the Second World War. Then, for the first time since the depression began, we were able to use and to expand our production to the full limit of our industrial ability. As a result we came out of that war richer in our productive capacity than at any time before. But after the Second World War the old religion took over. Since 1953 we have been progressively slowing down and increasingly unable to sustain the economic growth necessary for full employment.

Today we write about ourselves as an affluent society. But in 1960 there were almost 10½ million families (households of two or more persons) with annual incomes of under $4,000 before taxes. This means that one family in every four was living in poverty in the United States in 1960. Out of this group of families with under $4,000 a year, over 3,000,000 were living in actual deprivation with incomes of under $2,000 a year, and as for the unattached individuals almost 4,000,000 had annual incomes of under $2,000. These figures are taken from Leon Keyserling's pamphlet *Poverty and Deprivation in the United States,* written for the Conference on Economic Progress. To sum up, Leon Keyserling concludes that there were living in poverty 34,000,-000 people in families and 4,000,000 unattached persons. There were living in deprivation 37,000,000 people in families and 2,000,000 unattached persons. This makes a total of 77,000,000 people who are unable to attain what we like to think of as an American standard of living. They are unable to buy the products of our industrial economy. As a result the nation has lost in goods and services a staggering total of $387 billion from 1953 to the middle of 1962.

Yet the *Wall Street Journal,* in a typical editorial (July 26, 1962) attacking government spending in a period when our industrial plant is 75 percent idle, says with absolute religious conviction: "There is no visible lack of purchasing power today."

Our failure to realize our economic potential has occurred during a period when Western Europe has no problem of unemployment and has been operating its industrial plant, in many ways superior to ours in efficiency, at full capacity. This is today a constant source of bewilderment to Europeans. After a recent visit to the United States, Gunnar Myrdal said that the stagnant condition of the American economy was a menace to the prosperity of the Western world. He regarded it as inexcusable for so rich a country as ours to have so many slums, obsolete houses, inadequate schools, and inadequate social services. He attributed it to the illiteracy of our economic thinking. When asked to comment on Myrdal's observations all President Kennedy could say was this: "Well, I think it is regrettable that we have not been able to develop an economic formula which maintains the growth of our economy. If we were moving ahead at full blast today, of course, you would have full employment."

In July, when the President made that comment, the rosy January predictions of his economic advisers had collapsed. The Gross National Product, though it was the highest in our country's history, was billions of dollars short of the January prediction. There had been no change whatever in the problem of unemployment.

The reason why no acceptable formula has been developed to achieve full utilization of the tremendously increased capacity of the twentieth-century industrial revolution is that the majority of our respectable and conservative citizens are still obsessed with the economic folklore of the nineteenth century.

That folklore consisted of a series of very simple mental pictures. The government was pictured as the thrifty head of the family who balances his budget and saves money for the future. If he does not do so he goes bankrupt and his children suffer. The national debt which had been constantly increasing since the First World War was a mortgage on the property of every citizen, which sooner or later would have to be paid by the next generation. Prosperity and full employment could only be forthcoming by balancing the national budget and taking the burden of taxation from the backs of our taxpayers. The money and credit necessary to operate our economy and full employment would then be produced by private industry and our economy would begin to grow and expand, as it did in the nineteenth century. The idea that government credit or government debt could be used to create the purchasing power necessary to distribute the products of the twentieth-century industrial revolution was unsound, radical, crackpot, dangerous, and subversive. It was leading us straight to socialism. Such was the economic folklore of 1962.

When the President said that we had been unable to develop an economic formula which would maintain the growth of our economy he meant that we had no such formula which was consistent with our theology of balancing the fiscal budget. It was an admission that there was no way under the folklore of capitalism existing in 1962 in which we could maintain full employment and full utilization of our resources. We had to go on losing about $10 billion in goods and services every year, which wealth we might have had had our folklore allowed us to distribute it. The principle of balancing the fiscal budget was so sacred that any other course was economic sin and would inevitably lead to some sort of unspecified economic or social hell.

It was not true that no formula had been developed to maintain economic growth. It was only true that no *respectable* formula had been developed. For years a group of economists led by Leon Keyserling had advocated balancing the economic budget rather than the fiscal budget. By this they meant that on one side of the balance sheet the President should estimate the productive capacities of our national industrial plants. On the other side there should be listed the demands on that productive capacity for necessities such as schools, public works, water conservation, health, and so on through a long list. Congress could then formulate programs which would not put an inflationary burden upon our productive capacity but at the same time would utilize it to its fullest extent. France has such a plan. Germany, though without a formal plan, has for years thought in terms of production rather than money. In other words, balancing the economic budget consists in the establishment of economic goals and the implementation of those goals by practical methods.

But the trouble with this practical approach to the problem of maintaining economic growth is that there is no automatic fiscal principle by which it can be carried out. Of course the practical ad hoc approach is the one we use in time of war. In the last war we were able to allocate production between the war effort and consumers' goods. We not only maintained our economic growth but expanded it tremendously. Indeed, it was only the enormous spending of the World War which pulled us out of the depression. We also have no difficulty in applying the concept of balancing the economic rather than the fiscal budget in our program for the Alliance for Progress among Latin American nations. Here economic goals are set. Economic planning is the key to the solution; the economic budget rather than the fiscal budget is the center of the program.

But the approach to the problem of economic growth which is possible in time of war, or is freely used in the Alliance for Progress, is as yet impossible in the domestic economy of the United States in time of peace. We are obsessed with the dream of an automatic economy which operates without planning, and the center of the whole thing is the balanced fiscal budget.

12

Given a balanced fiscal budget the private economy is supposed, through credit mechanisms which it creates without government interference, to supply the purchasing power to operate the industrial plant of the twentieth century at full capacity. The fact that it has not been able to do so since 1929 is in conflict with this theory and, therefore, is ignored because it is inconsistent with our folklore.

The central idea of the economic folklore which frustrates our ability to use the capacity of the modern industrial revolution may be expressed as follows: Private enterprise with its tremendous variety of credit devices is able to supply the purchasing power which will not only utilize our full productive capacity but enable it to expand. It is the duty of the government to prevent that expansion from proceeding too rapidly. The government performs that duty by balancing the budget.

This was true before the First World War. But since the end of the First World War it has become increasingly apparent that private credit mechanisms are not by themselves sufficient to distribute the tremendously increased industrial capacity created by the twentieth-century scientific revolution.

The persistence of the idea that through the expansion of private credit alone the economy of the twentieth-century revolution can grow and be utilized to its fullest capacity is illustrated by a recital of our popular economic thinking during the boom of the 'twenties and through the depression. Before the First World War sound economic opinion estimated that a national debt of $500 million was all that our economy could safely absorb. But during the war our national debt grew from less than one billion dollars to the incredible sum of $26 billion in 1919. We followed our accepted theory. The sole function of government was to balance the budget. The Republican Administration reduced the national debt in ten years by $9 billion, saving about a billion dollars a year.

Then came the crash of 1929 and the depression which followed. There was not enough purchasing power to begin to take up the productive capacity we had achieved. But our economic folklore prevented us from seeing this outstanding fact.

13

Roosevelt ran for office on the tried and true principle of balancing the budget. It was not lack of purchasing power but rather lack of business confidence that was supposed to be the cause of prolonging the great depression.

Roosevelt was forced to abandon his devotion to the principle of a balanced fiscal budget in favor of measures which were absolutely required to keep people from starving. He was bitterly attacked on the ground that these measures were leading to inflation and would inevitably result in the destruction of the capitalistic system. The fear of inflation haunted the business community throughout the entire depression in spite of the fact that a realistic appraisal clearly showed that the only thing we had to fear was continued deflation and a sluggish, nonexpanding economy.

In 1937 Roosevelt did succeed in balancing his cash budget, that is, in taking out of the economy more money than the government was putting in. There followed the recession of 1938. But that recession was still not attributed to lack of purchasing power. Conservative economists and bankers pointed out that it was due to lack of business confidence as a result of Roosevelt's attack on the Supreme Court.

The war pulled us out of the depression. It gave us the greatest industrial plant the world has ever known. In spite of gloomy predictions to the contrary which were made by conservatives at the end of the Second World War the country enjoyed an unprecedented boom. Then in 1953 the conservative Republican Party took over, determined to combat inflation and to balance the national budget, and finally to stop inflation by stopping the money supply.

But it soon appeared that the program was impossible. The failure of the conservatives in power has been described by Edwin Dale, Jr., financial editor of the *New York Times*, in a brilliant book, *Conservatives in Power: A Study in Frustration* (Doubleday, 1960):

After five years of trying, the regime had produced (or found itself with), in fiscal 1959, the biggest budget deficit in peacetime history and the first really serious wave of "inflationary psychology" in modern times.

The only answer seemed to be more conservative than ever. Squeeze the budget—Russian challenge and depressing slums and dirty streams to the contrary notwithstanding. Stretch out the national debt at every opportunity—at the risk of even more uncertainty in the bond markets. Keep money tight and interest rates high—even with nearly five million people out of work in the winter of 1958-59. Keep trying to return functions to the states to relieve federal finance—even with the State of Michigan so tightly pinched for money that it had to appeal to large corporate taxpayers to pay in advance.

And given their view of the world and the dollar, the conservatives were right. The only cure for the disease was a stronger dose of the familiar medicine.

And so Eisenhower achieved through his budget-balancing policies the greatest peacetime deficit in our history and the greatest peacetime inflation.

The real difficulty is that we have failed to realize the tremendous productive capacity of the twentieth-century scientific revolution. That capacity is so great that the credit mechanisms invented by the private sector of the economy cannot fully employ it. Those credit mechanisms, which we will call the private printing of money, have never before in our history pumped as much money into the nation's purchasing power. The automobile companies print the money for even the lowest income groups to buy cars. FHA prints the money for private organizations to build houses. Never before in our history has the down payment on houses been so little or the mortgages so long that they outlast the houses themselves. Almost anyone can get an unlimited letter of credit for travel by joining something like the Diners' Club. Department stores are printing the money their customers use to buy goods through revolving credit accounts and whatnot. No one has to pay cash for anything but food. In fact, anything which can be capitalized and on which a dollar income may be attributed can be financed. And this financing, though fantastically unsound according to nineteenth-century standards, is actually working. It is a new type of currency based on faith that the consumer will have a job and pay the installments on his debt. And by and large that faith has been justified.

15

But this new reservoir of credit, vast as it is, has only kept our industrial plant running since 1953 at about 75 percent of its capacity and $10 billion a year in goods and services has been lost. We are as yet unable to think of our national wealth in terms of productive capacity. We are unable to utilize that productive capacity for pressing national needs such as schools, health, and education because it would unbalance the fiscal budget.

The Potomac River is a good illustration of this folklore. It is an open sewer. A vast recreation area badly needed has gone to waste. The more the sludge accumulates the greater will be the burden on posterity. We have the productive capacity to clean up this river and all the other rivers. But we cannot do so because it would be an intolerable burden on our taxpayers. According to our folklore there is only one economic situation which would justify cleaning up the Potomac, and that is if Washington, D. C., became a depressed area. In that case, perhaps, we might clean it up, not because the job itself was worthwhile doing but because the expenditures might prime the pump and get Washington on its economic feet again. But until Washington becomes a depressed area it is better to let the Potomac fill up with sludge so that it will remain a handy way of priming the pump in the future.

There seems no way, according to our present folklore of capitalism, to utilize our productive capacity to clean up the Potomac because it is a very necessary thing to do with respect to the health and recreation of our nation's capital.

In the nineteenth century our productive capacity was not enough for such public projects. To have engaged in them might have been inflationary. Today, when our productive capacity is so great that only 75 percent of it can be absorbed by the purchasing power created by private credit, we still consider it inflationary to utilize that capacity. We cannot accept as a rational plan for ourselves the basic formula which even the conservatives have been willing to accept for Latin America.

And thus the old folklore of capitalism which I attempted to describe in my book of a quarter-century ago still frustrates our economic growth. The fact that Western European economies are not so frustrated is a continuing source of bewilderment to us. We are at present sending economists to Western Europe to find out why those countries have no unemployment and are moving ahead at more than double our speed. I suggest that nothing will come of such economic inquiries. Each inquiring economist will look at Western Europe through the spectacles of a preconceived theory. He will then disregard all the facts which do not fit in with that theory. Finally he will come back with the report that the lesson we must learn from the booming economies of Western Europe is to balance our fiscal budget at home. Many reports of this character are already being published in our conservative journals. To paraphrase Karl Marx, "Economic theology is the opiate of the middle classes."

Each year more and more goods can be produced with less and less labor. For the past ten years we have been able to use only about 75 percent of what we can produce. As a practical matter it would not be difficult to avail ourselves of that unused production. As an ideological matter it is a present impossibility to carry on the public works and services which our economy could so easily afford. This is because private money and credit are not available for such things as conservation of our water supply, our health, our recreational facilities, and so on through a long list of public necessities. Things which cannot be bought and sold for dollars on the marketplace cannot be financed by private credit. Therefore, we must do without them even though this means a colossal waste of our real productive resources.

If it were just a matter of wasting resources perhaps we could live with it. The nineteenth century was an era of colossal waste. But the present industrial revolution is gradually destroying the purchasing power necessary to distribute its productive ability. This is in spite of fantastic credit schemes which provide private credit that a nineteenth-century banker would consider insane. And so the backlog of unemployment grows as our labor force increases. A new phrase has become part of our economic vocabulary, "structural unemployment." It means

17

that an incredibly rich country can find no ideological way of providing its citizens with the standard of living which it is physically capable of giving them.

The problem is a psychological one, not to be solved by either preaching or learning. It involves a recognition that things without a dollar value on the marketplace are nevertheless national assets of incalculable value. A trained scientist, engineer, or physician is an asset. The university that trains him is as valuable to our economy as a General Motors plant. An unskilled laborer, or an unemployed person, is a liability. A public debt owed by a nation to its own citizens is not a mortgage which their children must pay off. The building of necessary public works is an asset both for the present and the future.

It is this central idea that gives the Russian economy such strength as it has. It is the rigid and inflexible philosophy that such assets cannot be built or maintained by private enterprise that is the principal weakness of Russia. Budgets of course have to be balanced. But the budget of the twentieth century is a balance between productive capacity and the effective demands which are made on that capacity. When those notions become part of our folklore of capitalism the only limit on American progress will be the extent to which modern science can expand productive capacity.

How will this change come about? I expect that the process of the adjustment of inherited economic images to the reality of the vast potential productive capacity of the twentieth century may turn out to be as painful as it was during the great depression when we finally became acclimated to social security, unemployment relief, guarantee of bank deposits, the TVA, control of security markets, and so on through a long list of changes for which Roosevelt was so bitterly denounced. Basic economic beliefs are religious in character. We are struggling today through a period more like the period of the Reformation than any other period in history, but the frustrating effects of religious economic beliefs can be overcome, and in a period of revolutionary change they must be.

Delivering the Goods by Air: The United States Air-Cargo Industry, 1945-1955

John C. Bishop
Auburn University

ABSTRACT

The years 1945 to 1955 brought the beginnings of the American air-cargo industry. The origins of the leading all-cargo airlines are studied against the background of a postwar economy and a confusing regulatory system. The role of the CAB in shaping the new industry is emphasized.

The rapid and extensive development of aviation during World War II precipitated similar expansion of the United States air-cargo industry in the decade after 1945. The war left a legacy of proven aircraft, qualified pilots, and pent-up demand for goods and services. The fledgling industry also inherited competition from established land and water transportation systems, an uncertain government policy on regulating public service enterprises, and entrepreneurs with more enthusiasm than business experience.[1]

Cargo-flying experience was not in short supply. The Air Transport Command (ATC) and the Navy Air Transport Service (NATS) trained many of the leaders in the postwar civilian air-cargo industry. During World War II the ATC and NATS logged almost 2 billion miles ferrying aircraft and transporting personnel, munitions, and mail.[2]

Passenger airlines began flying cargo as early as 1944. American Airlines filed the first schedule of tariff rates for air cargo with the Civil Aeronautics Board (CAB) in 1944 and began its transcontinental DC-3 service on October 15, 1944. Transcontinental and Western Airlines (TWA) initiated transcontinental operations on July 1, 1945. United Airlines followed suit on February 1, 1946. Delta Airlines cultivated the regional market for air freight. By November 1944, Delta's Air-Cargo

40

Department, under the direction of Paul Pate, was successfully transporting perishable products like newspapers, shrimp, and plants--tomato plants from Tifton, GA, to Bowling Green, OH, for example.[3]

After the war, new airlines were established, and existing companies requested that the CAB control competition between conventional air carriers and the new all-cargo lines. Before regulation was begun, however, airfreight rates per ton-mile plummeted. United began flying cargo coast-to-coast in 1946 at 26.5 cents a ton-mile. A year later United's rate was 14 cents and American's was 11 cents.[4]

The fall in shipping rates was a market reaction to competitive conditions. Falling prices do not always reflect a rate war. The addition of new firms and the expansion of existing firms are normal in a market that generates economic profits--profits above the minimum the market must provide to continue the service. Firms competing for business lower their prices unless they can attract customers in other ways. Regulation is simpler than competition: by restricting entry of new firms into the market and limiting expansion of existing firms regulation can make price reductions unnecessary.[5]

The CAB estimated domestic demand for airfreight at a billion ton-miles annually for the years following World War II. As late as 1955 the total airfreight flown in the United States had not surpassed 300 million ton-miles. The following statement from the CAB illuminates the agency's role in limiting the development of the air-cargo industry:

> In deciding the present case we have not been unmindful of the foregoing principles. The certification of unsubsidized all-cargo carriers will require such carriers to bend all their efforts and to direct their abili- ties and skill to the full development of the airfreight potential. Such carriers will not be able to rely on passenger operations or mail payments to furnish the greater portion of their revenues. They will live and prosper only through their ability to develop an economic business and by constant search for new techniques, new business, and new equipment. To the extent that they succeed in such endeavors they will, by their example, benefit the presently certified carriers and air transportation as a whole; and new methods, equipment and managerial improvements will be made available to the entire industry. Thus, the cargo carriers will provide a valuable yardstick for measuring the alertness and efficiency of other carriers of cargo.[6]

The CAB expected all-cargo carriers to compete with existing certificated carriers and to adapt to a changing industry. Rates, routes, and ground service changes that were advantageous in the short run were outmoded by the time the all-cargo carriers received CAB permission to

41

21

adopt them. Furthermore, innovations produced by the all-cargo carriers were to be passed on free of charge to the passenger carriers.[7]

The U.S. Navy-Slick Airways charter service of 1951 is an example of a successful all-cargo operation. It was a fixed cost operation: the Navy paid the same fee whether or not the planes were full. The system was cheaper and more efficient than rail or truck transport. In April 1951, the air ton-mile cost to the Navy averaged 11.2 cents and the rail express ton-mile cost averaged 13 cents. This successful arrangement was built around high-load factors and high rates of aircraft utilization, and provided substantial savings to the Navy and profits to Slick. The Navy played the role of a freight forwarder, keeping the planes full and the flow of cargo steady. Although an isolated example, the Navy-Slick arrangement might have encouraged air-cargo development had the CAB permitted its extension to commercial enterprise.[8]

The CAB took a position on the origin of all-cargo freight:

> In view of the size of that potential, as reasonably estimated on the present record, there is no reason to believe that, if a limited number of all-cargo carriers which are now operating should be certificated, they will continue to develop their traffic from the cargo potential rather than by diversion from the certificated carriers. We are unable to accept the conclusion, therefore, that the certification of a few exclusive cargo carriers as a means of promoting and developing air traffic from the large airfreight potential would inflict a destructive diversion upon the existing certificated carriers. Any such conclusion would be at war with the facts of the present record, and could not qualify as a basis for the informed judgement which is expected of an administrative body charged with the important responsibilities which have been delegated to this Board.[9]

If CAB's estimate of one billion ton-miles of potential traffic annually was reasonable, what purpose aside from safety regulation could the agency's intervention serve?[10]

The CAB issued Economic Regulation 292.5 on May 5, 1947, and under it granted common carrier certificates to fourteen all-cargo firms. Only six survived until January 1949. In an attempt to strengthen Regulation 292.5, the CAB issued the Minimum Rate Order of July 1, 1948. The order set a fixed rate of 16 cents per ton-mile for the first 1,000 miles and 13 cents for each additional ton-mile. These rates were increased to 20 cents and 16.25 cents on September 21, 1953. The CAB rates were minimums, not maximums, and they became a price floor for air-cargo service.[11]

On April 24, 1949, the CAB designated four airlines to hold five-year, scheduled air certificates on an experimental basis. These were Slick

42

Airways, Flying Tiger Line, U.S. Airlines, and Airnews.[12] U.S. Airlines survived the 1945-47 rate cuts by subcontracting its business to other carriers. It resumed operations after the Minimum Rate Order and continued until the CAB withdrew its certificate on April 27, 1955. The firm's financial difficulties coupled with aircraft losses to force the CAB withdrawal.[13]

Airnews served fifty-six South Texas cities with two DC-3s that flew between San Antonio and Corpus Christi. The line was distinguished by its use of trucks to complement the planes. Unfortunately Airnews was unable to overcome chronic undercapitalization and voluntarily surrendered its certificate on October 12, 1951.[14]

At the age of twenty-five, Earl F. Slick, a former Yale University student and veteran of the ATC, founded Slick Airways in January 1946. Slick drew on his family's oil fortune to establish and fund his company. He began operation with ten Curtiss C-46Es. Close attention to costs paid off, and by 1951 Slick's was the leading cargo airline. In that year Slick Airways became the first firm to use Douglas DC-6As, one of the first four-engine aircrafts designed for cargo. After 1951 the firm suffered reverses in competing with the passenger carriers, especially American Airlines. On March 26, 1953, Slick agreed to merge with the Flying Tiger Line. The merger did not materialize for a variety of reasons, including problems in transferring pilot seniority.[15]

The strongest of the original four all-cargo firms was the Flying Tiger Line. Founded as the National Skyway Freight Corporation on June 25, 1945, Flying Tiger was the brainchild of Robert W. Prescott and the beneficiary of funding from Sam Mosher of Signal Oil. The thirty-two-year-old Prescott was a six-kill ace who flew with General Claire Chennault's Flying Tigers in China. He flew for Transcontinental and Western Airlines in 1942-43 and for China National Aviation Corporation in 1943-44. Although Flying Tiger got underway with stainless steel Budd RB-1 Conestogas, it moved to Douglas C-47s, Douglas C-54s, Curtiss C-46s, Douglas DC-6As, and Lockheed L.1049H Super Constellation freighters. The firm's early financial success came from a contract with ATC to provide crews and logistical support for that organization's thirty-two Douglas C-54s.[16]

Two other cargo airlines were financial successes in the first ten years after World War II. Riddle Airlines, later Airlift International, was incorporated in May 1945. It discontinued operations in 1947 because of CAB regulations, but was granted a temporary authorization in 1951 for a freight route to Puerto Rico. Authorization was expanded in 1955 to include a Florida service from Chicago, Detroit, Boston, and New York. Seaboard & Western Airlines (SWA), founded on September 16, 1946, was primarily an international carrier. The adoption of C-54s supported its move from an irregular carrier in 1947 to a fully certified, scheduled carrier in 1955. The financial success of SWA was linked to contracts with the International Relief Organization and the United States military.[17]

43

Air transport is best suited for carrying goods that are price inelastic in demand--a given percentage increase in price leads to a smaller percentage decline in sales. The time required to attain a good frequently influences its price elasticity. For example, an East Coast firm buying a machine part for inventory is unlikely to pay high airfreight rates to have it shipped from California. But if the part is needed to get an expensive piece of machinery into operation, the firm will pay more for the transportation, even if carrying costs exceed the price of the part. Further- more, the firm might find that the availability of airfreight sufficiently reduces the investment required for inventories to make air transport a viable alternative to lower-cost ground transport. Time influences the market for many items, including drugs, fruits and vegetables, meat, printed matter, nursery stock, and seafood.[18]

The ground transport industries were not concerned with the loss of high-bulk freight to the airlines, of course. The low-bulk items of high value and strong demand, however, support high freight rates and are thus coveted by carriers. The railroads began taking those goods from maritime shippers in the mid-1840s; the airlines began taking them from the railroads in the mid-1940s. The first ten years of airfreight proved that the market was sufficiently robust to support the cargo business of not only the passenger airlines but several all-cargo carriers as well.[19]

NOTES

The author acknowledges the help received on this project from W. David Lewis, Hudson Professor of History and Engineering, Auburn University.

1. "Air Freight Case," *Civil Aeronautics Board Reports* (July 1949): 572-646; "Railroads Move to Put CAA, CAB Under ICC," *American Aviation* (October 1945): 40; "Air Freight Rate Investigation," *Civil Aeronautics Board Reports* (July 1949): 340-362.
2. Oliver La Forge, *The Eagle in the Egg* (New York: Arno Press, 1972), 165-175.
3. R.E.G. Davies, *Airlines of the United States Since 1914* (London: Putnam, 1972), 424-425; W. David Lewis and Wesley P. Newton, *Delta: The History of an Airline* (Athens: University of Georgia Press, 1979), 102-103; "Air Cargo Anniversary," *New York Times* (October 15, 1949): 31; "Air Freight Case," 578.
4. Davies, *Airlines*, 425-427; "American, UAL Plan 25% Freight Rate Cut," *American Aviation* (June 1947): 17; "CAB Orders Cargo Rate Probe But Refuses to Suspend Tariffs," *Aviation Week* (October 1947): 53; "Air Freight Rates Cut," *New York Times* (February 25, 1950): 29; "Rank Cargo Carriers on Their Own," *Aviation Week* (April 1946): 41-43.
5. George Stigler, "The Theory of Economic Regulation," *Bell Journal of Economics* (1971): 1-18; "No End in Sight for Cargo Fight," *Aviation Week* (November 1948): 32-33; "CAB Reverses Self on Pay to Airlines," *New York Times* (May 18, 1949): 4; "'Regulars' Losing in Air Cargo Race," *New York Times* (March 29, 1948): 39.

44

6. "Air Freight Case," 581-589; Howard Lewis and James Culliton, *The Role of Air Freight in Physical Distribution* (Boston: Harvard University Press, 1956), 55.

7. "Air Freight Case," 589.

8. "Profitable Cargo at 11 Cents a Ton Mile!" *Aviation Week* (June 1951): 12-13.

9. "Air Freight Case," 586.

10. "Air Freight Case, 586.

11. Davies, *Airlines*, 427; Daniel S. Wentz, "Freight 'Rate War' Ends as CAB Sets Minimums," *American Aviation* (May 1948): 13; "CAB Sets First Floor for Air Freight Rates," *New York Times* (April 23, 1948): 47.

12. Davies, *Airlines*, 427-428; "Four All-Cargo Carriers Win 5-Year CAB Approval," *American Aviation* (May 1949): 14-15; "Rich Cargo," *Time* (May 1949): 8-9; "CAB Sets Up Airfreight Route Pattern," *Aviation Week* (May 1949): 12-13; "First 4 Cargo Airlines Chartered; CAB Lists New York as Terminal," *New York Times* (April 30, 1949): 1; "Three Air-Cargo Lines Get U.S.-Wide Runs in Federal Order for National 'Pattern'," *New York Times* (August 3, 1949): 45; "Air Freight Case," 597-609.

13. Davies, *Airlines*, 427-428.

14. Davies, *Airlines*, 427; "Air Freight Case," 597-609.

15. Davies, *Airlines*, 428-431; "Slick Airways Flies 5 C-46s, Awaits Conversion of 5 More," *American Aviation* (April 1946): 22; "Slick Airways," *Fortune* (July 1950): 70-75; "Flying Tiger Line, Slick Would Drop Merger," *New York Times* (September 22, 1954): 59; "Air Freight Case," 637-638.

16. Davies, *Airlines*, 431-437; "Air Freight Case," 635-636.

17. Davies, *Airlines*, 437-443; "Riddle Cashing in on Airfreight," *Aviation Week* (July 1954): 64-65.

18. Roger Leroy Miller, *Intermediate Microeconomics* (New York: McGraw-Hill, 1982), 200-250; John Frederick, *Commercial Air Transportation* (Homewood: Irwin, 1955), 432-438; James Haggerty, "Berlin Air Lift Tops Cargo Volume of All U.S. Airlines," *American Aviation* (December 1948): 11-12; "Greater Use of Airlines in State Held Possible," *New York Times* (September 8, 1952): 32; "Air Freight Case," 580.

19. Frederick, *Commercial*, 432-438; "Air Freight Case," 583.

45

Guns and Butter: The Pre-Korean War Dispute Over Budget Allocations:

Nourse's Conservative Keynesianism Loses Favor Against Keyserling's Economic Expansion Plan

By Lester H. Brune*

ABSTRACT. Focusing on the disagreement between *Edwin Nourse* and *Leon Keyserling*, two members of the first *Council of Economic Advisers*, the *Truman Administration's* gradual shift from Nourse's belief that a choice had to be made between *"guns or butter"* and Keyserling's claim that an expanding *economy* permitted large *defense expenditures* without sacrificing an increased standard of living is explained. In 1949, when Keyserling gained support from such presidential friends as *Dean Acheson* and *Clark Clifford* and persuaded the President, Nourse resigned as CEA Chairman, warning about the dangers of *budget deficits* and increased funding of "wasteful" defense costs. Keyserling succeeded to the chairmanship. He influenced Truman's *Fair Deal* proposals and the economic sections of *National Security Council* resolution 68 which, in April, 1950, asserted that the larger *armed forces* America needed would not affect *living standards* or risk the "transformation of the free character of our economy."

I

Introduction

SINCE 1950, "GUNS AND BUTTER" has become an axiomatic economic assumption by which the American public and its politicians justify obtaining the highest degree of military security without sacrificing the middle class welfare programs which provide high living standards. Politicians from Eisenhower to Reagan debate the proper proportions of guns relative to butter but do not question the presumption that the nation's economy can support both. The once traditional policy that nations must choose between "guns *or* butter" is almost forgotten.

Although some members of President Dwight D. Eisenhower's cabinet agonized over choices between guns or butter, the message that the nation could afford both developed in 1949, gained credence during the Korean War and suited well politicians who could campaign on the dual platform of protection from the communist menace without any burden or sacrifice on the part of

* [Lester H. Brune, Ph.D., is Oglesby Professor of American Heritage in the department of history, Bradley University, Peoria, IL 61625.] Research for this paper was assisted by a grant from the Harry S. Truman Foundation.

American Journal of Economics and Sociology, Vol. 48, No. 3 (July, 1989).

American citizens. Thus, advocates of guns *and* butter provided corporate liberals with political economic concepts which promoted social harmony at home and American military leadership of international capitalism's struggle against communism.[1]

The shift in the national outlook from the traditional choice of guns *or* butter to the contemporary belief in guns *and* butter originated in the pre-Korean years when the Truman Administration generated exaggerated fears of the communist threat while advocating the Fair Deal expansion of New Deal legislation. Although various individuals and groups played roles in this change of American political economic attitudes, this paper will focus on two members of the first Council of Economic Advisers (CEA) whose policy differences represented the alternative economic perspectives facing the nation: Edwin G. Nourse and Leon Keyserling.

II

The Shift from Conservative Keynesianism

NOURSE, THE FIRST CEA CHAIRMAN, was a highly respected insider among professional economists who boasted of being outside political circles. A former president of the American Economic Association, he had worked at the Brookings Institute as a specialist in agricultural economics. He applied Keynesian views to agricultural problems but was a conservative Keynesian who retained some classical views such as a balanced budget and the wastefulness of war. Nourse believed economists were scientists who should stay aloof from the political scene. Except for a brief period after he resigned as CEA Chairman and began to speak and write against "guns *and* butter" policies, Nourse maintained his political non-involvement.[2]

Representing the shift to new economic policies was the Vice Chairman of the first CEA, Leon Keyserling. In contrast to Nourse, Keyserling was an outsider in economic circles having never completed his doctoral dissertation because he went to Washington in 1933 where he became a confidant of Senator Robert Wagner and, later, an official of the National Housing Agency. In 1946, Keyserling became a member of the Wardman Park Hotel group, a coterie of Democratic Party liberals who influenced Harry Truman to accept the Fair Deal. Although he eschewed connections with Keynesians, Keyserling's advocacy of expansionist government economic policies accorded with the views of American Keynesians such as Alvin Hansen who accepted budget deficits to promote the economic growth of a healthy national economy.[3]

Thus, while Nourse and Keyserling each accepted John Maynard Keynes' concept of complementary action by government and business to promote economic soundness, they held divergent views on balanced budgets, causes of inflation, and especially the necessity of keeping peacetime defense costs low in order to maintain a sound, prosperous nation. Their differences became evident between 1948 and 1950 when the Truman Administration changed its program from demobilizing the armed forces and consolidating the New Deal programs to the Cold War confrontation of the Soviet Union and Fair Deal expansion of Franklin Roosevelt's programs.

Truman's decision to confront the alleged Soviet threat is generally better known than his acceptance of Fair Deal plans. A series of international events evolved into Cold War containment policies by 1950: the Truman Doctrine to aid Greece and Turkey, the Marshall Plan to reconstruct Western Europe, the communist coup in Czechoslovakia, the Berlin Blockade and formation of NATO and, most critical in 1949, the communist victory in China's civil war and the Soviet Union's successful test of an atomic bomb. These events eventually led Truman's National Security Council advisers to conclude in NSC-68 of April 1950 that the communist menace required a massive American military program in addition to the economic, political and military aid it had been supplying to the "free world."[4]

III

Truman's Fair Deal Program

THE SUCCESSFUL EFFORTS of the Wardman Park group in formulating Truman's Fair Deal program received less publicity than world events. Truman had been a "middle-way" Democrat as a senator and upon becoming president in 1945. This meant his economic ideas sometimes agreed with liberals like Senator Robert Wagner and sometimes with southern conservatives such as James Byrnes.[5]

Following the Republicans' congressional victory in 1946, a group of non-cabinet level Democrats began weekly meetings at the Wardman Park Hotel in order to coordinate efforts to encourage Truman to expand New Deal programs as the best way for winning reelection in 1948. Known as the Wardman Park or Ewing group for Oscar Ewing, Director of the Federal Security Agency, the group members with most direct access to the White House were Leon Keyserling and Clark Clifford, the presidential counselor. Appealing to Truman's humanitarian side, this group persuaded the President to veto the Taft-Hartley labor law in 1947 and to challenge Republicans by adopting the Fair Deal program.[6]

Truman accepted a broader domestic program more quickly than the large defense budgets which the Joint Chiefs of Staff desired. Believing in 1946 and 1947 that national prosperity precluded large defense budgets, Truman unified the armed forces in order to economize on defense and used economic aid to

29

Europe as the best means for building strong non-communist nations abroad.[7] Subsequently, at the end of 1948, Truman's post-war reconversion policies had performed remarkably well. Inflation was at 3%, gross national product had increased by 11.1%; unemployment ranged between 3 to 3.3%; and there was a budget surplus of $8.3 million.[8]

The first signs of the guns-butter dispute appeared in March 1948, when the Czechoslovakian crisis and the forewarnings of the Berlin blockade led Truman to obtain a $3 billion supplemental appropriation for the Pentagon. Neither Truman nor CEA Chairman Nourse thought this $3 billion would upset the "sound economy" but they soon discovered they had opened the door to greater military demands. Looking ahead to budgets beyond 1948, Truman insisted on a maximum defense budget of $15 billion for fiscal 1950, but the Joint Chiefs of Staff claimed the military additions of 1948 necessitated larger defense budgets of $18 billion or more by 1950 in order to sustain the 1948 increase. Truman and the Director of the Budget Frank Pace insisted on the maximum of $15 billion in 1950, a decision which caused the Navy and Air Force to scramble for more funds and stimulated an inter-administration conflict which NSC-68 hoped to resolve when it was prepared in April 1950.[9]

IV

Nourse Campaigns for Guns *or* Butter

IN 1948, HOWEVER, CEA Chairman Nourse began efforts to explain to the groups involved in the budget process that choices had to be made between guns or butter; that is between a sound domestic economy or "wasteful" expenses on the military. Soon after Truman asked Congress for the $3 billion supplement, a quarterly memorandum of the CEA warned that two points should be made clear to the military officers and the public. First, although present sound economic conditions would not cause the $3 billion to "swamp the economy," larger defense expenditures did require "systematic and vigorous discipline" in directing the nation's economy. Secondly,

> "Every citizen must recognize [the memorandum read] that further diversion of productive effort to military uses inevitably involves some sacrifice of civilian types of consumption. It is our particular application of the old alternatives of 'guns or butter.' All groups must share in the common burden of protecting our country. These economic facts of life should be proclaimed in working out the practical details of the defense program."[10]

Nourse's prescriptions of "vigorous discipline" and "sacrifice to share the burden" were not attractive political slogans. Consequently, throughout 1948 and 1949 Nourse's alarm increased because the Joint Chiefs of Staff interpreted the $15 billion not as a ceiling but as the bottom of an escalator rising to $18, $23 or $30 billion plus an estimated $17 to 22.9 billion for allocations of strategic materials and greater foreign economic and military aid for Europe. The Joint Chiefs of Staff argued that the Truman Administration's international commitments required larger budgets for the "balanced forces" of the Army, Navy and Air Force.

At the urging of Secretary of Defense James Forrestal, Nourse undertook speaking engagements before public audiences and private military groups seeking to educate them about the long-term negative effects of large peacetime defense expenditures. His efforts matched the forebodings of conservative groups such as the Eberstadt Committee of the Hoover Commission which claimed there was a Soviet communist plot to bankrupt America, a perspective shared by Forrestal.[11]

Nourse's analysis of the guns *or* butter issue was more sophisticated than that of the Eberstadt group. Emphasizing that all nations had limited economic resources, he argued that military demands required economic trade-offs which lowered domestic productivity. Addressing a Joint Conference of the Military Establishment on November 10, 1948, Nourse described four effects on business of large defense costs.

First, inflation—inflationary spirals resulted from large defense costs because the military competed with consumers for scarce resources. Raising taxes and higher interest rates for savings might offset inflation but high prices would raise defense costs further.

Second, shortages—there would be shortages of men and materials as defense projects diverted up to two million skilled workers and as more manufacturing and mining went to military machinery.

Thirdly, controls—government controls of strategic materials, wages, and prices, would be needed even for partial mobilization. This would "force us out of the free market procedures of a peacetime economy. . . ."

Finally, delayed domestic needs—peacetime economic objectives of the government would again be deferred as they were during World War II. This would threaten the nation's educational interests as well as projects such as streets, highways and public facilities. The skills of war engineering, Nourse said, do *not* benefit civilian activity.

In order to minimize war costs during peacetime, Nourse made four suggestions.

1. Apply wisdom by diplomats and the military to reduce national security costs to the lowest point.
2. Use military efficiency in spending which would "forego every outlay based on traditional practice, corps pride, or dispensable economy." That is, Nourse meant, stop interservice bickering and have all branches of the armed forces work for the national good.

3. Employ government finances and control measures to minimize the defense effects on business.

4. Require all Americans to make sacrifices and accept discipline to pay for war expenditures.[12]

Nourse's harsh economic prescriptions suited President Truman's conservative economic inclinations from 1946 to 1948. During 1948 and 1949, however, the President gradually accepted the more liberal economic expansion concepts of Leon Keyserling and the Wardman Park group. Initially, therefore, Truman's change represented his desire to enact Fair Deal legislation for he retained the $15 billion limit on defense costs for fiscal 1950 and cut them to $13 billion for 1951. Not until pressure from both the State and Defense Departments increased by April 1950 did Truman consider larger future defense expenditures related to Keyserling's guns *and* butter expansion formula.

V

The Split Among the Economic Advisers

TRUMAN'S ADOPTION of Keyserling's economic ideas became evident when Nourse resigned and Keyserling became acting chairman of the CEA in September, 1949. Nourse had become greatly disturbed by Keyserling's White House connections during and after the 1948 election campaign. He and Keyserling disagreed about testimony to congressional committees, Keyserling's advocacy of Senator James E. Murray's Economic Expansion Act of 1949, Truman's proposal to construct or operate steel mills, and the 1949 mid-year economic report. Nourse became aware of Keyserling's frequent and direct access to the White House through Clark Clifford and in August 1949 he decided to "step aside" so the President could have CEA members whose views he accepted.

Significantly, Nourse resigned as CEA Chairman during a council dispute over Truman's budget proposal for fiscal 1951. On July 1, 1949, Truman directed the CEA and the NSC to review the proposal for a $41.1 billion budget which had a $5 billion deficit despite proposed tax increases and a ceiling on defense spending of $13 billion. Because the NSC requested more funds for defense and foreign aid while the Clark-Keyserling liberals desired an economic stimulus to counteract signs of an impending 1949 recession, a deficit seemed justified. Therefore, Truman asked the council to advise him of the impact on the U.S. economy of the proposed budget, of substantial deficits for a period of years, and of moderate increases or decreases in the defense-foreign assistance appropriations.

After arguing for two months in seeking a unified response to Truman's request, the council members made two reports to the President: one by Nourse, the second by Keyserling and John D. Clark who was the other member of the CEA. Without considering possible defense increases, Nourse and Keyserling disagreed bitterly over the proposed $5 billion deficit. Nourse argued that there were no economic "panic" signs in mid-1949 and wanted a surplus in a year of good times. Keyserling believed the Fair Deal programs would stimulate the economy to avoid a recession by expanding production so that the budgets might balance again in 1952 or 1953. Clark, who failed to compromise their differences, sided with Keyserling because he thought inflationary booms were better than recessionary busts, and expanding the economy would bring full employment. Consequently, on September 2, for the first time in the three years of its existence, the CEA sent two conflicting recommendations to the president. Nourse hoped that Budget Director Frank Pace would sympathize with his minority views about the deficit.

During the intense debate over the proper response to Truman, Nourse decided to resign because he believed Keyserling represented Truman's changed attitude on deficits. On August 9 and, again, on September 9, Nourse sent the president a letter of resignation effective November 1. Because the White House staff wanted to wait for a good political time to announce the change and get a replacement, Nourse stayed on for two months.[13]

During his "lame-duck" months, Nourse had the opportunity to send one last vigorous memo to the NSC to oppose deficits and inflation. Responding to a September 26 draft of NSC-52/2, Nourse argued that a sound economy was an essential part of national security. While recognizing that the "guns or butter" choice was a "true economic dilemma," he urged the NSC leaders to weigh dangers on the economic front as well as the strategic and diplomatic fronts. Any final decision must, however, consider the effects of constant deficits on the "economic behavior of free men" and the "financial machinery" of the nation's total security.[14]

By mid-1949, Nourse's opposition to Keyserling's economic expansion concepts no longer had Truman's sympathy because Clifford, Keyserling and others had persuaded the president to promote Fair Deal policies. The liberal Democrats wanted to add at least $1 billion to domestic programs but Keyserling also believed larger military costs could be accommodated without sacrifices by the public. Thus, Keyserling's guns *and* butter analysis replaced Nourse's grimmer economic analysis of choosing between guns *or* butter.

In contrast to Nourse, Keyserling adopted Alvin Hansen's liberal Keynesian concepts to argue that the government should take action by planning with business and accepting temporary deficits in order to increase production and cut unemployment. Keyserling said a constantly expanding economy would end the cyclical fluctuation of prosperity and recession. Economists such as

Nourse, he said, worried too much about the scarcity of economic resources. Keyserling envisioned growth and prosperity for a limitless future because idle industry would be put to work and more jobs would bring full employment. For Keyserling, America's vast productive increase generated during World War II demonstrated what complementary action by business and government could achieve in peace as well as in wartime.[15]

Specifically in 1949, Keyserling advocated a ten year plan of economic expansion. Government policy should stimulate business activity to advance from the current GNP of $260 billion to $300 billion by 1954 and to $350 or $400 billion by 1958. With such growth, all families could have a minimum annual income of $4000; all retirees a pension of at least $100 per month. On October 14, 1949 *U.S. News and World Report* called Keyserling's ideas "Truman's 10 Year Plan: Something for Everyone," a perfect political program.[16]

VI

Truman's 10-Year Plan

KEYSERLING AND THE WARDMAN PARK GROUP persuaded Truman to embrace a Fair Deal vision of more butter. Two of Truman's speeches in September, 1949, substantiated the president's shift from the balanced budget to a deficit budget that would enact Keyserling's expanded economy concept. At Pittsburgh on September 5, Truman defended the Fair Deal program to "promote the welfare of all people" by greater economic benefits for labor and farmers, "better social security, improved education, and a national health program." The President criticized the "selfish interests" who used scare words about big government or complained that "they cost too much and we can't afford them."

Truman said:

> The selfish interests say we can't afford these programs during a boom because that would be inflationary. They say we can't afford them during a recession because that would be deflationary. They say we can't afford them during a war because we are too busy with defense, we can't afford them in time of peace because that would discourage business. So, according to the selfish interests we never can afford them.
>
> But the truth is, we can't afford not to put these programs into effect. We can afford them, we ought to have them, and we will have them.[17]

Although Keyserling's expanding economic ideas had been criticized by some commentators as visionary, Truman disagreed. On September 29, he told a Kansas City and national television audience that since 1890 the U.S. economy had grown tremendously and would continue to do so. The nation could attain a $300 billion economy and raise family incomes from $2000 to $4000 per family per year. "This," he said, "is not a pipe dream. It can be done. But it can't happen by itself. And it can't happen if we have a lot of 'pull-backs' at the helm of government."[18]

For Truman, the "butter" side of the fiscal program was easier to accept than larger defense costs. Having served during World War II as Chairman of Senate War Investigation Committee and criticized waste in defense contracts during World War II, Truman anticipated that the unification of the Department of Defense in 1947 would enable the military to make the hard choices needed to provide sound defense at the least cost. During 1948, the first Secretary of Defense, James Forrestal, applied these policies but ruined his sanity in trying to mediate the interservice rivalry for funds. Following Forrestal's resignation early in 1949, Louis Johnson became Defense Secretary and endeavored to achieve the military budget savings Truman desired.[19]

Johnson quickly discovered that deciding on military spending priorities by discriminating between essential and less essential weapons aroused anguished screams from the still disunited military officers and the political-industrial allies who lobbied for defense funds. Truman and Forrestal had upset the Air Force in 1948 by refusing to spend $822 million which Congress appropriated for a seventy-group force. On April 23, 1949, Johnson angered the Navy by halting construction of the super-airplane carrier, the prototype weapon the Navy wanted to enable it to compete with the Air Force as the primary instrument of strategic atomic attack on Russia.

Johnson's action precipitated the resignation of Navy Secretary John L. Sullivan as well as the "Revolt of the Admirals" who balked at Johnson's decision to rely on the Strategic Air Command as the most efficient weapon against the Soviet Union. Because Johnson's decision attempted to enforce Truman's $15 billion defense limit, Congress undertook a series of investigations of Truman's defense priorities. Throughout the remainder of 1949, congressional hearings gave the military-industrial critics of Truman's policies a stage for publicizing their demands for greater military expenditures to protect America from the communist menace.[20]

In an atmosphere which included interservice wrangling for defense funds, the signing of the NATO treaty, legislation giving $1.35 billion for Mutual Defense aid to Europe, the communist victory in China, and news of Russia's atomic success, Keyserling's concepts of unlimited economic potential was a breath of fresh air to a coterie of Truman's advisers in the State and Defense Department who wanted larger budgets for national security. With Secretary of Defense Louis Johnson committed to following Truman's orders for low, efficient defense budgets, the State Department under Secretary Dean Acheson became the leader in advocating greater military costs.[21]

VII

The Military Brush-up Prevails

PRESIDENT TRUMAN'S EFFORTS to contain military expenditures began to disintegrate between July 1949, and June 1950. Pressure from congress, the Joint Chiefs and Acheson as well as Keyserling's contention that the nation could afford both guns and butter eroded, even though it did not eliminate, Truman's instinctive concern for balanced budgets, tax policies to "pay-as-you go," and a preference for butter rather than guns.

The key document in Acheson's effort to increase military expenditures was NSC-68 of April 1950. This document originated from the military chiefs' effort to have the State Department define the nation's foreign policies so that the Joint Chiefs could determine what defense strategies to plan. In the State Department this proposal precipitated heated debate because the Director of the Policy Planning Staff, George Kennan, believed precise definitions of policy were both inappropriate and hazardous to the flexibility required by foreign service officers. Kennan also argued that the political-economic measures undertaken since 1947 were the best response to the current Soviet threat. He and other Soviet analysts did not anticipate that Russia would undertake a military attack in the near future and, therefore, communism's methods of internal subversion were best combated by economic not military solutions.

Kennan had been well accepted by Secretary of State George Marshall in 1947–48. Under Acheson, however, Kennan's ideas were less acceptable and during 1949, Paul Nitze gained in favor and eventually replaced Kennan as Director of Policy Planning in January 1950. Nitze, who in 1980 indicated that he had profited greatly from Keyserling's economic ideas, joined Acheson in arguing for greater military expenditures to combat the Soviet threat. Thus, by early 1950, Acheson outmaneuvered both Kennan and Louis Johnson in persuading Truman to approve a complete review of the nation's security policies.[21]

Nitze became Chairman of the State-Defense Department's study group which reviewed U.S. policy and completed NSC-68 late in March 1950. This document enunciated an exaggerated threat of the communist menace and used Keyserling's ideas of economic expansion to justify the build-up of all three branches of the armed forces. Unequivocally, NSC-68 declared the Soviet Union "is animated by a new fanatic faith, antithetical to our own, and seeks to impose its absolute authority over the rest of the world." Because the Soviets used both violent and non-violent methods according to the "dictates of expediency," the United States and its citizens stand "in their deepest peril."[23]

The Soviet challenge required an enlargement of the free world's military power which only the U.S. could undertake. Using Keyserling's ideas, the economic section of the report stated that with a dynamic level of economic growth providing a GNP of $300 billion per year "the necessary build-up could be accomplished without a decrease in the nation's standard of living because the required resources could be attained by siphoning off a part of the annual increment in the gross national product." Thus, the nation could afford both the Fair Deal and a larger military establishment without imposing hardship, denial and sacrifice on the American people. Guns *and* butter were both possible.[24]

As presented to President Truman on April 7, 1950, the exact costs of the military expansion were not given. In 1948 and 1949, the President had immediately rejected proposals for additional defense expenditures. He did not do so this time. On April 12, he informed the ad hoc NSC-68 study committee that before further consideration they should consult with such groups as the CEA and the Bureau of the Budget in preparing details of the military program and its costs.[25] During these committee deliberations in May 1950, the Defense Department proposed military costs of $40 to $50 billion by 1954 and $70 to $80 billion by 1958. The CEA became directly involved and Keyserling's staff advised the NSC how they could best justify greater military expenditures.

On May 8, 1950, Keyserling approved a memo by Hamilton Dearborn which represented the official CEA response to NSC-68. The CEA comments were designed to help the proposal based on the statement that the larger defense budgets would correspond to "a very rapid absolute expansion" of the total of all U.S. production. Such expansion would render supportable "any given level of defense outlays."

The CEA memo stated that the military could spend whatever costs necessary provided that the government's program embraced "not only the conduct of our foreign policy, but also the conduct of our domestic policy." Within a framework of economic expansion over a period of years, the council could estimate what the effects would be on consumption, price and allocation controls, cuts in other programs or tax increases. Together these careful considerations would ensure the "full achievement of our potential."

VIII

Cold War as a Counter-cyclical Strategy

THE CEA NEEDED NOTIONS of the magnitude and duration of the defense build-up in order to make specific recommendations for economic plans. Nevertheless the nation's capacity for growth enabled new costs to be accepted "without serious threat to our standard of living, and without risking a transformation of the free character of our economy."

Because Nourse and other conservatives did not appreciate the nation's capacity for growth, and therefore aroused fears of bankruptcy and government controls, the CEA memo ended by suggesting that these non-economic apprehensions would have to be reduced by education and persuasion to stress the nation's growth potential. In order to realize both the economic and military strength of the nation, these non-economic concerns must be recognized and overcome. In brief, the public and Congress will have to realize that both guns *and* butter are possible in the framework of the nation's ability to expand economically.[26]

Because the cost analysis of NSC-68 had not been completed and presented to Truman before the Korean War began, the fate of the NSC-68 military budget without wartime expansion cannot be known. Nevertheless, by May 1950, Keyserling's advocacy of budget deficits to stimulate economic growth in peace or war had become widely accepted in the Truman Administration and among many liberal economists. Truman had accepted Keyserling's deficits to encourage the Fair Deal program and while Keyserling's advice never spoke to the issue of military inefficiencies and the waste of interservice rivalries, the President might have accepted NSC-68 because of the advice of Acheson with whom he got along very well.

What is certain to historians is that after 1949–1950, America fought the Cold War with little attention to Edwin Nourse's concern for such terms as sacrifice, share the burden, minimize defense costs, or negative influences of national defense on the total economy. During the Vietnam conflict of the 1960s and the stagflation years of the 1970s, a few economists again studied the baneful long-term effects of "military Keynesianism."[27] Generally, however, Nourse's fears seemed to be obsolete. Even when economic competition intensified with other capitalist nations such as West Germany and Japan, few economists and almost no politicians blamed military costs as a principal culprit.

Rather, most Americans seemed to agree with a *U.S. News and World Report* prediction of May 19, 1950 in its "Tomorrow" column:

> Business won't go to pot as long as war is a threat, so long as every alarm can be used to step up spending-lending for defense at home and aid abroad. Cold War is almost a guarantee against a bad depression.[28]

NOTES

1. For a succinct explanation of corporate liberal views see Michael J. Hogan, "Corporatism: A Positive Appraisal," *Diplomatic History,* 10 (Fall, 1986), 363–72. Two important discussions of the political processes in formulating the defense budgets are Warner R. Schilling, "The Politics of National Defense: Fiscal 1950" and Paul Y. Hammond, "NSC-68: Prologue to Rearmament" in Schilling, Hammond and Glenn H. Snyder, *Strategy, Politics, and Defense Budgets* (New York: Columbia, 1962). These should be read together with the more recent essay by Samuel F. Wells, Jr., "Sounding the Tocsin: NSC 68 and the Soviet Threat," *International Security* 4 (Fall 1976), 116–58.

2. On Nourse's background see Edward S. Flash, Jr. *Economic Advice and Presidential Lead-*

ership (New York: Columbia, 1965), 20–21. Nourse describes economics as an objective science in his book *Economics in the Public Service* (New York: Harcourt, Brace and Co., 1953), 3–28. This volume and an earlier, more polemical book highlighted his efforts to counteract Keyserling's deficit spending ideas. The other book is Nourse, *The 1950s Come First* (New York: Holt and Co., 1951). At the time he made an oral history in 1972, he still emphasized his non-political connections, Nourse, Oral History Interview, March 7, 1972, transcript at Harry S. Truman Library (HSTL), 1–12. This interview also has autobiographical statements, 1–10.

3. Keyserling, Oral History Interview, May 3, 10, and 19, 1971, transcript at HSTL, 1–37; Cabell Phillips, *The Truman Presidency* (New York: Macmillan Co., 1966), 162 *ff.;* Flash, *Economic Advice,* 21–22.

4. For general accounts of the Cold War developments see Richard F. Haynes, *The Awesome Power: Harry S. Truman as Commander-in-Chief* (Baton Rouge: Louisiana State Univ. Press, 1973), 137–53; and John Lewis Gaddis, *The United States and the Origins of the Cold War 1941–1947* (New York: Columbia Univ. Press, 1972), 282–352. Of course, there are many studies of the beginnings of the Cold War.

5. Alonzo Hamby, "The Clash of Perspectives and the Need for a New Synthesis" in Richard S. Kirkendall, ed. *The Truman Period as a Research Field: A Reappraisal, 1972* (Columbia: Univ. of Missouri Press, 1974), 140–143. In this same volume, Barton Bernstein writes a "Commentary" which argues that Truman has no coherent liberal policy because of his "ideological confusion," 188 *ff.* Keyserling, *Oral History,* sees Truman as a "middle-way" liberal who shows his true colors after 1948, 69–74; also see James E. Webb, "Comments" in Francis H. Heller, ed., *Economics and the Truman Administration* (Lawrence: Regents Press of Kansas, 1981), 24–27.

6. Keyserling, *Oral History,* 73–74; Alonzo Hamby, *Beyond the New Deal: Harry S. Truman and American Liberalism* (New York: Columbia, 1973), 182–83, 293–303.

7. In his *Oral History Interview,* March, 1971, transcript at *HSTL,* Clark Clifford indicates that President Truman believed the U.S. won World War II despite the organization of the Army and Navy which fought each other as much as the enemy, 7 and 111–122; Haynes, *Awesome Power,* 93–115.

8. John W. Snyder, "The Treasury and Economic Policy," in Heller, ed. *Economics and the Truman Administration,* 24–27.

9. George M. Elsey papers, *HSTL,* Box 34, Statement by President to the Secretary of Defense, the Secretary of the Three Departments, and the three Chiefs of Staff, May 13, 1948. Truman stated that he had wanted only $1½ billion in March but had agreed to $3.481 billion. Now he noted the military projections were up to $18 to $20 billion for 1951 or 1952. Because this would require "large-scale deficit financing," Truman opposed it and insisted that $15 billion was a ceiling the military leaders must loyally support on orders of the commander-in-chief. Walter Mills, ed. *The Forrestal Diaries* (New York: Viking Press, 1951), 382–439. Forrestal's difficulty with the three services did not begin in March 1948 but occurred almost as soon as the Department of Defense began operation. The last seven chapters of the diaries are filled with interservice disputes.

10. Nourse, *Economics in the Public Service,* 213–214, quotes the April 7 memorandum. The CEA sent an initial memo to Truman on March 24, *HSTL,* President's Secretary File, Box 143.

11. For the estimates for 1950 fiscal year see Report to the NSC by Acting Executive Secretary (Lay), July 8, 1949 in *Foreign Relations of the United States* (FRUS) 1949, (Washington D.C.: Government Printing Office, 1973), I, 353. The Eberstadt Committee report is: U.S. Commission on Organization of the Executive Branch of Government, *The National Security Organization* (Washington, D.C.: GPO, 1949), 1–3. It spells out the need for adequate defense "without damaging or destroying our national economy." The report condemned interservice rivalry and called for greater authority for the Secretary of Defense. Millis, *Forrestal Diaries,* 288, 350.

12. Nourse, *Economics in the Public Service,* Appendix E, 485–495. A shorter version of this speech was printed in *Vital Speeches* 15 (May 1, 1949), 429–431.

13. Nourse, *Economics in the Public Service,* 238–51 and 279–85; Nourse, *Oral History, HSTL,* 22–23 and 59–62. Flash, *Economic Advice,* 24–26. After the announcement of Nourse's retirement, various opinion journals noted the differences he had with Keyserling. See for example: *Business Week,* "New Job for Economic Council," 49 (October 9, 1949), 26; *Nation,* "Dr. Edwin Nourse," 149 (October 29, 1949), 407; *Time,* "Too Old for Such Nonsense," 54 (October 31, 1949), 9.

14. *FRUS, 1949,* I, 394–396, "Memorandum by the Chairman of the CEA (Nourse) to the NSC," September 30, 1949.

15. Keyserling's general attitude on proper economic policy at this time may be found in a variety of articles and speeches he prepared from 1945 to 1950. Most notably see Keyserling, "Deficiencies of Past Programs and the Nature of New Needs," in Seymour Harris, ed. *Saving American Capitalism* (New York: Knopf, 1948), 275–84; Keyserling, "The Middle Way for America," *Progressive* 13 (May 1949), 5–9. On Keyserling's relationship to Keynesianism see: John K. Galbraith, "Came the Revolution," *New York Times Book Review,* May 16, 1965, Section 7, 1 and 34–39; Walter S. Salant, "Some Intellectual Contributions of the Truman Council of Economic Advisers to Policy-Making," *History of Political Economy* 5 (Spring, 1973) 36–49; Bertram Gross and John P. Lewis, "The President's Economic Staff During the Truman Administration. *American Political Science Review* 48 (March 1954), 114–30. On Alvin Hansen's ideas see Robert Collins, *The Business Response to Keynes, 1929–1964* (New York: Columbia, 1981), 10–20. Although he does not provide sufficient data for the assertion, James L. Clayton says that by 1950 most economists had abandoned the idea that wars had a negative effect on the economy. Clayton, "A General Introduction to the Readings" in James L. Clayton, ed. *The Economic Impact of the Cold War: Sources and Readings* (New York: Harcourt, 1970) 3–4. It may be more accurate to say that most Keynesians spoke of flexible budgeting but still differed on the effects of war, and when to permit deficits. See the articles in Arthur Smithies and J. Keith Butters, eds. *Readings in Fiscal Policy* (Homewood, IL: Richard Irwin, 1955), especially Jesse Burkland, "The Balanced Budget," 3–30; and Haskell Ward, "Fiscal Policy, Military Preparedness and Postwar Inflation," 155–69.

16. *U.S. News and World Report,* 27 (October 14, 1949), 18–20. Articles by Keyserling include: "A Policy for Full Employment" *New Republic* 121 (October 24, 1949), 13–15; "Planning for a $300 Billion Economy," *New York Times Magazine,* June 18, 1950, 9 *ff.;* "Strategy for a Depression-proof America," *United Nations World* 3 (July 1949), 36–41. Keyserling, *Oral History, HSTL,* 90–99, 157–58, 186–88. Also see: Hamby, *Beyond the New Deal,* 654–71.

17. *Public Papers of the Presidents, Harry S. Truman 1949* (Washington: GPO, 1964), 463.

18. *Ibid.,* 494.

19. See footnotes 7 and 9.

20. Haynes, *Awesome Power,* 120–27; Robert J. Donovan, *·Tumultuous Years: The Presidency of Harry S. Truman, 1949–1953* (New York: W. W. Norton, 1982), 105–13; Paola Coletta, *The United States Navy and Defense Unification, 1947–1953,* (Newark: Univ. of Delaware Press, 1981), 158–203; Paul Y. Hammond, "Super Carriers and B-36 Bombers: Appropriations, Strategy and Politics," in Harold Stein, ed. *American Civil-Military Relations* (Birmingham: Univ. of Alabama Press, 1963), 465–500.

21. After replacing George Marshall as Secretary of State in January, 1950, Acheson became a leader in arousing opinion about the Soviet threat and the need to have large U.S. military budgets and military aid to Europe under NATO. John Lewis Gaddis, *Dean Acheson, Vol. XVI of The American Secretaries of State and their Diplomacy* (New York: Cooper Square, 1972), 138–50. Donovan, *Tumultuous Years,* 159, notes that Acheson opposed restrictions on defense as unrealistic in July, 1949. Robert A. Pollard, *Economic Security and the Origins of the Cold War,*

1945–1950 (New York: Columbia, 1985) 222–42 emphasizes the State Department role under Acheson and Paul Nitze in changing from economic to military containment policies. In 1949, some observers also noted that Acheson, not Louis Johnson of the Pentagon, led the way in increasing military expenditures. See: I. F. Stone, *The Truman Economy* (New York: Random House, 1953), 74–77 reprinting an article of July 31, 1949 titled "From Butter to Guns"; "The Acheson Approach," *Progressive* 14 (April 1950), 3 and 14 (May 1950), 3–4.

22. Dean Acheson, *Present at the Creation* (New York: W. W. Norton, 1969), 344–53; John L. Gaddis, *Strategies of Containment* (New York: Oxford, 1982), 89–94. Hammond, "NSC-68: Prologue to Rearmament," 287–97; Wells, "Tocsin," 19–24; Donovan, *Tumultuous Years,* 158–61. The Kennan-Nitze differences may be read in detail in accounts of the PPS in *FRUS, 1949,* 399–403, 413–16; and *passim.* One of Kennan's main arguments against the military was that the JCS drew conclusions by assessing Russia's maximum capabilities and the nation's greatest danger *not* from the probable course of events, (*Ibid.* 402). Kennan resigned on September 29, 1949, effective June 1, 1950. Kennan's memoirs indicate he resigned because he was at odds with other senior officials of the State Department: *Memoirs 1925–1950* (Boston: Little-Brown, 1967), 468. Nitze recalled his talks with Keyserling in 1949–1950 in John Lewis Gaddis and Paul Nitze, "NSC 68 and the Soviet Threat Reconsidered," *International Security* 4 (Spring 1980), 173. In a 1954 article, two members of Keyserling's staff indicated the CEA helped meet the "special demand of international stress." Gross and Lewis, "The President's Economic Staff", 114–16. In 1965, Edward S. Flash Jr. had conjectured that the CEA must have influenced NSC-68 in *Economic Advice,* 38–39. On the same day he approved the review of national security, Truman ordered research to proceed on the super-hydrogen fusion bomb. Richard G. Hewlett and Francis Duncan, *Atomic Shield: A History of the United States Atomic Energy Commission, 1947–1952* (Washington, D.C.: U.S. Atomic Energy Commission, 1972), 369–416.

23. *FRUS-1950* (Washington: GPO, 1977) I, 237–38. Although much of its contents was leaked to the press, NSC-68 was not declassified until 1975 when it was first published in full in the *Naval War College Review,* "NSC-68" 27 (May–June 1975), 51–108. The quote cited is on page 53.

24. *FRUS-1950* I, 258; *Naval War College Review,* "NSC-68," 74.

25. Wells, "Tocsin," 137.

26. Memorandum by Dearborn to Executive Secretary of NSC, May 8, 1950 in *FRUS-1950,* 303–311. In a 1978 essay, Keyserling stated that even during the Korean War he urged a planning process to avoid economic controls and other trade-offs because a growth economy did not need these. He restated his idea that in the long contest with communism the government could not maintain the people's support by the "continuous imposition of hardship and denial but only by expanding the industrial base to avoid such burdens." Keyserling, "The Council of Economic Advisers Since 1946: Its Contribution and Failures," *Atlantic Economic Journal* 6 (March 1978), 22. On December 8, 1950, Keyserling approved major defense increases proposed in NSC 68/3 by saying there was no doubt they could "be maintained indefinitely without damage to civilian consumption" or sacrifice. The programs were he said, "about half way between 'business as usual' and a really large-scale dedication of our enormous economic resources to the defense of our freedoms. . . ." Keyserling's economic comparison point was America's World War II economic effort. See Memo by Chairman of CEA, December 8, 1950, *FRUS,* I, 427–31.

27. Clayton, *Economic Impact of the Cold War,* has excerpts of the critical writings on military costs during the 1960s. For a recent assessment by Seymour Melman who became the principal critic of military costs as detrimental to the U.S. economy, see "Limits of Military Power: Economic and Other," *International Security* 11 (Summer 1986), 72–87.

28. *U.S. News and World Report,* 28 (May 19, 1950), 7.

SOCIAL PROBLEMS, Vol. 30, No. 4, April 1983

THE MYTH OF CORPORATE CAPTURE:
REGULATORY COMMISSIONS IN THE UNITED STATES*

PETER J. FREITAG
Clarkson College of Technology

Popular wisdom has it that representatives of big business have "captured" the U.S. federal government, and social scientists have gathered much data to support this theory of "corporate dictatorship." While it has been widely assumed that federal regulatory commissions are no exception, this is the first study of the links between the corporate world and the seven biggest U.S. regulatory agencies. I analyze the careers of 341 commissioners to determine how many were recruited from business and how many returned to it after government service. I find that corporate domination of the commissions has been overestimated and that the agencies appear to be staffed by the representatives of smaller capitalist interests when they are staffed by members of the corporate community at all. The results cast new light on the thesis of "corporate dictatorship" and suggest that the cooptation of the commissions by business, if a reality, is accomplished through means other than the "capture" of agency personnel.

The structure of power of the United States was a subject of great controversy among sociologists from the 1950s through the 1970s. At issue was whether U.S. society could best be described as a "corporate dictatorship" (Domhoff, 1967, 1970; Mills, 1956) or a "pluralist democracy" (Keller, 1963; Rose, 1967). By the end of the 1970s, the large volume of data demonstrating the domination of non-economic institutions by corporate leaders strongly favored the "corporate dictatorship" view (Useem, 1979:553). Corporations appeared to have "captured" the federal government (Freitag, 1975; Kolko, 1969; Mintz, 1975; Zweigenhaft, 1975); concern was expressed over the "revolving door" between business and government (Hershman, 1977; MacNeil/Lehrer, 1976; *New York Times*, 1975). Though no studies were made of the federal regulatory commissions, few sociologists would have been surprised to find a high degree of personnel interchange between U.S. corporations and the agencies designed to regulate them.[1]

This paper fills a gap in the research on the structure of power in the United States by looking at the links between corporations and the so-called "Big Seven" federal regulatory commissions: Interstate Commerce Commission (ICC), Federal Trade Commission (FTC), Federal Power Commission (FPC), Federal Communications Commission (FCC), Securities and Exchange Commission (SEC), National Labor Relations Board (NLRB), and Civil Aeronautics Board (CAB). These commissions, like the dozens of smaller federal commissions and boards, have been established by legislative enactment and are independent of the supervision and control of the three major branches of government. Each is charged with carrying out legislative, administrative, and judicial functions. From five to 11 members, appointed by the president with

---

* An earlier version of this paper was presented at the 29th annual meeting of the New York State Sociological Association, Syracuse, October 1981. The author thanks Joyce Freitag, Judy Grant, Herman Lebovics, Mark Mizruchi, Charles Perrow, Michael Schwartz, Eugene Weinstein, and the anonymous *Social Problems* reviewers for their help. This research was supported by grants from the National Science Foundation (FOC 73–05606) and Clarkson College. Correspondence to: Center for Liberal Studies, Clarkson College, Potsdam, NY 13676.
1. For the purposes of the present study, no distinction is made between "predatory" regulation and "capture" regulation (Zerbe, 1980:343). In the former, regulation is viewed as having been established *originally* at the behest of the regulated group. In the latter, the process of regulation on behalf of the regulated comes about *after* an agency has been established. The "capture" of the commissions referred to in this paper applies equally to both phenomena and is employed, specifically, to deal with the incidence of personnel interchange.

Congressional approval, sit on each of the "Big Seven" commissions. They possess broad regulatory powers, including licensing, rate-making, and the control of business practices. I analyze the extent of corporate "capture" of these commissions by asking four questions: (1) What careers did commissioners pursue before and after their experience as federal regulators? (2) How many commissioners were employed by regulated industries? (3) To what extent did commissioners serve big business? (4) What trends existed in corporate "capture" of the commissions over time?

Analyzing the occupational backgrounds of political decision-makers can provide an important index of the representativeness and openness of government. As Mintz (1975:132) explained:

> Because background appears to be a factor in determining scopes of interest, it can be argued that individuals drawn from a similar stratum would be concerned with similar types of policy. Further, if government leaders are recruited from an extremely narrow portion of the population, it is unlikely that their policy views would coincide with those of the majority. In this case, no evidence would be found to support the pluralist notion of several groups competing on different issues. Rather, a consequence of unrepresentative recruitment would be a 'power elite' determining major policy in their own interests.

Specifically, a government leader with a background in business is likely to be sympathetic toward corporate interests. A regulatory commissioner with prior business experience is likely to accept the "themes that the industry is trying to get across" more willingly than someone without business experience (Representative Toby Moffett, quoted in MacNeil/Lehrer, 1976:5). This should be especially evident in commissions with "a well-defined area of responsibility" (Stigler, 1972:230). While the FTC, SEC, and NLRB control certain aspects of economic activity *throughout* the corporate sector, the remaining four commissions deal with *specific* industries and a *limited number* of firms. The ICC regulates carriers engaged in interstate commerce, including railroads, trucking companies, and bus lines; the FPC regulates companies involved in the sale or transmission of electric power or natural gas; the FCC regulates radio and television broadcasting, telephone, telegraph, and satellite communications firms; and the CAB regulates members of the interstate and international air transport industry. One would expect stronger corporate links in the four *industry-specific* commissions than in the three *cross-industry* commissions; the strongest links should be found in those commissions with a higher frequency and intensity of contact between regulator and regulated, and whose actions directly affect the vitality of an industry.

METHOD

I obtained directly from the regulatory agencies the names of the 341 commissioners who served on the "Big Seven" from 1887 (the year in which the first federal regulatory commission, the ICC, was created) until 1975. I compiled biographical information on these members from a variety of sources, including *The National Cyclopedia of American Biography, The Dictionary of American Biography, Current Biography, Standard and Poor's Register, Martindale–Hubbell Law Directory*, and the historical and contemporary editions of the various *Who's Who?* volumes. For those individuals not included in these standard references I turned to transcripts of nomination hearings, newspaper and periodical articles, news releases, biographical sketches provided by some of the agencies, and other accounts of the regulatory commissions. The difficulties I encountered in finding biographical information about the commissioners is significant in itself. Most commissioners were not well-known at the national level; appointment to a regulatory agency did not guarantee one inclusion in those sources which compile biographies of famous men and women.

I traced the occupational history of each commissioner from earliest reported position to service in the regulatory agency, and from the date of departure until death or 1975, the last year of the study. By coding the data to construct career lines for each individual, I identified 70 types of positions. Analysis of the data without further reduction would have proven quite cumbersome and yielded results so scattered that they would have had little meaning. Consequently, I collapsed the positions into seven broad categories, accounting for nearly 95 percent of the occupations reported (see Table 1).[2]

I determined the principal occupation of each commissioner prior to service in the regulatory agency by first ascertaining the initial occupational position held after the completion of schooling. This date of entry into the career line was then subtracted from the date of appointment to the commission to determine the duration of the career path prior to service in the agency. This served as the base figure for determining the individual's principal position. The occupational category in which the person was engaged for the largest percentage of the base time period constituted the principal position prior to service in the regulatory commission. Where tenure in an occupation was non-consecutive, I lumped together the time spent in the same category of position. To determine a commissioner's principal position after service I used the same method, employing as a base period the time between departure from the commission and either the year of death or, if the commissioner was still living, 1975.

Before Service   **CAREERS OF COMMISSIONERS**

Table 1 shows that most commissioners had not held previous positions in the industry they were regulating. In the "Big Seven" as a whole, 7.3 percent of the commissioners were principally employed by the industry which they were subsequently charged to regulate. The most heavily dominated commission was the SEC: 13.5 percent of its members were culled from corporate positions which were related to that agency's jurisdiction (securities, finance, brokerage, etc.). No more than 12.5 percent of the members of the other six commissions had been principally engaged by the regulated. Moreover, while differences between agencies were those of "degree" and not of "kind," the four industry-specific commissions exhibited slightly *lower* rates of "capture" than the cross-industry agencies.

In the seven agencies as a whole, 31.9 percent of the commissioners had worked previously in the corporate sector — if we include those employed in corporate law (19.9 percent) and other business enterprises (4.7 percent). By comparison, 35.5 percent served in government and 32.5 percent in occupations in other areas of the private sector, including unspecified law, higher education, journalism and publishing, and "other."[3] Among the agencies, previous employment in corporate enterprise ranged from a low of 17 percent in the FPC to a high of 50.1 percent in the SEC. With the exception of the CAB, industry-specific agencies were *less* likely to be staffed by representatives of the corporate sphere than cross-industry commissions.

After Service

Analyzing the positions held by commissioners prior to appointment cannot in itself demonstrate that a commission reflects a plurality of interests, because the previous careers of the commissioners may not indicate the social groups they represent while in office. Lubin (1968:59) suggests that:

Occupational histories of individual commissioners are often perplexing guides to their behavior — perhaps

---

2. The remaining positions, classified as "Other," were so diverse as to make further creation of categories unwarranted. The positions in this group ranged from service in municipal governments, the military, farming, ranching, and citrus growing to employment in religious groups, the entertainment field, cultural organizations, and philanthropic foundations. No single category could account for even 1 percent of the total.
3. Unspecified law denotes the practice of *non*-corporate law or service in a law firm for which no information on the type of practice was available.

TABLE 1

Percentage of Principal Positions Held by Commissioners Before and After Service, by Agency

	ICC		FTC		FPC		FCC		SEC		NLRB		CAB		TOTAL	
	Before	After	Before	After	Before	After	Before	After	Before	After	Before	After	Before	After	Before	After
Regulated Industry	4.9	22.9	5.8	12.8	2.4	20.0	6.3	25.7	13.5	30.2	12.5	12.0	8.8	17.2	7.3	20.9
Other Business	6.1	4.2	0.0	0.0	0.0	8.0	6.3	0.0	3.9	2.3	3.1	4.0	14.7	17.2	4.7	4.5
Corporate Law	13.4	29.2	25.0	48.7	14.6	32.0	20.8	40.0	32.7	41.9	18.7	24.0	14.7	34.5	19.9	36.5
Unspecified Law	26.8	16.7	11.5	10.3	21.9	8.0	12.5	5.7	5.8	4.7	6.3	0.0	26.5	10.3	16.7	8.6
Government	31.7	16.7	40.4	15.4	43.9	16.0	33.3	11.4	32.7	20.9	50.0	32.0	20.6	10.3	35.5	17.2
Higher Education	4.9	6.3	3.9	2.6	4.9	8.0	6.3	5.7	3.9	0.0	6.3	4.0	8.8	3.5	5.3	4.1
Journalism/Publishing	4.9	2.1	5.8	7.7	7.3	0.0	4.2	2.9	0.0	0.0	0.0	0.0	2.9	3.5	3.8	2.5
Other	7.3	2.1	7.7	2.6	4.9	8.0	10.4	8.6	7.7	0.0	3.1	24.0	2.9	3.5	6.7	5.7
Total*	100.0	100.2	100.1	100.1	99.9	100.0	100.1	100.0	100.2	100.0	100.0	100.0	99.9	100.0	99.9	100.0
(N)	(82)	(48)	(52)	(39)	(41)	(25)	(48)	(35)	(52)	(43)	(32)	(25)	(34)	(29)	(341)	(244)**

Notes:

* Percentages may not add up to 100 because of rounding.

** Ninety-seven individuals were eliminated in the analysis of subsequent positions because they died in office, retired, were still in office, or simply "dropped out of sight."

45

because a commissioner is an upward mobile who adopts the values, attitudes, and behavior of the social stratum *toward which he desires to gravitate* . . . (emphasis added).

Thus, to determine accurately the extent to which business has "captured" the "Big Seven," we must consider what becomes of commissioners after service. As Fellmeth (1970:20) points out, "it must influence a high Commission official's judgment to know that he may get a lucrative industry position when he retires from the Commission." Since government service cannot offer the financial rewards of the private sector, it is commonly acknowledged that many individuals use their experience on commissions as a "stepping stone" to better-paying careers in industry. A commissioner who makes decisions which affect an industry or a particular firm may feel the need to consider the impact of those decisions on future employment opportunities. Further, when this pressure is felt by a *group* of individuals, each expecting a later career in industry, the group may serve to encourage conformity to business values (Edelman, 1967:53).

Table 1 shows that almost three times as many commissioners left government for jobs in the regulated industries (20.9 percent) as were recruited from them (7.3 percent). Moreover, 36.5 percent went on to positions as corporate lawyers and 4.5 percent to careers in other businesses. In sum, then, 61.9 percent of the commissioners spent the majority of their careers after service in the corporate world. While 35.5 percent of the commissioners were employed in government prior to service on one of the "Big Seven," only 17.2 percent returned to government careers after service. Similarly, while 32.5 percent began their careers in the non-corporate private sector, 20.9 percent returned to it.

Among the individual commissions a similar pattern is evident. Each agency sent from 50 to 75 percent of its members on to careers in the corporate world, with the exception of the NLRB, which sent 40 percent. Commissioners on industry-specific agencies did not exhibit closer ties to corporate interests than their colleagues in cross-industry commissions. Yet, one distinction is worth noting. The commission most heavily linked to corporations is the SEC, while the NLRB is the least linked. Given that the former regulates corporate finance and the latter relations between labor and management, spheres of influence may be reflected in patterns of personnel interchange. Perhaps the power of the corporation is manifest in that area of greatest concern to its operation, while labor demonstrates similar control over that agency most closely aligned to its activity. If this is the case, patterns of "capture" may provide evidence of differing priorities among economic interests.

The analysis of subsequent careers shows that corporate lawyers are the "high priests" of the commissions (Matthews, 1954). More commissioners in each agency went on to careers in corporate law than in any other field, and 36.5 percent of all the commissioners followed this career path. This is not surprising. Prior experience in the commissions provides access to information, knowledge of procedures, and an "old-boy" network unavailable to "outside" lawyers. Retiring commissioners are extremely desirable candidates for positions in corporate law firms. Upon leaving office, many commissioners establish private practices specializing in handling cases before the agencies they served.

In sum, while commissioners are recruited from diverse occupational backgrounds, most follow careers in the corporate sector after service. This suggests that the "corporate dictatorship" thesis *may* apply to the "Big Seven." However, there is no conclusive evidence that the commissions are dominated by individuals sympathetic to regulated interests, as many journalists and social scientists assume. In fact, only 7.3 percent of the commissioners came from regulated industries, and only 20.9 percent left to join them. This counterintuitive finding merits further examination. Perhaps the study of *primary* careers is too stringent a test to reveal the ties which exist between the regulators and the regulated. A broader question may prove more useful: How many commissioners served in the regulated industries at *any* time and in *any* capacity?

TABLE 2

Percentage of Commissioners Who Served in the Regulated Industry
or in Big Business, *by Agency and Time*

		Before Only	After Only	Before and After	Total*	(N)**
ICC:	Regulated Industry	11.0	19.5	9.8	40.2	(82)
	Big Business	7.3	8.5	4.9	20.7	
FTC:	Regulated Industry	13.5	25.0	5.8	44.2	(52)
	Big Business	5.8	15.4	7.7	28.8	
FPC:	Regulated Industry	2.4	14.6	17.1	34.2	(41)
	Big Business	2.4	9.8	2.4	14.6	
FCC:	Regulated Industry	10.4	33.3	6.2	50.0	(48)
	Big Business	8.3	4.2	8.3	20.8	
SEC:	Regulated Industry	9.6	17.3	26.9	53.8	(52)
	Big Business	15.4	19.2	15.4	50.0	
NLRB:	Regulated Industry	15.6	3.1	21.9	40.6	(32)
	Big Business	0.0	3.1	9.4	12.5	
CAB:	Regulated Industry	2.9	17.6	14.7	35.3	(34)
	Big Business	5.9	17.6	8.8	32.4	
TOTAL:	Regulated Industry	9.7	19.6	13.8	43.1	(341)
	Big Business	7.0	11.1	7.9	26.1	

Notes:
  * Rank percentages may not equal totals because of rounding.
  ** Number of cases on which percentages are based.

EMPLOYMENT BY REGULATED INDUSTRIES

If the "Big Seven" were staffed by individuals who worked for, or anticipated employment in, the industries which they were supposed to regulate, then the "corporate dictatorship" view would be strongly suggested. Since the previous analyses did not demonstrate the "capture" of the commissioners, I introduced a more lenient definition of service in a regulated industry, attempting to include as many of the commissioners as possible. I included: (1) individuals who had been employed in the regulated industries at any time in their careers; (2) lawyers who had served as counsel to a company in a regulated industry or who had been members of law firms (or maintained private practices) engaged in regulatory law or in areas related to the regulated industries; and (3) any other individuals who had served in the regulated industry (as an advocate of a corporation or of an industry-wide association), regardless of duration of service, size of firm, or time relative to agency tenure.

Even with these expanded criteria, the results hardly support the "capture" thesis. Table 2 shows that fewer than one-half of all the regulators also served the regulated in some manner. In only two agencies, the FCC and the SEC, did more than half the commissioners ever work for the regulated industry. As in the first analysis, more commissioners worked for the regulated industries after government service (19.6 percent) than prior to it (9.7 percent). The one exception was the NLRB: 15.6 percent of its commissioners worked for regulated interests prior to service and only 3.1 percent after.

The most surprising result is the small number of commissioners who were drawn from *and* returned to the regulated industries — the so-called "revolving door" phenomenon. In all, 13.8 percent of the commissioners returned to the regulated industries, from a high of 26.9 percent in the SEC to a low of 5.8 percent in the FTC.

Since the results of this analysis did not demonstrate that representatives of regulated interests "dominate" the "Big Seven," I next asked whether the commissions were dominated by agents of *big business*, those Useem (1978, 1979) calls the "inner group" of the capitalist class.

SERVICE IN BIG BUSINESS

While Useem defines the inner group "as the set [of] people who are in a position to exercise simultaneous influence over the activities of at least *several* major business firms" (Useem, 1978:226; emphasis added), I sought only to determine whether business *elites* served on the "Big Seven." I deemed that the ability to shape the policy of a *single* major corporation was a sufficiently robust indicator of business elite membership. If the commissioners were affiliated with the top U.S. firms they possessed at least the *potential* to influence regulatory policy so as to make it correspond to the needs of big business. Thus, the presence of business elites among the regulators would reaffirm the existence of a "power elite" (Mills, 1956) or "governing class" (Domhoff, 1970) in the United States.

I judged individuals to have served big business if they were either "corporate elites" or "superlawyers."[4] I counted commissioners as members of the corporate elite if they were, at any time, an officer or director of a major U.S. corporation. I defined these corporations as those listed by *Fortune* from 1955 to 1975 as the "Top 500" industrials; "Top 50" commercial banks, insurance companies, diversified financial companies, retailers, transportation firms, utilities, and miscellaneous firms; and the leading investment banks from 1960 to 1969, obtained from *A Decade of Corporate and International Finance* (Hillstrom and King, no date). Prior to 1955 I defined major U.S. corporations as: the 200 largest non-banking corporations (for 1932) compiled by Rochester (1936); the top 200 non-financial corporations (for 1937) compiled by the Temporary National Economic Committee (1940); rail companies mentioned in various editions of *Poor's Manual of the Railroads of the United States*; leading motion-picture industry companies listed by Rochester (1936:186); and corporations identified through the use of histories such as Myers' *History of the Great American Fortunes* (1936), Josephson's *The Robber Barons* (1934), and Lundberg's *America's 60 Families* (1937) and *The Rich and the Super-Rich* (1968). Clearly, this technique is less preferable than the use of systematic listings of firms, but in the absence of listings such as *Fortune's*, I tried to be as inclusive as possible in order to overcome the limitations of the method.

I considered a commissioner to be a superlawyer if he or she was a lawyer in a major corporate firm identified by Smigel (1964), Goulden (1972), Green (1975), Hoffman (1973), or Mayer (1967); or was a lawyer in a firm which comprised 50 or more individuals, as listed in various editions of the *Martindale–Hubbell Law Directory*; or was "house counsel" to a major corporation as defined above. Where the above criteria could not be applied, I examined the biographies of the commissioners to determine whether they were major corporate lawyers. Again, I tried to be as inclusive as possible.

The results of this analysis, shown in Table 2, are surprising. In all, 26.1 percent of the commissioners served big business at some time during their careers. Only in the SEC were more than a third of the commissioners linked with major corporate interests. These findings cast my previous results in a new light: the commissions appear to be staffed by representatives of *smaller* capitalist interests when they are staffed by the members of U.S. business *at all*.

Differences among commissions do not alter the overall picture. Only in the SEC was there a high level of interchange both with the regulated industry *and* big business. For the remaining agencies, even when ties to the regulated were relatively high (as with the FCC), there is little

---

4. The term *superlawyer* is taken from Goulden (1972) and is used here to denote those individuals whose law practices (at any time in their careers) would be likely to include them among the "inner core of the power elite" (Mills, 1956:289).

TABLE 3

Percentage of Commissioners Who Were Members of the Corporate Elite
or Superlawyers, *by Agency*

	Corporate Elites*	Superlawyers	(N)**
ICC	12.2	8.5	(82)
FTC	9.6	19.2	(52)
FPC	7.3	7.3	(41)
FCC	4.2	16.7	(48)
SEC	21.2	28.8	(52)
NLRB	3.1	9.4	(32)
CAB	23.5	8.8	(34)
TOTAL	11.7	14.4	(341)

Notes:

* Those individuals who were both members of the corporate elite and superlawyers were included only in the former category.

** Number of cases on which percentages are based.

evidence to demonstrate the dominance of major corporate interests. With the exception of the SEC, about one-quarter (73 of 289) of the regulators were, at one time, "interlocked" with big business. Only for the FTC and the CAB do the figures for individual commissions slightly exceed this bench mark. The influence of big business is not felt more heavily in industry-specific than cross-industry commissions, and there is no clear pattern of corporate dominance.

This is further confirmed by the evidence shown in Table 3. Of the commissioners who served in big business, fewer than half (11.7 percent of *all* agency members) were corporate elites. If any of the individuals under study are to be considered members of the inner group of the capitalist class, they are to be found among these 40 representatives of the "higher circles" of corporate power. But, by any reasonable standard of domination, this figure is low. For example, Freitag (1975:141) found that 62 percent of U.S. Cabinet members (from 1897 to 1973) also served as corporate directors or officers of major U.S. corporations, and an additional 14 percent served as corporate lawyers.

The regulatory commissions' corporate ties do not appear to be with businesses which dominate the corporate economy. Either we must conclude that small firms have, to some extent, "captured" the commissions or we must reject the "corporate dictatorship" thesis in the sphere of federal regulation. In either case, I must agree with Herring (1936:23) who, examining the biographies of members of the FTC a half-century ago, observed that regulatory commissioners have been largely "men of character and importance, but of 'local' character and 'local' importance." Yet, this failure to demonstrate the corporate "capture" of the "Big Seven" may only be the result of the lengthy time period of this study. Perhaps the early years of regulation in the United States were marked by a separation of commissioners and corporate leaders, only to be supplanted by increased interchange of personnel between the commissions and the corporations.

TRENDS IN CORPORATE CAPTURE OVER TIME

According to the "life cycle" theory of government regulation (Bernstein, 1955), a commission goes through stages of development, beginning with a period in which the agency strongly advocates the "public interest" and culminating in the establishment of a cooperative relationship between the regulators and the regulated. If this model applies to the corporate "capture" of the "Big Seven," we should find increasing personnel interchange as the commissions get older.

To test for this phenomenon, I divided the "life cycles" of the commissions, from their dates of inception until 1975, into "early" and "late" periods. For each time period, I tabulated the

TABLE 4

Percentage of Commissioners Who Served in the Regulated Industry or in Big Business, over Time and by Agency

	Early Period	Late Period	Total
ICC	(1887–1931)	(1931–1975)	(1887–1975)
Regulated Industry	39.0	41.5	40.2
(N)*	(41)	(41)	(82)
Big Business	22.0	19.5	20.7
FTC	(1915–1944)	(1945–1975)	(1915–1975)
Regulated Industry	52.0	37.0	44.2
(N)*	(25)	(27)	(52)
Big Business	28.0	29.6	28.8
FPC	(1930–1952)	(1953–1975)	(1930–1975)
Regulated Industry	18.8	44.0	34.2
(N)*	(16)	(25)	(41)
Big Business	6.2	20.0	14.6
FCC	(1934–1954)	(1955–1975)	(1934–1975)
Regulated Industry	53.6	45.0	50.0
(N)*	(28)	(20)	(48)
Big Business	10.7	35.0	20.8
SEC	(1934–1954)	(1955–1975)	(1934–1975)
Regulated Industry	59.3	48.0	53.8
(N)*	(27)	(25)	(52)
Big Business	51.8	48.0	50.0
NLRB	(1934–1954)	(1955–1975)	(1934–1975)
Regulated Industry	52.6	23.1	40.6
(N)*	(19)	(13)	(32)
Big Business	15.8	7.7	12.5
CAB	(1938–1956)	(1957–1975)	(1938–1975)
Regulated Industry	42.9	23.1	35.3
(N)*	(21)	(13)	(34)
Big Business	38.1	23.1	32.4
TOTAL	Early Periods	Late Periods	Total
Regulated Industry	46.3	39.6	43.1
(N)*	(177)	(164)	(341)
Big Business	25.4	26.8	26.1

Note:
* Number of appointments in each time period on which percentages are based.

number of appointments and the percentage of individuals having served in the regulated industry or big business. If it takes time for a close relationship to develop between commission and industry, we should find a greater percentage of regulated industry and big business representatives in the second half of an agency's existence.

Table 4 shows that none of the commissions revealed a clear trend toward increased overlapping membership over time. In fact, *no* clear pattern of domination is present. There is little evidence to support a "life cycle" theory. Overall, there is a *smaller* percentage of industry representation in the later years (39.6 percent) than in the earlier years (46.3 percent), and a relatively *even* distribution of big business domination (26.8 percent in the later periods; 25.4 percent in the earlier periods). For individual commissions, only the ICC and the FPC show an increase in the proportion of regulated industry personnel, and only the FTC, FPC, and FCC demonstrate higher percentages of big business presence. The SEC, NLRB, and CAB indicate concurrent *declines* in industry *and* major corporate "capture." In the analysis over time there is no noticeable difference between the industry-specific and cross-industry commissions.

CONCLUSION

The results of this study of U.S. regulatory commissioners are difficult to evaluate because there is no universal standard by which to gauge the "capture" of government by corporate interests. But, as Kerbo and Della Fave (1979) indicate, it is perhaps best to consider the question of elite domination as one of *extent* or *degree*. In this sense, the findings of the present investigation are quite dissimilar to those revealed in studies of other governmental leaders in the United States. When the social backgrounds and corporate links of key foreign policy decision-makers (Kolko, 1969), members of Congress (Zweigenhaft, 1975), Cabinet officers (Freitag, 1975; Mintz, 1975), and the occupants of numerous other posts in the federal government (Domhoff, 1967, 1970; Mills, 1956) were examined, a preponderance of members of the upper social class and economic elite was discovered. In contrast, the present study offers results which resemble more closely those of Dye (1976) and Dye *et al.*, (1973), that "there is both concentration and specialization in the nation's institutional elite structure" (Dye *et al.*, 1973:28). While there is *some* evidence to indicate that commissioners are tied to the corporate world, notably after government service, the extent of such links is limited.

The "negative" findings of the preceding analyses are counterintuitive for four reasons. First, they contradict previous studies of other political elites which have demonstrated a corporate "takeover" of positions in the U.S. federal government. Second, they do not support the widely held belief that there is a "revolving door" between the regulatory agencies and the regulated. Third, *big* business "capture" of the commissions is found wanting. Fourth, differences among the commissions and differences over time do not account for the nature of the results.

The data presented here cannot *disprove* the "corporate dictatorship" or "life cycle" perspectives on government regulation of industry. Rather, they reject one version of those theories; namely, that business domination of the regulatory mechanism is accomplished through the interchange of personnel between the corporate and government spheres. Neither can these results support a view of regulation in the "public interest." The absence of business representatives on the commissions does not, alone, permit the conclusion that the agencies reflect a plurality of interests. Given that even pluralists accept the premise that "the 'controlled' thus control the 'controllers' " (Rose, 1967:100), these findings may simply indicate that direct participation by capitalists is unnecessary in the realm of regulatory relations.

There are, perhaps, more effective and unobtrusive means by which corporate interests control regulatory policies and the decisions of the regulators. Clearly, commissioners who come from regulated industries or expect future employment there may show support for those industries while in office. But it is also the case that there is "a potential for corruption from people who don't come from the regulated industry" (John Hill, quoted in MacNeil/Lehrer, 1976:6). The possibilities for exerting such influence derive from several sources: commissioners attend conferences and conventions of the regulated industries (often at industry expense), meet privately and socially with industry representatives, receive gifts from industry personnel, and are subject to "personal lobbying" through many other forms of informal interaction. Likewise, the theory of the "life cycle" of regulatory commissions may be true, despite the failure of these results to demonstrate an increasing trend in personnel "capture." The passage of time may allow the regulated to strengthen their *organizational* ties with the regulators, irrespective of the presence or absence of "corporate types" among the commissioners. Finally, the *structure* of regulatory control in a capitalist economy may severely limit the possibility for commissions to act in a manner which *curtails* the power of private enterprise.

The question of the cooptation of the regulatory commissions by corporate interests awaits further detailed study by social scientists. This analysis of the leadership of the commissions can only serve to show that "the foxes have not taken over the hen house."

REFERENCES

Bernstein, Marver H.
   1955   Regulating Business by Independent Commission. Princeton, N.J.: Princeton University Press.
Domhoff, G. William
   1967   Who Rules America? Englewood Cliffs, N.J.: Prentice-Hall.
   1970   The Higher Circles: The Governing Class in America. New York: Vintage Books.
Dye, Thomas R.
   1976   Who's Running America? Institutional Leadership in the United States. Englewood Cliffs, N.J.:
           Prentice-Hall.
Dye, Thomas R., Eugene R. DeClercq, and John W. Pickering
   1973   "Concentration, specialization, and interlocking among institutional elites." Social Science
           Quarterly 54 (June):8-28.
Edelman, Murray
   1967   The Symbolic Uses of Politics. Urbana: University of Illinois Press.
Fellmeth, Robert C.
   1970   The Interstate Commerce Omission: The Public Interest and the ICC. New York: Grossman
           Publishers.
Freitag, Peter J.
   1975   "The Cabinet and big business: A study of interlocks." Social Problems 23 (December):137-152.
Goulden, Joseph C.
   1972   The Superlawyers: The Small and Powerful World of the Great Washington Law Firms. New
           York: Weybright and Talley.
Green, Mark J.
   1975   The Other Government: The Unseen Power of Washington Lawyers. New York: Grossman
           Publishers.
Herring, E. Pendleton
   1936   Federal Commissioners: A Study of Their Careers and Qualifications. Cambridge, Mass.: Har-
           vard University Press.
Hershman, Arlene
   1977   "Regulating the regulators." Dun's Review 109 (January):34, 36.
Hillstrom, Roger, and Robert King (eds.)
   No date 1960-1969: A Decade of Corporate and International Finance. New York: IDD, Inc.
Hoffman, Paul
   1973   Lions in the Street: The Inside Story of the Great Wall Street Law Firms. New York: Saturday
           Review Press.
Josephson, Matthew
   1934   The Robber Barons: The Great American Capitalists, 1861-1901. New York: Harcourt, Brace.
Keller, Suzanne
   1963   Beyond the Ruling Class: Strategic Elites in Modern Society. New York: Random House.
Kerbo, Harold, and L. Richard Della Fave
   1979   "The empirical side of the power elite debate: An assessment and critique of recent research." The
           Sociological Quarterly 20 (Winter):5-22.
Kolko, Gabriel
   1969   The Roots of American Foreign Policy: An Analysis of Power and Purpose. Boston: Beacon
           Press.
Lubin, Martin
   1968   "Political socialization of independent regulatory commissioners in the United States and their
           behavior." Master's thesis, Department of Political Science, University of Illinois, Urbana.
Lundberg, Ferdinand
   1937   America's 60 Families. New York: Vanguard Press.
   1968   The Rich and the Super-Rich. New York: Bantam Books.
MacNeil/Lehrer Report
   1976   "Revolving door policy." Transcript, WNET/WETA. Air Date: November 9. Educational Broad-
           casting and GWETA.
Matthews, Donald R.
   1954   The Social Backgrounds of Political Decision-Makers. New York: Random House.
Mayer, Martin
   1967   The Lawyers. New York: Harper and Row.
Mills, C. Wright
   1956   The Power Elite. New York: Oxford University Press.
Mintz, Beth
   1975   "The President's Cabinet, 1897-1972: A contribution to the power structure debate." Insurgent
           Sociologist 5 (Spring):131-148.

Myers, Gustavus
    1936   History of the Great American Fortunes. New York: Modern Library.
    [1909]
New York Times
    1975   "Previous industry links noted among U.S. regulatory aides." September 7:36.
Rochester, Anna
    1936   Rulers of America: A Study of Finance Capital. New York: International Publishers.
Rose, Arnold M.
    1967   The Power Structure: Political Process in American Society. New York: Oxford University Press.
Smigel, Erwin O.
    1964   The Wall Street Lawyer: Professional Organization Man? New York: The Free Press of Glencoe.
Stigler, George J.
    1972   "The process of economic regulation." Antitrust Bulletin 17 (Spring):207-235.
Temporary National Economic Committee
    1940   The Distribution of Ownership: The 200 Largest Non-Financial Corporations. Monograph #29. Washington: U.S. Government Printing Office.
Useem, Michael
    1978   "The inner group of the American capitalist class." Social Problems 25 (February):225-240.
    1979   "The social organization of the American business elite and participation of corporation directors in the governance of American institutions." American Sociological Review 44 (August):553-572.
Zerbe, Richard O., Jr.
    1980   "The costs and benefits of early regulation of the railroads." Bell Journal of Economics 11 (Spring):343-350.
Zweigenhaft, Richard
    1975   "Who represents America?" Insurgent Sociologist 5 (Spring):119-130.

THE AMERICAN REVIVAL OF ANTITRUST: THEORIES OF
EFFICIENCY VERSUS REPUBLICAN VALUES, 1948–1968

Unlike British postwar policymaking, American antitrust, of course,
built upon a long-established tradition. Returned to office in 1948,
the Truman Administration attempted to revive antitrust enforcement. Until the Korean conflict compelled a change in
priorities, the Justice Department and the FTC pushed for a return
to policies more consistent with the republican values associated with
Brandeis, while the Democratic Congress amended the Clayton law
with the Celler-Kefauver Anti-merger Act of 1950. The Republican
Eisenhower Administration, moreover, succeeded in winning from
the federal courts victories supporting the old policy and the new
law. Sustained in sweeping terms by the Supreme Court, the
Kennedy and Johnson Administrations maintained policy continuity
with their successors. Generally, Democrat and Republican
presidents respected the interests of small business in merger cases
and defended competition in cartel suits. In addition, after Truman,
all three Justice Departments opposed fair trade laws and other
antitrust exemptions. The mix of policies reflected the ambiguous
political status of large and small business, while the resulting
tensions gave rise to economic theories emphasizing efficiency. The
interplay of government policies, interests, and theory facilitated the
conglomerate mergers of the 1960s.

After Truman's election victory the relation between antitrust and
big business remained ambivalent. In part, popular distrust of big
government limited the Administration's effectiveness. Pressure
from large and small business groups, antagonistic newspaper
editorials, and division within the Administration prevented passage
of legislation which would have established a Small Business Agency.
There was widespread resistance also to government prosecution of
the A & P Company solely because of bigness. The public and
Congress opposed the Small Business Agency as indicative of the
slide toward collectivism and the A & P prosecution as an ill-
conceived attack on consumers. On the grounds of free enterprise
and states' rights, however, Congress established new antitrust
exemptions, first in the fields of cooperative rate-making practices

known as the basing-point system and second in the states' Fair Trade Laws.[92]

The antimerger amendment to the Clayton Act also received serious consideration. Theoretically, the legislation avoided the "big-government" stigma because it increased federal antitrust authority to protect small firms in the name of free enterprise, without enlarging the size of the federal bureaucracy. During 1949 there was a recession which continued until the Korean conflict. While the new Democratic congressional majority supported antimerger legislation, the environment of uncertainty led a Republican Senator to admit that rising "antibigness" criticism was not politically partisan, but consistent with a long American tradition. The critics directed their antagonism not toward merchandizing firms such as A & P, but at such corporate giants as General Motors and DuPont. Most of the modest-sized enterprisers represented by the Small Business Federation were within the distribution sector; since the TNEC they had pressured Congress to close the Clayton Act's asset-loophole. Also, unlike the proposal for the small business administration, the antimerger provision did not suggest the need for increased taxes to fund a new agency.[93]

Nevertheless, the law was the object of contention. The leading proponents were Congressman Emmanuel Celler and Senator Estes Kefauver who supported much the same measures which Congress had rejected in 1947. *Business Week*, *Fortune*, and principally Republican conservatives retorted that these proposals were based on resistance to bigness per se. According to the rule of reason, they rightly claimed, bigness in and of itself was not "bad." Celler and Kefauver, the FTC, the Council of Economic Advisors, and their small-business constituents repudiated this argument. Appealing to the distrust of bigness, the FTC's economist Corwin Edwards said, "From an economic standpoint, all businesses reach a point where they begin to lose their efficiency because of their size." Similarly, Celler stated, "The individual and small business man cannot flower amidst the weeds of monopoly."[94] Kefauver and Celler argued further that the antimerger amendment to the Clayton Act was indispensable for the very reason that the federal courts in such cases as *Columbia Steel* had made the prevention of merger by government prosecution virtually impossible. With Truman's support, Celler's House Committee conducted the most thorough investigation of mergers since the TNEC.[95]

After protracted debate and parliamentary maneuvering Congress

55

passed and Truman signed in December, 1950 the Celler-Kefauver
Antimerger Act. Yet, during the rest of Truman's Administration,
the new Act and antitrust generally was relatively quiescent. The
Korean conflict, combined with conflicts within the Justice
Department, limited the implementation of a coherent enforcement
strategy. The various cases the Justice Department and the Antitrust
Division had initiated against the big firms remained active. After
1950, however, the Administration's main antitrust activities
involved efforts to provide small firms with a fair proportion of
military contracts. Thus, despite the enactment of the most stringent
antitrust measure since the Sherman Act, and the Justice Department's willing return to a Brandeisian "big-is-bad" philosophy,
American antitrust enforcement suffered the same fate as Thurman
Arnold's activism of twenty years earlier.[96]

President Dwight Eisenhower consummated and extended what
the Truman Administration had begun. Numerous studies by
economists supported the view that the Antimerger Act facilitated
the merger movement which began in the mid-fifties and peaked at
the end of the 1960s. The polls of business opinion, as well as the
business press indicated that antitrust generally and the law
governing mergers in particular, influenced the increase of mergers.
Even so the advice corporate lawyers gave their clients rested upon
the substantive action of the Justice Department and the courts.[97]
Shortly after Eisenhower took office in 1953, Attorney General
Brownell set out a broad enforcement policy. Brownell noted that
the press, lawyers, business leaders, and the general public expressed
heightened interest in vigorous antitrust enforcement. Accordingly,
the 1952 Platform Pledge of the Republican Party included an
antitrust plank. The Party pledged equality of enforcement,
simplication of administration, assistance to business seeking good-
faith compliance, and "an *uncompromising determination* that there
shall be no slackening of effort to protect free enterprise against
monopoly and unfair competition; and most certainly – no winking
at violations of the law and no wholesale dismissal of pending
suits."[98]

Brownell explained how the Administration intended to fulfill this
pledge. He supported the recommendations of expert legal and
business groups for legislation streamlining, simplifying, and exp-
editing antitrust prosecutions. As one who was "proud of...
American capitalism," Brownell said he was nonetheless "old
fashioned enough to believe... that this control should be in keeping

with a middle-of-the-road political philosophy... aimed primarily at the elimination of predatory practices." Quoting a law professor Brownell emphasized that big business had "made no important managerial policy or decision without conscious consideration of the prohibitions of the antitrust laws." The Attorney General expressed sympathy also for the "continual cry of little business that, being unable to pay large retainers to insure proper advice, it [was] the recipient of by far an undue proportion of criminal prosecutions, because of the average small business-man's inability to determine without advice whether his conduct [was] within or without the law."[99]

In the tradition of the TNEC Brownell also proposed the appointment of the "Attorney General's National Committee to Study the Antitrust Laws."[100] The publication of the Commission's report in 1955, coincided with the rise of merger activity.[101] Partisan criticism arose in Congress because of the delay. Nevertheless, an internal memorandum of September, 1953 expressed the Administration's view that the wait for the report was justified "by the great desirability of resolving uncertainty confronting business management as a means for stimulating investment and high employment as well as vigorous competition."[102] Newspapers and experts anticipated that the report would have significant impact on business structure and conduct. During the spring of 1955 the Eisenhower Cabinet considered the Commission's findings prior to publication. The Commission favored adherence to the rule of reason as applied in the *Columbia Steel* case. Bigness was not unlawful, yet enforcement of the Antimerger Act was especially necessary in cases involving vertical and horizontal mergers. The report did not mention conglomerate mergers.[103]

In addition, the Commission urged a "harmonization" of the goals of the Clayton, Robinson-Patman, and Sherman Acts. It recommended the repeal of the "fair trade" exemption, but few changes were proposed in patent law. Although the Commission rejected establishing an antitrust exemption for agreements involving foreign trade, it recommended careful attention to the needs of exporters within the existing legal framework. Finally, the report supported technical modifications of antitrust procedures, indicating that there should be greater reliance on advice and negotiation, especially through consent decrees. Government and private law suits, of course, were important, but because they often were drawn out it was necessary to rely more upon negotiation.[104]

57

Throughout the remaining years of Eisenhower's presidency the Commission's report guided the course of antitrust action. Within the Administration, private memoranda recognized the political usefulness of following the recommendations pertaining to small enterprise. Since the 1930s the Democrats had gained support among farmers and modest-sized retailers and wholesalers in small farming communities which were traditionally Republican constituencies. The middlemen were divided concerning fair trade laws, but generally favored Robinson-Patman. Farmers had no set position for or against the latter law; they opposed, however, fair trade statutes. Accordingly, the Administration concluded that fair trade "acts operated to the detriment of free competition" and so their repeal seemed "advantageous"; yet there was to be little interference with Robinson-Patman. The Justice Department also attacked price-fixing agreements in the name of "fighting inflation."[105] In quiet cooperation with the FTC the Justice Department negotiated important consent decrees, including one with RCA which placed valuable patent information in the public domain. The Administration also decided that vital elements of the international petroleum cartel did not violate the antitrust laws.[106]

The Commission's Report also pointed out the importance of antitrust to international business generally. Following the Commission's recommendation the Administration's Council on Foreign Economic Policy (CFEP) established an interdepartmental Task Force in spring, 1955 which included representatives from the Department of State, Justice Department, FTC, Treasury, and the National Security Council. Arguing that the law of European nations permitted greater trade restraints, American foreign-business interests such as the Chamber of Commerce of London contended that the antitrust laws hurt their competitiveness. Throughout the remainder of the Eisenhower Administration the Task Force studied this and related issues. The resulting report concluded that the nation's foreign trade, investment, and the exchange of technology were being adversely affected by the uncertainty of the law. Also, antitrust enforcement in some situations created foreign relations and national security problems with which neither the Attorney General nor the President has sufficient statutory authority to cope. There was disagreement, however, over whether to establish an administrative mechanism for "advance consultation" between business and the antitrust enforcement agencies. Brownell opposed establishing such a process without legislation, and he had higher legislative priorities of his own. Finally, the relevant government departments merely improved the means of disseminating antitrust information to foreign businesses.[107]

By Eisenhower's second term a high priority was antimerger litigation. In April, 1957 the Executive Assistant to Brownell wrote to the White House that the "most important immediate objective of the Antitrust Division ... [was] to obtain an authoritative court ruling on the Anti-merger statute." The Division had reached agreement "with counsel for Bethlehem and Youngstown to speed up consideration of that merger case, which will be a test case for all industry ... result[ing] in a speedy court decision on the main legal problems troubling corporate officials regarding mergers."[108] As this case and others proceeded, the Government won a noteworthy victory against DuPont, which required the firm to divest its share in the General Motors Corporation. Notwithstanding this decision, however, the necessity of an authoritative test of the Antimerger Act remained. "Striking and surprising" as the Court's *DuPont* decision was, a memorandum observed, "it will have little practical effect in both the short term and the long term." The decision might "become a factor in businessmens' decisions respecting new vertical acquisitions." But congressional unwillingness to fund an "antitrust crusade," combined with the closely divided Court handing down the decision made revolutionary consequences unlikely. Finally, the "1954 [Brown] decision on school segregation provides some lessons with respect to the speed of implementation of 'revolutionary' court actions."[109]

By the end of the Eisenhower Administration, Brownell's Antitrust Division began fulfilling the Celler-Kefauver Act's promise. Antitrust enforcers took as their point of departure the recommendations of the Antitrust Commission Report. The Antitrust Division and the FTC thus sought to undercut the legal basis of horizontal and vertical mergers. Generally they succeeded. The Department's famous DuPont victory was less important than its blocking of a merger between Bethlehem and Youngstown Steel. Brownell won the sort of case Clark had lost in *Columbia Steel*. Once corporate lawyers realized that vertical and horizontal mergers were unlikely to survive legal prosecution they advised their clients that conglomerate mergers were safe. Significantly, the Antitrust Commission had not mentioned conglomerate mergers, so the Eisenhower

Administration's antimerger policy encouraged a new merger wave. Meanwhile, in the prosecution of price-fixing agreements, the opposition to Fair Trade, and the reform of antitrust technicalities the Eisenhower antitrust officials sought to win over small business.[110]

Notwithstanding a contrary public image, the transition from Republican to Democratic antitrust enforcement was characterized by continuity. During the Kennedy Administration, the media dramatized several confrontations between Attorney General Robert F. Kennedy and certain business leaders. Yet, concerning the enforcement of antitrust itself, the reality was more prosaic. Lee Loevinger, former judge of the Minnesota Supreme court and Kennedy's first Assistant Attorney General of the Antitrust Division, said that between the two Administrations, "I don't think there was any dramatic change in policy." According to Loevinger his Republican predecessor, Robert T. Bicks, "did pretty well. I think that he ran away with it a little bit, and he probably went beyond what the Eisenhower Administration really wanted as an antitrust policy." In addition, many of the lawyers and staff Bicks employed remained under Loevinger.[111]

Loevinger and his successor William H. Orrick, Jr., as had Brownell, tried to balance coercion and restraint. The Kennedy Administration's official position was that "far from being natural enemies, government and business" were "necessary allies" in making the "free enterprise system" work. In practical terms this meant that over two-thirds of the Division's civil cases ended up in consent decrees. To facilitate the negotiational process with adequate safeguards, however, Loevinger initiated a procedure requiring public disclosure prior to entering a decree. More quietly, the Justice Department and the FTC maintained a liaison permitting private parties to submit a request for merger clearance from either agency. The Division also significantly influenced passage of the "most significant" antitrust measure since the Antimerger Act, the law for civil investigative demand. Growing out of Loevinger's recommendations, Celler and Kefauver supported the law which strengthened the Division's investigative authority, particularly where firms sought clearance to merge. Loevinger and Orrick also emphasized the education of business leaders and their lawyers through numerous public presentations.[112]

Loevinger also implemented the Republican recommendation of

creating a Foreign Commerce section within the Antitrust Division. Before Brownell took significant action on the Task Force Report of the CFEP, the Eisenhower presidency ended. As a United States representative to the Organization of Economic Cooperation and Development committee studying international restrictive practices, Loevinger understood legal issues involving foreign commerce. It was not surprising, therefore, that he implemented the Republican initiative. Among the units of the Antitrust Division, the Foreign Commerce Section coordinated matters relating to international business of foreign nationals, maintained liaison with the State Department and other federal agencies on similar matters, and carried out the Justice Department's responsibilities in connection with the OECD. The Section was small and rarely involved in litigation.[113] Loevinger observed that its existence indicated neither a "more nor less rigorous attitude toward antitrust enforcement in foreign trade, but rather a recognition of the growing importance of international trade and an effort to develop greater knowledge and expertise in this area."[114]

Efforts to maintain a balanced policy carried over into prosecutions. As Loevinger said, the "question, basically, came down to the relative emphasis that you give to pricefixing cases on the one hand and merger cases on the other." The former included the more easily won "conspiratorial action cases," whereas the latter were the harder merger cases. Initially, "congressional antitrust liberals" criticized the Justice Department's emphasis on price-fixing cases. By the time Orrick replaced Loevinger in 1963, however, the Division had "brought more merger cases than in any comparable period before or since."[115] The Court's acceptance of the federal government's arguments in these cases made it "clear" Orrick concluded, that both horizontal and vertical "anticompetitive mergers" were "now effectively prohibited by antitrust laws." As a result, he predicted an "increase in conglomerate mergers." The conglomerates were "subject to antitrust laws, but their effect on competition is more complex and therefore more difficult to establish."[116]

The search for balance reflected mixed political tensions. The Kennedy Administration's antitrust enforcement, like that under Eisenhower, recognized that on most issues small business was a divided constituency. Accordingly, the Kennedy Justice Department followed its predecessor by opposing fair-trade legislation, vigorously prosecuting price-fixing conspiracies, and working to streamline technical procedures in order to reduce the advantages large firms had in the market for lawyer services. Although not without qualification, the Federation of Small Business on the whole approved of these outcomes. Antimerger policy remained ambivalent. Publicly disclaiming support for the theory that "bigness is bad," the government actively encouraged or at least did not resist administrative procedures which facilitated advanced approval of mergers. Yet in defense of competition it attacked increased corporate concentration, overcoming adverse decisions in federal district courts to win in the Supreme Court. The result under Kennedy was the same as under Eisenhower: horizontal and vertical mergers steadily declined while conglomerate mergers increased. Antitrust liberals applauded the former and criticized the latter.[117]

The Court's landmark *Brown Shoe* decision of 1962 facilitated the antimerger policy. Initiated during the Eisenhower years, the *Brown Shoe* case applied the ALCOA "economic-effects" theory to prevent a merger of the fourth and twelfth largest shoe producers which would have established retail control of a market share totaling only 8 percent. Nevertheless, the Court decided that because the firm's increased horizontal and vertical concentration significantly enlarged its market share in various local markets, the merger violated the Celler-Kefauver Act. Said Loevinger, the decision, "prohibits acquisitions, either of stock or assets, where competition in *any* line of commerce in *any* section of the country may be substantially lessened. The test as stated in the Senate Report on the [Celler-Kefauver] Bill is whether there is a reasonable probability that competition *may* be lessened." *Brown Shoe* shaped the course of the Court's antimerger decision-making for nearly a decade.[118]

Even so, the Kennedy Administration's antimerger enforcement reflected a distrust of bigness. As had every Antitrust Division head since Thurman Arnold, Orrick insisted that this pro-competition policy rested on a rigorous analysis of economic effects. The Antitrust Division, Orrick affirmed, had "no authority to balance any violation of the law against the social, political, and economic benefits which we feel might be derived from a merger."[119] The string of cases from *Brown Shoe* on, however, indicated that a basic distrust of increased concentration and greater corporate size was central to the government arguments the Court adopted. It was noteworthy that most federal district courts rejected these arguments, making victory contingent upon a favorable review by the Supreme Court. The working assumption shared by both the antitrust prosecutors and the Court was that competition resulted from limiting the number of big firms and increasing or maintaining the number of small ones.[120]

The continuity of postwar antitrust enforcement continued during the Johnson Administration. Ramsey Clark, who followed Nicholas Katzenbach as Attorney General, supervised first Harvard Law School antitrust expert, Donald Turner, and later Turner's executive assistant, Edwin M. Zimmerman, as head of the Antitrust Division. Despite the personnel changes the mix of cases fit the pattern established since the late 1940s: the bulk involved price-fixing while the number of antimerger suits steadily rose. As had their Republican and Democratic predecessors, Clark and Turner opposed fair trade laws. Although unsuccessful on that point, they blocked attempts by the auto industry to establish antitrust exemptions for research in connection with automobile safety legislation. They also won Congressional approval for strengthened procedures in merger investigations. Through the Divisions' Foreign Commerce Section and other units in the Department, discussions with British and EEC officials on restrictive practices increased. Following the lead of the White House and State Department, Clark and Turner approached the international petroleum cartel with flexibility. On the whole, the Johnson Administration's antitrust policy successfully reconciled diverse political pressures, particularly those arising from small business.[121]

There was innovation in the field of mergers. Clark, like Katzenbach, continued to win victories in the Supreme Court applying the Antimerger Act to vertical and horizontal mergers. Yet beginning in 1965 the numbers of conglomerate mergers climbed significantly, peaking three years later. Accordingly, when Clark became Attorney General in early 1967, he called for increased prosecution of the conglomerates. As the business press and polls of business leaders showed, however, successful antitrust prosecution of vertical and horizontal mergers on grounds of their anti-competitiveness had facilitated conglomerate mergers for the very reason that uncompetitive effects were difficult to prove. Indeed, the Orrick Antitrust Division initiated very few such prosecutions because the connections between conglomerates and established antitrust competition doctrines were so complex. Undaunted, Clark attempted to persuade first Turner and then Zimmerman that stepped-up prosecution of conglomerates was vital.[122]

Turner's stance on the conglomerate issue was influential. At Harvard he had co-authored a seminal article which argued that contemporary antitrust competition doctrine permitted prosecution of conglomerates on very limited grounds. A court might accept proof of uncompetitive effects arising from "potential competition," "decisive competitive advantage," and "reciprocity." During the mid-1960s the FTC applied a "reciprocity" theory to block the merger of a producer of processed foods, Consolidated Foods, and Gentry, a manufacturer of dehydrated onion and garlic. The FTC used the same theory to prevent the merger of General Dynamics and Liquid Carbonic Company. As a result, Turner's ideas received close scrutiny from antitrust lawyers representing business and the government.[123]

"Reciprocity" and the other doctrines looked to economic effects. But the underlying presumption against concentration was consistent with a general distrust of bigness. Turner was concerned that this distrust might result in an antitrust policy based on social and political goals. Favoring a policy of support for the interests of consumers as defined by economic analysis, Turner resisted using his theories to launch a general attack on conglomerate "super concentration." He stated, "One cannot support an attack of much greater depth on conglomerates without trenching on significant economic and other values, and therefore without an unprecedented reliance on judgments of an essentially political nature."[124]

Turner denied that social or political value provided an adequate basis for antitrust policy. He told a meeting of the ABA's Antitrust Section, that achieving "order" in antitrust law was unlikely until "we can succeed in disentangling it from many policy considerations having little or nothing to do with the protection of competition." Antitrust enforcers "should not attack a merger simply because the companies are large in the absolute sense, and we should not attack aggressive but fair competitive conduct simply on the basis that some competitors are hurt." Turner observed, however, that lawyers could use these same arguments to defend increased corporate concentration. Since becoming head of the Division in 1965, he said, proponents defended contemplated mergers on the "grounds that it would promote the national defense, assist in solving the balance of payments problem, reduce unemployment and contribute to the

Administration's anti-poverty program. I fully expect to hear before long that a merger should be allowed because it will contribute to the President's program for making America beautiful."[125]

The tension between the policy preferences of Clark and Turner was evident in the Merger Guidelines of 1968. One of the most important innovations of postwar merger policy, the merger guidelines proposed statistical concentration levels that determined the basis for bringing an antitrust suit. Following the tests established in *Brown Shoe*, the basic criteria were related to market structure. "As the market share of firms increased, their ability to acquire a firm in the same market without fear of recrimination decreased," explained one expert. "In a market where concentration had increased 7 percent in the past ten years, an acquisition of only 2 percent was enough to prompt an antitrust suit." According to *Business Week*, Turner's Guidelines made "no sweeping changes." But the *Antitrust and Trade Regulation Review* observed that the guidelines made "a significant contribution to what has come to be known as the 'numbers game' – the use of market share figures to show a merger's anticompetitive effect."[126]

Turner's merger guidelines grew out of his experience as head of the Antitrust Division. Near the start of his term in 1965 he preached how important to the enforcement of antitrust was publicity. In their role as business advisors the antitrust bar was especially vital. Significant, too, was the research and writing of legal academics. Publication of the "Government's views" thus "speeds up the process of development of the law by laying the basis for a continuing dialogue among Government, the bar, business groups and the academic profession." Publication also generated "empirical data that will help us to decide whether tentative positions have gone too far or not far enough." In time, however, the pressure from "lawyers and/or their business clients ... requesting general advice or 'guidelines'" became sufficiently great that Turner refused private appointments with these individuals or groups. The need to reconcile this pressure with the commitment to publicity facilitated the formulation of the guidelines.[127]

The Guidelines codified the tension between economic and sociopolitical values which had characterized the government's antitrust policies and the Court's merger decisions since ALCOA. The theoretical preoccupation with competition obscured the conflict between the triumph of oligopoly in American big business and the persistent distrust of concentration indicated by the continuing attack on horizontal and vertical mergers. Thus the "order" Turner sought to create in antitrust law assumed that limiting levels of corporate concentration did not interfere with the scale and organizational economies which resulted in benefits to consumers. Ultimately, however, this vision of competition was unable to escape the value judgments inherent in the determination of what exactly were appropriate concentration levels. The complexity of the problem was suggested by the attempt to distinguish between anticompetitive effects in horizontal and vertical mergers on the one hand and conglomerates on the other.

92 Branyon, "Antimonopoly Activities," 65–98, 133–208.

93 *Ibid.*, 78–83, 123–133.

94 Fligstein, *Transformation of Corporate Control*, as quoted, 188, 189.

95 *Ibid.*, 190.

96 *Ibid.*, 197; and notes 92, 93.

97 Fligstein, *Transformation of Corporate Control*, 195–225, 230–238. For an overview of the Eisenhower antitrust policy see: Theodore Philip Kovaleff, *Business and Government During the Eisenhower Administrative: A Study of the Antitrust Policy of the Antitrust Division of the Justice Department* (Athens, Ohio, 1980).

98 "Our Antitrust Policy," Friday, 26 June 1953, 2, 3. Neil Jacoby, Box 3, EPL.

99 *Ibid.*, 6.

100 Kovaleff, *Business and Government*, 17–48.
101 See note 92.
102 Neil H. Jacoby to Arthur F. Burns, 21 September 1953, Neil Jacoby Box 3, File "Antitrust," EPL.
103 Note 100. See also Robert Gray to Brownell [no date]; and "Preview of the Report of the Attorney General's Committee to Study the Antitrust Laws," 16 March 1955, White House, Cabinet, 1953–1960, Box 1. File "Antitrust," EPL.
104 *Ibid.*
105 *Ibid.*; and see Lubel, *Future of American Politics*, 167, 170–171; Estes Kefauver, "Anti-Trust Laws: Progress in Reverse," *The New Leader*, 28 February 1955, 12–14.
106 Brownell to Eisenhower, 15 September 1954, Areeda Papers, Box 5, File, "Antitrust (Oil) Cartels," EPL; Harold H. Healy to A. J. Goodpaster and Albert P. Toner, 19 February 1958, White House Staff Research Group, Box 13, File "Justice," EPL.
107 The CFEP files are extensive in the Eisenhower Library. For summary see "Report of the Antitrust Task Force of the Council on Foreign Economic Policy," CFEP Records, 1954–1961, Box 4, File 524, EPL.
108 Harold, H. Healy to A. J. Goodpaster and Albert P. Toner, 9 April 1957; Healy to Goodpaster and Toner, 17 December 1956, White House Office Staff, Box 12, File "Justice 1–100," EPL.
109 Irving H. Siegal to Paul W. McCracken, "A Note on the Supreme Court Decision in DuPont Case," 17 June 1957, Areeda Papers, Box 5, File "Antitrust," EPL.
110 Note 97.
111 "Oral History Interview with Lee Loevinger," 13 May 1966, 7, 8, 9, quote at 10, KPL.
112 *Ibid.*, quote at 4, 12, 22–23.
113 *Ibid.*, 40–44.
114 "Summary of Discussion with Assistant Attorney General Lee Loevinger … Concerning the Policies, Operation and Organization of the Antitrust Division," 28 January 1963; quote at 5, Personal Papers of Ramsey Clark, Box 40, JPL.
115 "Oral History Interview with Loevinger," 12,
116 "The Antitrust Division – Should its Powers be Expanded or Restricted?" 5, 6, Orrick Papers, Box 15, drafts of talk for Meeting of the Commonwealth Club, 9 March 1965, KPL.
117 *Ibid.*, Fligstein, *Transformation of Corporate Control*, 201–203.
118 Fligstein, *Transformation of Corporate Control*, as quoted 201, and text, 201–203.
119 "The Antitrust Division – Should its Powers be Expanded or Restricted?" 7, 8, Orrick Papers, Box 15, drafts of talk for Meeting of the Commonwealth Club, 9 March 1965, KPL.
120 Note 118; and Neale and Goyder, *Antitrust Laws*, 186.
121 "Justice Department History Antitrust Division," "Administrative

History of the Justice Department," Volume 8, Part 12; James M.
Frey to James Gaither, 25 November 1966, Office Files of James
Gaither, Antitrust General, JPL; *Attitudes of Independent Business
Proprietors Toward Antitrust Law, 1943 to 1963* (National Federation of
Independent Business, San Mateo, California, 1963).

122 Fligstein, *Transformation of Corporate Control*, 203–206; notes 116–119;
"Conglomerates Beware," *Forbes*, 1 November 1967, 27 30.
123 Fligstein, *Transformation of Corporate Control*, 204–206.
124 *Ibid.*, 205–206.
125 "Address," Delivered before Antitrust Section of the ABA, Miami,
Florida, 10 August 1965, at 8–9, Personal Papers of Ramsey Clark,
Box 40, "Antitrust Division 1965," JPL.
126 As quoted, Fligstein, *Transformation of Corporate Control*, 219, 220.
127 "Address," Miami, 10 August 1965, 6–7; Turner to Clark, 7 December
1965, Clark Papers, "Antitrust Division," Box 40, JPL.

4

What Happened to the Antitrust Movement?

Notes on the Evolution of an American Creed

Richard Hofstadter

I

The antitrust movement is one of the faded passions of American reform, but historians have neglected to tell us very much about its fate. The writers of general history books deal with the antitrust issue in connection with the rise of the great corporations and the passage of the Sherman Act and then, again, in discussing antitrust sentiment in the Progressive era and the enactment of further regulatory laws. Most of them touch on it briefly once more, when they discuss the New Deal antitrust revival associated with Thurman Arnold and the T.N.E.C. Then, for the most part, they drop the subject. Presumably they drop it not because they imagine that antitrust has lost its role in our society, but rather because it is no longer the object of much public attention.

Although it may seem superficial of historians to be influenced by such a criterion, I have come to realize that in their neglect of this matter there is a certain self-protective wisdom at work. In our time, the issue of the regulation of monopoly and competition has acquired a complexity, both legal and economic, that the historian is ill-equipped to handle. It is much simpler for him to sweep the whole thing under the carpet. And in his willingness to do so lies one key to the disappearance of the antitrust issue from our politics. In this matter the historian too is a layman who shares the general public bafflement. He sympathizes with the common retreat from an issue that has become a maze of technical refinements in which specialists alone can find their way.

Perhaps the essence of the problem can be put this way: once the United States had an antitrust movement without antitrust prosecutions; in our time there have been antitrust prosecutions without an antitrust movement.

Like all such formulas, this one oversimplifies considerably, but it has the merit of putting in stark outline a puzzling episode in the history of reform. In 1890, when Congress passed the Sherman Act, many Congressmen believed that they were responding to an overwhelming public demand; it is the presence of this kind of influential and active sentiment that I mean, when I speak of a social movement. During the mid-nineties, when the depression made other issues more urgent, there was a brief lapse of interest in the "trust problem"; but then a new outburst of business consolidation between 1898 and 1904 quickened it into life again. During the Progressive era, strong public sentiment against big business made itself felt almost everywhere. Often a common hostility to big business was the one link that bound together a variety of interest groups whose views on most other issues diverged widely. The Progressive era, which culminated with the passage of the Clayton Act and the creation of the Federal Trade Commission in 1914, probably marks the high point of anti-big-business sentiment in our history.

But the early accomplishments of antitrust, hampered as it was by the courts and by administrative lassitudes, were slight. Historians have often made sport of the contrast between aspiration and performance, particularly of the reputation of Theodore Roosevelt as a trustbuster, which survived his repeated repudiations of the trustbusting philosophy. They have enjoyed pointing out that under his regime the Antitrust Division of the Justice Department sallied out against the combined might of the great corporations with a staff of five lawyers and four stenographers.

Roosevelt and his contemporaries witnessed the first of three phases in the history of antitrust. In the first, from about 1890 to 1914—the era of the founding fathers of antitrust—the opening steps were taken, in statutes and in the courts, to define what form the antitrust efforts of the federal government might take and to see how they would work. The second phase, lasting from the First World War to about 1937, might be called the era of neglect. Enforcement during the conservative 1920's was almost minimal, and in its opening years the New Deal actually suspended the antitrust laws to accommodate the N.R.A. codes. The present phase, from 1937 onward, is marked by a considerable revival, which stems from the New Deal's reactivation of the Antitrust Division and from the T.N.E.C. investigation. It is characterized by a sharp legal and administrative increase in antitrust activity. But this has taken place without any corresponding revival of public sentiment against big business, indeed in the face of a growing public acceptance of the large corporation. In this phase, antitrust concern has been confined to small groups of legal and economic specialists, who carry on their work without widespread public interest or support.

Whereas the first of these phases was characterized by tentative efforts at enforcement with nearly negligible results, and the second by minimal or token enforcement, the latest turn in antitrust is relatively vigorous. Here prosecutions may serve as a rough index. During all the years from 1891 to 1938, the government instituted an average of nine cases a year. The peak years in this half century were 1912 and 1913, with 29 and 27 prosecutions. For about 30 years after these dates the typical load was about a dozen cases, often considerably fewer, and the objects of prosecution were not often vital points in American industry. In 1940, with the Roosevelt-Arnold revitalization well under way, the number of cases jumped to 85—only two short of the number instituted during the entire first *two decades* of the Sherman Act. After that the number fluctuated, but stayed at a considerably higher level than before 1938.[1] In 1962 the Antitrust Division,

[1] On prosecutions to 1940 see Walton Hamilton and Irene Till, *Antitrust in Action*, T.N.E.C. Monograph No. 16 (Washington, 1940), esp. pp. 135–143; see also *United States versus Economic Concentration and Monopoly*, a Staff

employing 300 lawyers and working with a budget of $6,600,000, instituted 92 cases. Figures, of course, are crude, but a qualitative analysis of the legal victories of the antitrust revival would show that it has won decisions from the courts, particularly since 1940, that have amplified the possibility of enforcement. Despite the collapse of antitrust feeling both in the public at large and among liberal intellectuals, antitrust as a legal-administrative enterprise has been solidly institutionalized in the past quarter of a century. The antitrust enterprise thus appears to be a case of magical levitation, and it seems incumbent upon us to find out what is holding it up.

II

The antitrust movement and its legislation are characteristically and uniquely American. Perhaps this is attributable to the particularly flagrant form that monopoly took in America during the early years of its development. It may also be said that no other people has taken the principle of economic competition so earnestly as to try to underwrite it by statute, although in recent years some European countries have begun to show interest in the American approach to the subject, and we may see more of this in the future. The idea of competition as a means of social regulation—as an economic, political, and moral force—has grown stronger roots in the United States than elsewhere, partly because it has had little to compete with in the way of aristocratic, militaristic, or labor-socialist theories. Founded to some degree in the common-law tradition whose injunctions against restraint of trade proved an inadequate basis for the protection of competition, the antimonopoly tradition rested intellectually upon classical economic theory and upon the pluralism of American democratic thought.

But in America competition was more than a theory: it was a way of life and a creed. From its colonial beginnings through most of the nineteenth century, ours was overwhelmingly a

---

Report to the Monopoly Subcommittee on Small Business, House of Representatives (Washington, 1946), pp. 276–289.

nation of farmers and small-town entrepreneurs—ambitious, mobile, optimistic, speculative, antiauthoritarian, egalitarian, and
competitive. As time went on, Americans came to take it for
granted that property would be widely diffused, that economic
and political power would be decentralized. The fury with
which they could be mobilized against any institution that even
appeared to violate these expectations by posing a threat of
monopoly was manifest in the irrational assault on the Bank of
the United States during Jackson's presidency. Their most respected thinkers habitually assured them that the order of society
that they enjoyed was God-ordained or natural, and they probably thought it would last forever.

Then, with extraordinary rapidity as historical time is reckoned, that order was overwhelmed by the giant corporation. In
the last three decades of the nineteenth century a wholly new
economic order came into being. An American born in 1828,
the year of Jackson's election, came of age in a society in which
the old small-enterprise economy, however dynamic and expan-
sive, had kept its fundamental pattern more or less intact. But
in his mature years he would have watched that economy fast
becoming obsolete, and if he lived as late as 1904, he would have
seen industry concentrated to a degree unthinkable even during
most of his adult life. This economic transformation happened
so fast that the mind could not easily absorb it. An entire
people could hardly be expected to cease overnight to dream the
dream of the small entrepreneur. In 1900 the problem of big
business and the threat of monopoly were still so new that it was
hard to get one's bearings. Bigness had come with such a rush
that its momentum seemed irresistible. No one knew when or
how it could be stopped.

It is hardly surprising that the men of the first antitrust generation made some frightening projections into the future. A
nation that had gone so fast from competitive small enterprise to
corporate giantism might readily develop with equal speed from
corporate giantism to a system of monopolistic tyranny. Hence,
discussions of big business in the last decades of the nineteenth
and the opening decade of the twentieth century are full of
anxious prognostications, most of them plausible enough at the

time; however, hardly any of them have been realized. In 1890
and even in 1914, bigness had not yet been domesticated either
as a force in the economic world or as a factor in the American
imagination.

Since it had been widely assumed that competition, being
"natural," would be largely self-perpetuating, the classical theory
had not reckoned with the possible necessity of underwriting
competition by statute. But as soon as it became clear that
the common-law tradition against restraints on trade had ceased
to have any force and that state laws on the subject were altogether inadequate to the purpose, the demand arose for federal
action. George Gunton thought in 1888 that "the public mind
has begun to assume a state of apprehension almost amounting
to alarm," and that the social atmosphere was "surcharged with
an indefinite but almost inexpressible fear of trusts." [2] Senator
Sherman warned his colleagues that "the popular mind is agitated with problems that may disturb the social order," singling
out inequities of wealth and the formation of combinations of
capital so great that they threatened to produce "a trust for every
production and a master to fix the price for every necessity of
life." Congress must heed the appeal of the voters, he said, "or
be ready for the socialist, the communist, and the nihilist. Society is now disturbed by forces never felt before." [3] Historians,
like contemporaries, have differed as to how imperative the
demand for federal action was. In a careful survey of articulate
opinion on the "trust" problem in 1890, Hans B. Thorelli concludes that public demand, though perhaps less than an irresistible tide, was too strong to be ignored by the politicians.

Historians have often doubted that the Congress of 1890 meant
the Sherman Act to be a serious threat to trusts and have suggested that it was cynically offering a sop to public sentiment.

[2] Quoted by G. W. Stocking and M. W. Watkins, *Monopoly and Free Enterprise,* Twentieth Century Fund, New York, 1951, p. 257.

[3] *Congressional Record,* 51st Cong., 1st sess. (March 21, 1890), p. 2460. "Although this body is always conservative," Sherman said hopefully, "yet, whatever may be said of it, it has always been ready to preserve not only popular
rights in their broad sense, but the rights of individuals as against associated
and corporate wealth and power."

The plutocratic character of that Congress lends some credence to this view, as does the observation of Senator Orville Platt, at one point in the debate, that the conduct of the Senate during the previous days was "not in the line of honest preparation of a bill to prohibit and punish trusts" but was merely an effort "to get some bill headed 'A bill to punish trusts' with which to go to the country." [4] These circumstances of its origins have helped to confirm many historians in their suspicion that antitrust was, from beginning to end, only a charade.

But there is also reason to believe, on the contrary, that most Congressmen thought of the competitive order in business as being the cornerstone of the whole democratic way of life and that they thought of themselves as making the first tentative step in formulating a policy for the control of trusts, which, if it could be put on sound constitutional footing, might serve as the basis for litigation and perhaps subsequent statutory changes. Admittedly, they were breaking new ground. Senator Hoar said that Congress was entering a wholly new field of legislation and that "the opinions of Senators themselves, of able and learned and experienced lawmakers, were exceedingly crude in this matter." [5]

It is true, of course, that Congress emerged with a statute written in the most general terms, which for many years was emasculated by judicial decisions and administrative lethargy. But it is very likely that, with its broadly worded prohibition of conspiracies in restraint of trade and of efforts to monopolize, Congress was attempting to lay down a declaration of policy that would serve as a guide to future action in much the same flexible way as the Constitution itself had served the country after 1787. Many Congressmen doubtless believed that the self-enforcing fea-

---

[4] Hans B. Thorelli, *The Federal Antitrust Policy*, Johns Hopkins, Baltimore, 1955, p. 198. There is a mass of information about the antimonopoly aspects of the American tradition in Arthur P. Dudden's unpublished doctoral dissertation, *Antimonopolism, 1865–1890*, Michigan University, 1950. On contemporary views, see also Sanford D. Gordon, Attitudes towards Trusts prior to the Sherman Act, *Southern Economic Journal*, XXX (October 1963), pp. 156–167.

[5] *Congressional Record*, 51st Cong., 1st sess. (April 8, 1890), p. 3146.

tures of the law would be far more effective than they actually
were—that is, that the triple-damage suits authorized for victims
of restraints of trade would cause businessmen themselves to
carry on a good deal of the policing of the economy.   Perhaps
the problem confronting Congress can be reconstructed with
greater sympathy if we try to imagine whether a drastically different law would have been passed by a wholly populistic and
militantly anti-big-business Congress, and whether such a law
could have been expected to receive a more successful implementation than the Sherman Act in the hands of the subsequent
administrative officers and judges.

One may say with reasonable assurance that the confusion of
Congress over the economic significance of antitrust mirrored a
more general confusion in American society.   The goals of antitrust may be classified under three headings.   The first were economic.   The classical model of competition confirmed the belief
that the maximum of economic efficiency would be prompted by
competition, and at least some members of Congress must have
been under the spell of this intellectually elegant model, insofar
as they were able to formulate their economic intentions in any
abstract terms.   The second class of goals was political; the antitrust principle was intended to block private accumulations of
power and protect democratic government.   The third was social
and moral; the competitive process was believed to be a kind of
disciplinary machinery for the development of character, and the
competitiveness of the people—the fundamental stimulus to
national morale—was felt to need protection.

Among the three, the economic goal was the most cluttered
with uncertainties, so much so that it seems to be no exaggeration
to regard antitrust as being essentially a political rather than an
economic enterprise.[6]   A fundamental difficulty in economic

6 Hans B. Thorelli, after examining carefully the Congressional debates
over the Sherman Act, concludes, p. 227, that "The Sherman Act is not to be
viewed exclusively as an expression of economic policy," and that in safeguarding the rights of the common man in business it "embodies what is to
be characterized as an eminently 'social' purpose." Thorelli believes that
Sherman and many of his contemporaries in Congress saw the legislation as
"an important means of achieving freedom from corruption and maintaining freedom of independent thinking in political life."

thought, troubling from the very start, arose over the relative claims of combination and competition. The Sherman Act was framed and debated in the preexpert era. Economists as a professional group were not directly consulted by the legislators. But even if they had been, they would have given mixed and uncertain advice. A few years earlier the American Economic Association had been founded by men in revolt against the classical tradition and laissez-faire doctrines, although, of course, many economists of the older school were still ensconced in universities and colleges. Economists were hardly strangers to the argument that the competitive order, far from being fixed in a permanent, beneficent, self-sustaining equilibrium, might have a strong tendency toward self-liquidation. One of the early historicists, E. Benjamin Andrews, argued in 1893 that laissez-faire was no more than a systematized expression of anarchy, and warned, the following year:

Bills have been brought before half the legislatures of the Union to free competition by making trade syndicates absolutely illegal. To my mind there is no question that such legislation will be vain. The age of competition as we have known it is gone forever. As well try to waken the dead.[7]

The more influential voice of Richard Ely was also raised in protest against the ideal of pure competition. He was among those who insisted that size should not be equated with monopoly, and long before Thurman Arnold he held that antitrust legislation was not only futile but actually encouraging to monopoly, because it caused business leaders to replace "soft" combinations by "hard" combinations in the form of mergers.[8]

No consensus was to be had on the proper line of governmental action on trusts or on the kind of law Congress should pass. Nearly all economists believed that attempts simply to prohibit combinations by law would be futile. There was a growing disposition to consider that both competition and combination needed some measure of control and that neither could be elimi-

[7] Thorelli, *op. cit.*, pp. 112n, 316.
[8] *Ibid.*, pp. 314–315.

nated by law. In this sense, as William Letwin has pointed out, the counsel that was available from the economists, however much attended to or ignored, shared the ambiguity that the legislators themselves could feel as lawyers:

The economists thought that both competition and combination should play their parts in the economy. The lawyers saw that the common law permitted combination in some instances and prohibited it in others. Congressmen seized on this hidden agreement, and set out to construct a statute which by the use of common law principles would eliminate excesses but allow "healthy" competition and combination to flourish side by side.[9]

If one gives due regard to the uncertainties of the matter and to the improbability that any attempt at a quick solution would be effective, one may arrive at a more charitable judgment of the Congress of 1890. Its members were probably trying to lay down general guidelines by means of which their successors might evolve a policy that would give society the advantages of both competition and combination. As Senator Sherman said, "All that we, as lawmakers, can do is to declare general principles." [10] These principles could hardly have been enunciated in more sweeping language than that used in the Sherman Act. Presumably, many Congressmen hoped that the courts would find a way of striking at the notoriously unfair methods of competition that had already been used to build such companies as Standard Oil and the National Cash Register Company, without barring useful consolidations or even such restrictive agreements as were intended to eliminate intolerably rigorous competition.

This original uncertainty about the economic rationale for antitrust continued to haunt well-intentioned progressives in the years before the First World War. The vagueness and inconsistency so often expressed by intelligent and relatively candid political leaders during this era must be taken as a reflection not

---

[9] William Letwin, Congress and the Sherman Antitrust Law, 1887–1890, *University of Chicago Law Review*, XXIII (Winter 1956), p. 247.

[10] *Congressional Record*, 51st Cong., 1st sess. (March 21, 1890), p. 2460. Sherman was here conceding the difficulty of defining in law the precise difference between legal and illegal combinations, and expressing a preference for leaving such decisions to the courts in particular cases.

on the calibre of the leadership but rather on the intrinsic difficulty of the problem.

Theodore Roosevelt represents, on this count, a maximum of shrewdness combined with a minimum of anxiety. With the exception of railroad regulation, Roosevelt was not profoundly interested in the economic issues that agitated the American public during his presidency; indeed, he was quite candid in confessing his reluctance to tackle them head-on. When in difficulties, as in 1907, he was disposed to trust to the judgment and the political and financial leadership of the conservatives in the Senate or the economic powers in Wall Street. However, he saw the trust problem as something that must be dealt with on the political level; public concern about it was too urgent to be ignored. He understood how important it was to assure the public that the government of the United States had the will and the power to assert its authority over large corporations. Accordingly, his antitrust prosecutions, although few, were in some cases appropriately spectacular. When he assessed the significance of the Northern Securities Case, he did not say that it would open the way to a general assault on bigness, but rather that it was important for showing that "the most powerful men in this country were held to accountability before the law." His fundamental solution for the problem—that bigness must be accepted as a part of the modern industrial and social order, and that its behavior should be subjected to administrative control under full publicity—comes somewhat closer than the views of most of his political contemporaries to anticipating the future course of antitrust procedure.

Roosevelt was accompanied, or perhaps followed, by a school of liberal publicists—among them Charles R. Van Hise, Herbert Croly, and Walter Lippmann—who accepted his conviction that the Sherman Act philosophy was the product of what he called a "sincere rural Toryism" long since outgrown. Lippmann, in one of the most penetrating attacks on the antitrust philosophy, characterized it as the philosophy of "a nation of villagers." This school of Progressives saw the Western world as entering upon a new era of organization and specialization for which the old competitive philosophy was hopelessly retrograde. Some of them, notably Croly and Van Hise, also saw small-scale business as inadequate to the task of competing in the world's markets, which they believed to be a necessity of the American situation. In retrospect, they appear more sophisticated and prophetic than those who put great stock in the Sherman Act as a force for actual dissolution. They foresaw the decline of antitrust as a movement, and in some instances recognized that if the Sherman Act persisted it would be as a basis for occasional *ad hoc* regulatory suits rather than as an instrument for dismantling the corporate economy.

Woodrow Wilson spoke more feelingly for the "rural Toryism" and the village democracy, which seem to have been at the center of popular antitrust feeling; but by the same token he illustrated more clearly than Roosevelt their intellectual difficulties. Speaking in the campaign of 1912, which afforded a full-dress display of the differences between the two schools of thought on trusts, he asserted that he too was not against size as such. He was all for bigness as an inevitable and natural growth, whenever it was the outcome of superior efficiency. But he was against "the trusts," which had grown out of illicit competition. He was never very successful, however, in explaining why a business that had become large through legitimate methods might not become just as menacing to competition as one that had grown large through illicit competition. His statement, "I am for big business and I am against the trusts," seems hardly more than an attempt to evade the argument that there is a self-liquidating threat inherent in competition.[11]

[11] For Woodrow Wilson's position on monopoly, see *The New Freedom*, Doubleday-Page, New York, 1913, pp. 163–222. William Diamond, in *The Economic Thought of Woodrow Wilson*, Johns Hopkins, Baltimore, 1943, makes it clear that in his earlier years Wilson had been committed to the evolutionist acceptance of size but became more devoted to the competitive principle as he came before the public eye and as he accepted the advice of Brandeis. By 1913 he seems to have been persuaded that dissolution was an essential tactic. "Real dissolution in the case of the trusts is the only thing we can be satisfied with," he wrote privately, and he indicated that this was part of a program necessary "to satisfy the conscience of the country." *Ibid.*, p. 112.

III

The political and social arguments against monopoly were pressed with greater clarity than the economic argument and with hardly less fervor.   Antitrust must be understood as the political judgment of a nation whose leaders had always shown a keen awareness of the economic foundations of politics.   In this respect, the Sherman Act was simply another manifestation of an enduring American suspicion of concentrated power.   From the pre-Revolutionary tracts through the Declaration of Independence and *The Federalist* to the writings of the states' rights advocates, and beyond it into the era of the antimonopoly writers and the Populists, there had been a perennial quest for a way of dividing, diffusing, and checking power and preventing its exercise by a single interest or by a consolidated group of interests at a single center.   Hence, the political impulse behind the Sherman Act was clearer and more articulate than the economic theory.   Men who used the vaguest language when they talked about "the trusts" and monopolies, who had not thought through the distinction between size itself and monopolistic practices, who had found no way of showing how much competition was necessary for efficiency, who could not in every case say what competitive acts they thought were fair or unfair, or who could not state a rational program that reconciled their acceptance of size with their desire for competition, were reasonably clear about what it was that they were trying to avoid: they wanted to keep concentrated private power from destroying democratic government.

One of the glories of the competitive model had been that it purported to solve the question of market power by denying any particular location to it.   The decisions of the market were beautifully impersonal, since they were only the averagings of the decisions of thousands of individuals, none of whom enjoyed any decisive power.   The market mechanism suggested that power was not really exercised by anyone.   With the perfect impersonality of Adam Smith's "invisible hand," the market made decisions that ought not be vested in the hands of any particular man or body of men. Hence, the market mechanism met the desire for the diffusion of power and seemed to be the perfect economic counterpart of American democratic pluralism.

Where power *must* be exercised, it was agreed that it should be located in governmental and not in private hands. But the state governments were inadequate; in sheer mass, business enterprises already overshadowed them. Charles William Eliot pointed out as early as 1888 that the large corporations, considered as units of economic organization, had already begun to tower over the states. A Boston railroad company, for example, employed 18,000 persons and had gross receipts of about $40,-000,000 a year, as compared with the Commonwealth of Massachusetts, which employed 6,000 and had receipts of $7,000,000.[12] Even individually, some corporations were big enough to dominate state governments, and if they should combine among themselves, they might come to dominate the federal government as well.

The existence of the industrial combinations and the threat that under one auspice or another—perhaps that of the investment bankers—there would come about someday a combination of the combinations that would be stronger than civil government itself provoked a fear that haunted the minds of the writers of the industrial era, including many whose social views were as conservative as Eliot's. The fundamental fear of private power was well put by William Jennings Bryan, in a speech delivered at the Chicago Conference on Trusts in 1899:

I do not divide monopolies in private hands into good monopolies and bad monopolies. There is no good monopoly in private hands. There can be no good monopoly in private hands until the Almighty

[12] C. Eliot, The Working of the American Democracy, *American Contributions to Civilization,* Century, New York, 1907, pp. 85–86. Three-quarters of a century later the T.N.E.C. found that, as economic units, only ten states had assets greater than the two largest corporations, and that more than half the states were completely overshadowed in size by private businesses. *Final Report and Recommendations,* pp. 676–677; David Lynch, *The Concentration of Economic Power,* Columbia University Press, New York, 1946, pp. 112–113.

sends us angels to preside over the monopoly. There may be a despot who is better than another despot, but there is no good despotism.[13]

And the general sense that the dire economic and political consequences of monopoly were as one was incorporated in the Democratic platform of 1900:

> Private monopolies are indefensible and intolerable. . . . They are the most efficient means yet devised for appropriating the fruits of industry to the benefit of the few at the expense of the many, and unless their insatiate greed is checked, all wealth will be aggregated in a few hands and the Republic destroyed.[14]

The most articulate expression of the Progressives' case against the political power of monopoly was made by Woodrow Wilson in 1912. It was the burden of his case, as against T. R., that once the existence of large-scale combinations is accepted, their regulation by government becomes impossible, because the political power of business combination will be great enough to nullify all attempts at its control. Wilson played artfully on the fears and suspicions of the small entrepreneurs. Even some very powerful men, he said, knew that "there is a power somewhere so organized, so subtle, so watchful, so interlocked, so complete, so pervasive, that they had better not speak above their breath when they speak in condemnation of it. . . . They know that somewhere, by somebody, the development of industry is being controlled." [15] He pictured concentrated capital as being already in control of the government: "The masters of the government of the United States are the combined capitalists and manufacturers of the United States. . . . The government of the United States at present is a foster-child of the special interests." [16]

This would have to be the state of affairs until the combinations were not only unseated by the people, but were also dissolved—until "this colossal 'community of interest'" was dis-

---

[13] Thorelli, *op. cit.*, p. 336.

[14] Kirk H. Porter and Donald B. Johnson, *National Party Platforms*, University of Illinois Press, Urbana, Ill., 1956, p. 114.

[15] Wilson, *op. cit.*, pp. 14, 62.

[16] *Ibid.*, pp. 57–58.

entangled. It was a thing that the laws must "pull apart, and gently, but firmly and persistently dissect." Otherwise, under Roosevelt's plan for accepting and regulating monopolies, there would only be a union between monopoly and government: "If the government controlled by the monopolies in its turn controls the monopolies, the partnership is finally consummated." "If monopoly persists, monopoly will always sit at the helm of the government. I do not expect to see monopoly restrain itself. If there are men in this country big enough to own the government of the United States, they are going to own it." [17]

The third objective of antitrust action, hardly less important than the others, was psychological and moral. It sprang from the conviction that competition has a disciplinary value for character, quite aside from its strictly economic uses. America was thought to have been made possible by the particular type of character that was forged by competitive individualism, a type that had flourished in the United States because competitive opportunities had been so widespread that alert men could hardly fail to see them, to grasp and use them, and, hence, to be shaped by them. The American male character was believed to have been quickened and given discipline by the sight and pursuit of opportunity. For this process to take place it was important that business be carried on fairly—the sporting vocabulary was never far below the surface—and that newcomers be able to enter the game as entrepreneurs on reasonably open terms.

The significance of this faith that competition could be relied upon to form character can be fully grasped only if we bear in mind the Protestant background of our economic thinking. Economists themselves had not been in the habit of analyzing economic relationships in purely mechanical and secular terms, and what may be said of them on this count can be said with greater force about laymen, when they thought about economic issues. Behind the American way of thinking there lay a long Protestant tradition, which tended to identify economic forces with religious and moral forces and which regarded economic

[17] *Ibid.*, pp. 118, 207, 286. For a later statement of this view see the dissenting opinion of Mr. Justice Douglas in *U. S. v. Columbia Steel Co.*, 334 U. S. 495 (1948).

processes from the standpoint of their contribution to the discipline and development of character. The economic order was not merely an apparatus for the production of goods and services; it was a set of rules for forging good conduct. Everyone is familiar, I believe, with the proposition that some of the concepts of classical economics were shaped under the influence of a kind of prudential morality in which savings and abstinence were not merely instruments of economic analysis but moral sanctions. In our time we have heard conservatives frankly condemn government fiscal policy that deviates from the prudential rules suitable to a family budget by appealing to the Puritan tradition. Such critics are the legitimate heirs of the men of the nineteenth and early twentieth centuries, who saw the protection of competition and its incentives as a safeguard of national morale, as a means for mobilizing and rewarding the industrious and the prudent and for penalizing those whom William Graham Sumner called "the poor and the weak, the negligent, shiftless, inefficient, silly, and imprudent . . . the idle, intemperate, and vicious." [18]

Here again one looks to Woodrow Wilson for the most articulate expression of this emphasis on the economic foundations of character and especially to the masterful speeches of 1912 in which he expressed his concern for "the beginner," "the man with only a little capital," "the man on the make," upon whose genius he thought the country had always been built. "The treasury of America," he argued, "lies in those ambitions, those energies, that cannot be restricted to a special favored class." It rests upon the inventiveness and the energy of "unknown men" and would lose its force, if the economic order ceased to stimulate such inventiveness and energy. It was possible, he hinted, that under large-scale organization the country would turn its back on its past, which he evoked in poignant terms:

. . . the ancient time when America lay in every hamlet, when America was to be seen in every fair valley, when America displayed her great forces on the broad prairies, ran her fine fires of enterprise up over the mountainsides and down into the bowels of the earth, and eager men

[18] William Graham Sumner, *What Social Classes Owe to Each Other*, 1883 Edition, Yale University Press, New Haven, Conn., 1925, p. 21.

were everywhere captains of industry, not employees; not looking to a distant city to find out what they might do, but looking about among their neighbors, finding credit according to their character, not according to their connections, finding credit in proportion to what was known to be in them and behind them, not in proportion to the securities they held that were approved where they were not known.[19]

The prospect that these "fine fires of enterprise" were about to be quenched suggested that the old kind of character would be destroyed, that the old America was about to die—a reason even more imperative than mere industrial efficiency for seeking out the possibilities of antitrust action.

The inherited belief that small property and small business opportunity have forged the American character, which might well lose its form without the discipline imposed by a particular variety of entrepreneurial competition, is one that has never died out. Near the end of World War II the Small Business Committee of the Senate put this faith clearly when it said that the pursuit of opportunity by the small business owner

. . . has been a great motive force among our people. It stimulates expression of the fundamental virtues of thrift, industry, intelligence, schooling, home ties, and family pride—in short, those fireside virtues which have counted for so much in developing our strength and character.[20]

The preservation of small business opportunities, as a member of the S.E.C. put it in 1945, is more important than any economic goal; it is "a goal which transcends economic and political forms and processes as such, and remains fundamentally concerned with the character of the men and women who comprise the nation." [21]

IV

There are two salient differences between the problem of bigness as it was perceived about sixty years ago and as it is per-

[19] Wilson, *op. cit.*, pp. 18–19.

[20] Quoted in John H. Bunzel, *The American Small Businessman*, Knopf, New York, 1962, p. 84.

[21] Rudolph L. Weissman, *Small Business and Venture Capital*, Harper, New York, 1945, p. 164.

ceived now; the first is that it is no longer a new problem, and the second is that the economy has performed in a way hardly dreamed of before World War II. In 1964 we are as remote in time from the passage of the Sherman Act as the men of 1864 were from the first term of George Washington. The public has had almost three-quarters of a century of experience in living with big business, and analysts of the big business problem no longer make the same frightening projections as to its future dangers that could be made with entire plausibility sixty or seventy years ago. At the same time, the public is hardly unaware that a great rise in mass standards of living has occurred during the period in which the economy has been dominated by the big corporation. Whatever else may be said against bigness, the conception of monopolistic industry as a kind of gigantic, swelling leech on the body of an increasingly deprived and impoverished society has largely disappeared.

About the change in public attitudes from those prevailing sixty years ago we can only make an educated guess. Today we can check our impressions of the public mind against opinion polls; for the earlier era we have impressions alone. But it is very difficult for anyone who reads widely in the political literature of the period 1890–1914 to believe that public concern today over big business has anything like the sense of urgency that it had then. In 1951 the Institute of Social Research of the University of Michigan published the results of an illuminating survey, *Big Business as the People See It*. Its findings show some residues of the old popular suspicion of bigness, but the noteworthy thing is public acceptance. Americans have always had to balance their love of bigness and efficiency against their fear of power and their regard for individualism and competition. The survey indicates that this ambivalence has been largely resolved in favor of the big business organization.

A quarter of the population, as represented in the Institute's national sample, showed some concern over big business and an awareness that it had an important effect on their lives. But a substantial majority reacted favorably to big business. Asked to give a general characterization of its social effects, the respondents answered as follows:

The good things outweigh the bad things   76%
They seem about equal   2%
The bad things outweigh the good things   10%
Don't know   5%
Confused; evaluation not ascertainable   7%
                                          _____
                                           100%

Plainly, big business was not a scare word to the public at large. Eighty-four per cent of those polled reacted without apparent emotion to the questions, and only a small minority reacted unfavorably. Questioned on particulars, respondents spoke with especial favor of the productive powers of big business and its ability to give jobs and keep prices down. The most critical responses about big business dealt mainly with its effect on "the little man" and the destruction of competition. Very little concern was expressed about the power of big business over its workers (it is commonly regarded as a good employer), and surprisingly little about its influence on government.

Whereas fifty years before, fear of an indefinitely continued increase in the political power of big business was commonplace, the typical expectation expressed in the poll of 1951 was that the power of big business would decline, and properly so. As in the Progressive era, there was a strong preference for a balance of power and a conviction that wherever there must be a clear preponderance of power it should rest in governmental and not private hands. But the existing state of business power was not widely considered to be dangerous. In fact, big business power was regarded as being third in rank among five forces—behind national government and labor unions and ahead of state governments and smaller business. Stronger feeling was shown against labor unions than against big business. Although there was a fraction of the public that saw big business as more powerful than labor unions and would have liked to see the situation reversed, there was a fraction almost twice as large that saw the unions as more powerful and preferred to see the situation reversed.[22]

[22] Burton R. Fisher and Stephen B. Withey, *Big Business as the People See It,* Survey Research Center, University of Michigan, Ann Arbor, 1951, *passim.*

The findings of the Michigan group were not widely at variance with those of Elmo Roper, who a few years earlier had collated the responses of the public over a span of 15 years to questions about business. Roper found that "the public has mixed feelings about big business. There is pride over the achievements of big business but some apprehension over the possible abuses of power inherent in big business." The public was disposed to want a watchdog set upon the amoral and greedy elements in business, but only about a fourth of the respondents were found to believe that the disadvantages of bigness overshadow whatever advantages there might be.[23]

To what can we attribute this public acceptance of big business? Not much, I believe, to the efforts that big businessmen have made to cultivate a favorable "image" for the large corporation. As the fate of the postwar campaign to sell "free enterprise" suggests, such efforts can miscarry badly when they represent nothing more than an attempt to make the public take seriously the blather with which business sometimes comforts itself.[24] What has really made bigness palatable more than anything else is the remarkable performance of the economy since the beginning of World War II. Something too must be credited to the emergence of countervailing bigness in government and labor, whose effects on public attitudes emerge clearly from the Michigan survey. Moreover, anyone who is aware of the historical circumstances under which hostility to big business flourished must be aware that big business has not lived up to the horrifying billing that it got in the age of the muckrakers. It is not merely that no business today treats competitors as they were treated in the early days of the National Cash Register Company or Standard Oil. What is important is that a whole range of fears, expressed in the Progressive generation and based largely upon preoccupation with an unknown future, has vanished. We now live in that future, and although it has fears of its own—

[23] Elmo Roper, The Public Looks at Business, *Harvard Business Review*, XXVII (March 1949), pp. 165–174.

[24] William H. Whyte, Jr., is eloquent on the failure of one such campaign in *Is Anybody Listening?*, Simon and Schuster, New York, 1952.

nightmarish beyond anything anticipated in the days of Bryan and Wilson—they are of a wholly different origin. Probably the worst of the Populist-Progressive nightmares was the notion, expressed in the Pujo Committee's inquiry, in Brandeis's *Other People's Money,* in Wilson's speeches, and in Jack London's *The Iron Heel,* of the formation, under the auspices of the investment bankers, of a giant syndicate, a combination of the combinations, which would rule the country with a tyrannical grip. The self-financing character of the great corporations, the survival of competition in investment banking, and the failure of investment banking to remain a power of the first order after the crash of 1929 have set this spectre to rest.

If no sinister central syndicate had to be feared, it did at least seem reasonable at the turn of the century to anticipate a steady, growing concentration of industry that would eventually deprive the country of every advantage of competition. And here, insofar as the antitrust enterprise was directed against size itself or against concentration, it was beaten before it ever got started; American industry was already highly concentrated in 1904, when T. R. was boasting about the lessons of the Northern Securities Case. But insofar as the Progressives were worried about what the economists later came to call "workable competition" in industry, they might well have been reassured as time went on. The investigations of such economists as M. A. Adelman, G. Warren Nutter, and George J. Stigler have cast considerable doubt on the idea that either the scope of monopoly or the degree of concentration has, in fact, grown since the beginning of the century. "The extent of concentration," Adelman concluded in an important study, "shows no tendency to grow, and it may possibly be declining. Any tendency either way, if it does exist, must be at the pace of a glacial drift." [25] Measuring monopoly

[25] M. A. Adelman, The Measurement of Industrial Concentration, *Review of Economics and Statistics,* XXXIII (November 1951), pp. 269–296. See also the discussion by Adelman and others, *ibid.,* XXXIV (May 1952), pp. 156 ff.; G. Warren Nutter, *The Extent of Enterprise Monopoly in the United States, 1899–1939,* University of Chicago Press, Chicago, 1951; and George J. Stigler, *Five Lectures on Economic Problems,* Longmans, London, 1949, pp. 46–65.

is an undertaking of considerable complexity, and the issues are controversial.   But it is at least safe to say that no one who has due regard for the difficulties of the problem can any longer raise alarmist cries about the rapid growth of monopoly without flying in the face of much formidable testimony.

Another cause of concern, very real to many men in the Progressive era and rather quaint from today's perspective, had to do with the progress of industry.   "Monopoly," warned Wilson in 1912, "always checks development, weighs down natural prosperity, pulls against natural advance."   In the past, he said, competitive America had produced or developed the steamboat, the cotton gin, the sewing machine, the reaper, the typewriter, the electric light, and other great inventions, but the day was at hand when monopoly might end all this.   "Do you know, have you had occasion to learn, that there is no hospitality for invention nowadays?   There is no encouragement for you to set your wits at work. . . . The instinct of monopoly is against novelty, the tendency of monopoly is to keep in use the old thing, made in the old way. . . ."   Only a restoration of freedom could unleash American inventiveness again: "Who can say what patents now lying, unrealized, in secret drawers and pigeonholes, will come to light, or what new inventions will astonish and bless us, when freedom is restored?" [26]   To two generations that since 1912 have been astonished and blessed almost to death by inventions, such rhetoric can no longer be alarming or inspiring; it is merely a curiosity.   Today the public needs no persuading that it is the large corporations, with their programs of research, that are technologically progressive.   As Galbraith has remarked, the showpieces of American industrial progress are, in the main, those dominated by a handful of large firms, and "the foreign visitor, brought to the United States by the Economic Cooperation Ad-

---

However, on the identity of the largest firms and the mobility of firms into positions of leadership, see Norman R. Collins and Lee E. Preston, The Size Structure of the Largest Industrial Firms, *American Economic Review*, LI (December 1961), pp. 986–1003. Fritz Machlup, *The Political Economy of Monopoly*, Johns Hopkins, Baltimore, 1952, pp. 469–528, is instructive on the difficulties of the subject.

26 Wilson, *op. cit.*, pp. 265–266, 270.

ministration, visits the same firms as do attorneys of the Department of Justice in their search for monopoly." [27]

Another typical fear expressed in Progressive writing was that the possibility of individual advancement would be frozen out, that the upward social mobility that had refreshed and inspired American development in the past would come to an end, when the business of the country was fully dominated by the large corporation. I know of no very certain information on how the American public regards the prospects for social mobility today, although our concerted scramble for educational position and advantage suggests that the middle-class public and even much of the working-class public are rather well aware that mobility still exists; they are also aware of the mechanisms through which it can be pursued. What can be said with greater confidence is that informed observers no longer speak so glibly of the decline of mobility or opportunity.

Indeed, there is strong evidence that the opportunity of middle- or lower-class men to rise to top positions in business has somewhat increased over what it was fifty or sixty years ago,[28] and there is some reason to believe that the increase, or at least the persistence, of occupational opportunity has, in fact, impressed itself on the public mind. In fact, the modern corporation has proved to be a better medium for social mobility and opportunity than the old system of individual and family entrepreneurship, whose openness in this respect was always much exaggerated. Oddly enough, the concentration of capital and the divorce of ownership from the entrepreneurial function may prove in the long run to be more conducive to the lowering of social tensions and to political stability than diffused ownership.[29] The ways of

[27] John Kenneth Galbraith, *American Capitalism*, Houghton Mifflin, Boston, 1952, p. 96; cf. Joseph A. Schumpeter, *Capitalism, Socialism, and Democracy*, Third Edition, Harper, New York, 1947, pp. 81–82.

[28] For a good review of the relevant findings, see Seymour M. Lipset and Reinhard Bendix, *Social Mobility in Industrial Society*, University of California Press, Berkeley and Los Angeles, 1960, Chapter 3.

[29] For a shrewd and heretical statement on the political and social effects of the large corporation, see M. A. Adelman, Some Aspects of Corporate Enterprise, in Ralph Freeman, ed., *Postwar Economic Trends in the United States*, Harpers, New York, 1960, pp. 289–308.

achieving occupational advancement and economic success have changed; individual entrepreneurship is a much less sure and satisfactory path as compared with bureaucratic careers. The acquisition of specialized skills has become more important, and with it the seizure and exploitation of educational opportunities.

I do not mean to suggest that the old ideal of self-employment or the old confidence in the entrepreneurial path to success has been entirely abandoned in favor of the bureaucratic career. The incidence of self-employment and the population that actually lives by the competitive ideal have shrunk very considerably in the three-quarters of a century since the Sherman Act; but most of this is attributable to the numerical decline of family farmers, who in 1890 still comprised nearly half the population and today comprise about a tenth. The farmers, with their contemporary dependence on subsidies and governmentally administered prices, can hardly be looked upon any more as vigorous exponents of the competitive way of life. But the dream of self-employment that dominated the agrarian-entrepreneurial society of the nineteenth century is still alive. It has been estimated that about 20 to 30 per cent of the American working force has been at some time or another self-employed.[30] The growth of small businesses over the past dozen years or so has roughly kept pace with the growth of the adult population, and the aspirations of small business have been institutionalized in Senate and House committees as well as in some antitrust activities.

But although small business holds its place as a segment of the economy itself, its role as a sector of society committed to the entrepreneurial ideal has declined. Small business can no longer be idealized for its independence and hardihood or its devotion to competitive principles. It, too, looks to government intervention for sustenance, whether in the form of resale price maintenance, anti-chain-store legislation, or the Small Business Administration. Small business, which used to be, as one writer has put it,[31] "a symbol of opportunity, enterprise, innovation, and achievement" and of "an independent way of life," has been

[30] Lipset and Bendix, *op. cit.*, pp. 102–103.
[31] Theodore O. Yntema, in the Foreword to A. D. H. Kaplan, *Small Business: Its Place and Problems*, McGraw-Hill, New York, 1948, p. vii.

driven largely into the marginal areas of economic life, where it often tries to maintain itself by waging its own assaults upon the competitive principle. Various segments of small business, in their pressure for support for the Robinson-Patman Act of 1936 and the Miller-Tydings Amendment of 1937, have shown how quickly they can be rallied against competition, when it impinges upon their own interests. Vigorous advocates of the Sherman and Clayton Acts where big business is affected, they turn their backs on competitive virility when it suits their purposes. If there is anything rarer than a small businessman who will question the merits of competition, it is one who can understand and abide competition when it really afflicts him.[32]

Not only can the small businessman not purport, in the eyes of any well-informed observer, to be a vigorous and consistent exemplar of the competitive ideal; he can no longer be idealized by progressive-minded men from other walks of life, as he could, say, in the era when Woodrow Wilson waxed rhapsodical about the new men out of "unknown homes" who really made America. In the United States and elsewhere, liberal intellectuals now cock a suspicious eye at him, if not as a potential stronghold of support for fascist movements, at least as the backbone of the reactionary wing of the Republican party. An occasional big business leader may stand out for his enlightenment and urbanity, as compared with the small businessman, who more often than not proves to be a refractory antiunion employer, a parochial and archaic opponent of liberal ideas, a supporter of vigilante groups and of right-wing cranks.[33] As a figure in our economic society, the small businessman still plays a part of some considerable importance, but as a partner in the American liberal coalition, he has all but disappeared, and with him has gone much of the pristine antibigness feeling of the Progressive tradition.

Still, the conviction that American democracy will survive only if small business enterprise survives to sustain the American char-

---

[32] For an amusing illustration of this incomprehension of competition, see the testimony before the T.N.E.C. quoted in David Lynch, *op. cit.*, pp. 155–156.

[33] On the politics of small business, which, of course, still has a liberal minority wing, see Bunzel, *op. cit.*, Chapter 5.

acter has not disappeared. It has been inherited from the Progressives of yesterday by the conservatives of today. It appears to be, as we shall see, a conviction that flourishes less among the young than among the old, who are often troubled that they cannot persuade their juniors of its importance. "For the development of self-reliance," say two authors of a manual for small business operation, "for making men as well as money, small business excels." [34] In 1936, when the Robinson-Patman Act was under consideration, this effort to underwrite the middleman was touted by the Chairman of the House Committee on the Judiciary as a potential bulwark of the democratic order: "There are a great many people who feel that if we are to preserve democracy in government, in America, we have got to preserve a democracy in business operation. . . . We must make some effort to *maintain the yeomanry in business.*" [35]

In the 1940's and 1950's there has been much evidence of a widespread uneasy conviction that years of war, depression, and bureaucratic expansion have finally drained away the old regard for entrepreneurship among the young, and that the spirit that animated the old competitive ideal has finally succumbed to the world of the large corporation. The signs and portents are numerous, but a memorable article of 1949 in *Fortune* may be taken as a landmark. Surveying "The Class of '49," *Fortune's* editors pointed out that it was perhaps the most significant college graduating class in our history. It was one of the largest, most mature (with a high proportion of veterans) and responsible; but its distinguishing feature was its aversion to risk, its passion for security. "The class of '49," the editors reported, "wants to work for somebody else—preferably somebody big. No longer is small business the promised land. As for the idea of going into business for oneself, the idea is so seldom expressed as to seem an anachronism." Only in the Southwest, which seems socially and intellectually to lag behind the rest of the country, was there

[34] Pearce C. Kelley and Kenneth Lawyer, *How to Organize and Operate a Small Business,* Prentice-Hall, Englewood Cliffs, N. J., 1949, p. 11.

[35] Quoted in Merle Fainsod, Lincoln Gordon, and Joseph C. Palamountain, Jr., *Government and the American Economy,* Norton, New York, 1959, p. 549; italics added.

any sign of significant exceptions to this generalization. The generation who had been impressionable children during the depression and who had come of age in the shadow of the war rendered a firm verdict in favor of security, service, and the good life (measured in modest income expectations) rather than risk, self-assertion, and the big prizes. The emergent young man, the editors reported, "is not afraid of bigness; where his father of the twenties, fearful of anonymity, was repelled by hugeness in an organization, he is attracted." [36]

This was the response of a generation raised in an economy of giant corporations, educated very often in universities with thousands of students, disciplined by army life, and accustomed to the imperatives of organization, mass, and efficiency. No doubt they often saw in big businesses the promise of laboratories and market research to which the atmosphere of the universities had already accustomed them. Because of its army experiences, the class of 1949 may have been unusually security-minded, but there is no reason to doubt that its acceptance of large organization represented a secular trend. Not long after the *Fortune* piece appeared, the Youth Research Institute Survey put to 4,660 high school and college seniors, recent college graduates, and veterans the question: "Do you feel that you will be able to achieve all of your economic desires by working for someone else?"   61.1 per cent said yes, 20.4 per cent no, and 18.5 per cent were uncertain.[37]   In his essay, "The Found Generation," an analysis of the expressed life ideals of the class of 1955, David Riesman revealed not only a bland acceptance of the large corporation as a place in which to do one's life work but also a depressing complacency about the terms and rewards of the corporate life. The class of 1949 had at least been aware of making a somewhat difficult choice in which their individuality might be at stake. The class of 1955 took the bureaucratic career for granted.[38]

It is this acceptance of the bureaucratic career that, more than

[36] The Class of '49, *Fortune* (June 1949), pp. 84–87.

[37] William H. Whyte, Jr., *The Organization Man*, Anchor Books, New York, 1957, p. 79n.

[38] David Riesman, The Found Generation, in *Abundance for What?*, Doubleday, New York, 1964, pp. 309–323.

anything else, tells us why there is no longer an antitrust movement. It is far more revealing than the law cases or the books on the control of monopoly. It is also a perfect illustration of how the problems of yesterday are not solved but outgrown. Only a few people today are concerned about how to make the large corporations more competitive, but millions are concerned about how they are going to live inside the corporate framework. The existence and the workings of the corporations are largely accepted, and in the main they are assumed to be fundamentally benign. What is questioned, when anything is questioned, are matters of personal style: what can be salvaged, in the way of either individualism or individuality, in an age in which the big corporation has become a way of life? It is this concern that marks the transition from an age in which *The Curse of Bigness* and *Other People's Money* set the tone of the prevailing anxieties to one in which everyone reads *The Lonely Crowd* and *The Organization Man.*

Long-prevailing systems of values do not usually go under without a fight, and along with the new acceptance there is a good deal of uneasiness about the corporate life. The young may be losing the concern of their elders with the virile prerogatives of enterprise. Certainly they are now much more disposed to ask of the economic order not whether it is raising a nation of enterprising and hardy men but more matter-of-factly whether it is maintaining an adequate level of employment and producing a sufficient increase in the Gross National Product. But there is a persistent uneasiness, which has its manifestations both on the left and the right. The left, if it can be called that, rebels in the name of nonconformity and opts out of the whole bourgeois world, and we get the beat and the hip. The right rebels in the name of the older individualism, which believed that economic life should inculcate discipline and character, and we get Barry Goldwater and his enthusiasts. Though they would hate to admit it, they are both bedeviled in different ways by the same problem; each of them is trying to make its variety of nonconformism into a mass creed, which is a contradiction in terms. The beats opt out of corporate uniformity in uniforms and erect themselves into a stereotype. The right-wingers sing their praises of individualism in dreary, regimented choruses and applaud vigilantes who would kill every vestige of genuine dissent.

In politics, of course, it is the right-wingers who really count—it is they who have the numbers, the money, the political leverage. They can also invoke the greater part of the old American pieties and can appeal to the kind of old-fashioned American who believes that federal fiscal policy can be discussed in language suitable to family budgets. Much of our conservative writing echoes with concern over the decline of the older kind of economic morale, which it identifies with small entrepreneurship. But conservatives understandably fear to make the large corporation the object of their criticism; this smacks too much of subversion. They have a safer and more congenial outlet for their animus against the organization of modern life in the form of denunciations of big government. In this way, the large corporation escapes its proper share of odium. But, historically, it was the giant corporation far more than governmental policy that eclipsed the old-fashioned economic morality.

Oddly enough, although it is primarily conservatives who are profoundly disgruntled with the style of contemporary economic life, many liberals complete the paradox by springing to its defense and, in particular, to the defense of bigness. As we have seen, there was always a large number of Progressive intellectuals who preferred to accept corporate organization and to whom the possibilities of rationalization and order were more appealing than the competitive ideal. Today it is men of such views who seem to have inherited what is left of American liberalism. Of course, big business still holds a place as a negative symbol in the liberal creed, and the liberal creed still gives a certain ritualistic compliance to the anti-big-business sentiment that was once very close to the heart of Progressivism. But by and large, as Carl Kaysen has remarked, "today's liberals have abandoned the symbol of competition without much struggle." [39]

Some of the most striking efforts to reconcile us to the business structure have been written in recent years by liberals who derive

[39] Big Business and the Liberals, Then and Now, *New Republic* (November 22, 1954), pp. 118–119.

from the New Deal tradition. If, in 1953, one read a paean to big business asserting, among other things, that the emotional antagonism to which it was subject was based on "abuses long since corrected"; that the big business leader is "a man with a strong and practical sense of responsibility to the public, and an awareness of the ethics of present-day business competition"; that "big business has performed economic wonders with one hand tied behind its back"; that it has actually increased competition and multiplied small enterprises; that "size is our greatest single functional asset"; that big business nourished diversity; that "we are living in what is probably the most highly competitive society men have ever known"; that big business research has multiplied opportunities for small business enterprise; that ill-considered antitrust prosecutions have "grave implications for national security"; and that "in Bigness we have the material foundation of a society which can further the highest values known to men, values we describe as spiritual," [40]—one no longer expected to find that one had been reading a speech by a General Motors or A. T. and T. director and was not at all surprised to learn that the author was David E. Lilienthal, once one of the most outspoken democratic idealists of the New Deal bureaucracy and a former disciple of Brandeis.

Lilienthal's innocent rhapsodies to big business may perhaps be taken as the effusions of one who had been reshaped by his experiences in giant public enterprises like the T.V.A. and the A.E.C.[41] But there is also A. A. Berle, Jr., another New Dealer, who held his first job in Brandeis's office and whose public career was marked by friendships with Robert La Follette, George Norris, and Franklin D. Roosevelt. In his most recent works Berle has been speculating about the possible development of a corporate conscience and arguing that the contemporary business power system is governed by public consensus. In his *Power*

[40] David E. Lilienthal, *Big Business: A New Era*, Harper, New York, 1953, pp. 5, 7, 27, 33, 36, 47, 190, and *passim*.

[41] For critiques see Lee Loevinger, Antitrust and the New Economics, *Minnesota Law Review*, XXXVII (June 1953), pp. 505–568, and Edward S. Mason, *Economic Concentration and the Monopoly Problem*, Harvard University Press, Cambridge, Mass., 1957, pp. 371–381.

Without Property he urged liberals to reconsider their former, and historically justified, antipathy to big business and to judge it in the light of its achievements in increasing income and distributing property.[42]   Finally, there is John Kenneth Galbraith, whose book, *American Capitalism,* has probably done as much as any other work to reconcile the contemporary liberal mind to the diminished role of competition as a force in modern economic society by offering, as an alternative account of the mechanism by which market power is controlled in the public interest, the principle of countervailing power.   Of course, neither Berle nor Galbraith advocates doing away with the antitrust laws—Galbraith, in fact, argues that in the main federal antitrust policies have helped to produce countervailing power, where it has not emerged spontaneously [43]—but the net effect of their view of our society is to lower the premium upon competition and to turn attention to other economic and social mechanisms that promise to control excessive market power.

To say all this is not to say that liberal intellectuals have ceased to be critical of business civilization or, on occasion, of big business.   But a variety of other issues—foreign policy, urban development, civil rights, education, and the like—have become more central, and where these issues are concerned, liberals do not always find themselves in a simple antagonistic confrontation with big business, as they so often did in the past.   Their criticisms of business civilization now rest more on cultural than economic grounds.   The last thing they are interested in is the restoration of competition as the solution to the evils that they see.[44] They are not even particularly titillated by such a thing as the General Electric–Westinghouse scandal, although it may confirm their estimation of the kind of behavior to be expected of businessmen.   In short, that "gale of creative destruction" about

[42] *Power Without Property,* Harvest Books, New York, 1959, pp. 11–16.

[43] Galbraith, *op. cit.,* p. 151.

[44] Nor are contemporary radicals.   The most full-throated indictment of the ruling element in big business that has been written in our time, C. Wright Mills's *The Power Elite,* does not concern itself even fleetingly with the problem of market power.   The Sherman and Clayton Acts are not mentioned in its index.

which Joseph Schumpeter wrote so eloquently, when he described the progressive character of capitalist technology, has driven both the liberal and the conservative ideologies before it.

V

It is easier to account for the decline of the antitrust movement as a matter of public sentiment than it is to explain the persistence and growth of the antitrust enterprise as a legal and administrative fact. But the fate of antitrust is an excellent illustration of how a public ideal, vaguely formulated and often hopelessly at odds with stubborn realities, can become embodied in institutions with elaborate, self-preserving rules and procedures, a defensible function, and an equally stubborn capacity for survival.

The antitrust revival originated in the closing phases of the New Deal. It was a response to the recession of 1937–38, which itself brought about a crisis in the thinking and the political strategy of the New Dealers. The recession gave to the Brandeis liberals, who had always been present in New Deal councils, a chance to reassert their competitive ideas and their suspicion of big business. In 1934, long before the cartelization of the N.R.A. was abandoned, the economist Gardiner C. Means, then economic adviser to the Secretary of Agriculture, had prepared a memorandum on administered prices that provided the economic rationale for a new approach to the depression. Early in 1935 this memorandum was published by the Senate.[45] Means contrasted market

45 Gardiner C. Means, *Industrial Prices and Their Relative Inflexibility*, Senate Doc. No. 13, 74th Cong., 1st sess. Parts of this document, along with later papers on the same theme, are reprinted in Means's *The Corporate Revolution in America*, Crowell-Collier, New York, 1962. For a critique and some reflections on later interest in the theory, see Richard Ruggles, The Nature of Price Flexibility and the Determinants of Relative Price Changes in the Economy, in *Business Concentration and Price Policy*, Princeton University Press, Princeton, N. J., 1955, esp. pp. 443–464, and the conflicting views expressed by economists before the Kefauver Committee, *Administered Prices*, Hearings before the Subcommittee on Antitrust and Monopoly of the Committee on the Judiciary, United States Senate (Washington, 1957).

prices, which were made and remade in the market as the result of interactions between buyers and sellers in the fashion of traditional economic theory, with administered prices, which were set by administrative action and held constant for a considerable period of time. Market prices are flexible and respond readily to a fall in demand; administered prices are rigid. Means considered the disparity between flexible and rigid prices to be an important aggravating force in the depression. Although he did not identify administered prices with monopoly, he focused attention once again on those industries in which market power was sufficiently concentrated to make administered prices possible. Some of his contemporaries seized upon the conception as a rationale for stepping up antitrust activity, and Franklin D. Roosevelt invoked it in his message of 1938, calling for the creation of the T.N.E.C. At the same time, other New Deal theorists, notably Assistant Attorney General Robert Jackson, who was then head of the Antitrust Division of the Department of Justice, and Secretary of the Interior Harold L. Ickes, became convinced that the organized power of big business was attempting to sabotage reform through a "strike of capital" and that a new assault on business power must be undertaken as a basis for further attempts at recovery. The old argument that business power was a threat to democratic government itself thus entered into Roosevelt's T.N.E.C. message.

The new attack on business power took two forms; the first was the elaborate, if inconclusive, T.N.E.C. investigation, which yielded a mass of factual information, much of it new, but no programmatic proposals in which the investigators themselves had any confidence.[46] The second was the stepping up of anti-

___

[46] Early in its *Final Report,* the Committee confessed that its members "are not rash enough to believe that they can lay down a program which will solve the great problems that beset the world, but they are convinced that the information which this committee has assembled, when eventually properly analyzed and disseminated, will enable the people of America to know what must be done if human freedom is to be preserved." *Final Report and Recommendations of the Temporary National Economic Committee,* 87th Cong., 1st sess., Sen. Doc. No. 35, p. 4. In short, the Committee did not know what precisely to make of its own data but hoped that in due time

trust activity under the leadership of Thurman Arnold, the new chief of the Antitrust Division. Congress doubled appropriations for Arnold's division in 1939 and then doubled them again in 1940. Between 1938 and 1943 its staff grew almost fivefold.

In retrospect it is instructive to see what results came from uncertain and, at times, ill-considered beginnings. Today the Jackson–Ickes view of the recession seems quite partisan and fanciful; the T.N.E.C. investigation, for all the information it gathered, was from a pragmatic point of view a fiasco; the value of Means's emphasis on administered prices is highly controversial among economists; and Thurman Arnold's experiment with antitrust enforcement can be judged, at least from one angle of vision, as a substantial failure. And yet, as in the case of so many of the gropings of the New Deal, there was a valuable outcome, which in this case can best be got at by looking at the core of success wrapped up in Thurman Arnold's frustration.

Arnold's story is replete with ironies. He had written of the antitrust enterprise with a devastating note of mockery, and the appointment of a man with such views, especially by an administration that had only recently resorted to the wholesale cartelization of the N.R.A., was looked at askance by antitrust-minded senators as a possible effort to sabotage the Antitrust Division. But Arnold proceeded to recruit and inspire a splendid staff and to rehabilitate the entire antitrust function. His goal was not to attack bigness or efficient mass production or efficient marketing, but rather to discipline the pricing policies of business at the vital points where abuses seemed most important. Antitrust was thus to become an instrument of social and economic policy, aimed to stop firms from setting prices above reasonable levels, to prevent businesses from holding new processes off the market, and to reduce unemployment. All this was to be achieved not so much by isolated cases or by responding to this or that complaint, but rather by systematic action against whole industries—motion pictures, petroleum, radio broadcasting, drugs, housing.

the public would. See the penetrating critique by two members, Isador Lubin and Leon Henderson, *ibid.*, pp. 51–52.

From a short-run point of view, Arnold's regime could be judged a failure. His program for housing was spiked when the Court made it impossible to act effectively against the labor unions, which constituted a lynch-pin of restraint of trade in that industry; his plan for the food industry lost its point during the war; his program for transportation was put off by the War Production Board.[47] He could not wholly reform a single industry, much less bring about important general structural changes in the economy. And yet he succeeded in demonstrating the usefulness of the antitrust laws. In actually *using* the Sherman Act, thanks to the enlarged staff that Congress had given him, he showed for the first time what it could and could not do. Although it could not alter the fundamental character of the economy or make it less liable to cyclical instability (as Arnold had promised in his book, *The Bottlenecks of Business*), it could significantly affect the conduct of business within the framework of the existing structure. Arnold's Division soon won a number of decisions from the courts—particularly in the Alcoa case of 1945 and the American Tobacco case of the following year—that opened new possibilities for enforcement. It won from Congress a permanent reversal of the former policy of niggardly support. And finally, it put the antitrust enterprise on such a footing that it could flourish under both Democratic and Republican regimes; the return of the Republicans under Eisenhower did not bring a remission of efforts to use the Sherman Act or retrenchment of the Antitrust Division. Instead, it set up the Attorney General's National Committee to Study the Antitrust Laws, which in 1955 returned a unanimous judgment in favor of antitrust policy and of the current state of case law, which had tightened enforcement. Although the Committee did not make any dramatic recommendations for more rigorous enforcement, the effect of its work was to reaffirm the bipartisan character of the antitrust commitment by ratifying the achievements of Democratic administrations in the preceding fifteen years.[48]

[47] See Corwin D. Edwards, Thurman Arnold and the Antitrust Laws, *Political Science Quarterly*, LVIII (September 1943), pp. 338–355.

[48] *Report of the Attorney General's National Committee to Study the Antitrust Laws* (Washington, 1955).

What makes it possible to institutionalize antitrust activities. at the higher plateau that has been maintained since 1938 is not a consensus among economists as to its utility in enhancing economic efficiency, but a rough consensus in society at large as to its value in curbing the dangers of excessive market power. As in the beginning, it is based on a political and moral judgment rather than the outcome of economic measurement or even distinctively economic criteria. "It must be recognized," says Professor Edward S. Mason, "that there is an element of faith in the proposition that maintaining competition substantially improves the efficiency of resource use." The option for a minimal level of competition to be underwritten by public policy, although it can be backed by substantial economic arguments,. "rests basically on a political judgment," write Carl Kaysen and Donald F. Turner in their inquiry into trust policy: "In our democratic, egalitarian society, large areas of uncontrolled private power are not tolerated." "We found," write Dirlam and Kahn in their book, *Fair Competition,* "that the decisions [of courts and commissions] could not be fully understood or fairly appraised by economic standards alone. Hence we concluded that the appropriate question for economists to ask about antitrust policy is not whether this is the most efficient way of structuring or reorganizing the economy, but the inverted one: Does antitrust seriously interfere with the requirements of efficiency?" "The rationale of antitrust," writes A. D. Neale, a British student of the American experience, "is essentially a desire to provide legal checks to restrain economic power and is not a pursuit of efficiency as such." "For most Americans," concludes Professor Galbraith, "free competition, so called, has for long been a political rather than an economic concept." [49]

In any case, the state of antitrust enforcement seems to correspond with a public consensus. Economists and lawyers differ profoundly on how effective the antitrust laws have been and on

[49] Edward S. Mason in the Preface to Carl Kaysen and Donald B. Turner,. *Antitrust Policy,* Harvard University Press, Cambridge, Mass., 1960, p. xx; *ibid.,* p. 5; A. D. Neale, *The Antitrust Laws of the U.S.A.,* Cambridge University Press, Cambridge, 1962, p. 487; Galbraith, *op. cit.,* p. 27.

how effective they could be if they were more amply enforced,[50] but there is hardly a major industry that has not seen a significant lawsuit or two, and in most industries in which intervention might be thought desirable, government intervention has had more than negligible effects.[51]   It is also one of the strengths of antitrust that neither its effectiveness nor its ineffectiveness can be precisely documented; its consequences rest on events of unknown number and significance that have *not* happened—on proposed mergers that may have died in the offices of corporation counsel, on collusive agreements that have never been consummated, on unfair practices contemplated but never carried out. Liberals can support it because they retain their old suspicion of business behavior, and conservatives support it because they still believe in competition, and they may hope to gain an additional point of leverage in the battle against inflation.   No one seems prepared to suggest that the antitrust enterprise be cut back drastically, much less abandoned, and Congress has consistently supported its enlarged staff.   The existing state of enforcement conforms to the state of the public mind, which accepts bigness but continues to distrust business morals.   Even business itself accords to the principle of antitrust a certain grudging and irritated acceptance.   Visitations by the Department of Justice are a nuisance, lawsuits are expensive, and prosecution carries an unpleasant stigma, but the antitrust procedures can be considered an alternative to more obtrusive regulation such as outright controls on prices.   At any rate, big business has never found it necessary or expedient to launch a public campaign against antitrust enforcement; the pieties at stake are too deep to risk touching.

A final element in antitrust enforcement rests on the fact that the government itself is now a major consumer, and the points of exposure of industrial prices to official concern and reaction have been multiplied.   One of the reasons for the antitrust re-

[50] See, for example, the symposium, Dexter M. Keezer, ed., The Effectiveness of the Federal Antitrust Laws, *American Economic Review,* XXXIX (June 1949), pp. 689–724.

[51] See the industry-by-industry survey in Simon N. Whitney, *Antitrust Policies: American Experience in Twenty Industries,* 2 vols., Twentieth Century Fund, New York, 1958.

vival in 1938 was the irritation of government officials over the prevalence of what seemed to be collusively priced bids. With his book, *The Bottlenecks of Business,* Thurman Arnold hoped to mobilize the consumer behind the new phase of antitrust enforcement—a forlorn hope when one thinks of the historical passivity of American consumers. But the presence of the government as consumer has perhaps supplied some of the leverage he was looking for.

Antitrust reform is not the first reform in American history whose effectiveness rested less upon a broad movement of militant mass sentiment than upon the leadership of a small group of influential and deeply concerned specialists. In passing from a phase in which it was largely an ideology to one in which it has become largely a technique, antitrust has become, like so many other things in our society, differentiated, specialized, and bureaucratized. No layman can any longer concern himself very much with the immense body of case law that has been built up over the decades or with the truly formidable literature of relevant economic analysis and argument that has grown up since the 1930's. Of necessity the potentialities of antitrust action have become the almost exclusive concern of a technical elite of lawyers and economists. Indeed, the business of studying, attacking, defending, and evaluating oligopolistic behavior and its regulation has become one of our small industries, which gives employment to many gifted professional men. The volume of books and articles in this field and the large number of entrants indicate that this industry, at least, is workably competitive.

By Burton I. Kaufman

ASSOCIATE PROFESSOR OF HISTORY
KANSAS STATE UNIVERSITY

Oil and Antitrust: The Oil Cartel Case and the Cold War*

❡ *Nowhere was the postwar growth of multinational corporations more dramatic than in the petroleum industry. The major oil companies of the western nations were soon banded together in a complex of joint exploration, producing, refining, and marketing organizations. But efforts to advance criminal prosecution of the American companies under the antitrust laws soon ran head-on into overriding considerations of national security. The hardening of the Cold War, complicated by internal political weaknesses in Iran, persuaded .both President Truman and President Eisenhower to soft-pedal litigation. In the end, criminal prosecution of joint production enterprises became civil suits against marketing and pricing agreements, which were settled by consent decree. This, according to Professor Kaufman, amounted to attacking "the tail but not the head or body of the energy tiger."*

In 1918 Congress passed the Webb-Pomerene Act exempting certain business combinations engaged in foreign commerce from the provisions of the antitrust laws. The purpose of this legislation was to encourage small businessmen to enter the field of foreign commerce by allowing them to form joint selling agencies in competition against foreign buying cartels. Although never very successful, the measure was the government's first meaningful effort – aside from the Sherman, Clayton, and Federal Trade Commission Acts – to legislate on foreign antitrust questions.[1]

Business History Review, Vol. LI, No. 1 (Spring, 1977). Copyright © The President and Fellows of Harvard College.

° This essay is based in large measure on the Department of Justice Files relating to the Oil Cartel Case, 1940s to 1968, file number 60–57–140, Washington, D.C. The file consists of several thousand pages of bound documents as well as several hundred thousand pages of supporting documents, most of which are still in file cabinets and cartons in a Department of Justice storeroom. The Department of Justice made this material available to the author through the Freedom of Information Act. The author wishes to acknowledge the cooperation of the Department of Justice in making this material available. He also wishes to express his appreciation to the Bureau of Grants and Research of Kansas State University for two grants that made the research for this essay possible. Except where otherwise noted, the materials cited in this essay are the bound documents in file 60–57–140 and are cited as DOJ, 60–57–140.

[1] On the Webb-Pomerene Act, see Burton I. Kaufman, *Efficiency and Expansion: Foreign Trade Organization in the Wilson Administration, 1913–1921* (Westport, Conn., 1974), 214–210. See also Wilbur L. Fugate, *Foreign Commerce and the Antitrust Laws* (Boston, 1973) 223–254.

As the United States expanded abroad after 1918, foreign trade issues became manifold. This was especially true for the period following the end of World War II when the growth of multinational corporations changed the entire nature of foreign commerce. Not only did government and business leaders debate the value of the Webb-Pomerene Act, but they also gave increased attention to such other matters as foreign subsidiaries, foreign and foreign–related joint ventures, patents and technology, and trademarks in foreign commerce.[2]

For the most part, the courts applied a rigorous interpretation of the antitrust laws, even narrowing the scope of dealings that could take place between a parent company and its foreign subsidiaries or between two subsidiaries of the same parent company.[3] Likewise, the Truman and Eisenhower administrations advocated, at least in theory, strong support for stringent enforcement of the antitrust laws abroad as well as at home. For example, the Federal Trade Commission (FTC) issued a series of reports indicating that major industries had violated the antitrust laws by restraining foreign commerce.[4] The Department of Justice increased the number of its prosecutions involving overseas trade,[5] while Truman and Eisenhower made clear their own support for international free trade by attacking a number of trade practices, including the establishment of world monopolies and cartels. As Truman explained his position in 1949, "[Trade] agreements do not touch certain important obstacles to the expansion of world trade. Subsidiaries, cartels, and many other devices have important effects in limiting trade or creating disadvantages for one country as compared with another."[6]

Even more important than antitrust questions in determining policy toward foreign trade, however, was growing national concern about the hardening Cold War with the Soviet Union. Simply stated, administration and other public leaders, believing that the United

---

[2] Fugate, *Foreign Commerce and the Antitrust Laws, passim.* Kingman Brewster, Jr., *Antitrust and American Business Abroad* (New York, 1958), *passim.*

[3] Mira Wilkins, *The Maturing of Multinational Enterprise; American Business Abroad* (Cambridge, Mass., 1974), *passim.*

[4] Federal Trade Commission, *Report on the Copper Industry* (Washington, D. C., 1947); Federal Trade Commission, *Report on the Sulphur Industry and International Cartels* (Washington, D. C., 1947); Federal Trade Commission, *Report on International Electrical Equipment Cartels* (Washington, D. C., 1948); Federal Trade Commission, *Report on International Steel Cartels* (Washington, D. C., 1948); Federal Trade Commission, *Report on Fertilizer Industry* (Washington, D. C., 1950); Federal Trade Commission, *Report on International Cartels in the Alkali Industry* (Washington, D. C. ,1950).

[5] Wilkins, *The Maturing of Multinational Enterprise,* 292–300; Fugate, *Foreign Commerce and the Antitrust Laws,* esp. 444–447.

[6] *Public Papers of the Presidents of the United States: Harry S. Truman,* 1949 (Washington, D. C., 1964), 233–235. On Eisenhower's views, see especially, *Public Papers of the Presidents of the United States; Dwight D. Eisenhower,* 1954 (Washington, D. C. n.d.) 352–364.

States had the responsibility for containing Soviet (communist) expansion throughout the world, subordinated questions of foreign commerce, including antitrust matters, to the exigencies of national defense and security as they saw them. The result was internal tension in the administration and a bifurcation of policy — on the one hand, prosecuting violators of the antitrust laws while, on the other, allowing, even encouraging, violations when they were conceived to be in the interests of national defense and security. Such was the case where the nation's petroleum industry was concerned.

In 1952, the Truman administration began the process of bringing criminal indictments against the nation's five major oil companies, Standard Oil of New Jersey (Jersey), Socony Mobil (Socony), Standard Oil of California (Socal), Texaco, and Gulf Oil. The administration accused these multinational giants, along with Royal Dutch Shell and Anglo-Iranian Oil (now British Petroleum) with violation of the nation's antitrust laws by having engaged in a worldwide combination to restrain and monopolize the United States's domestic and foreign commerce in crude oil and petroleum products. The administration hoped to obtain relief by forcing divestiture of the defendants' joint production, refining, pipeline, and marketing operations. However, faced with the exigencies of the Cold War after 1950 and seeking to use the major oil companies for foreign policy purposes (such as preventing the spread of communism in that area, assuring America's control of the world oil trade, and securing a reliable source of crude oil for the United States and its allies at reasonable prices), the Truman and Eisenhower administrations so altered and narrowed the scope of the antitrust proceedings that the defendants were able to maintain their hold on Mideast oil even up to 1968 when the Justice Department decided to drop its proceedings against the last defendants, Socal and Socony.

INVESTIGATIONS OF THE OIL INDUSTRY

The Department of Justice had been concerned for some time about the foreign operations of the oil companies. As early as 1942, in a separate suit, the Justice Department had charged Jersey with having illegally arranged with the German chemical trust, I. G. Farben, not to compete against it in chemicals in return for the latter's agreement not to compete in oil. During the preparation of the case, documents were uncovered revealing an arrangement between Jersey and Royal Dutch Shell for maintaining their respective marketing positions as provided for in an earlier pact known as the

OIL AND THE COLD WAR   37

"As Is" agreement. Jersey signed a consent decree enjoining it from participating in this agreement or from otherwise restricting American foreign commerce. However, the Justice Department obtained information after World War II indicating that "As Is" was still operating. The information included evidence that Jersey and Royal Dutch Shell had been conducting meetings about their "As Is" positions as well as a letter from a Czechoslovakian subsidiary of Socony making a direct reference to the current marketing position of Shell under "As Is." On the basis of this information, an official of the Department's Antitrust Division, Robert Nitschke, recommended at the beginning of 1947 that the Justice Department seek grand jury authorization to begin an investigation of what he referred to as the "As Is" cartel; the investigation was to include not only Jersey, Royal Dutch Shell and Socony, but also Socal, Anglo-Iranian Oil, Gulf, and Texaco.[7]

Nitschke's recommendation was rejected by his superior, Assistant Attorney General Graham Morrison, for several reasons. In the first place, Morrison felt that the Justice Department simply lacked sufficient evidence to ask a grand jury for an investigation of the oil industry. As he told Nitschke, there was still inadequate proof that restraints of trade or enjoining of competition existed within the oil industry.[8]

At least as important in rejecting Nitschke's proposal, however, was the peculiar position of oil among largely unregulated industries. In public as well as in private circles the oil industry was widely regarded as an essential public utility requiring government support, including diplomatic assistance in developing foreign sources of oil. Even Truman agreed with this since he encouraged the expansion abroad of American oil interests.[9] Morrison was reluctant, therefore, to engage in what many within the administration, perhaps the president himself, might regard as a precipitous action against the oil industry. Nitschke's recommendation, he pointed out, "completely ignores the fact that distribution of oil both foreign and domestic is in fact a quasi-public utility business although not usually

[7] Frank W. Gaines to Robert Nitschke, October 4, 1946; Nitschke to Graham Morrison, January 31, 1947, DOJ, 60–57–140.

[8] Nitschke to John F. Sonnett, June 4, 1947, *ibid.* Morrison's response to Nitschke is in long hand at the end of Nitschke's memorandum.

[9] One reason why Truman encouraged the expansion of American oil interests was his fear that without an American presence in the Middle East, especially in Iran, the region might fall to the communists. According to one of his advisers, George Elsey, Truman went to the globe in his office during a meeting to discuss the Korean situation in late June, 1950. Putting his finger on Iran, Elsey noted, the president said "Here is where they [the communists] will start trouble if we aren't careful . . . if we just stand by, they'll move into Iran and they'll take over the whole Middle East." Papers of George Elsey (Harry S. Truman Library, Independence, Missouri).

recognized as such and is inately [sic] by nature of a monopolistic character."[10]

Not until five years later did the administration follow up Nitschke's recommendation. By this time strong pressures had developed within administration and government circles for a grand jury investigation of the oil industry as a preliminary to bringing criminal antitrust indictments against the oil majors. The purchase in 1947 of a 40 per cent interest in the Arabian American Oil Company (Aramco) by Jersey and Socony created an uproar in the Senate, where a special committee headed by Owen Brewster of Maine sought an investigation of the multinationals operating in the Mideast. Previously owned by Texaco and Socal alone, Aramco enjoyed a monopoly of the vast Arabian oil fields. Texaco and Socal agreed to the purchase in order to raise capital for increased production and for the construction of new pipelines. The effect of the sale appeared, however, to be the joining of four of the majors (and former competitors) into one huge cartel dominating Mideast oil production, refining, and distribution. Furthermore, the Brewster Committee was annoyed at what it believed to be excessive prices for Persian oil delivered by Aramco to the Navy and the American public. The Committee therefore urged Attorney General Tom Clark to look into the Aramco purchase, clearly anticipating that such an investigation would lead to antitrust action against the oil majors.[11]

In 1949 the Federal Trade Commission (FTC) undertook its own investigation of the oil industry as part of the series of studies it was making on the foreign trade practices of the nation's leading industries, including copper, electrical equipment, steel, and fertilizers. As the FTC noted in explaining the reasons for its study of oil, the Commission regarded international petroleum operations as constituting "one of the most important of the international cartels."[12]

The following year the FTC completed its investigation. As in its earlier reports, the Commission reached no conclusions about violations of the antitrust laws; nor did it make any recommendations about possible criminal indictments against the oil companies. But it left little doubt where it stood on these matters. Concentration in the form of jointly–owned subsidiaries and affiliated companies was

[10] Nitschke to John F. Sonnett, June 4, 1947, DOJ 60–57–140.

[11] Brewster to Clark, November 14, 1947, *ibid*. See also George P. Comer to John Ford Beecher, June 7, 1948, and Comer and Haldon R. Mohar to Herbert Borkland, September 1, 1948, *ibid*.

[12] Senate Select Committee on Small Business, Commission Print No. 6, *The International Petroleum Cartel: Staff Report to the Federal Trade Commission* (Washington, D.C.),

"probably more widespread in the international petroleum industry than in any other field of enterprise," it concluded.[13]

The National Security Council (NSC), Central Intelligence Agency (CIA), Department of Defense, and other agencies and individuals concerned with national security matters tried to keep the report (marked "classified") from being made public, regarding it as a threat to national security in the Mideast. At a special meeting on May 6, the White House's Intelligence Advisory Committee, on which many of these agencies and individuals sat, advised against releasing the report in any form, noting that its release would "greatly assist Soviet propaganda, would further the achievement of Soviet objectives throughout the world and [would] hinder the achievement of U.S. foreign policy objectives, particularly in the Near and Middle East."[14]

Nevertheless, the pressures against the oil companies had grown too great by this time to prevent further disclosures of their foreign operations. Rumors of the FTC's findings had already begun to circulate in official Washington, and the Judiciary Committees of both the Senate and the House were seeking access to its report (which was the reason for the Intelligence Advisory Committee's meeting). Furthermore, the Justice Department had accumulated sufficient evidence by now to recommend to President Harry Truman a grand jury investigation of the oil companies' overseas operations.[15]

The president's position in this developing struggle over foreign oil policy was ambiguous. As already mentioned, Truman supported the general proposition of expansion of American oil interests abroad. Moreover, as subsequent events soon showed, the president was heavily influenced by his national security advisers who were recommending a "hands off" policy toward oil abroad. However, the president was also committed to breaking up international cartels, which posed a challenge to the nation's stated commitment to the principles of free trade. In this respect, he shared a prevalent sentiment within administration and congressional circles for helping small business by strengthening the antitrust laws against big business, domestically as well as internationally.[16]

Faced with what seemed to be overwhelming evidence of an in-

13 Senate Select Committee on Small Business, Commission Print No. 6, *The International Petroleum Cartel*, 1.

14 John Edgar Hoover to the Acting Attorney General, May 7, 1952, DOJ, 60–57–140.

15 W. B. Watson Snyder to H. G. Morison, January 23, 1952; *"Memorandum for the Attorney General"*, January 24, 1952; W. B. Watson Snyder to Mr. Hodges, September 11, 1950, *ibid.*

16 More work needs to be done on Truman's policy toward trusts, but see, for example, Alonzo L. Hamby, *Beyond the New Deal: Harry S. Truman and American Liberalism* (New York 1973), 46–47.

ternational petroleum conspiracy to restrain American foreign and domestic commerce, the president decided he had to take action. On June 23, 1952 he ordered a grand jury investigation of the oil industry for the purpose of bringing criminal indictments against the multinational giants. A high ranking official of the Justice Department's Antitrust Division, Leonard Emmerglick, was put in charge of the investigation and subpoenas were served upon twenty-one companies, including all the majors, asking them to produce thousands of documents on their foreign and domestic operations.[17]

THE IRANIAN CRISIS

Within a few months Truman reversed himself and ordered that the investigation be dropped. In place of criminal action he recommended that the Justice Department consider a civil suit having more complex search procedures and carrying milder penalties. Fearing the expansion of Soviet influence in the Mideast as a result of a decision by Iran in 1951 to nationalize British Petroleum holdings in that country, Truman followed the counsel of his national security advisers who not only recommended strongly against prosecuting the Mideast oil companies, but who, in fact, hoped to use them for foreign policy purposes.

The problem in Iran developed largely as a result of British Petroleum's refusal to grant Iran a larger share of its oil profits. British Petroleum responded to the nationalization by placing a boycott on Iranian oil and then threatening legal action against any oil company that attempted to break the boycott.[18] From the beginning of the crisis, administration leaders, especially those in the Department of Defense and State and the NSC, warned of the growing influence of the Soviet Union in Iran (whose government was headed by the nationalist Prime Minister Mohammed Mossadegh) and of the dangerous precedent that Iranian nationalization might set for other oil producing countries. No worse harm could be done to American oil interests abroad and to American foreign policy, they argued, than to bring criminal indictments against the oil majors, which would be fodder for the Soviet propaganda machine

[17] Senate Foreign Relations Committee, Subcommittee on Multinational Corporations, *Committee Print, Multinational Oil Corporations and U. S. Foreign Policy*, 57–58. See also statement of Leonard J. Emmerglick, Senate Foreign Relations Committee, Subcommittee on Multinational Corporations, *Hearings, Multinational Corporations and United States Foreign Policy*, Part VII (Washington, D. C., 1974), 103–107.

[18] This incident is covered in numerous works on Mideast oil interests. One of the most recent is Christopher T. Rand, *Making Democracy Safe for Oil: Oilmen and the Islamic East* (Boston, 1975), 135–136. See also Robert Engler, *The Politics of Oil: A Study of Private Power and Democratic Directions* (New York, 1061), 203 204.

and which might lead to further nationalization of American foreign oil interests. Oil company spokesmen took up the same themes, even linking the FTC report on international petroleum with the nationalization of British Petroleum, despite the fact that the report was not published until a year after nationalization had taken place.[19]

As the crisis in Iran continued, a number of the same administration leaders sought to use the oil companies to achieve two foreign policy objectives: first, to make oil available to Europe from other producing countries, and then to win an American oil presence in Iran. In 1951, Attorney General J. H. McGrath approved a voluntary agreement permitted under the Defense Production Act, which had been passed after conflict broke out in Korea in 1950 and which allowed the President to grant antitrust exemption to voluntary agreements among industries deemed essential to national security. The agreement that McGrath approved authorized the formation of a Foreign Petroleum Supply Committee to channel supplies of petroleum to areas short of oil as a result of the Iranian stoppage. Later, as it became apparent that the Teheran government would never permit British Petroleum to return to Iran alone, Truman even instructed Secretary of State Dean Acheson to open discussions with the American majors and British Petroleum in hopes of reaching an agreement whereby American oil companies might enter Iran as part of an international consortium.[20]

Before any agreement with the oil companies could be worked out, Truman left office. But first he held a lengthy meeting of the NSC in which the Departments of Defense, State, and Interior recommended dropping the criminal investigations of the oil companies and the Justice Department urged their continuation. A few days later Truman made his decision. In a letter to Attorney General James P. McGranery, the president wrote: "As a result of factors which have emerged since the institution of the current grand jury investigation of the international activities of the major oil companies,

[19] See, for example, "Conference with representatives of the Department of State," prepared by George H. Schueller, August 13, 1952. According to Schueller, during this conference Robert Eakins, chief of the Department of State's Petroleum Policy Staff, thus suggested the Middle East situation as one problem on which there should be close consultation. He emphasized the delicate nature of this problem, the presence of national security interests, and the importance of keeping oil interests in the Middle East in the hands of United States nationals. DOJ, 60–57–140. See also "Memorandum re Pending Criminal Proceedings Against Oil Companies," January 21, 1953, ibid. For the oil company's campaign against the FTC report, see "Editorials, News Stories, Articles, and Other References Indicating Attacks on FTCs Oil Cartel Report," October 17 and December 16, 1952, Stephen J. Springarn Papers, Box 47 (Harry S. Truman Library, Independence, Missouri). See also Engler, The Politics of Oil, 209–212.

[20] "Memorandum for the Secretary," November 26, 1952, DOJ, 60–57–140. See also W. B. Watson Snyder to H. G. Morison, January 23, 1952 and George B. Haddock to Newell A. Clapp, August 22, 1952, ibid; Emanuel Celler to Harry S. Truman, OF 134–138, Harry S. Truman Papers (Harry S. Truman Library, Independence, Missouri).

I am of the opinion that the interest of national security might be best served at this time by resolving important questions of law and policy involved in that investigation in the context of civil litigation rather than in the context of criminal proceedings." [21]

The Justice Department yielded to the president by dropping its criminal investigation. Not until President Eisenhower had been in office for three months did the Department even resume its case, this time filing a civil action with the federal district court of Washington, D.C. in which it charged an international conspiracy by the major oil companies to restrain American foreign and domestic commerce by controlling the world's production, refining, and distribution of oil. Two months later the court transferred the case to the Southern District of New York for final disposition. [22]

By following the advice of his national security advisers, Truman had seriously damaged the Justice Department suit even before it was filed. In simplest terms he helped develop a defense for the oil companies against Justice Department charges of antitrust violations. The oil companies were serving a vital national function abroad, they were now able to argue, helping to protect the free world against communist inroads. To attack the oil companies on obscure and unfounded grounds of conspiring to control world markets and to restrain world trade was to invite Soviet expansion into the Mideast and other oil producing regions. Besides, the government had just granted the oil majors antitrust immunity on the grounds of serving the national interest. How could that same government now seek to prosecute the oil companies for violating the national interest through an alleged antitrust conspiracy? These themes oil company executives would continue to stress for the next fifteen years. [23]

The Justice Department was fully aware of the implications of Truman's actions for their suit against the oil majors. During the Iranian crisis, the Department had agreed only reluctantly to the Defense Production Act exemption of oil from the antitrust laws, emphasizing the limited nature of the exemption and providing for government supervision of the proceedings of the Foreign Petroleum Supply Committee established according to the provisions of the Defense Production Act. More important, at the meeting before Truman's decision to drop criminal proceedings against the oil

---

21 Truman to McGranery, January 12, 1953, DOJ, 60–57–140.

22 Engler, *The Politics of Oil*, 216–217.

23 See, for example, Oscar John Dorwin to Assistant Attorney General, May 23, 1957 and Dorwin, "Memorandum for the Department of State of the Views of the Texas Company," June 25, 1958; Herman J. Schmidt to Secretary of State, June 5, 1958; Oscar J. Dorwin to Lee Loevinger, November 15, 1961; David Haberman for files, January 24, 1962, DOJ, 60–57–140.

majors, Department officials had warned of the danger of relying on private business interests to carry out national policy. Nevertheless, the Department's hands had been tied by the national security considerations growing out of the hardening Cold War.[24]

ACTIONS UNDER THE EISENHOWER ADMINISTRATION

The Justice Department fared little better under the new administration, through whose actions the Department was forced ultimately to limit its suit to marketing and price-fixing arrangements only. In these matters the Department did achieve some notable successes, forcing the breakup of a major marketing organization, Stanvac, which was jointly owned by Jersey and Socony, and the partial breakup of a second marketing firm, Caltex, jointly owned by Texaco and Socal. The Department also ended a number of anticompetitive marketing arrangements, involving Gulf, Texaco, British Petroleum, Royal Dutch Shell, and Jersey. However, these were very limited victories since the basic structure of oil operations abroad — joint production, refining, and transportation — remained untouched. The result was that while some antitrust relief was obtained and certain cartel arrangements broken, the oil majors succeeded in keeping their firm grip on Mideast oil through most of the 1960s, dictating world prices and keeping independents out of the region.

It would be easy to attribute this success to the warm relationship that existed between the oil industry and the Eisenhower Administration. Certainly the Department of Interior, many of whose top officials were closely tied to the major oil companies, played an obstructionist role throughout most of the antitrust proceedings, defending the actions of the oil majors in the Mideast, and even refusing to make available to the Justice Department requested documents on oil operations abroad. Furthermore, President Eisenhower himself enjoyed friendly personal relations with a number of oil leaders, who had an opportunity to influence his oil policies.[25]

The final outcome of the oil cartel case was far more involved,

---

[24] "Report of the Attorney General to the National Security Council Relative to the Grand Jury Investigation of the International Oil Cartel — January 1, 1953" and "Memorandum for the Attorney General" by Robert S. Cutler, DOJ, 60–57–140. See also W. B. Watson Snyder to H. G. Morison, January 23, 1952, *ibid.* The Justice Department had quite early taken the position that it would not use private interests for public policy purposes. See, for example, Johnston Avery to John C. Stedman, May 31, 1949, *ibid.*

[25] The Department of Interior had been uncooperative and defensive of the oil companies even before the civil suit was filed. See Secretary of Interior Oscar L. Chapman to Attorney General James P. McGranery, January 17, 1953, *ibid.* See also Clarence A. Davis (Acting Secretary of Interior) to Attorney General Herbert Brownell, Jr., May 1, 1956, *ibid.* See also Robert Engler, *Politics of Oil*, esp. 92–94, 126–128, 245–246, and 358–359.

however, than this analysis suggests. For one thing, such an explanation assumes a homogeneity of oil interests during the 1950s (and into the 1960s) that never existed. Congressional hearings in the 1950s reveal that the story of American oil in that decade was one of bitter warfare between producer and refiner, major and independent, distributor and consumer, each seeking to protect its own interest against the other, generally through complex and varying alliances. Moreover, to the extent that Eisenhower participated in this maze, it was to support independent domestic producers who felt threatened by increased imports of cheap foreign oil by the majors.[26]

More fundamental to the disposition of the oil cartel case was the intrusion of the Cold War into domestic policy. Like his predecessor, Eisenhower subordinated antitrust considerations to the exigencies of the Cold War. In the process he encouraged and then approved arrangements among the oil majors that practically assured that their dominance of foreign oil would be protected from antitrust attack.

That foreign policy rather than antitrust considerations would continue to determine the final outcome of the cartel case was made clear soon after the Justice Department filed its civil suit. Department officials decided to confine their action to those firms headquartered and doing their principal business in the United States, thereby excluding as defendants, British Petroleum, Royal Dutch Shell, and even Aramco. This decision was reached at the highest levels of government and under great pressure from the Department of State, which was concerned by the policy implications of a more generalized antitrust case. By approving an NSC memorandum stating "that the enforcement of the antitrust laws of the United States against the western oil companies operating in the Near East [were] to be deemed secondary to the national interest," Eisenhower made clear that he was in full agreement with this approach to the suit.[27]

In fact, Eisenhower's major concern relative to the cartel case was a favorable settlement of the oil impasse in Iran. Accepting as his own Truman's plan of gaining an American presence in Iran, Eisenhower appointed Herbert Hoover, Jr. as his personal emissary to travel between the American majors, British Petroleum, and the

[26] Senate Committee on the Judiciary and Senate Committee on Interior and Insular Affairs, *Joint Hearings, Emergency Oil Lift Program and Related Problems* (Washington, D. C., 1957). See also Engler, *Politics of Oil*, 78–79, 143–146, 231–237 and 355–371.

[27] Senate Foreign Relations Committee, Subcommittee on Multinational Corporations, *Committee Print, Multinational Corporations and U. S. Foreign Policy*, 65–66. See also Walter Bedell Smith to Attorney General Herbert Brownell, Jr., April 27, 1953 and Wilbur L. Fugate to Stanley L. Barnes, January 24, 1956, DOJ, 60–57–140.

Teheran government in order to establish an international consortium to work the Iranian oil fields.[28]

The oil majors, which had abundant supplies of oil elsewhere, including the United States, were by no means eager to enter an Iranian consortium. They made it clear to the administration that they would do so only in the interest of national security, that is, to protect American interests against communist expansion, and only if they were promised antitrust immunity in the production of Iranian oil. "I note that 'the National Security Council has determined that it is the security interests of the United States that United States petroleum companies participate in an international consortium to contract with the Government of Iran'," the chairman of the Board of Texaco, J. S. Leach, wrote to Undersecretary of State Walter Bedell Smith in February, 1954, "We, of course, desire to cooperate in every way with the National Security Council. . . . However, as we wish to be quite sure that the Attorney General is satisfied that all final agreements which are executed pursuant to the proposed plan will not separately or collectively constitute a violation of the antitrust laws, or create a violation of antitrust laws not already existing, we feel that we should not become finally obligated under any agreement or understandings in pursuance of such plan, until they have been first examined and approved by the Attorney General." [29]

The Eisenhower Administration bowed to these demands of the oil majors. The Department of Justice granted a newly formed Iranian oil consortium consisting of British Petroleum, Royal Dutch Shell, the five American majors, and a number of smaller independents antitrust immunity in the exploration, production, and refining of Iranian oil.[30]

Eisenhower's decision to permit the formation of the Iranian consortium (which was reluctantly approved once more by the Justice Department on the grounds of national security) undercut much of the Department's case against the majors. While Attorney General Brownell gave only a qualified opinion of the consortium's legality and reserved the right to prosecute the case, his opinion had an

[28] See various memoranda in Senate Foreign Relations Committee, Subcommittee on Multinational Corporations, *Committee Print, The International Petroleum Cartel, the Iranian Consortium and U. S. National Security* (Washington, D. C., 1974), 33–95.

[29] Leach to Smith, February 16, 1954. DOJ, 60–57–140. See also Smith to Leach, January 28, 1954, *ibid.* According to the Department of Justice, following the Iranian embargo, a group of oil company representatives, known only by the initials, "G.A.C.," began operating in New York City as a private purchasing agency to fill the orders of alleged cartel members for shipment to Europe. Spot shortages of oil in the United States were alleged to be due to the purchasing activities of G.A.C., "Memorandum for the Attorney General," June 24, 1952, *ibid.*

[30] W. B. Watson Snyder to Assistant Attorney General Stanley N. Barnes, September 16, 1954, DOJ, 60–57–140.

obvious detrimental effect upon the government's case against joint exploration, production, and refining, since it was not prepared to prosecute the very actions that it had just encouraged and sanctioned in the name of the national interest. Officials within the Justice Department's Antitrust Division, who were responsible for bringing the case to trial, were fully aware of the difficult position in which they had been placed as a result of the Iranian settlement. While officially still seeking redress in these areas, as well as in marketing and price-fixing, they actually narrowed their action to the last two points only.[31]

The suit itself moved slowly through the courts from 1954 to 1960. With considerable success the oil companies fought a series of legal skirmishes in an effort to prevent disclosure of the details of their foreign operations. Their most compelling argument — and one which weighed heavily with the courts — was that production of documents located abroad would be resisted by host governments as violating national sovereignty. In this argument the companies were supported by the British, French, and Dutch governments, which refused the release of any documents.[32]

During the "Suez Crisis" of 1956, following the second Arab-Israeli War, the case was suspended for nearly a year. Once more responding to the fear of an oil shortage in Europe (as a result of the closing of the Suez Canal and the cutting of the Iraq pipeline to the Mediterranean), the administration actually granted the defendants and co-conspirators immunity from the antitrust laws in order to establish the Middle East Emergency Committee (MEEC). This committee was part of a plan of action to meet Europe's oil needs, a plan permitted under the Defense Production Act of 1950, which, it will be recalled, granted antitrust immunity in instances in which national security was involved. Through MEEC the oil companies were permitted to work together in lifting oil to Europe without fear of antitrust prosecution.[33]

LIMITING ACTION TO JOINT MARKETING AND PRICE FIXING

Toward the end of 1957 the Justice Department, willing by this time to settle its case in return for relief in matters of joint marketing

---

[31] *Ibid.*

[32] Wilbur Fugate to Victor R. Hansen, June 3, 1957, DOJ, 60–57–140. See also Max Freeman to Leonard Emmerglick, October 16, 1953; Barbara J. Svedberg for files, June 27, 1956; Oscar John Dorwin, "Memorandum for the Department of State of the Views of the Texas Company," June 25, 1958; Wilbur Fugate to Lee Loevinger, April 13, 1961, *ibid.*

[33] Senate Committee on the Judiciary and Senate Committee on Interior and Insular Affairs, *Joint Hearings, Emergency Oil Lift Program and Related Problems,* esp. 1–9, 762–869 and 1003–1336; Senate Committee on the Judiciary, *Petroleum, the Antitrust Laws and Government Policy* (Washington, 1957), 19–22, 25–26, and 51–55. See also Engler, *The Politics of Oil,* 305–307.

and price fixing only, decided to begin formal consent negotiations with the defendants. The crisis of the previous year made a settlement of the case seem imperative. Presiding Judge John Cashin urged an out-of-court settlement, noting that a public trial would have dangerous foreign policy implications in the Mideast and Venezuela. Attorney General Brownell, who now applied his own pressure for a settlement, made much the same point, while also emphasizing the national security importance of government–industry cooperation in foreign oil producing regions.[34]

Gulf Oil, which had been the most cooperative of the defendants in producing foreign documents — and against whom the government admitted it had one of its weakest cases [35] — appeared ready to settle, probably because it had less to lose than the other majors. The government's suit against Gulf rested largely on the latter's agreement with Royal Dutch Shell to sell Shell virtually its entire production of Kuwait oil, which Shell then marketed in the Eastern Hemisphere, allegedly according to "As Is" stipulations. The government sought to end this agreement (which also contained marketing prohibitions against Gulf in Shell territories) while requiring Gulf to set aside a portion of its Kuwait production for sale to independents. Foreign marketing was involved only indirectly in the case against Gulf. According to the government, Gulf shared profits and losses with Shell on its Kuwait oil. Gulf was willing to settle, therefore, provided the consent agreement protected Gulf's sales to Shell without forcing Gulf to admit to a joint marketing conspiracy.[36]

Jersey also seemed willing to settle with the government. Because of national security reasons, the government by 1957 had reduced its case against Jersey from sixteen points to only eight. While none of these called for divestiture or dissolution of Jersey's widely diversified joint producing, refining, or pipeline ventures abroad, they did call for relief in the areas of marketing and price-fixing. Substantial differences still remained between Jersey and the government on a number of issues involving these matters, such as the government's insistence that Jersey limit the amount of offtake (oil) it took from any of its joint production companies. However, Jersey consented to a number of government demands, the major one being the separa-

[34] Wilbur Fugate for files, April 12, 1957; Oscar John Dorwin to Victor R. Hansen, May 23, 1957; "Memorandum for the Attorney General," June 20, 1957; Wilbur Fugate for files, December 3, 1957, DOJ, 60–57–140.

[35] Wilbur Fugate to Stanley L. Barnes, November 3, 1955, *ibid.*

[36] Wilbur Fugate to Robert A. Bicks, November 15, 1957; Wilbur Fugate for Files, November 6, 1957; Wilbur L. Fugate to Robert A. Bicks, October 30, 1957; Wilbur Fugate for Files, November 25, 1957; Wilbur Fugate to Victor R. Hansen; December 5, 1957, *ibid.*

tion of the marketing assets of Stanvac, a joint Jersey-Socony company and one of the major marketing companies east of Suez.[37]

Actually, dissolution of Stanvac as a joint marketing venture would have been far less injurious to Jersey than to Socony since the former (unlike Socony) was strong enough to compete on its own against Stanvac's principal business rivals, Royal Dutch Shell and British Petroleum. Nevertheless, the government considered Jersey's concession on Stanvac a major breakthrough in its cartel case. Notwithstanding remaining differences, a settlement with Jersey seemed possible. Justice Department officials were persuaded that such an agreement along with one from Gulf would force the other defendants to come to terms. "Defendants Socony, Socal and Texaco have informed us that they are not interested in a consent judgment, at least at present," Assistant Attorney General Victor Hansen remarked in urging continuation of negotiations with Jersey. "However, a consent judgment with Jersey, and perhaps Gulf, might result in change of position by the other defendants." [38]

What Hansen failed to comprehend was the recalcitrance of the other defendants, especially Socal and Socony. None of these companies was as strong as Jersey abroad and each relied heavily on its jointly–owned subsidiaries in order to meet competition overseas. Without Stanvac, Socony's position east of Suez would be jeopardized. Likewise, Texaco and especially Socal depended on their marketing subsidiary, Caltex, to sell their share of Aramco's offtake. Unwilling to agree to the breakup of Stanvac or Caltex or to major changes in ownership and operations, as insisted upon by the government, the three defendants rejected consent settlements.[39] For its part, the Justice Department, having decided earlier not to settle with one defendant without reaching agreement with all (since any later court judgment might affect prior consent agreements), dropped its negotiations with Gulf and Jersey.[40]

Even as these negotiations had been taking place, a number of congressmen, including Senators Joseph O'Mahoney of Wyoming and Estes Kefauver of Tennessee, who had learned of the talks, had

[37] Wilbur Fugate for Files, April 4, 1957; "Memorandum for the Attorney General," June 20, 1957, ibid.

[38] "Memorandum for the Attorney General," June 20, 1957.

[39] Wilbur Fugate for Files, December 3, 1957; Oscar John Dorwin to Assistant Attorney General, May 23, 1957, ibid. See also Robert A. Bicks for Files, December 6, 1957 and Barbara J. Svedberg for Files, June 27, 1956. The latter memorandum concerns a discussion that Svedberg had with Texaco's chief counsel, Oscar John Dorwin. According to Svedberg, Dorwin remarked, with reference to breaking up Caltex that "they [Texaco] would carry the case to the Supreme Court on this issue alone, that they would 'go on like this for ten or fifteen years before breaking up Caltex.'"

[40] Wilbur Fugate for Files, December 4, 1957 and Robert Bicks for Files, December 6, 1057, ibid.

begun to complain about the possibility of an out–of–court settlement of the cartel case. As members of the Senate's Antitrust and Monopoly Subcommittee, which was investigating the MEEC, they were persuaded that the issues involved in the cartel case were too important, both from the point of view of foreign policy and the national economy, not to be decided publicly. As O'Mahoney wrote to Attorney General William P. Rogers in November, 1957 with respect to the case, "This is a question of foreign policy. It may be a question of national security, and it is surely a question of antitrust law and policy." [41]

Nevertheless, the general sentiment within the administration, government, and business remained one of settling without public trial, especially since concern was growing in public and private circles that the Soviet Union might seek to unbalance the western marketing structure by dumping its own surplus supplies of oil on the West. Gulf and Jersey were already willing to settle provided some unresolved differences and minor technicalities in language could be worked out. At the same time, lawyers for the three other defendants pressed the foreign policy importance of not embarrassing the oil companies through public disclosure of their activities while at the same time noting their own contribution to national security by providing the western world with oil at stable prices and preventing the spread of communism. Administration officials for the most part appear to have accepted the industry's arguments. [42]

The major break in the cartel case came finally in 1959 when, after years of delay, Judge Cashin ordered the defendants to produce foreign documents in response to government interrogatories. In reaching this decision, which was made only after obtaining State Department approval, Cashin was clearly trying to apply pressure on the defendants to reach settlement without having to go to trial. According to the prosecuting attorney, Wilbur Fugate, Cashin had told him earlier that while he (Cashin) thought an order to produce foreign documents "might hurt the companies in their dealings with foreign governments," he also believed that "the overhanging threat of an order might induce the defendants to settle the case." At the same time, Cashin applied pressure on the Justice Department for a quick settlement. [43]

[41] O'Mahoney to Rogers, November 20, 1957, *ibid.* See also Kefauver to Assistant Attorney General, December 27, 1957; Victor Hansen to O'Mahoney and to Kefauver, January 7, 1958, *ibid.*

[42] See, for example, Wilbur Fugate to W. Wallace Kirkpatrick, November 10, 1960 and Oscar J. Dorwin to Assistant Attorney General Lee Loevinger, November 15, 1960, *ibid.*

[43] Wilbur Fugate to Robert A. Bicks, December 10, 1959, *ibid.* See also Fugate to Bicks, June 26, 1959; Fugate to Victor Hansen, January 19, 1959; Fugate to Lee Loevinger, April

Cashin's decision to threaten the oil companies while continuing to press the Justice Department for a settlement broke the impasse that had developed following the negotiations of 1957. Although Socal, Socony, and Texaco continued to hold out against a consent agreement, the latter two softened their position. For example, Socony worked out a plan under which Jersey would take over Stanvac facilities in a majority of countries and Socony in the remainder. Socony would be compensated for the imbalance through various offtake and other product deals involving both companies' producing and refining facilities throughout the world. Joint activities, including marketing, would continue in such places as Pakistan, the Philippines, Australia, and, at least temporarily, Japan.[44]

Significantly, the Justice Department made it clear to Jersey that it "did not see any insuperable obstacles to a decree along the lines ... mentioned," although it continued to object to a number of aspects of this arrangement, such as the exchange deals involving crude and products, and the fact that Jersey would obtain all Stanvac's assets in particular countries. Justice's position represented a substantial reversal of its earlier policy of 1957 when it refused to countenance Jersey's unilateral control of any of Stanvac's former assets. Significantly also, Justice appeared ready to drop its previous position of insisting upon consent agreements with all defendants rather than settling with one or two only in the hope that the others would follow.[45]

THE SETTLEMENTS

With all parties in the cartel case more amenable to settlement (except for Socal, which remained intransigent over the breakup of Caltex) the Justice Department reopened its consent talks with the defendants. After some negotiation, it reached settlement with Jersey and Gulf very much along the lines of the 1957 agreements except with respect to Stanvac. By the settlement reached with Jersey in November, 1960, Jersey consented to the breakup of Stanvac as a joint marketing venture with Socony. However, the judgment provided for a division of Stanvac's marketing assets only rather than a separation of all Stanvac's assets, which included transportation and

13, 1961; Herman J. Schmidt to Secretary of State, June 5, 1958; "Draft Memorandum of the Department of State Regarding the Plaintiff's Motion for Production of Documents," July 11, 1958; Robert Murphy to Victor R. Hansen, September 16, 1958; "Memorandum for Attorney General," September 19, 1958, *ibid.*
44 Wilbur Fugate for Files, November 13, 1959, *ibid.*
45 *Ibid.*

refining facilities. The Jersey decree also enjoined agreements and combinations between Jersey and any of its competitors to fix prices, agree upon quotas, or regulate production of foreign oil. Combinations involving Jersey (apart from permitted joint production and refining ventures) were also prohibited from allocating or limiting production of crude oil in any foreign country and from limiting the United States' imports and exports of crude oil and petroleum products. Jersey was also enjoined from agreeing with competitors to exclude third persons from competition in a foreign country in the production, refining, distribution or sale of crude oil. Finally, the multinational giant was prohibited from using exchanges of crude oil or products as a means of implementing divisions of markets or restricting imports into the United States.[46]

The Gulf decree followed very much the same lines as the Jersey settlement, except that in the case of Gulf, no marketing subsidiary was involved. However, Gulf had to consent to eliminate the restrictive marketing provisions of its contract with Royal Dutch Shell for Kuwait oil while setting aside 100,000 barrels per day of Kuwait production for a period of ten years for sale to independent companies.[47]

In presenting the consent settlements to Judge Cashin for his final approval and then releasing their terms to the press, the Justice Department purposely sought to avoid any reference to the foreign policy and national security considerations that had guided the course of the cartel case and determined its final outcome; instead, with State Department concurrence, it chose to mask the true purpose behind the settlements by presenting them strictly as victories for free trade at the expense of multinational cartels. However, those responsible for bringing about the final settlement made clear privately that foreign policy considerations — and not free trade — had been the principal cause for the settlements. "I do not intend to bring into my statement anything about national defense security factors or relations with foreign nations," Fugate explained to his superior, W. Wallace Kirkpatrick, in outlining the remarks he proposed to make to Cashin:

> If questioned as to why joint production, refining and pipeline ventures abroad were expressly not included in the judgments, I could remind the Court that we have previously taken the position that the

[46] Wilbur Fugate to Robert A. Bicks, November 17, 1960; Fugate to Lee Loevinger, April 13, 1961, ibid. See also Fugate to Bicks, October 3 and 10, 1960; Fugate to William D. Kilgore Jr., June 19, 1962, ibid. For the Department of Defense's agreement to the consent proposal, see Vice Admiral Burton B. Biggs to Robert A. Bicks, November 3, 1960, ibid.
[47] Wilbur Fugate to Robert A. Bicks, October 3 and 10, 1960; Fugate to Lee Loevinger, April 13, 1961, ibid.

legality of such joint ventures was mentioned in the complaint as having been used to implement the over-all conspiracy charged. . . . I could say, if pressed, that we did not consider that the case necessarily called for divestiture or separation of these joint interests, and, moreover, that there were questions of jurisdiction and foreign law involved. . . .

[The national defense argument which I would not go into, is, in a nutshell, that separating these joint interests at this time might jeopardize the position of United States oil companies abroad vis-à-vis the Russians.] [48]

As for the press release to the public, the State Department vetoed any language that appeared embarrassing to American oil interests abroad, such as the fact that Stanvac had had a billion dollars in sales the previous year. Instead, State chose to stress the fact that the settlement opened up markets to smaller American and foreign companies.[49]

Once the Justice Department reached settlement with Jersey and Gulf, the remainder of its case against Texaco, Socal, and Socony proved anticlimactic. Soon after the Jersey-Gulf settlements, Texaco indicated that it was also ready to negotiate a final consent agreement. Actually Texaco was finding its marketing relationship with Socal an increasing burden since Socal was insisting on a 50 per cent share of certain of Texaco's planned ventures abroad such as in refining. Texaco was eager, therefore, to divest itself of Caltex, believing that it was sufficiently strong on its own by now to compete abroad.[50] Moreover, the Jersey-Gulf settlements increased the public pressure on Texaco for a settlement. The major obstacle to an agreement was Texaco's desire to be able to enter joint ventures with other defendants and co-conspirators, action which the Justice Department expressly opposed. Also, Socal remained unwilling to break up Caltex, which was the government's principal objective in its suit against Texaco. Finally, however, Texaco yielded to most of the government's demands. In 1963 the corporation reached an agreement largely along the lines of the previous settlements with Jersey and

[48] Fugate to Kirkpatrick, November 10, 1960, *ibid.* According to Fugate, in accepting the consent settlements, Judge Cashin himself "commented on the critical situation existing in the Middle East and in foreign countries generally, and stated again to counsel for the other defendants that he thought that from the point of view of national defense and preserving American interests abroad, it was very important that the case be settled as to the other defendants." Fugate to Robert L. Bicks, November 17, 1960, *ibid.*

[49] Wilbur Fugate to W. Wallace Kirkpatrick, November 8, 1960, *ibid.*

[50] David I. Haberman for Files, December 7, 1961 and December 14, 1962, *ibid.* See also Oscar John Dorwin to Lee Loevinger, November 15, 1961 and Loevinger to Dorwin, December 4, 1961; Wilbur Fugate to Loevinger, December 12, 1961, *ibid.*

OIL AND THE COLD WAR   53

Gulf, except that Texaco obligated itself to cooperate with the government in bringing about the dissolution of Caltex.[51]

As for the two remaining defendants, they held periodic negotiations with the Justice Department in the years after 1963 in which they evinced some interest in settlement, especially since by now Socony had agreed to the divestiture of Stanvac and Texaco was seeking to break up Caltex. In 1967 Socal even acquiesced in the voluntary dissolution of Caltex's European assets, including all refining, marketing, and transportation properties in twelve European countries. But Socal would not agree to a similar dissolution in the sixty countries east of Suez or in France, Spain, and Turkey where Socal felt its marketing position was too weak to compete successfully without Caltex.[52]

Why Socony failed to agree to a consent settlement is not entirely clear except that its lawyers apparently felt the Justice Department would never take its case to trial, having gained the dissolution of Stanvac and the partial dissolution of Caltex and having won concessions in the areas of joint marketing and price-fixing.[53] In this judgment Socony's lawyers were correct. Despite the obvious limitations that dismissal of the case against Socony and Socal presented, even in the areas of markets and prices, and despite the possibility that dismissal might be construed by other defendants as cause to seek release from their previous consent settlements on the grounds of equity, the Justice Department decided in 1968 to drop its case against Socal and Socony. As one Department official, David I. Haberman, explained as early as 1966, by this time the case had become stale and the Department had "achieved just about all the really practical relief [it] could ever hope to gain even after successful litigation against Socony."[54]

Moreover, Justice lawyers dismissed as unlikely the possibility that the other defendants would use the dismissal of the suit against Socal and Socony as reason to overturn their own cases. As Haberman also pointed out, with much insight, the consent settlements protected these companies in their joint production, refining, and pipeline ventures abroad; the agreements amounted to giving these

[51] David I. Haberman to William D. Kilgore, Jr., March 1, 1963, *ibid.* Fugate, *Foreign Commerce and the Antitrust Laws,* 209.

[52] David I. Haberman to Alan Dobey, May 9, 1966, DOJ, 60–57–140. See also unpublished manuscript prepared for Socal by Neil H. Jacoby, "Post-War Changes in the Foreign Oil Industry" (1963) and Wilbur Fugate to Lee Loevinger, December 12, 1961, DOJ, 60–57–140.

[53] David I. Haberman to Alan A. Dobey, May 9, 1966, *ibid.* See also Wilbur Fugate to Donald F. Turner, February 14, 1967; press release of January 24, 1968, *ibid.*

[54] Department of Justice press release, January 24, 1968; David I. Haberman to Allan A. Dobey, May 9, 1966, *ibid.*

arrangements unofficial government sanction.[55] Foolish indeed would be the oil company executive who would risk losing this sanction by attacking the consent agreements on the grounds of equity.

This latter point goes to the heart of the oil cartel case and points out the fundamental weakness of the government suit after the Iranian settlement of 1954. Joint marketing and price-fixing agreements were only the most burdensome and difficult to maintain of the many parts of a scaffolding by which the oil majors controlled the world's flow of oil. Once these vertically integrated multinational giants had achieved control over the bulk of foreign crude through a complex of interlocking joint production, refining, and pipeline ventures abroad, the rest of their joint operation was really superfluous. They had achieved the stability of flow and, hence, of prices, that had been the purpose of the original "As Is" arrangements. No settlement that attacked the tail but not the head or body of the energy tiger could have more than a limited cosmetic effect in unsettling the stability of local market prices and conditions in the world's consuming nations.[56]

CONCLUSION

The oil cartel case has importance even beyond its eventual impact upon international markets and price structures. In the first place, it presents an excellent study of the way in which the Cold War intruded into the domestic affairs of the United States, modifying and distorting long held principles and programs in behalf of the enlarged postwar concept of national interest and security. In the oil cartel case, the nation's commitment to antitrust in foreign as well as domestic commerce was made subordinate to a perceived Soviet threat in the third world and to the need to assure a cheap supply of energy in the presence of the expanding Cold War.

Moreover, while the outcome of the case was largely determined by considerations of national security, it was also part of a continuing pattern of tension, frustration, and constraints within which antitrust action had developed and operated in the United States. In this

---

55 David I. Haberman to Alan A. Dobey, May 9, 1966, *ibid.* It is perhaps significant in this respect that in 1968 counsel for Jersey made it clear to the Justice Department that Jersey did not desire dismissal of its consent settlement since "Jersey's overseas operations [were] presently guided by the provisions of the Jersey decree." David I. Haberman for Files, March 1, 1968, *ibid.*

56 As David I. Haberman of the Public Counsel and Legislative Section of the Justice Department pointed out in 1966, "the real key to the economic power wielded overseas by the Cartel case defendants together with British petroleum and Shell at least since World War II, has resided in the complex of closely interlocked *joint* ventures which they control at some of the very industrial levels we have been foreclosed from challenging, viz., crude production and refining." Haberman to Alan A. Dobey, May 9, 1966, *ibid.*

respect it was an element of a yet larger pattern of private partnerships, cooperative arrangements, and government–sanctioned cartelization that has characterized federal oil policy since the beginning of the century. As Gerald Nash has written about American oil policy, "The first six decades of the twentieth century witnessed the development of a consensus by business and government concerning the ends and means of public policy. . . . If monopoly gave rise to the antitrust movement in the United States . . . oligopoly resulted in making government an arbiter." [57]

No one need doubt, therefore, Truman's and Eisenhower's sincerity in advocating free trade even as they followed contrary policies with respect to oil. No less an advocate of international free trade than Woodrow Wilson had supported antitrust immunity for certain combinations engaged in export trade when he deemed it in the national interest. In Truman's and Eisenhower's case, as in Wilson's, considerations of national interest instead of free trade ultimately determined their foreign economic policies and programs to the benefit of the oil industry.[58]

[57] Gerald D. Nash, *United States Oil Policy 1890–1964;* (Pittsburgh, 1968), 238.
[58] Kaufman, *Efficiency and Expansion*, 213-216.

THE ANTITRUST RECORD OF THE
EISENHOWER ADMINISTRATION

by

THEODORE P. KOVALEFF*

When the Eisenhower administration took office in early 1953, the climate of opinion was not favorable to antitrust. During the depression, the government had experimented by first substituting the regulatory Blue Eagle of the National Recovery Administration [NRA] for the enforcement of the antitrust statutes;[1] and then when that had failed, using the tools of the Temporary National Economic Committee, it had tried a vigorous policy of trade regulation. Neither had been very successful in prodding the economy forward. With the advent of peace and the concomitant reorientation of national priorities after World War II, many people in and out of government began to look at the antitrust statutes very carefully. In Congress, there was an accumulation of proposed

---

* Professor of History, Barnard College, Columbia University.

EDITOR'S NOTE: Portions of this paper were delivered at the 1973 Convention of the American Historical Society and the 1973 meeting of the Business History Conference.

[1] Created as a result of the National Industrial Recovery Act of 1933, the NRA established production codes and quotas for all phases of industry. Parallels between the NRA and Mussolini's program have been noted by Mariano Pierro, *L'Esperimento Roosevelt e il Movimento Sociale Negli Stati Uniti d'America* (Milan, 1937), see esp. 316-489; see also Arthur Schlesinger, *The Coming of the New Deal* (Boston, 1965), 153. When the NRA was unanimously declared unconstitutional by the Supreme Court (*United States* v. *A.L.A. Schechter Poultry Corp.*, 295 U.S. 374 [1935]), Pres. Franklin Roosevelt upbraided it for its "horse and buggy" decision. Historians today agree that he was aware that the NRA was not working, that its chief, General Hugh Johnson was uncontrollable, and that, in general, the NRA "had reached the end of its usefulness"; see, for instance, Raymond Moley, *The First New Deal* (New York, 1966), 294; Ellis Hawley, *The New Deal and the Problem of Monopoly* (Princeton, 1966), 130-135; Paul Murphy, *The Constitution in Crisis Times: 1918-1969* (New York, 1972), 142-143. Rexford Tugwell describes the decision as "opportune," suggesting that it rescued Roosevelt "from an embarrassment." *The Democratic Roosevelt* (Baltimore, 1969), 385.

amendments to the antitrust corpus awaiting action.[2] Law
and business journals presented articles on the subject and
even popular mass culture periodicals treated the topic from
every possible perspective. Perhaps the only point of agreement of all these writers was that the antitrust laws were
not understandable and that something should be done.[3]

Of all the studies, the most important was the seminal contribution of S. Chesterfield Oppenheim, professor of law at
the University of Michigan, entitled "Federal Antitrust Legislation: Guideposts to a Revised National Antitrust Policy."[4]
It obviously influenced the new Attorney General, Herbert
Brownell, for one of his first acts was to announce the formation of a committee to study the antitrust laws. Modeled along
the lines suggested in Oppenheim's article, the Attorney General's National Committee to Study the Antitrust Laws was
not formed to advocate repeal of the laws because "American
business generally joins the public in support of a federal
antitrust policy."[5] Rather it was constituted to determine
"how the new administration might best answer the insistent
public demand for review and clarification of the Federal
Antitrust Laws and Policies. . . . Antitrust enforcement officials may well be aided by a comprehensive review of enforcement problems and practices."[6] Oppenheim envisioned that

---

[2] Herbert Brownell to author, April 11, 1974.

[3] Benjamin Wham, "The Growth of Antitrust Law: A Revision
is Long Overdue," 38 A.B.A.J. 934-935 (1952); H. Graham Morison,
"Is the Sherman Act Outdated?" I. J. Pub. L. 323-334 (1952); John
McDonald, "Businessmen and the Sherman Act," 41 *Fortune* 104-114
(1950). See also the five-part series by David Lilienthal in 129
Collier's Weekly (May 31-June 28, 1952).

[4] 50 Mich. L. Rev. 1139-1244 (1951).

[5] Herbert Brownell, "Our Antitrust Policy," speech to the Fourth
Circuit Judicial Conference delivered at White Sulphur Springs,
West Virginia on June 26, 1953. The papers of the Antitrust Division
of the Department of Justice are housed in the Federal Records
Center, Suitland, Maryland. They will be cited as Antitrust Papers:
Subject. Unless otherwise designated, the materials consulted are part
of Accession #70A4771. A copy of the Brownell speech is included
in Antitrust Papers: Attorney General's National Committee to
Study the Antitrust Laws (AGNC), file 60-414-0, section 123, "Antitrust Investigations."

[6] Brownell to Oppenheim, July 2, 1953, Antitrust Papers:
AGNC, section 432, "Antitrust Committee: Journal #1."

the group's report would also be useful to all practicing lawyers, not just the antitrust specialists. Further, he hoped that most topics could be handled in such a way that the average businessman or Congressman could utilize the study.[7]

Led by Oppenheim and co-chaired by the Hon. Stanley Barnes, Assistant Attorney General in charge of the Justice Department's Antitrust Division, the Committee was composed of lawyers, academicians, economists, and a minimal number of government officials. In an effort to obtain the "best minds" for the Committee, Oppenheim requested nominations from people in government, the bar, business, labor and education. He has stated that there was no effort by the administration to "stack" the Committee. Furthermore he asserts that at no time did members of the top echelon of the administration suggest that any particular person be named to the Committee; all they requested was that certain geographic areas of the country be better represented.[8] Communications in the Eisenhower papers, however, indicate that several White House staff members did press for the appointment of certain people.[9] With the exception of Stephen P. Ladas, who was named as a "conferee" and not as a member, no White House-backed personnel were chosen.[10] On the other hand, it is significant that Bob Ladd of Vice-President Richard Nixon's office left a message for Oppenheim stating that "[Nixon] would appreciate it if you could give him [Robert Graham] extra special consideration."[11] Subsequently Graham was appointed to the Committee.

---

[7] Transcript of the meeting of the Attorney General's Committee, October 14, 1953, 10-11, Antitrust Papers: AGNC, section 16.

[8] S. Chesterfield Oppenheim to author, April 23, 1971: Hearings on H. 114 before the Select Committee on Small Business, 84th Cong., 1st Sess. pt. 1, at 812. From a political viewpoint the request was understandable; however, it did create practical problems in that antitrust practitioners tended to be concentrated in the New York, Washington, D.C., Chicago and California areas.

[9] Eisenhower Papers (Abilene, Kansas), General File 15-M-1, Box 285, "Endorsements, Members"; see also Antitrust Papers: AGNC, section 431, "Correspondence #2: Antitrust Committee."

[10] Antitrust Papers: AGNC, section 19, "Advisory Committee: Suggestions for Membership," section 313, "Foreign Commerce Group: AG's Committee."

[11] Memo dated August 7, 1953, Antitrust Papers: AGNC, section 431, "Correspondence #2: Antitrust Committee."

The group's findings appear to have been uninfluenced. Nowhere in the entire file is there a communication suggesting any pressure by the government. Rather the Committee influenced the administration. Attorney General Brownell stated that antitrust was "the most important and difficult problem" facing him and that he looked to the Committee "for help and guidance." [12] Eisenhower also indicated the significance he attached to the findings when he urged the Committee "to get going on it [the report]." [13] The administration followed the deliberations closely, and, to help avoid any outside pressure on the members of the Committee, it was very diligent in its efforts to avoid any premature release of any information. [14] Further illustrating the importance of the Committee is the fact that the White House made it a policy not to support proposed changes in the antitrust statutes until after the publication of the report. [15] In this way the administration could have "expert advice." [16] It subsequently submitted or backed bills implementing many of the 86 proposals made by the Committee.

The Report of the Attorney General's National Committee to Study the Antitrust Laws[17] was a smashing victory for antitrust in that it advocated a stricter enforcement of the laws and most of the changes which it recommended would have strengthened them. Members of the Antitrust Division of the Department of Justice even now refer to it often;[18] and it has played an important role in the development of

---

[12]   Memo dated October 16, 1953, Antitrust Papers: AGNC, section 354, "Administrative and Enforcement Group: Attorney General's Committee."

[13]   Transcript of the meeting of Attorney General's Committee October 14, 1953, 92-3, Antitrust Papers: AGNC, section 16.

[14]   See, for instance, "Preview of the Antitrust Report (for the Cabinet)." Written on the cover is "Recipients of this paper are requested to take special measures to protect its contents from premature release," March 16, 1955, Antitrust Papers: AGNC, section 1-B.

[15]   Memorandum to Arthur Burns from Melvin de Chazeau and Fritz Machlum. Eisenhower Papers, Official File 149-A, "Monopolies: Antitrust (1)."

[16]   Brownell to author, April 11, 1974.

[17]   Washington, D.C., 1955.

[18]   Badhia Rashid to author, July 8, 1971; Keith Clearwaters to author, August 23, 1973.

antitrust codes by the Common Market and other industrialized nations. As late as 1970, the Spanish Ministry of Commerce requested copies of the work.[19] The business community, as represented by the National Association of Manufacturers, found the study useful for it provided standards of guidance to the courts and enforcement agencies; and, by restating in more comprehensible terms many of the "heretofore confusing antitrust doctrines," it served as a "valuable aid to a better understanding of the antitrust laws." [20]

The report and its reception by the administration raised the morale of the career people in the Antitrust Division of the Justice Department.[21] Additionally Barnes, himself, brought a new vitality to the Division. When Barnes assumed leadership, he found that the average case from filing to final judgment lasted over five and a half years; one case had even been filed back in 1938. Such actions often became stale; they were also very expensive to try for it cost the government in the neighborhood of one quarter million dollars to litigate a medium-sized antitrust suit.[22] Thus one of Barnes' first priorities as chief of the Division was reducing delay.[23] One means was recourse to consent decrees. A product of negotiation and a certain amount of compromise between the government and the defendant, the decree, once entered, carried with it the force of a litigated judgment. Not only did it treat a current situation, it also could and often did include clauses which covered possible future situations. The con-

---

[19] "Attorney General's National Committee to Study the Antitrust Laws," File 4, 60-414-0. Department of Justice files, Records Administration's Office, Washington, D.C.

[20] National Association of Manufacturers Papers, folder 100-NN: 1955: Publications: Antitrust Laws: "The NAM Law Department Reviews the Antitrust Laws: The Report of the Attorney General's Committee." (The Papers of the NAM are located in the Eleutherian Mills Historical Library in Greenville, Wilmington, Delaware.)

[21] Brownell to author, April 11, 1974.

[22] Lamar Cecil, "Remedies in Antitrust Proceedings: Fines and Imprisonment," 5 *A.B.A. Antitrust Section* (August 18-19, 1954), 123. The figures have not been adjusted to compensate for the shrinking value of the dollar.

[23] Stanley Barnes, "Antitrust in 1954," speech delivered before the New York State Bar Association Section on Antitrust Law in New York City, January 26, 1955.

sent decree mechanism was an important tool for the government, for it provided effective enforcement without the cost in time, manpower and money of a protracted trial. The meetings negotiating the consent decrees were informal. Under Barnes, the government's conferees were directed to appear in shirtsleeves in the hope that such an unstudied atmosphere would lead to more give-and-take than might prevail in more formal negotiation. Barnes emphasized that thereby "The Division may strike down violations in areas otherwise . . . beyond its reach." [24] All the advantages, however, did not redound to the government. While litigated government antitrust actions were *prima facie* evidence in subsequent private treble damage actions arising out of the same basic facts, consent decrees were not, and consequently any defendant who agreed to a consent decree greatly increased the work and sharply diminished the chances of success for any future treble damage claimant. Furthermore, a consent decree did not garner as many headlines as did an antitrust conviction.[25] Wide use of consent decrees did have the unquestioned benefit of substantially reducing the backlog of cases and allowing more productive allocation of Antitrust Division resources.

The Division used another time- and money-saving device on the order of the consent decree: the "prefiling conference." After investigating a particular situation and preparing a proposed complaint, the Department would then notify the prospective defendant of the Division's intentions. It then summarized the nature and grounds of the charges to provide the defendants with some frame of reference. If they wished to start negotiations toward a possible consent decree, prior to the filing of the complaint, Barnes' Division was ready to confer with them in an effort to work out an acceptable solution. The agreement would dispose of the problems raised on the complaint, while at the same time safeguarding both the public and corporate interest. The benefits accruing to both

---

[24] Stanley Barnes, "Settlement by Consent Judgment," 4 *A.B.A. Antitrust Section* (April 1-2, 1954), 10.

[25] Sometimes, additionally, a company was able to negotiate an agreement which has subsequently been seen to be too lenient, thus necessitating a second, more costly and difficult case, see for example today's actions against American Telephone and Telegraph Corp. and the International Business Machines Corp.

sides were identical to those gained by the signers of consent decrees.

The 1954 *Eastman Kodak* case[26] is important because it illustrates the operations and thought processes of the administration and the antitrusters. The action commenced with the use of the prefiling procedure and, from then on, negotiations moved smoothly, demonstrating how good will and sincerity on both sides of the conference table can ameliorate many difficult and complex problems. In short order the government obtained a consent decree providing effective relief: The restoration of competition in the film developing market without adversely affecting the profitability of Kodak.

In detail, the *Kodak* case began with an investigation arising from a number of private complaints regarding the company's monopoly of the processing of amateur color film.[27] The findings suggested that Kodak had monopoly power in processing and that its practice of controlling the resale price of its color film under fair trade laws amounted to an unfair trade practice since the price of developing was included in the cost of the film itself.[28] Thus, almost all Kodacolor and Kodachrome film sold in the United States was processed by Kodak after it had been exposed. As the independent photo finisher had no opportunity to process the film, the public was paying the company a tariff for film development which was not determined by the competitive forces of the marketplace.

In July 1954, the Antitrust Division notified the officials of Kodak of the intended complaint, and furnished them with a copy. Shortly thereafter the company advised the Department that it wanted to try to work out a consent decree prior

---

[26]   1954 Trade Cases, par. 67,920.

[27]   See especially memo dated June 21, 1952 to William Dixon concerning complaint letter from a private citizen, William Drewry, Antitrust Papers: Kodak, Accession #70A4771, file 60-42-18.

[28]   Fair trade laws only cover commodities in "free and open competition with commodities of the same general class produced and distributed by others." The difficulty lay in the fact that processing is not a commodity, and "even if so, the processing aspect is not in free and open competition." Memo dated May 5, 1954 to Barnes, Antitrust Papers: Kodak. Fair Trade was largely abolished in 1975 when the Congress rescinded the enabling legislation which gave the States the power to authorize it.

to the filing of the complaint.[29] By mid-August, the parameters of the negotiations had been set. At conferences lasting until early December, officials of both sides formulated
provisions of the decree which were entered in the federal
court at Buffalo on December 21, 1954, simultaneously with
the filing of the complaint.[30]

Using the technique of prefiling, in less than six months,
after 104 hours of negotiations,[31] the government was able to
enter a decree which, saving the costs of time and trial, afforded satisfactory relief. The judgment required Kodak to
cancel its fair trade contracts covering its color film, and it
enjoined the signing of any such new contracts in the future.
Additionally, and a key factor for Barnes and Brownell, the
decree prohibited Kodak from selling its color film with the
processing charge included in the sales price, or from any
other type of tying together of the price of the film and its
subsequent processing. This clause of the decree would have
been nearly meaningless had there not been an enabling section stating that independent film processors would obtain,
upon written request, licenses at reasonable royalty under
the Kodak processing patents. As even the license to use certain techniques was useless without technical know-how, the
decree directed Kodak to make available scientific manuals
which could be used by new entrants in the processing field.
In order that Kodak not overlook any critical aspect, the
decree stipulated that the company permit independent processors to send technical personnel to observe the methods
and machines utilized at the Kodak plants in Rochester,
Chicago, and Palo Alto. Additionally, the company was required to sell all materials necessary for the processing of
its amateur color film. To ensure that the independents would
be able to garner at least 50 percent of the market, part of
the decree included the stipulation that seven years from the
effective date of the judgment, Kodak would be forced to

---

[29] Letter of Carl Nixon, General Counsel for Eastman Kodak, to
Barnes, July 17, 1954, Antitrust Papers: Kodak.

[30] Report of Barnes to files, December 23, 1954, Antitrust Papers:
Kodak.

[31] Barnes to Frederick Mullen, Director of Public Information of
the Department of Justice (December 23, 1954), Antitrust Papers:
Kodak.

divest itself of a number of facilities so that it would control less than 50 percent of the domestic capacity for processing the film. Illustrating the flexible attitude of the Eisenhower era Antitrust Division, the decree also included a clause protecting the company: If, at the specified date, Kodak still controlled more than the agreed-upon market share, but if it could prove that it had taken no restrictive actions and that all purchasers had had the option of having their film processed by an independent company, the Division would take no further action.[32]

The decree was far from popular. In the Justice Department files, there are scores of letters attacking the settlement as "antibusiness" and "communistic."[33] Although understanding that certain dislocations were necessary to restore competition, according to Barnes, even "President Eisenhower . . . complained to me . . . about the inconvenience . . . of certain provisions of the Eastman Kodak decree."[34] Brownell asserts with pride that the great number of new entries in the processing field directly resulting from the decree established real competition in an industry where there had been none before.[35]

The Sherman Act cases, garnering the most headlines during the Eisenhower presidency, were a group of 20 actions which have come to be known collectively as the *Electrical* cases. These alone are enough to illustrate the vigor of the antitrust program.

For years the Antitrust Division had been watching the various members of the heavy electrical industry.[36] There were several instances during the 1940's when the companies

---

[32] 1954 Trade Cases, par. 67,920; "Kodak News" (December 21, 1954), (Distributed by Press Relations Department); Antitrust Papers: Kodak.

[33] Antitrust Papers: Kodak.

[34] Barnes to author, May 7, 1971.

[35] "The Reminiscences of Herbert Brownell," 341, in the Oral History Collection of Columbia University.

[36] The earliest file is dated 1902. An index as of March 5, 1956 is located in Antitrust Papers: Heavy Electrical Power Equipment Industry (Electrical), Accession #70A4771, file 60-230-27.

were caught for fixing prices, but each time when they agreed to abandon the practice, the charges were dropped.[37] In 1949, the Division launched an inquiry into the business of electrical transformers. Although by 1951 not enough evidence had been uncovered to support criminal indictments, the action was kept alive in the civil sphere. Barnes subsequently closed the investigation.[38] In mid-1954, there was another inquiry which focused on the problems of identical bidding and allocation of customers. It studied a total of 1,989 bids and concluded that 1,048 "were identical with one or more companies." [39] But the mere existence of identical bids by themselves proves neither price fixing nor collusion. In certain instances conscious parallelism in pricing is both explainable and permissible.

As a result of large increases in the prices of heavy electrical equipment, in 1957 the Tennessee Valley Authority [TVA] enlarged the number of companies eligible to bid on its jobs. Several of the companies admitted to the bidders list were foreign and they consistently submitted prices which, even after adjustments for the "Buy American" laws, were far lower than those of the American manufacturers.[40] Almost immediately there was agitation to limit the importation of foreign electrical generating equipment. The National Electrical Manufacturers Association and General Electric spearheaded the attack using such devices as an avalanche of letters to public officials and intense lobbying efforts, all endeavoring to prove that the high price of American labor

---

[37] Memo dated January 27, 1956, Antitrust Papers: Electrical.

[38] Barnes memo dated November 21, 1953. Antitrust Papers: Transformers and Power Line Lightning Arresters, Accession #70A4771, file 60-9-78.

[39] Barnes memo to files dated July 22, 1954; Hansen memo to J. Edgar Hoover dated July 18, 1957, Antitrust Papers: Electrical.

[40] A non-American manufacturer had to pay 15% customs duty; 50% of the machinery had to be delivered in high cost American ships; additionally, a 20% differential was allowable (6% for Buy American, 6% for a contract to a company located in areas of high unemployment, 8% "to cover the cost of sending men to make a general factory inspection."), Testimony of Alan Barraclough of English Electric, Ltd., before Grand Jury #4 empaneled April 21, 1960, *in re* Electrical Suppliers Industry, located in Antitrust Papers: Electrical, Accession #64A580, file 60-230-45.

led inexorably to the cost differentials. Not to "Buy American" was unpatriotic and, worse, it denied jobs to deserving citizens. Even some unions boarded the bandwagon.[41] But after extensive economic analysis, Albert Fitzgerald, president of the United Electrical, Radio and Machine Workers of America, was able to counter the argument and prove that the difference in bid prices "would cover the actual wage cost differential almost 17 times over." [42]

Undoubtedly the publicity had an effect on the antitrust investigation. The TVA had to reply to the electrical equipment company attacks, and it released a statement noting the similarity in bids it had been receiving over the previous few years. An enterprising newspaperman, Julian Granger, picked up the material. Unaware that the Antitrust Division was studying the subject, he wrote a series of articles in the *Knoxville News-Sentinel.*[43] Subsequently, the *Washington Daily News,* its Scripps-Howard sister paper, carried the story.[44] This account may have been responsible in part for the inquiry instigated by Senator Estes Kefauver's Subcommittee on Antitrust and Monopoly. Being from Tennessee, his interest may have been sparked by the possibility of making some home state headlines in time for the presidential primary election in 1960. The Antitrust Division also was interested and contacted the TVA on June 1, 1959.

The material supplied by the TVA, plus the publicity, convinced William Rogers, the Attorney General, that enough improprieties did exist to merit a full scale investigation. This yielded results which suggested that a grand jury be empaneled to inquire into the practices of the industry. At this juncture, Kefauver dropped his investigation and turned

---

[41] See folders of letters, Official File 149-B-2, Box 789, folder entitled "Heavy Electric Power Equipment"; 102-I, Box 439, 1959, folder I; Box 440, 1959, folder II, Eisenhower Library.

[42] Albert Fitzgerald to author, December 8, 1971; letter to all public officials dated March 23, 1959 (copy in Antitrust Papers: Electrical) and made public at press conference March 26, 1959.

[43] *The Knoxville News-Sentinel,* May 17, 1959, May 18, 1959, May 19, 1959.

[44] *Washington Daily News,* May 20, 1959.

over his findings to the Justice Department.[45] The amount of material uncovered by the grand jury was so great that two others were empaneled. The number was increased until at one point there were actually five separate grand juries probing the electrical industry.

The investigations found 20 separate conspiracies and General Electric was a member of all but one of these. Some of the violations were long-lived, one being traceable to the heyday of NRA,[46] but the Justice Department concentrated on the most recent to prove its charges. The violations were so blatant that in one conspiracy the perpetrators even had formulated a set of rules for themselves:

1) Minimize phone calls

2) Use plain envelopes if mailing materials

3) When registering at a hotel, do not include the company's name

4) Endeavor not to travel together

5) Do not eat together

6) Leave no wastepaper behind after a meeting in a hotel room.[47]

In another intrigue, low bids were set on the basis of the conspirator's market share under a formula utilizing the various phases of the moon. When the final numbers were tabulated, a total of 32 corporations were involved as defendants or coconspirators, and 48 individual defendants were also included. Almost every large manufacturer of electrical equipment was cited at least once.

---

[45] See Hearings on S. 57 before the Subcommittee on Antitrust and Monopoly of the Senate Committee on the Judiciary, 86th Cong., 1st Sess. pt. 13.

[46] "A Theory for Computing Damages Sustained by the United States and Tennessee Valley Authority in the Direct Purchase of Power Transformers," 2 (a memorandum dated July 25, 1961), Antitrust Papers: Electrical, file 60-230-55.

[47] Hearings on S. 52 before the Subcommittee on Antitrust and Monopoly of the Senate Committee on the Judiciary, 87th Cong., 1st Sess. pt. 27, at 17,394-17,396.

The new acting Assistant Attorney General in charge of the Antitrust Division, Robert Bicks,[48] displayed great enthusiasm and vigor as he personally handled large segments of the project. That the government was determined to block the easy escape route for the electrical companies was illustrated by its opposition to the court's acceptance of a *nolo contendere* plea. In this situation undoubtedly private suits would ensue, and like consent judgments in civil actions, *nolo* pleas could not be entered as *prima facie* evidence in subsequent private treble damage suits. In an unprecedented move, both Bicks and Rogers went before the court and urged Chief Judge J. Cullen Ganey not to accept any *nolo* pleas. Bicks personally argued that since the cases included charges that ranked them among the most serious in the entire 70-year history of the Sherman Act, the acceptance of a *nolo* plea would be highly inappropriate. Second, he wanted the record to be available so that injured parties could sue to recover treble damages. Finally, he noted that there was more stigma attached to the plea of guilty than to that of *nolo*. Attorney General Rogers, in an affidavit, emphasized that since each conspirator knew he was violating the law, and in view of the severity of the crime, acceptance of a *nolo* plea would essentially mean that in the future there could be no other plea.[49] The power of the government's argument was such that Judge Ganey rejected many of the *nolo* pleas and many of the defendants then pleaded guilty. Fines of nearly $2 million were imposed and 31 company executives were sentenced to jail for 30-day periods; only seven were actually incarcerated, the rest being given suspended sentences. But the imposts were small compared to the costs of the private suits which were direct outgrowths of the government actions.

---

[48] When Barnes resigned to accept a position on the U.S. Court of Appeals for the Ninth Circuit [California], he was replaced on July 13, 1956 by Victor Hansen who remained there until April 20, 1959. Although not nominated to fill the spot until July 15, 1960, Robert Bicks served as the Acting Assistant Attorney General as soon as Hansen resigned. Bicks remained in the "acting" capacity because he was never able to obtain Senate confirmation.

[49] Rogers to author, October 22, 1974. Also see Charles A. Bane, *The Electrical Equipment Conspiracies* (New York, 1973), 1-22; Attorney General Rogers' affidavit is reprinted in Clabault and Burton, *Sherman Act Indictments: 1955-1965* (New York, 1966), 58-62.

In all, 1,912 private damage suits were filed, reducing the profits of Westinghouse and General Electric, alone, by nearly $200 million.[50]

Although the Eisenhower administration vigorously enforced the Sherman Act phase of the antitrust laws, it was in the area of Clayton Act enforcement that it made its greatest contributions. In 1950, Congress had passed the Celler-Kefauver amendment to Section 7 of the Clayton Act,[51] but until the Republican administration came into office, the new statute was unused. According to H. Graham Morison, a former chief of the Antitrust Division during the last years of the Truman presidency, there was no occasion to use the bill;[52] however, the succeeding administration managed to find many opportunities, some even dealing with situations dating back to the Truman era. In so doing, the Justice Department played a major role in defining the parameters of the law.

Conforming to the Eisenhower administration's policy of streamlining and improving the operation of government, the Antitrust Division introduced what became known as "merger preclearance." Under this, two merging companies requested a government clearance, and after a thorough study of all the economic and competitive problems peculiar to the industry, the government would clear or indicate its opposition to the merger. All that the clearance guaranteed was that the Division would not institute proceedings at that time. If the competitive situation changed, or if later investigation revealed that the facts were either inaccurate or incomplete, the clearance could be withdrawn.[53] This innovation is a good example of the philosophy of the Eisenhower administration:

---

[50] James Bruce (Litigation and Antitrust Counsel of General Electric) to author, March 11, 1975; Westinghouse Electric Company prospectus dated March 29, 1967, "Statement of Current and Retained Earnings," footnote 16; General Electric Company prospectus dated April 25, 1967, "Statement of Current and Retained Earnings," 4; Bane, 82-83.

[51] 15 U.S.C. 18.

[52] H. Graham Morison to author, July 15, 1971.

[53] Brownell speech delivered to the National Industrial Conference Board in Philadelphia, Pennsylvania, November 17, 1955.

Help those who are cooperative to stay within the confines of the law.

In early 1955, after the Attorney General's Committee had completed most of its work, the Justice Department filed four important complaints alleging violation of Section 7. Each presented "distinctive factual differences"[54] and illustrated the attitude of the Justice Department toward mergers.

The first case was directed against Schenley Industries for its "acquisition of a controlling interest in one of its prominent competitors, the Park & Tilford Distillers Corporation."[55] Since repeal of the 18th Amendment, Schenley, according to the complaint, had acquired more than 50 companies involved in the production and distribution of alcoholic products. Not only had Schenley grown in this period, but other companies had also expanded and the industry had become increasingly concentrated, with four big companies in 1955 accounting for 75 percent of the industry's sales. The Justice Department marshalled an impressive array of statistics to prove that the merger was anticompetitive.[56]

The complaint against General Shoe Corporation for its acquisition of Delman, Inc. was based on the contention that it was the 18th in a series of take-overs dating back to 1950, and the cumulative effect of all the mergers produced the type of result that Congress had intended to outlaw when it amended Section 7 in 1950.[57]

Within a month of the *General Shoe* filing, the Department of Justice announced the filing of a third Section 7 case, charging that the Hilton Hotels Corporation had violated the antimerger act when it acquired the Hotel Statler Corporation. Even though the two companies were among the largest hotel

---

[54] 1955 Att'y Gen. Ann. Rep. 168.

[55] Department of Justice, "Immediate Release," February 14, 1955.

[56] Memos dated December 30, 1954, January 31, 1955, and complaint dated February 8, 1955, Antitrust Papers: Schenley, Accession #64A580, file 60-0-37-57.

[57] Memos dated May 18, 1953, August 12, 1953, December 18, 1953, March 2, 1955 in file 60-0-37-22; memos dated January 12, 1955, March 3, 1955 and complaint dated March 29, 1955, Antitrust Papers: General Shoe, Accession #70A4771, file 60-0-37-53.

chains in the world, their merger would not materially affect the hotel business as a whole, for even their combined share was but a small percentage of the entire industry. The Justice Department was aware of this fact and based its complaint on a different and much smaller market—the convention hotel market. In that area, the two companies were major factors and competed directly in four cities.[58] Here then the key question was the precise definition of the word "market."

A much less complicated case, against Minute Maid Corporation, was important because the Department of Justice used the device of prefiling, and was able simultaneously to file a consent judgment. Minute Maid, a major producer in the concentrated frozen juice market, had acquired the Snow Crop Division of Clinton Foods, and the consolidated entity controlled 35 percent of the total industry capacity. According to the consent judgment, Minute Maid was obliged to dispose of the facilities it had obtained from Clinton Foods; also included in the agreement were other clauses, among them one which enjoined the corporation from acquiring any stock or interest in any other companies in the field, except upon application to the court and a showing that such an acquisition would not lessen competition or tend to create a monopoly.[59]

None of the first three cases was decided in the courts. In the *Hilton Hotels* case a consent judgment was entered in which the government received substantially everything for which it had asked.[60] Less than two weeks later the Department of Justice announced the entry of a consent judgment ending the government's case against General Shoe. Although the decree allowed the Delman acquisition to stand, it forbade the company from acquiring any corporations in the industry

---

[58] Memos dated August 27, 1954, January 18, 1955, and complaint dated April 27, 1955, Antitrust Papers: Statler-Hilton, Accession #70A4771, file 60-0-37-48.

[59] Memos dated December 10, 1954, December 15, 1954, January 7, 1955, Antitrust Papers: Minute Maid, Accession #70A4771, file 60-0-37-513, Department of Justice, "Immediate Release," September 7, 1955; 1955 Trade Cases, par. 68,131.

[60] Agreement dated February 6, 1945 in Antitrust Papers: Hilton; Department of Justice, "Immediate Release," February 6, 1956; 1957 Trade Cases, par. 68,253.

without the approval of the government or the court. In only one instance could General Shoe take over companies with government approval: if the acquired corporation were facing imminent bankruptcy and if it had made efforts to sell out to other companies first. In order that markets not be foreclosed to smaller shoe companies, the judgment required that for five years, General Shoe be bound to purchase 20 percent of its shoes from other manufacturers.[61]

The last of the original Section 7 cases, the one challenging Schenley's acquisition of Park & Tilford, ended April 3, 1957, also with a consent judgment. At first glance the decree does not appear to have offered much relief. It amounted to an injunction enjoining Schenley from making any acquisitions of any whiskey distillers or distributors.[62] Upon closer inspection the agreement appears logical and appropriate. At the time of the acquisition Park & Tilford was losing money on its distilling operations, but was making money distributing foreign lines; after the merger, the company lost most of its distributorships, and thus was a losing proposition as a whole, and was no longer a viable entity. The Schenley-Park & Tilford decree illustrated the flexibility of the Eisenhower anti-trusters, a sharp contrast to the rigidity displayed by some of their predecessors who, for instance, continued a case against the Cement Institute after it had been dissolved.[63]

---

[61] No final copy of the February 17, 1956 consent agreement is in Antitrust Papers: General Shoe; but see Department of Justice, "Immediate Release," February 17, 1956; 1956 Trade Cases, par. 68,271.

[62] No copy of the consent judgment is in Antitrust Papers: Schenley, but see memo dated February 6, 1957; Department of Justice, "Immediate Release," April 3, 1957; 1957 Trade Cases, par. 68,664.

[63] The Cement Institute, Inc. was the principal motivating force behind the conspiracy to fix the price of delivered cement by means of the "basing point" system. Because of the filing of the complaint in 1945, the Institute dissolved itself in 1946. Although the challenged practices were subsequently abandoned, it was not until 1953 that the case was dismissed. Two memos dated August 6, 1953, Antitrust Papers: Cement Institute, Accession #64A580, file 60-10-27. The use of the "basing point" system for determining prices was determined to be illegal in *Federal Trade Commission* v. *Cement Institute*, 333 U.S. 683 (1948).

While the amended Section 7 had been applied with a great deal of success in four cases, legal scholars realized that although negotiated settlements were useful to other companies as guidelines, consent decrees did not create legal precedent, and thus they were useless except for dealing with a problem at hand. An adjudicated Section 7 judgment against a major company would be pivotal, for it would establish the legal parameters of the new law. Although the first four cases had been against large companies, none was so large as to make a sizable contribution to the gross national product of the United States. Thus, when the subject of merger between Bethlehem Steel Corporation and Youngstown Sheet and Tube Company was broached to the Division, there was no "jawboning" or threats; instead, Brownell practically dared the two companies to consummate what would have been in terms of dollar assets the largest merger in United States history.[64] The idea of merging the two steel companies was not new; indeed it had its roots back at least to 1928.[65] The marriage had first failed because of the opposition of Cyrus Easton, who wanted Youngstown as a merger partner for his own Inland Steel Company.[66] Later the economic slowdown caused by the depression short-circuited it. At no time did the government act to contravene it.

Rumors of the merger surfaced in 1954, and almost immediately the entire administration was interested. Eisenhower made a special request for information, and subsequently on September 10, 1954 there was a top secret meeting at the

[64] "Bethlehem-Youngstown: Controversial Engagement," 55 *Fortune*, 145 (1957). (In constant dollars, however, the 1901 merger creating United States Steel was bigger.) See also "The Reminiscences of Herbert Brownell," 340, in the Oral History Collection of Columbia University. Subsequently Brownell slightly modified his stance. ("It wasn't a dare, it was a warning on what we felt was a serious violation of the law. . . . It was a real landmark case.") Brownell to author, April 11, 1974.

[65] "The Bethlehem Youngstown Case," *Barron's*, X (September 29, 1930), 24.

[66] Francis Davis, Jr. (President of United States Rubber) to Irenée du Pont (March 19, 1930), Series J, Accession #1034, File 217. Papers of Irenée du Pont, folder 3, "United States Rubber Company." (The papers are located in the Eleutherian Mills Historical Library, Greenville, Wilmington, Delaware.)

White House at which Barnes and several cabinet members were in attendance.[67] They appear to have decided to send a letter of disapproval in response to the two companies' request for premerger clearance.[68]

By the time the merger was formally announced, Barnes had been replaced by Victor Hansen, who believed that the merger must not be allowed and that if the present laws were inadequate to forestall the marriage, then Congress should be requested immediately to strengthen the antimerger provisions of the Clayton Act.[69]

The argument of each side was extremely simple. Bethlehem contended that the merger would actually increase competition because the new company would be able to compete more effectively with United States Steel; and further, it posited that even after the merger, United States Steel would be the biggest factor in the steel business. Opposed to this stance was that of the federal government, which asserted that the linkup would eliminate competition between the second largest steel maker, Bethlehem, and the fifth largest, Youngstown. This would aggravate the already high concentration in the industry as, for instance, the ingot capacity of Bethlehem would increase from 16 percent to 20 percent of the national total. Although it felt that these factors alone made the merger illegal, the government also included sophisticated market breakdowns and product analyses in its case.[70]

Both sides were eager for a speedy decision. The steel makers had plans involving the consolidated properties; and, should the merger not be approved, they had contingency expansion programs. On the government side, there were other factors besides saving time, money and manpower favoring a speedy resolution of the case. Hansen wanted to

---

[67] Memo of call from White House, August 3, 1954; Barnes confidential memo of September 2, 1954, Antitrust Papers: Bethlehem-Youngstown, Accession #70A4771, file 60-0-37-29, Eisenhower Papers, Central Files: OF-5, Report of the Department of Justice—April 21, 1954-September 30, 1954.

[68] Draft of letter of disapproval, September 28, 1954, Antitrust Papers: Bethlehem-Youngstown.

[69] Victor Hansen to author, June 16, 1971.

[70] 1958 Trade Cases, par. 69,189; 168 F. Supp. 576.

find out as quickly as possible about any limitations in the amended Section 7. The merger agreement was entered on December 11, 1956, and in the same month the lawsuit was filed. It was settled in December 1958 after a trial that lasted but 19 days. Each party limited its stipulations to 140 pages, and in the end the court proceeded to accept the government's contention that the merger would definitely have an adverse effect on competition, thus violating Section 7. The two companies elected not to exercise their right of appeal, and the government then had adjudicated guidelines for future merger actions, albeit enunciated on the district court level.[71]

For all their activism, the Eisenhower antitrusters did not attack every merger which came before them. At almost the same time that it turned down the steel merger, the Department granted pre-merger clearance to two consolidations in the automobile industry: that of the Packard Motor Car Company with the Studebaker Corporation into the Studebaker-Packard Corporation,[72] and that of the Hudson Motor Car Company and the Nash-Kelvinator Corporation into the American Motors Corporation.[73] The Justice Department reasoned that the small car makers were becoming relatively smaller. In 1949, they had had a meager 14.5 percent of the market, but by 1954 that share had dwindled to slightly more than 4 percent. At that point, some of the companies were actually operating at a loss. It was hoped that the merger would revitalize these lagging concerns. By giving them a broader asset base, allowing them to save money by eliminating duplicate facilities, and assuring them a wider dealer network, the Justice Department felt that the mergers would allow them to compete more effectively with the Big Three. The marriages were possible, also, because there were no

---

[71] In affirming a district court decision (179 F. Supp. 721 [November 20, 1959]) holding Brown Shoe Company's acquisition of G.R. Kinney Corporation to be in violation of Clayton Act Section 7, the Supreme Court (370 U.S. 294 [1962]) finally provided the Antitrust Division with definitive guidelines.

[72] See memo of June 18, 1954 to Ephraim Jacobs recommending clearance (initialed by Barnes), Antitrust Papers: Studebaker-Packard, Accession #70A4771, file 60-0-37-27.

[73] Memo to Jacobs and approved by Barnes, January 7, 1954, Antitrust Papers: Nash-Hudson, Accession #64A580, file 60-0-37-21.

other smaller firms that would be put at a competitive disadvantage. According to Herbert Brownell, these mergers actually intensified competition.[74] It appears that the Justice Department would have been willing to allow a subsequent merger between Studebaker-Packard and the newly-formed American Motors Corporation if the car makers had requested it. The grounds for allowing such a further concentration in the auto industry were that "such action will increase rather than lessen competition. Furthermore, to permit such further consolidation of independent companies will tend to lessen the control of the existing 'Big Three.'"[75]

In the last years of the Eisenhower administration the trend toward increasingly energetic enforcement of Section 7 of the Clayton Act's restriction on corporate mergers and acquisitions continued unabated. After several appeals the government was finally successful in obtaining a verdict directing that duPont divest itself of the shares it held in General Motors.[76] Perhaps even more important, however, was the attitude of Robert Bicks, Hansen's successor. Convinced that Section 7 represented a prime weapon for what he called prophylactic antitrust, he endeavored to implement the statute forcefully in those sectors of the economy that were not already highly concentrated.[77]

It is in this framework then that the actions taken with regard to the oil industry must be considered. Far from concentrated, it consisted of many competitive units at each level of operations—production, refining and retailing. Bicks' goal was to preserve the existing structure by means of Section 7, so that in the future the industry would not be concentrated as were steel or aluminum. Thus the Division

---

[74] Brownell speech delivered to the Small Business Administration, National Council of Consultants in Washington, D.C. on July 14, 1955 and speech delivered to the National Industrial Conference Board in Philadelphia, Pennsylvania on November 17, 1955.

[75] Memo to Barnes, August 19, 1954, Antitrust Papers: Studebaker-Packard.

[76] *United States* v. *E.I. du Pont de Nemours and Co., et al.,* 353 U.S. 586 (1957) and 366 U.S. 316 (1961).

[77] Robert A. Bicks to author, June 10, 1971; Richard A. Smith, "What Antitrust Means under Mr. Bicks," 59 *Fortune* 270 (1960).

opposed the Standard Oil Company of Ohio merger with Leonard Refineries. Within three weeks the companies shelved their plans.[78] When Texaco, Incorporated, a crude deficit firm, announced that it planned to merge with the Superior Oil Company, a company with excess crude production capacity, the Justice Department indicated its opposition. Besides stating that competition would be adversely affected, the antitrusters cited their fear that the marriage would incite a wave of other mergers in the industry.[79] Upon being informed of the government attitude, the two companies abandoned their plans, and the government won a major victory without having to waste the time and expense of a protracted court fight. Had the Eisenhower administration not had a strong record in the field of antitrust, it is unlikely that the situation would have resolved itself so easily.

The Eisenhower antitrust policy was important because it revived interest in the field. The administration enforced the Sherman Act vigorously and it applied the newly amended Clayton Act in such a manner that antitrust became a major factor for industry to consider. From the relatively small early cases through the larger *Bethlehem-Youngstown* merger case, and other unfinished actions such as *Brown Shoe*,[80] the government played a key role in establishing the new parameters of the laws—boundaries which would last long after the administration left office.

---

[78] Memorandum to the Attorney General (William Rogers), December 28, 1959, and Bicks' memo of January 21, 1960 entitled "Lessons to be Learned," Antitrust Papers: Sohio-Leonard, Accession #70A4771, file 60-0-37-352.

[79] Bicks to author, June 10, 1971; memo to Bicks dated September 14, 1959, and memorandum for the Attorney General dated September 29, 1959, Antitrust Papers: Texaco-Superior, Accession #70A4771, file 60-0-37-302.

[80] Antitrust Papers: Brown-Kinney, Accession #70A4771, file 60-0-37-81.

Bulletin of the
History of Medicine

THE AMERICAN ASSOCIATION FOR THE HISTORY OF MEDICINE

THE JOHNS HOPKINS INSTITUTE OF THE HISTORY OF MEDICINE

VOLUME 53   SUMMER 1979   NUMBER 2

THE FDA's REGULATION AND CONTROL OF ANTIBIOTICS IN THE 1950s

THE HENRY WELCH SCANDAL, FÉLIX MARTÍ-IBÁÑEZ, AND CHARLES PFIZER & CO.*

RICHARD E. McFADYEN

The discovery and widespread production of antibiotics such as penicillin, tetracycline, streptomycin, and others mark a dramatic page in the history of modern medicine.[1] This rapid increase in the number of antibiotics pouring onto the American market after the Second World War put new responsibilities on the Food and Drug Administration to control and regulate these new antibiotics properly. In the more than a half century since the passage of the first Pure Food and Drugs Act, the Food and Drug Administration had never been tainted with an internal scandal. But in late 1959 and early 1960, a high official of the FDA, Dr. Henry Welch, was charged with serious instances of conflict of interest involving the regulation of antibiotics. The Welch scandal had a number of significant ramifications. Although the Welch case proved to be an isolated episode, it seriously damaged the reputation and morale of an agency that had had a long, proud history of consumer protection. The Welch scandal alerted the agency to the dangers of becoming too closely intertwined with the industry it was supposed to regulate. In addition, the Welch scandal, along with Senator Carey Estes Kefauver's investigation into the pharmaceutical industry and with the

* Presented at the 51st annual meeting of the American Association for the History of Medicine, Kansas City, May 11, 1978.

[1] For more on the history of antibiotics see Harry F. Dowling, *Fighting Infection: Conquests of the Twentieth Century* (Cambridge: Harvard University Press, 1977).

thalidomide scare,[2] did much to awaken the agency to the need to revamp federal legislation regulating the booming antibiotics field.

At the beginning of the 1950s, Dr. Henry Welch found himself in a key position in the development of antibiotics. Welch, who held a Ph.D. in bacteriology from Western Reserve (he was not an M.D.), had joined the FDA in 1938. In 1943, at the request of the Army, the FDA, under the guidance of Dr. Welch, undertook the task of developing standards and tests to insure the safety and efficacy of each batch of penicillin. With the arrival of the commercial production of penicillin, the FDA was empowered to certify each batch of penicillin produced.[3] Welch became director of the Division of Penicillin Control and Immunology, later in 1951 renamed the Division of Antibiotics.[4] Rapidly within the next five years or so newly discovered antibiotics, such as streptomycin, tetracycline, bacitracin, and chloramphenicol, were added to the certification lists.[5]

In his position in the FDA, Dr. Welch by the early 1950s was on the cutting edge of new developments in antibiotics. He himself had published widely in the field and was well on the way to establishing himself as a major figure in this new and growing area.[6] Thus it was not surprising that in 1950 Dr. Welch was approached by Dr. Henry J. Klaunberg to edit a new journal dedicated to the growing field of antibiotics. At the same time, Klaunberg suggested that Welch, along with Dr. Charles Lewis, also of the FDA, might author a book on antibiotic therapy for the physician. Both the journal and the book were to be published by the Washington Institute of Medicine. Welch requested permission from his superiors to undertake these outside activities pointing out that he would receive an honorarium for editing the journal, if successful, and the usual author's percentage on the book. In due time, Welch received permission to proceed from the then commissioner of FDA, Dr. Paul B. Dunbar.[7]

By October 1950, the new journal, called *The Journal of Antibiotics,* made its first appearance. The journal boasted a distinguished editorial board in-

[2] For a more complete discussion of the thalidomide episode see Richard E. McFadyen, "Thalidomide in America: a Brush with Tragedy," *Clio Medica,* 1976, *11*: 79-93. See also *Suffer the Children: The Story of Thalidomide,* by the Insight Team of *The Sunday Times* of London (New York: Viking Press, 1979).

[3] In 1945 the Food, Drug, and Cosmetic Act was amended to require certification of penicillin. U.S. Congress, Senate. *Administered Prices Hearings before the Subcommittee on Antitrust and Monopoly of the Committee on the Judiciary,* 86th Cong. 2nd sess., Part 23, 13075-76; hereafter cited as Administered Prices.

[4] *Ibid.,* 12634.

[5] *Ibid.,* 13076. Under the Kefauver-Harris Amendments of 1962, all antibiotics were added to the certification list.

[6] For a list of Welch's publications see *ibid.,* 13081-93.

[7] *Ibid.,* Part 22, 11926-38; also for a chronology of Welch's outside activities see Part 23, 12949-52.

cluding five Nobel Prize winners and such stellar names in the history of antibiotics as Sir Howard W. Florey, Dr. Selman Waksman, and Sir Alexander Fleming. Work moved rapidly ahead on the book, *Antibiotic Therapy*, by Welch and Lewis which was published in 1953.[8] In the first two years of his editorial duties, Welch received only $150 for his efforts; by 1952, his endeavors were a little more lucrative, but the $3270.59[9] he received was within the limits of an honorarium. But by 1952, a series of events radically changed Welch's relationship with his publisher, setting him on the road to potential conflict of interest charges.

In 1952, Welch's publisher, the Washington Institute of Medicine, under Dr. Klaunberg, fell into bankruptcy. As a result, Klaunberg sold all rights to Welch's book to Welch and his new partner, Dr. Félix Martí-Ibáñez. The two men now set up a new corporation, Medical Encyclopedia, which was to publish the book as well as other monographs. Around the same time, Dr. Martí-Ibáñez also took over control of the Washington Institute of Medicine, which published Welch's journal. Although Welch was not an owner of the Washington Institute, he was now in a position to benefit greatly monetarily from its editorship.[10]

Welch and Martí-Ibáñez realized the vast commercial potential represented by the growing market for antibiotics. They now proceeded to exploit Welch's position and prestige in the field of antibiotics through their various publishing enterprises. Articles and editorials which dealt favorably with a company's drug products could potentially be sold as reprints to companies who would distribute them, along with advertising material, to doctors. In addition to the very lucrative reprint business, the journals (a second one was created in the mid-1950s) also carried advertisements from the drug companies. Rather rapidly Welch, the chief regulator of the antibiotics industry, found himself in the position of chief editor of "scientific papers" frequently sponsored by drug companies and which were to appear in his journals supported by the companies' own advertising and bulk purchases of reprints. Incredibly, this arrangement went on for almost a decade.

One venture envisioned by the two men was the publication of a series of monographs recounting the history and use of particular antibiotics to doctors. By 1958, MD Encyclopedia, Inc., was publishing over 10 different volumes edited by Welch on various antibiotics including penicillin, Ter-

---

[8] See *ibid.*, Part 23, 12260, 13078.
[9] For an account of Welch's earnings see *ibid.*, Part 23, 12323.
[10] See *ibid.*, 12261-86, also 12949-50.

ramycin, and aureomycin.[11] The publishers were not hesitant in sending unpublished manuscripts to drug companies to determine if they might be interested in sponsoring the publication of the volume by buying advance copies of the book. In one case, the advertising department of Charles Pfizer and Co. informed Martí-Ibáñez that they were not interested in buying reprints of a manuscript dealing with carbomycin because "the paper is extremely conservative" and besides not much emphasis was being put on the drug by the Pfizer sales planning group. A book on Terramycin might be more favorably received, however. The following year, a book on Terramycin was published by MD Encyclopedia.[12]

Martí-Ibáñez and Welch felt it necessary to keep a semblance of objectivity to their work, turning down a request by Pfizer to substitute their trade name "Terramycin" wherever the generic name "oxytetracycline" appeared in the monograph.[13] But the monograph did appear under Pfizer's trade name with its generic name in parenthesis, prompting a reviewer to comment: "The book tries to sell Terramycin rather than critically appraise it. . . . "[14]

The author of the monograph on Polymycin, another volume in the series, was upset by the commercialization of his manuscript at the hands of Welch as editor. He wrote Martí-Ibáñez: "I am quite unhappy about your repeated reference to Pfizer products—these were not in my manuscript. . . . They give the impression that the book is written for the benefit of Charles Pfizer and Co., rather than for physicians."[15]

By 1953, the first journal, now named *Antibiotics and Chemotherapy,* had become a financial success. Although the paid circulation of the journal was small (only 3,000 copies a month at the end of the decade),[16] Welch and Martí-Ibáñez had found other ways to make their journal profitable. The journal made money in three ways: (1) advertising revenues from drug companies, (2) the sale of reprints to companies, and (3) payments for the addition of extra pages.

Later investigation revealed that MD Publications realized a total of $309,898 from advertising revenues in its journals from 1953 to 1959. But surprisingly the sale of reprints was far more lucrative, bringing in total sales of $685,760. Obviously major drug companies found reprints published in a

---

[11] For a list of their books see *ibid.,* 13062.

[12] See letter, Chas. Pfizer & Co., Inc., to Martí-Ibáñez, Feb. 4, 1955, *ibid.,* 13156.

[13] Letter, Martí-Ibáñez to George E. Peabody, Feb. 15, 1956, *ibid.,* 12480.

[14] *Ibid.,* 13053. The review appeared in the *Archives of Internal Medicine,* Aug. 1957.

[15] See letter, Ernest Jawetz to Martí-Ibáñez, Feb. 7, 1956, *ibid.,* 13025.

[16] *Ibid.,* 12635.

journal edited by the FDA's top antibiotics regulator extremely valuable. The total revenue resulting from extra page charges amounted to $69,454.[17] Far from receiving just an honorarium, Dr. Welch was to receive 7½ percent of the net advertising revenues, and most interestingly, a 50 percent cut of net income from the sale of reprints as well as 25 percent of the extra page revenue.[18]

Welch, from 1953 to 1960, earned a total of $287,142.40 for his editorial efforts. Of this sum the largest part came from the journals, some $224,016.70. At this rate, he was averaging over $35,000 a year with his worst year at a little over $13,000 and his best at over $50,000.[19]

With the continued growth of their journal, Martí-Ibáñez decided that it would be desirable to start a second journal. *Antibiotics and Chemotherapy* would continue to focus on laboratory and *in vitro* reports, but a new journal was needed to bring papers of a more clinical nature directly to physicians. With this aim in mind, a second journal, first called *Antibiotic Medicine,* was created in 1954. But after a year of publication the second journal was having trouble establishing a readership. It was decided to change the name of the journal to *Antibiotic Medicine and Clinical Therapy* which would broaden the editorial content of the journal, therefore making the journal more attractive to a wider range of advertisers. The journal would also become a controlled circulation periodical sent free to 60,000 doctors on a trial basis for a year and a half, after which some 23,000 doctors opted to continue to receive the journal on a complimentary basis.[20] In October 1956, Martí-Ibáñez attempted to market a British edition of their second journal, *Antibiotic Medicine and Clinical Therapy*. After only one year of existence, the British edition was discontinued due to lack of advertising support or subscription revenue.[21]

The difficulties faced by Welch and Martí-Ibáñez in winning acceptance for their new magazine reveal the length to which the two would go to prejudice the journals' editorial content to satisfy the advertisers. Evidently some question was raised by at least one concerned person regarding the ability of the journal to maintain its objectivity. Dr. Harry Dowling of the University of Illinois Medical School, a member of the editorial board of both journals, questioned what effect transforming the journal into a controlled circulation periodical might have on its editorial policy. Martí-Ibáñez

[17] *Ibid.,* 12678-79.
[18] See *ibid.,* Part 22, 11937.
[19] *Ibid.,* Part 23, 12678.
[20] *Ibid.,* 12356-66, 12950.
[21] *Ibid.,* 12680.

assured Dowling, "We will carefully preserve the good scientific standing and the recognition that the journal has earned. . . . "[22] But Dowling's fears were very well founded.

Clearly the dependence of the journal on advertising and reprint revenues prejudiced the editorial policy, both in terms of article contents and editorial statements. Martí-Ibáñez clearly saw the American and British version of AM&CT as a forum in which manufacturers could publish clinical studies they had sponsored. In a letter to Welch, Martí-Ibáñez pointed out that the journal offered a sponsoring company "the opportunity to publish . . . any important clinical papers" as well as "important news about its products" in a special clinical newsletter section. Although he continued "it would be better for the sponsoring company not to announce to the readers that they are sending the journal . . . as this would somehow weaken the impact of their papers in the journal."[23]

In the American edition, Welch evidently made a practice of allowing advertisers to review editorials *before* they were published, soliciting their comments as well as reprint orders on upcoming editorials.[24] Likewise the scope of the journal was widened beyond antibiotics to include hormones, vitamins, and other chemotherapeutic agents in the hopes of attracting greater advertising.[25] One company promised increased advertising if the journal promised "that there will be articles on vitamins and nutrition."[26]

Invariably, critics noticed the declining scientific quality of the journal and questioned the rigor and objectivity of its content. One critic wrote, "I have been so disappointed with many of the articles . . . (T)here have been far too many with little or no scientific merit. This is not only my own opinion, but it seems to be shared by all with whom I have discussed the subject, and there have been a good many." The writer was particularly disturbed by an article discussing antibiotic-vitamin combinations.[27]

In addition to their book and journal publishing ventures, Welch and Martí-Ibáñez also arranged an annual antibiotics symposium to be jointly sponsored by Martí-Ibáñez's MD Publications and the Food and Drug Administration. From 1953 to 1957 the symposium, which was chaired by Dr. Welch, received the blessing of the FDA. The proceedings were then col-

[22] See letter, Martí-Ibáñez to Harry Dowling, June 15, 1959, *ibid.*, 12490-91.
[23] See letter, Martí-Ibáñez to Welch, April 13, 1956, *ibid.*, 12426.
[24] See letters, *ibid.*, 13166, 13174.
[25] *Ibid.*, 13172-73.
[26] *Ibid.*, 13172, also see 13179.
[27] See letter, William W. W. Kirby to Welch, July 13, 1956, *ibid.*, 13191-2; also see 13206-07 and 13250.

lected and published as the "Antibiotics Annual" by none other than Medical Encyclopedia, the firm in which Welch owned a half interest.[28]

As with their other endeavors, Martí-Ibáñez was not bashful at all regarding manipulating the symposium to the advantage of large drug companies, therefore boosting sales of the "Antibiotics Annual" and reprints from it. In a long letter to Welch, outlining plans for the second symposium, Martí-Ibáñez commented, ". . . we have a unique opportunity to slant the papers of the Symposium in whatever direction we feel will be most useful to the audience of our publications." Among his many plans for the symposium, Martí-Ibáñez envisioned an increased number of "official" cocktail parties hosted by large drug companies. No wonder that one doctor returning from a trip to Europe reported, "The Europeans have a strong feeling that our Antibiotics Symposium is little more than a parade of new products and testimonials . . . without first class scientific data. . . . "[29]

By the mid-1950s, elements within the drug industry itself were becoming concerned regarding Welch's outside financial activities. In June of 1956, John Connor, Chairman of the American Drug Manufacturers Association's committee on FDA-NIH Relationships, expressed concern to HEW secretary, Marion B. Folsom, and commissioner of the FDA, George Larrick. The following month Connor met with Welch and Dr. A. H. Holland, medical director of the FDA, to discuss the matter. Welch again assured all parties that he received only an honorarium for his editorial services and that he did not make any effort to encourage the industry to use his journals for advertising purposes.[30]

Welch evidently felt that he had convinced Connor. Connor, however, was far from satisfied; he thought that Welch had agreed to state in a letter what he had told Connor regarding his outside activities. Martí-Ibáñez and Welch exchanged letters outlining Welch's activities, but the letters were left in HEW files and not distributed publicly. Connor felt Welch had reneged on his promise to publish his letter of explanation. In a last effort to clear the air, Connor urged that the industry group place the matter before Secretary Folsom and Larrick for final action. Connor commented, "My own view is

[28] *Ibid.*, 12636-37.

[29] See letter, Martí-Ibáñez to Welch, March 10, 1954, *ibid.*, 13022-24 and letter, William P. Boger to Welch, June 3, 1959, *ibid.*, 13031-32.

[30] Chronological Summary A: Inquiry by Mr. John Connor, American Drug Manufacturers Association, Respecting Outside Activities of Dr. Welch and Responses of FDA Thereto. (Undated). National Archives, Washington, D.C.

that other committee members will be quite surprised and shocked at the growing extent of Henry Welch's personal profitable enterprises."[31]

The industry group, however, felt that they had done all they could to bring the problem to the attention of HEW-FDA authorities. Despite the industry efforts, FDA management apparently felt it unnecessary to press Welch on the matter any further ignoring Connor's warning that it was "unsound for an important government official in a position like Dr. Welch's to have outside business interests that depend for their success on the financial support and backing of the very industry members whose activities he regulates or controls to such an important extent."[32]

Later investigation was to reveal how far Welch would compromise his scientific standing to benefit himself financially. In the mid-1950s a debate was taking place concerning the so-called synergistic effect to be derived from the use of combination drugs. In his opening remarks at the 1956 Antibiotics Symposium, Welch threw his support behind the use of combination drugs marketed in fixed ratios, heralding the arrival of "a third era of antibiotic therapy." Welch's advocacy of combination drugs caused quite a controversy at the symposium, spilling over into the editorial pages of his journals. Welch reprinted his symposium endorsement of combination drugs as an editorial in *Antibiotic Medicine and Clinical Therapy*. This action prompted Dr. Maxwell Finland to continue criticism that he, as well as others, had raised regarding the use of antibiotics in fixed combination. In a strong editorial in a subsequent issue of Welch's journal, Finland charged that "much of the clinical information presented at the symposium had the sound of testimonials rather than carefully collected and adequately documented scientific data." He further warned that "scientific publications have the duty to protect the medical profession and the public against the abuse of preliminary scientific information. . . . "[33]

In the following year, Welch was so determined to back up his endorsement of combination drugs that he put the FDA's own antibiotic research team on the job of demonstrating the synergistic powers of certain antibiotic mixtures. The research team's results were presented at the next year's antibiotic symposium.[34]

[31] Letter, John Connor to Dr. Karl Bamback, Sept. 13, 1956, National Archives.

[32] Chronological Summary A. Op. cit.

[33] For a copy of Welch's opening remarks see Administered Prices, Part 23, 12844-45, for essentially the same statement in his journal, see pp. 12846-47. For Finland's editorial see, 12925-28.

[34] See *ibid.*, 12860-80. For the results see *ibid.*, 12881-92.

Subsequent investigations revealed at least one major reason for Welch's keen interest in combination drugs. Senator Estes Kefauver's investigation into the drug industry showed that Welch had allowed Charles Pfizer and Co. to edit his opening remarks to be delivered at the 1956 Symposium.

Members of Pfizer's advertising staff inserted into Welch's speech the phrase "a third era of antibiotic therapy" which the Pfizer staff had previously decided would be the theme of the upcoming campaign for their new combination drug, Sigmamycin (a combination of oleandomycin and tetracycline). Dr. Welch's opening remarks, including the reference to "a third era of antibiotic therapy," were delivered at the symposium and were included in that year's *Antibiotic Annual.* Subsequently Pfizer purchased over 260,000 copies of reprints of Dr. Welch's opening remarks from his company, Medical Encyclopedia, Inc., for distribution at home and abroad.[35]

Due to some questioning of the desirability of the FDA's jointly sponsoring the Antibiotics Symposium with a private company, the agency ended its sponsorship after 1957. Welch, however, was allowed to remain chairman of the symposium, and FDA personnel were authorized to participate.[36] FDA management remained oblivious to Welch's financial dealings. The agency continued to accept Welch's statement that he received only an honorarium, and no effort was made to determine if he profited from advertising or reprint revenue.

Finally, in February 1959, John Lear, science editor of the *Saturday Review,* broached the subject of the possibility of conflict of interest regarding Welch's dual roles as regulator and editor. In a private interview with Welch, Lear pressed Welch about his financial arrangements. Welch again claimed that he received only an honorarium for his efforts, and he did not intend giving up his editorial position.[37]

The Lear article brought the question of conflict of interest into the public eye. As a result of the article and a number of letters from interested congressmen as well as queries from the press, HEW Secretary Arthur Flemming began looking into the matter. In the spring and early summer the investigation was slowed when Dr. Welch suffered a heart attack. By May Flemming had determined that the matter could only be settled by writing new policy regarding outside activities. Top FDA-HEW officials now began studying whether honorariums, advertising revenues, and sales of reprints were common practice in scientific publishing. But still Welch was being

---

[35] *Ibid.,* Part 22, 11967-70, 11997, 12014-15.

[36] *Ibid.,* Part 23, 12561, 12585, 12951.

[37] John Lear, "The Certification of Antibiotics," *Saturday Review,* Feb. 7, 1959, 43-48.

treated with kid gloves. Top FDA management refused to ask Welch the really hard questions: namely, how much he actually received and what was the formula for his payments.[38]

As late as June 1, 1959, the FDA still had no clear understanding as to how the journals were financed. Larrick, on a speaking trip to Florida, stopped to visit Welch who was recuperating in Miami. Only then did Larrick learn that the *Journal of Antibiotic Medicine and Clinical Therapeutics* was a controlled circulation journal whose principal revenues came from advertising and reprints. But Larrick was misled by Welch's statement that the journal consistently lost money. Larrick, ever reluctant to push Welch, failed to determine that it was the first journal which was the really lucrative vehicle.[39]

By October 1959, Secretary Flemming had formulated new policies greatly tightening outside activities, and thus requiring Welch to resign his editorial position and sever all ties with Medical Encyclopedia. In his press conference announcing the changes, Flemming, however, complimented Welch for being "one of the outstanding scientists at the present time"; he further stated, "No one has intimated any actual conflict of interest."[40]

It took the Kefauver investigation into the Welch case in May and early June of 1960 to reveal finally the degree to which Welch had indebted himself to major drug manufacturers. In turn the Kefauver investigation clearly demonstrated the lengths to which Welch had gone to endorse combination drugs for the benefit of Pfizer.[41]

A week before the Kefauver committee released the real amount of Welch's "honorarium," Welch filed for retirement on grounds of disability. The day after the release of the Kefauver findings (May 18), Welch, under orders from Secretary Flemming and Larrick, resigned. There was no way to deny him his federal disability pension which had been granted before the disclosures were made.[42]

The Kefauver revelations alerted Flemming to the possibility of further cases of conflict of interest in the agency and to the need to revamp the agency's regulatory powers, especially regarding drugs.

Two outside committees were appointed to probe the workings of the FDA to evaluate the performance of the agency. A panel of distinguished

[38] Administered Prices, Part 23, 12951, 12959-63, for copies of congressional inquiries see 12969, 12975-82.

[39] Memo, George P. Larrick to Charles Miller, June 1, 1959, *ibid.*, 12964.

[40] *Ibid.*, 12952, 12966.

[41] The investigation into the Welch affair can be found in *ibid.*, Part 22, with a mass of supporting documents in Part 23.

[42] *Ibid.*, Part 22, 12086-88.

scientific experts reviewed the policies and procedures of Welch's Antibiotic Branch and the New Drug Branch generally giving them an acceptable rating. But the panel also pointed out that the agency needed to increase its statutory powers in areas concerning the regulation of drug advertising and the control over the proof of drug efficacy. Most importantly the agency needed the proper budgetary allowances to keep abreast of the most recent advances in its regulatory field.[43]

A second committee spent six months trying to locate other possible conflict of interest cases and determining if the agency worked too closely with the drug industry. A careful examination of key FDA employees revealed that no present employee of the FDA presented a potential conflict of interest problem. But the experience of being required to divulge one's personal finances and having to prove one's integrity had a damaging effect on morale in the agency. The second committee did find, however, that due to increased responsibilities and decreased resources, the FDA in the fifteen years since the end of the war had moved too close to the drug industry. The committee felt that the agency needed to depend less on industry self regulation and act more aggressively in the consumer's interest.[44]

In the end, the Welch scandal proved to be an isolated case. But the episode did force the agency to revitalize its regulation of drugs, leading to the most comprehensive revision of the food and drug law since 1938. Indeed in the aftermath of the passage of the Food and Drug Amendments of 1962 (the Kefauver-Harris Amendments) the agency has been accused of being overly cautious in its regulation and introduction of new drugs.

[43] For the full report of this investigation see: *National Academy of Sciences–National Research Council Report of Special Committee Advisory to the Secretary of Health, Education and Welfare to Review the Policies, Procedures, and Decisions of the division of Antibiotics and the New Drug Branch of the Food and Drug Administration.* U.S. Congress, Senate. *Drug Industry Antitrust Act Hearings before the Subcommittee on Antitrust and Monopoly of the Committee on the Judiciary on S. 1552,* 87th Cong., 1st and 2nd sess., (1961), Part 2, 459.

[44] For the second report see: "Report to the Secretary of Health, Education, and Welfare Concerning the Food and Drug Administration," *ibid.,* 471-72, 474.

Conflict of Interest:
Promoting and Regulating the Infant
Nuclear Power Industry,
1954-1956

By

GEORGE T. MAZUZAN*

I N recent years the issue of atomic power, with its attendant controversial safety considerations, has become a major national issue. The controversy has been highlighted by demonstrations at reactor sites and in Washington, D.C., by innumerable articles and editorials, by the popular film, *The China Syndrome,* and most of all by the 1979 Three Mile Island reactor accident. Most arguments on the current issue demonstrate a lack of attention to the earlier history of America's atomic policies in which lie the roots of the present debate. This essay fills part of that void through discussion of the first two years of the United States Atomic Energy Commission (AEC) regulatory activities as they evolved after passage of the 1954 Atomic Energy Act. By assigning the AEC both promotional and regulatory responsibilities, the statute made inevitable a conflict of interest in the duties of the agency which both helped and hindered objective analysis of safety issues for the next twenty years.[1]

*The author is Chief Historian at the United States Nuclear Regulatory Commission. He wishes to thank J. Samuel Walker of the NRC for his suggestions on the manuscript.

[1]For the history of atomic energy development through 1952, see *A History of the United States Atomic Energy Commission,* vol. 1, *The New World, 1939-1946,* by Richard G. Hewlett and Oscar E. Anderson, Jr. (University Park, Pa., 1962), and vol. 2, *Atomic Shield, 1947-1952,* by Hewlett and Francis Duncan (University Park, 1969). The 1954 act is documented in *Legislative History of the Atomic Energy Act of 1954,* 3 vols., compiled by Madeleine W. Losee, Public Law 703, 83rd Congress (Washington, D.C., 1955). The Historical Office of the Department of Energy, the successor to the Atomic Energy Commission office, is continuing work on the history of the AEC. DOE historians have nearly completed a manuscript covering AEC activities during the Eisenhower Administration, but this will not incorporate the AEC regulatory functions. The Historical Office of the Nuclear Regulatory Commission is writing that history.

1

The Historian

The Atomic Energy Act of 1946 created the AEC. That law mandated the agency to continue the government's monopoly over atomic technology, a feature that dated from the Manhattan District atomic bomb project of the war years. Government concern in the immediate postwar years centered on continued bomb development and production. While the law allowed the possibility of widening the technology's use for peaceful purposes by private enterprise, it remained too restrictive to permit the development of an atomic power industry. Not until the early 1950s did the Commission, prodded by influential members of the industrial and electric power communities and by key members of the prestigious Congressional Joint Committee on Atomic Energy, make the first serious moves toward breaking the government monopoly and allowing private enterprise to exploit the new reactor technology.[2]

In 1950, Charles A. Thomas, president of Monsanto Chemical Company, proposed direct participation by industry in power reactor development. In 1951, the AEC, prompted by the Thomas proposal and a similar joint proposal by the Dow Chemical Company and the Detroit Edison Company, established an Industrial Participation Program that invited private enterprise to study the agency's classified atomic reactor technology data in order to determine whether private development and construction of different types of reactors should proceed.[3] Initial industry enthusiasm produced four project feasibility studies under the program in 1951, enough to encourage the AEC to issue a second invitation the following year.[4]

While industry and the AEC were developing this new climate for reactor development, the Congressional Joint Committee added its influence to the process. In December 1952, it published a special report, *Atomic Power and Private Enterprise,* a collection of recent historical documents on the subject, which included the positive results of an

[2]Hewlett and Duncan, *Atomic Shield,* 435-38, 494-95, 512, 514, 517, 590; George T. Mazuzan and Roger R. Trask, "An Outline History of Nuclear Regulation and Licensing, 1946-1979," unpublished manuscript, Historical Office, Nuclear Regulatory Commission, 13-16.

[3]Thomas to Sumner T. Pike, 20 June 1950, with encl., "Proposal for Industrial Development of Atomic Power"; J. W. Parker to Gordon Dean, 11 December 1950. AEC/DOE; AEC Press Release no. 341, 28 January 1951, AEC/NRC. When the AEC was disbanded in 1975, the agency records were divided between the Nuclear Regulatory Commission and the Energy Research and Development Administration that subsequently became part of the Department of Energy. AEC records located in the NRC files are designated AEC/NRC and those located in the Department of Energy are designated AEC/DOE.

[4]In addition to the two proposals mentioned above, the other two were from the Commonwealth Edison Company/Public Service Company of Northern Illinois, of Chicago, and the Pacific Gas and Electric Company/Bechtel Corporation, of San Francisco. AEC Press Release no. 373, 16 May 1951; no. 417, 6 April 1952, AEC/NRC.

2

informal opinion poll of "company executives, Government officials, scientists, lawyers, and others" conducted in the fall of 1952. Executive sessions and public hearings followed in the late spring and summer of 1953 eliciting testimony from more than fifty individuals representing forty-six companies, groups, organizations, and government agencies. In closing the hearings, New York congressman and Joint Committee chairman W. Sterling Cole noted that the testimony would be analyzed to prepare possible legislation amending the 1946 act.[5]

The documents and testimony produced obvious points of agreement. Gordon Dean, the retiring chairman of the AEC, and Lewis L. Strauss, the new chairman, testified on the importance of the promotion of atomic power. Scientific and engineering opinion held that the goal was technologically attainable. Industry had indicated enthusiastic interest. Furthermore, the long-range viewpoint saw hydrocarbon fuels as a diminishing natural resource; consequently steps should not be deferred in development of atomic power with its promise of both cheapness and unending source. In addition, and perhaps most important, both men emphasized that the nation's prestige would suffer if it lost its leadership in atomic power development.[6] All who testified seemed to agree that atomic power was important to the future economy not only of the United States but of the entire world. Most agreed that in order to bring about power reactor development, continued government assistance was necessary, particularly in the areas of research and development, investment, national health and safety, and defense and security. As Cole strongly suggested, the AEC should develop clear plans for "research and development in the field of atomic power components, pilot plants, and prototypes" so that private companies would have guidelines in planning for their own participation.[7] Clearly, then, the climate existed for promotion of reactor technology by the private sector.

The 1952 election of the conservative and business-oriented Dwight D. Eisenhower administration gave an additional boost to the movement. The president's Atoms for Peace speech at the United Nations on December 8, 1953, and his subsequent State of the Union and budget messages in January 1954 alerted the nation that his administration would endorse a policy of greater emphasis on peaceful and private uses of atomic energy.[8]

[5]U.S. Congress, Joint Committee on Atomic Energy (JCAE), *Atomic Power and Private Enterprise*, 82nd Cong., 2nd sess., December 1952; idem, *Atomic Power Development and Private Enterprise*, Hearings . . ., 83rd Cong., 1st sess., 24 June - 31 July 1953. The Cole statement is on page 570.

[6]JCAE, *Atomic Power Development*, 5-13, 562-67.

[7]*Ibid.*, 571.

[8]Mazuzan and Trask, "An Outline History," 23-24; *The Public Papers of Dwight D. Eisenhower, 1953* (Washington, D.C., 1960), 813-22; U.S. Congress, House, House Doc. 328, 83rd Cong., 2nd sess., 17 February 1954.

3

The Historian

In February 1954, the administration sent legislation to the Congress amending the Atomic Energy Act of 1946. But the Joint Committee took the lead in forging an entirely new bill. Over the course of a hot, humid Washington spring and summer, it redrafted the bill several times, held hearings, and presented legislation for full debate. Congress passed and Eisenhower signed the Atomic Energy Act of 1954 into law in August.[9]

The statute made the Atomic Energy Commission responsible for both promoting and regulating a new private atomic industry. A key section summed up these two basic functions of the Commission. It encouraged "widespread participation in the development and utilization of atomic energy for peaceful purposes to the maximum extent consistent with the common defense and security and with the health and safety of the public." Additional paragraphs told the Commission how to carry this out: through research activities including assistance to private enterprise, by providing to industry government-owned "special nuclear materials" (plutonium, uranium-233, and uranium enriched in the isotope 233 or in the isotope 235) used as fuel in power reactors, by releasing hitherto classified "restricted data" for use in domestic development of atomic facilities, through licensing of private atomic plants, and by continued inspection of such facilities and enforcement of the Commission's regulations.[10]

The promotion of a private atomic industry thus became a major policy of the Commission and the Joint Committee. Various program divisions in the agency geared up for this new challenge—to put atomic energy to work for wider use. The engineers and scientists in the agency's far-flung laboratories and offices as well as the Washington-based commissioners enthusiastically saw this as an exciting adventure filled with almost unending possibilities.

The new act, nonetheless, recognized the dangerous nature of the technology and included regulatory provisions. Throughout, the words "health and safety of the public" acknowledged potential hazards and underscored the basic general goal of the Commission's regulatory function.[11]

The question facing the agency was how to wear both the promotional and the regulatory hats without doing injustice to one or both functions. Commissioner and atomic scientist Willard Libby, in an early 1955 discussion on establishing the regulatory framework within the agency, expressed a feeling that was widespread in the Commission: "Our great hazard is that this great benefit to mankind will be killed aborning by unnecessary regulation. There is not any doubt about the practicability of isotopes and atomic power in my mind. The question is whether we can get it there in our lifetime." One

[9]*Legislative History of the Atomic Energy Act of 1954.*

[10]Atomic Energy Act of 1954, 68 stat. 919 (1954). The government owned all special nuclear material until 1964 when the act was amended to allow private ownership.

[11]*Ibid.*, secs. 2, 3, 11, 53, 81, 103, 104, 161.

4

Nuclear Power Industry, 1954-1956

logical way to balance the two would have been for the lawmakers to create separate promotional and regulatory agencies. That idea had crossed their minds when they discussed the proposed act with the commissioners.[12] But in 1954 there were compelling reasons to combine the two functions in a single agency. Technical manpower was at a premium. Two separate agencies would of necessity have drawn from the same pool of human resources with the real possibility of shortchanging each other. The technology itself—still experimenting with reactor designs to see which one or two would be the most feasible for widespread use—was in such an early stage that two organizations, one performing the research and development, the other regulating, would have worked at cross-purposes, maybe frustrating the overall goal of building a viable atomic industry. Consequentially, viewed in the context of those times, the risk of a conflict of interest, by making one agency perform two contradictory functions, appeared a small price to pay for the overall benefits derived.

Prior to passage of the 1954 act, no central regulatory office existed in the AEC. The safety of reactors — a major concern — was solely a government problem since all reactors were owned and operated by the agency. The AEC had handled reactor safety by establishing, in June 1947, a blue ribbon advisory group known as the Reactor Safeguard Committee. Composed of some of the nation's best atomic experts and chaired by physicist Edward Teller, the committee evaluated and audited technical health and safety factors of reactor hazards and submitted advisory recommendations to the general manager, the agency's chief operating officer. Teller, chairman for six years, described those early times: "The committee was about as popular—and also as necessary—as a traffic cop. Some of my friends, anxious for reactor progress, referred to the group as the Committee for Reactor Prevention, and I was kidded about being assigned to the AEC's Brake Department."[13]

The agency broadened safety considerations in the fall of 1950 by creating a second advisory group, the Industrial Committee on Reactor Location Problems, to balance the "technical and scientific aspects of reactor hazards, as developed by the Reactor Safeguard Committee, against the nontechnical aspects of reactor locations." This new committee drew its members from wider fields of the scientific and industrial communities. The group reviewed, for example, the problems of specific reactor locations, taking into account such matters as the density of surrounding population, property values, and hydrological and seismic factors. Recognizing that the responsibilities of the

---

[12]Commission Meeting (CM) 1085, 8 June 1955; JCAE, transcript of executive session, 3 May 1954, 135-36, AEC/DOE.

[13]Hewlett and Duncan, *Atomic Shield*, 186-87; "The Evolving Role of the Advisory Committee on Reactor Safeguards," 11 March 1974, ACRS File, AEC/NRC; Edward Teller and Allen Brown, *The Legacy of Hiroshima* (Westport, Conn., 1975), 102.

5

two committees were becoming more closely related, the Commission merged their functions in July 1953 and reorganized them into the Advisory Committee on Reactor Safeguards.[14]

The Safeguards Committee was influential in several areas of reactor safety. AEC general counsel William Mitchell, reporting to the Joint Committee in 1955 on the safety features of the new regulatory program, observed with considerable pride that the "extraordinary reactor safety record" owed much to the "strict criteria laid down by the Reactor Safeguards Committee."[15] Since all safety questions were referred to that group prior to enactment of the 1954 act, it was logical that the committee would continue to play an important role in safety matters in licensing procedures once the 1954 law was enacted.

After 1954, practical reasons prevented the Safeguards Committee from continuing as the only group reviewing reactor hazards. Its members were part-time consultants and the workload under the expanded reactor program began to place an increasing burden on them. Recognizing this problem, general manager Kenneth Nichols established a full-time Hazards Evaluation Staff to analyze reactor hazards.[16]

The Hazards Evaluation Staff was part of an evolving reorganization that began shortly after the passage of the 1954 act. Although the AEC had administered limited licensing functions under the 1946 law, these were peripheral to the act's primary national defense objectives of producing weapons-grade nuclear material and building atomic bombs. The previous licensing activities had involved control of isotopes and source material available for research; domestic and export control of production facilities for fissionable material and important component parts; and control of access to AEC-held patents. The 1954 law greatly broadened the scope of the licensing program, but the objectives of the earlier, more limited licensing functions still applied: protecting national security by regulating the distribution and use of certain materials and equipment, protecting health and safety, and stimulation of private enterprise toward use of materials, information, and techniques developed in the infant atomic energy program.

To build a functional regulatory organization and to develop the rules necessary to proceed with licensing, general manager Nichols

[14]CM 499, 27 November 1950; Report to the AEC of the 17th Meeting of the Reactor Safeguard Committee, 27 August 1952; CM 855, 25 April 1953; AEC 661, 2 July 1953; CM 884, 7 July 1953, AEC/DOE; AEC Press Release no. 491, 9 August 1953, AEC/NRC. The Safeguards Committee became a statutory committee in 1957.

[15]JCAE, *Development, Growth and State of the Atomic Energy Industry*, Hearings..., 84th Cong., 1st sess., 31 January 1955, 9. These "202" hearings were annual affairs required under section 202 of the 1954 act (cited hereafter as JCAE, *"202" Hearings*).

[16]AEC 661/4, 15 April 1955, AEC/DOE.

6

appointed Harold L. Price, an agency attorney, to serve as his special assistant on regulations. Price, a University of Virginia law school graduate, had practiced law privately for a short time before joining the Department of Agriculture in 1936. He subsequently served in the general counsel's office of the War Production Board and was general counsel in the Civilian Production Administration before joining the AEC in 1947 as the chief law officer at the Oak Ridge Operations Office. In 1951 the Commission appointed him deputy general counsel. Price was an indefatigable worker with good organizational ability. His appointment in 1954 was the beginning of a lengthy career as the chief regulator in the AEC.[17]

In June 1955, Price recommended that the Commission create a Division of Civilian Application not only to carry out licensing functions but also to promote the civilian uses of atomic energy.[18] His report specifically noted the Joint Committee's emphasis on and encouragement of maximum participation by private interests in its recent first annual hearings on "Development, Growth and State of the Atomic Energy Industry." Joint Committee members frequently commented at those hearings on the need for the AEC to keep licensing regulations and procedures as simple as possible and to process licenses expeditiously to encourage private participation. This congressional pressure had a bearing on the type of licensing structure the AEC established.[19]

By the end of 1955, Price had organized the Division of Civilian Application, which included as a key unit the former Hazards Evaluation Staff. The small technical staff of this branch reviewed the safety implications of all applications for reactor construction. Its goal was to satisfy for the agency that there was "reasonable assurance" that any given reactor could be operated safely and that any unresolved safety problems could be mitigated during the construction period before an operating license was issued.[20]

Other units in the Washington-based Division of Civilian Application assumed both regulatory and promotional responsibilities. The Licensing Branch carried out the administrative work on licenses for reactors, operators, and nuclear materials. The Foreign Activities Branch administered requests from Americans to engage in overseas activities. The Policy and Program Branch determined the need for new

[17]AEC Press Release no. 575, 22 October 1954; no. 615, 30 March 1955, AEC/NRC; interview with Robert Lowenstein, Washington, D.C., 27 March 1979. Price headed the AEC regulatory function until his retirement in 1971.

[18]AEC 804, 16 March 1955; CM 1068, 22 March 1955; AEC 804/1, 18 May 1955; CM 1089, 14 June 1955, AEC/DOE.

[19]AEC 804/1, 18 May 1955, AEC/DOE; JCAE, "202" Hearings, 84th Cong., 1st sess., 31 January - 3 March 1955.

[20]Organization Chart, Division of Civilian Application, January 1956, AEC/DOE.

7

regulations and assisted companies and persons wishing to engage in atomic energy activities. The Isotopes Extension, located at the Oak Ridge Operations Office, handled applications for stable isotopes, radioisotopes, and irradiation services.[21]

While Price was developing this organization in 1955, he also implemented the regulatory program through the writing and issuance of its regulations. Shortly after the 1954 act had become law, Nichols had outlined for the commissioners the major problems facing the AEC in licensing reactors. The greatest obstacle, he thought, would be the complexity of licensing activities, particularly in terms of procedural problems and the immediate and long-term development of regulations. For example, no regulations were in effect in the areas either of domestic and foreign distribution of special materials or of operator's licenses. And where regulations presently existed, in such areas as domestic and foreign distribution of source materials, production of special nuclear materials, commercial licenses, and construction permits, considerable revision would be required. By Nichols's estimate, at least "six months of solid work" lay ahead on the preparation of the new regulations.[22]

The Commission approached its regulatory responsibility well aware of the effect its rules would have on the growth of the industry. The 1954 act underscored the Congress's regulatory philosophy by directing the AEC to impose the minimum amount of regulation and terms on a licensee while fulfilling its obligations to protect the health and safety of the public. Chairman Lewis Strauss later told the Joint Committee that AEC regulations "should not impose unnecessary limitations or restrictions upon private participation in the development of the atom's civilian uses, that they should not interfere with management practices, and that such regulations should be enforceable in a practical and uniform manner."[23] Developing these regulations became an important aspect of Harold Price's job. To write clear regulations that covered the necessary legal, safety, and technical points, yet still allowed flexibility for the developing industry, proved to be a difficult task. Even so, Price and his colleagues felt pressure from the commissioners as well as the industry to turn regulations out as rapidly as possible.[24] Key rules were issued during 1955 and early 1956, and others followed in succeeding years.

One significant regulation can be used to exemplify the conflict of functions between promotion and regulation inherent in the agency. The regulation governing production and utilization facilities covered all types of atomic reactors, including those used for "producing" special nuclear materials (i.e., plutonium, uranium 233, 235) and for

[21]*Ibid.*; Hewlett and Duncan, *Atomic Shield*, 252-53.
[22]AEC 23/14, 13 September 1954; CM 1024, 14 September 1954, AEC/DOE.
[23]JCAE, *"202" Hearings*, 84th Cong., 2nd sess., 7 February 1956, 6.
[24]*Ibid.*, 84th Cong., 1st sess., 1 January 1955, 56-59.

8

"utilizing" atomic energy in electric power generation as well as for research purposes. The regulation itemized the data a company had to provide in order to receive a permit to start plant construction, and later to operate it. The general standards by which the agency judged an application were national security and public health and safety.[25]

Promising power reactor designs were being developed, but it was by no means clear in the mid-1950s that one or two particular designs would become the mainstays of the industry. Under the 1954 act, the AEC had authority to build large-scale reactors for research and development purposes as long as it did not do so for the sole purpose of generating or selling power. Under the leadership of Chairman Strauss, the AEC vigorously pursued a national policy that reflected the philosophy of the 1954 act, i.e., that competitive industry would bring about economic atomic power faster than any government-run program. In January 1955, the agency announced a plan to implement this policy, which it named the Power Demonstration Reactor Program, "designed to open the way for American industry to develop, fabricate, construct, and operate experimental reactors."[26]

Throughout the demonstration program, from 1955 to 1963, the AEC offered funding to private companies for conducting research and development on proposed reactor designs, waived charges for the loan of source and special nuclear fuels for up to seven years, and provided free research and development in government laboratories for certain mutually agreed-upon projects. The Commission justified these federally provided incentives because private industry took on the economic risk of the proposed projects. Several reactor designs were tried during the period, including the fast-breeder; the sodium-cooled, graphite moderated design; the organic moderated model; the heavy water design; and the gas-cooled reactor. By the end of the program in 1963, however, the light water reactor family (boiling water and pressurized water designs), developed earlier by Captain Hyman Rickover's atomic submarine program using the pressurized water reactor, had emerged as the future workhorse of the nuclear industry.[27]

In order to accommodate the various designs of prototype reactors expected under the government's Power Demonstration Reactor Program as well as those developed solely through private initiative, the production and utilization regulation allowed the developers to

[25]AEC 23/24, 16 December 1955, AEC/DOE.

[26]AEC Press Release no. 589, 10 January 1955, AEC/NRC.

[27]Frank G. Dawson, *Nuclear Power, Development and Management of a Technology* (Seattle, 1976), 76-101; Robert Perry, *Development and Commercialization of the Light Water Reactor, 1946-1977* (Santa Monica, 1977), 10-24; Irvin C. Bupp and Jean-Claude Derian, *Light Water: How the Nuclear Dream Dissolved* (New York, 1978), 33-36; Richard G. Hewlett and Francis Duncan, *Nuclear Navy, 1946-1962* (Chicago, 1974), 225-57.

9

experiment as they progressed in their construction. The AEC issued a conditional or provisional construction permit even though all the technical information required for the application was not initially submitted. The qualification was that the "Commission is satisfied and that it has sufficient information to provide reasonable assurance that a facility . . . can be constructed . . . without undue risk to the health and safety of the public and that the omitted information will be supplied."[28]

Both the developer and the AEC considered this provision necessary. The fact that the developer would be issued a permit, albeit conditional, would give him some assurance that his construction permit would eventually be converted to an operating license. For the agency, issuing a conditional construction permit provided the flexibility to promote the proposed reactor designs that had not yet proven themselves while at the same time it assured, within a reasonable doubt, that the outstanding safety questions would be resolved by the time the reactor was ready to operate.

Outstanding safety questions were, however, the heart of the problem. To determine what constituted a reasonable doubt about hazards in such a dangerous technology was the key to the agency's safety mandate. C. Rogers McCullough, an expert in reactor safety and chairman of the AEC's Safeguards Committee, told the Joint Committee in May 1956 that the "way we determine that the hazard is acceptably low is purely a matter of judgment." He believed that the probability of a major accident "involving presently operating reactors is quite low." And he noted that "for the first time in any industrial development an attempt is being made to foresee the possible accidents or disasters, and to take positive steps to prevent them." The introduction of this new philosophy posed difficult problems which, he said, the AEC and industry had to solve.[29]

McCullough reminded the Joint Committee of the AEC's excellent reactor safety record, which boded well for the future. "Careful reactor design by competent people, careful, conscientious, and skillful operation, and adequate maintenance—and I would like to add, a good deal of luck," he said, were the general conditions that would prevent future accidents. Nonetheless, McCullough acknowledged the risk involved. "We think the risk we are running there has been reduced to what we call acceptable. But there is some risk. We cannot convince ourselves that it is zero."[30]

The AEC recognized that the conditional construction permit that allowed reasonable doubt on safety was not the ideal licensing procedure. But it was pragmatic. Given the hazards involved, the fact

[28]AEC 23/24, 16 December 1955, AEC/DOE.
[29]JCAE, *Government Indemnity for Private Licensees and AEC Contractors against Reactor Hazards*, Hearings . . ., 84th Cong., 2nd sess., 1956, 46-47.
[30]*Ibid.*, 49-50.

10

that many of the power reactors under consideration were still in a development stage, and the fact that useful standards or codes could be finalized only as facilities became standardized and experience gained, the AEC maintained a flexible position. And the Commission believed its safety provisions were adequate. General manager Kenneth E. Fields, who replaced Nichols in May 1955, reassured the Joint Committee that the agency's hazards program carefully evaluated every atomic reactor to ensure that all potential hazards had been recognized, ascertained that "all reasonable steps" had been taken to "minimize the probability of the occurrence of an accident," and assured that if an accident did occur its consequences would be minimal. The agency, Fields testified, drew on the technical competence of designers and operators as well as on the agency hazards staff, and inspectors checked constantly on the reactor operator for compliance with the agency's rules and regulations. In closing, he noted that the conditional permit was the type "that we will probably have to issue for all the power demonstration reactors, and even for many of the research, testing and medical reactors, for the next few years."[31]

The AEC, as well as the atomic industry, recognized that an accident could destroy the fledgling industry or at least set it back many years. Excessive caution, though, in not recognizing the established essentials of reliable, safe reactor design and operation or in overloading the machines with unnecessary and expensive safeguards, might also have a negative impact on development. Dealing realistically with unanswered safety questions posed the major task for the agency.

The problem facing both the AEC regulators and applicants was a lack of definitive safety standards and criteria against which to judge an application. A growing technology with many reactor designs all in the developmental stage made it difficult to apply uniform regulatory standards. Although the experience gained by the mid-1950s had answered many technical questions, it had not given the certainty needed for clear-cut standards. This placed immense pressure on the hazards staff and their colleagues in the development divisions to give individual attention to the detailed design of each new reactor application. In spite of these uncertainties, Fields reassured the Joint Committee that the agency's technical staff was competent to review the hazards reports that were required with each application.[32]

Ultimately, both the AEC and industry wanted specific standards and guides to assist not only developers but also the agency staff in judging reactor applications. These could not be created immediately, but to postpone issuing reactor construction permits would be counter-

[31]*Ibid.*, 63-64.

[32]JCAE, *A Study of AEC Procedures and Organization in the Licensing of Reactor Facilities*, Committee Print, 85th Cong., 1st sess., 1957, 106; JCAE, *Government Indemnity and Reactor Safety*, Hearings . . ., 85th Cong., 1st sess., 1957, 54.

11

productive to the AEC's main objective of encouraging atomic industry development. Harold Price highlighted the dilemma. "Right now," he told the Joint Committee in 1956, "each reactor is a separate problem from the safety standpoint. They are all based on different design concepts. And we will have to look at them under the kinds of procedures and rules on a case-by-case basis." Price cited as an example the issue of reactor siting. "We don't say that a reactor has got to be located according to some specific rules. We look at the location in combination with containment. A particular location we might find was all right with twice as much containment as would be necessary, perhaps, in a more isolated location." He concluded that reactor development could proceed without standardized codes or formulas at little or no risk to the public safety.[33] The big loser, if delay was based on future standardization, was the rapid pursuit of the technology by private enterprise.

One critical element missing in safety standards development was an independent safety research program. The AEC conducted extensive safety related research, but its regulators lacked authority to control the direction, magnitude, and type of research carried out. Safety research was a part of the Division of Reactor Development's ongoing general research and development programs at the agency's various national laboratories and testing sites. These were performed on a specific safety program basis and, in some instances, on an individual reactor project basis. For example, the agency's Borax I test reactor and the Experimental Breeder Reactor were, in part, experiments in obtaining safety information. The AEC used the Borax reactor, a boiling water reactor designed for the study of its operating characteristics, for several years until the fuel elements in the core had been nearly exhausted metallurgically. In a final experiment, the atomic scientists intentionally allowed the reactor to destroy itself in order to confirm certain characteristics during an accident. Over a period of years the AEC's experimental breeder, located at the government's reactor testing center in Idaho, went through a series of tests that included operating through a zone of temperature instability combined with rapid power increases which produced important safety information. In addition, the Division of Reactor Development tested design or construction problems and established programs to experiment with metal-water reaction, metal-ignition, reactor fuses, containment, and reactor instrumentation and control.[34] It accumulated valuable safety data from these experiments.

Although the AEC was concerned enough about safety issues to spend an increasing amount of money on research projects, the

[33]JCAE, *Government Indemnity for Private Licensees,* 65.

[34]JCAE, *Government Indemnity and Reactor Safety,* 47-53; Richard G. Hewlett, "The Experimental Breeder Reactor No. 1: The Life Story of a Nuclear Reactor," unpublished manuscript, Historical Office, DOE.

12

regulatory division had no direct control over them. The hazards evaluation staff in the Division of Civilian Application received research results from the Reactor Development Division staff as well as from applicants for production and utilization facilities, licensees, and reactor manufacturers. In those days, when the agency placed top priority on the successful development of an atomic industry, there was a need for highest-level coordination in the entire atomic energy program. To maintain flexibility, to cut red tape, and to increase administrative efficiency, safety research was a part of the development program.[35] But in retrospect, the organizational structure pointed toward considerable lack of control on the part of the regulators to determine their own objective safety conclusions and perhaps impeded earlier development of some standards. In the long run, this situation gave some credence to later charges of conflict of interest between regulation and development.

In February 1955, a short time before leaving the agency, Kenneth Nichols told the Commission that the idea regarding regulations development "was to get into the licensee's business as little as possible." He continued, "That is particularly [true] in the light of the recent hearings where I think the majority of the Joint Committee feel that way."[36] Using that philosophy as its guide, the agency established what it thought was a workable regulatory program that protected health and safety while at the same time it provided the flexibility to develop a private, peaceful use of the atom.

Thus, the Atomic Energy Commission was statutorily obligated to both promote and regulate a novel, highly dangerous technology. Both promotional and regulatory activities were essential to the agency and to the private sector that would make use of the new energy source. Both aspects, however, were affected by several subtle factors that made a larger conflict of interest inevitable. The need for efficiency in promotion of the technology necessitated that regulatory action be a dual and somewhat overlapping function. Shortage of technical manpower at the government's disposal combined with promoters who needed to know what the regulations were and how they would be applied seemed reason enough to organize the agency with both regulatory and promotional elements.

In spite of the fact the regulators would, in the end, determine whether the technology was feasible by implementing their regulations, the AEC's organizational framework signified that regulation was secondary to promotion. Regulation was necessary, but it seemed like a stigma and lacked the glamor of the promotional side.

The 1954 law and the manner in which it was implemented emphasized that safety questions had to be resolved to ensure the growth and efficacy of the technology. The burden for safety fell primarily on

[35]JCAE, *A Study of AEC Procedures*, 9-10.
[36]CM 1061, 23 February 1955, AEC/DOE.

13

the scientists and engineers who designed the facilities, but the regulators had to approve those designs. How to answer complex safety questions in order to protect the public without stymieing reactor development was the central problem facing the early regulators. They chose the less-than-ideal conditional construction permit as the best available solution.

An excellent previous reactor safety record gave both the agency and the atomic industry confidence that current safety problems could be solved. Although both promoters and regulators acknowledged the possibility of a serious atomic reactor accident, they considered it remote, and the experience to date encouraged them to proceed with development although clear-cut standards had not been formulated in many areas. They believed that by moving with the same caution they had used in the past, they could virtually guarantee the health and safety of the public and help sustain atomic power's growth and usefulness.

The early history of nuclear regulation highlights the difficulty of discharging the dual mandate that the AEC received in the 1954 Atomic Energy Act—to promote the new atomic power industry and to protect public safety. The organization, regulations, and research procedures the agency established show that it tipped the balance in favor of promotion. Nonetheless, that inclination reflected the assumptions, concerns, and priorities of the times in which the atomic industry came into existence and set the general tone for atomic reactor development and regulation over the next twenty years.

14

A Critique of Governmental Intervention in Transport

Government in the United States has intervened in transport in two fundamental ways. First, all through its almost 200 years of existence, government has granted financial and other public aids to encourage development of new and more efficient transport facilities. Since 1920, governments have invested heavily to provide highways, inland waterways, and airways and airports under government enterprise conditions. Such intervention can be termed promotional or developmental action. Second, for about 100 years, governments have intervened to regulate common carriers (and more recently, contract carriers) on various economic grounds. These include the failure of the market under monopoly or partial monopoly conditions to limit rate and service discrimination or the markets' assumed failure under conditions of excessive, or "destructive", competition to yield normal competitive returns to carriers, stable services and rates, and efficient divisions of traffic and allocations of resources.

Both forms of government intervention have powerfully influenced the development of transport systems and the rates and services rendered to national, regional and state economies. This paper reviews whether government regulatory and promotional policies have primarily been directed toward national economic development or regional, state and urban area development. To the extent possible, it also discusses the sense in which national, regional or local planning was involved either in regulating carriers or in aiding and developing private or public transport facilities. Finally, the paper comments on the directions that regulatory and promotional policy should take to solve the outstanding issues of the day. At this point, the paper focuses more closely on how changes in government interventional

---

*Proceedings of a Conference on Regional Transportation Planning, ed. by Joseph S. DeSalvo (Santa Monica, Calif.: The Rand Corporation, 1971), pp. 233-308. Also in Perspectives on Regional Transportation Planning, ed. by Joseph S. DeSalvo (Lexington, Mass.: D.C. Heath and Company, 1975), pp. 229-290.

371

policies can help to solve the great urban and regional transport development needs of the future.

General Nature of the Influences of Government Intervention in Transport

In terms of transport's role in influencing economic development, perhaps the promotional policies of governments have been more significant than their regulatory activities. Thus, state entrepreneurship in building the Erie Canal and other canals in the first half of the last century made possible the exchange of large volumes of goods between the Atlantic Seaboard and the rich but underdeveloped lands west of the Allegheny Mountains. Governments' free-entry, eminent-domain and other encouragements to railway building in the last century, especially the Federal land grants, had an even wider geographical impact on population settlement, development of resource-orientated industries, growth of new cities, and rapid economic and political integration of the continental and highly specialized economy of the United States.

In the last 50 years, the role of government promotion has been even more prominent in transport development and it has had a greater impact on the transport supply system. Most significantly, the state and Federal governments have cooperatively engaged in the greatest long-term investment program in U.S. transport history, building the Federal-aid highway systems. Starting with the paving of principal intercity and interstate routes in the 1920s and the 1930s, that program has continued since World War II with great enlargements in the capacity of the primary highways. With almost continually rising Federal financial support in huge annual volumes since 1956, this government enterprise has revolutionized the relative transport roles of the major modes; substituted pervasive competition for monopoly as the most prevailing natural condition of transport markets; added greatly to decentralization of cities and the decline of villages and small towns; and has made the highways overwhelmingly dominant in the transport of persons and in short-haul transport of goods.

Likewise, the growing role of the inland waterways in both short-haul and long-distance transport of raw materials, liquid products and heavy semi-manufactures has been based on Federal enterprise and investment in inland waterway channels and locks. And Federal enterprise and investment in the civil airways and in some large airports and growing Federal aid to major airports made possible the great growth of long-distance passenger travel by air at speeds unattainable in surface transport. As a consequence of the gigantic Federal and state investments and aids to the new modes, however, a sharp decline in the railroads' role in intercity passenger travel, small-shipment traffic, and in short- and medium-distance freight markets has gradually taken place[1].

Government economic regulation was the second principal form of intervention in transport to emerge. Originally, it came in response to marked monopoly or cartel conditions in many transport markets after the railroads superseded the canals, restricting wagon road transport to gathering and distribution functions. Early state com-

372

missions and the Interstate Commerce Commission were organized to equalize market access for small shippers, communities served only by rail and producing areas far from markets. This principally involved elimination of rate and service discrimination that could not reasonably be justified.

Until 1920, regulatory intervention controlled the excesses of monopoly power and monopoly discriminating rates. It did not rationalize the competitive structure of railroads between major centers or producing areas, nor break up rate cartels. Regulation affirmatively influenced the economic organization of the railroads only after the Transportation Act of 1920, and regulation's marked influence on the economic structure of regulated trucking and on the intermodal division of traffic and revenues came only after passage of the Motor Carrier Act of 1935. However, regulation of the conditions for airmail contracts by the Post Office Department and of entry and mergers by the Civil Aeronautics Board beginning in 1938 markedly influenced the market structure of air transport almost from the beginning.

The promotional and allocative functions of economic regulation, which came late and are highly controversial today, were based on entirely new concepts of transport regulation. The promotion of air transport by the Civil Aeronautics Act of 1958 best exemplifies the new developmental objective of regulation. Minimum rate control by the ICC after 1935 and 1940 to prevent price competition from allocating traffic and revenues between the railroads and their intermodal competitors furnishes the best example of the exercise of the allocative function between modes of transport.

Use of economic regulation in recent decades for transport promotional and allocative purposes has much in common with promotional policy in transport. Whether or not designed to be complementary, both types of intervention have emphasized rapid development of air, highway and inland waterway transport through a variety of government controls and subsidies. In addition to contributing flexible schedules, higher speeds, and comfortable or protective services and some gains in economy, these government-promoted changes were important factors in the long and gradual decline in the railroads' role, and in their lessening ability to introduce technological innovations, replace capital and continue customary services.

In view of the mixed results of government transport intervention, several questions seem pertinent. Has the use of promotional and regulatory intervention to foster rapid development of the newer modes of transport been fully economic? Have those policies made the best use of scarce resources invested in transport? Have the impacts on national, regional and urban development been wholly desirable and entirely economic? Or can some of the more urgent transport problems of the day, such as traffic congestion, lack of modal alternatives in urban communities, inadequate rail investment and modernization, and the external diseconomies of transport be ascribed significantly to those promotional and regulatory policies? Can today's urban, regional and national development and resource-use problems be satisfactorily solved without major changes in transport policies?

373

Criticism of the effects of transport regulation has mounted and become widespread in recent years, bringing the role and accomplishments of carrier regulation into sharp controversy. Discussion will focus on the changing nature of economic regulation, the effects of regulatory policies, and the changes essential to promote more efficient use of resources committed to transport. Emphasis will be placed on the regulation of surface carriers of freight, the area in which the economic costs of misallocated traffic are the greatest. Although resource misallocation in the sense of inefficient market structures and excess capacity from service competition exist in the airline field, airline regulation will be treated only briefly as it is concerned with intercity passenger travel and contributes only slightly to misallocations of freight traffic.

Effects of Railroad Regulation to 1935

The prime period of Federal rail regulation was between 1887 and 1935. During the early years of that period, the ICC was criticized for being ineffective in controlling rate discrimination and high rates. The courts had declared that the ICC lacked the power to prescribe maximum rates and to deal effectively with long-haul, short-haul discrimination. Explicit grant of those powers to the ICC by the Hepburn and Mann-Elkins Acts in 1906 and 1910, respectively, started regulation on a path toward some alleviation of discriminatory conditions and excessive rates.

Soon, however, World War I intervened to disrupt transport conditions and to necessitate government operation of the railroads from 1917 to 1920. By the time the railroads regained private ownership in 1920, the rise of new modes was changing intercity transport from an industry of many monopoly markets and cartel rate-making into one of pervasive competition, with monopoly markets gradually becoming exceptional.

Nevertheless, some generalizations on the nature and effects of early regulation are tenable. First, although some recent historians have reinterpreted regulatory history in finding that ICC regulation strengthened the railroad cartels in price fixing[2], it remains clear that the public tasks assigned by the Act to regulate Commerce of 1887 were those of limiting monopoly and discriminating rates and of encouraging as much competition between railroads and between rail and water carriers as possible. Regulation was distinctly shipper-or-consumer motivated in its rationale. To the extent it was effective, it substituted for competitive forces that were not strong or pervasive enough to limit rates to costs and to prevent uneconomic discrimination.

Long before regulation became tolerably effective in terms of its original purposes, a discriminating freight rate structure had been fashioned by the forces of rail monopoly at intermediate points, route competition, market competition, and the carriers' profit interest in increasing utilization by quoting low rates on agricultural and extractive commodities over long distances and assessing high

374

rates on short-haul movements and on high-value commodities. The ICC basically accepted that rate structure as fitting the railroads' economic characteristics and as promotive of national and regional economic development, changing it only as to details[3]. In times of rising prices, the ICC limited general rate increases and the profitability of the railroads, but the ICC seldom reduced the general level of rates, even during the Great Depression. By controlling personal, long-short haul, commodity and place discrimination to an extent, the ICC widened the competitive opportunity of particular shippers, communities, and regions, especially for shippers of agricultural and extractive products located far from their markets.

Unquestionably, the railroad discriminating rate structure facilitated the economic integration of the continental U.S. It fostered much regional specialization, afforded wide markets for both extractive and manufactured products, and stimulated large-scale production in industry. Consequently, it promoted the national and regional development that already was taking place on the basis of other economic factors. Under the influence of low rates on foods and raw materials from western and southern origins and its early start in manufacturing, the Northeast developed as the core economic region of the country with most of its manufacturing, its largest cities, and about half of the population. The value-of-service rate structure assisted the South, Southwest and West to develop basically as agricultural and extractive regions.

This national economic structure, with large-volume movements of extractive products eastward and northward to the Northeast and reverse large flows of manufactured products to the outlying southern, southwestern and western regions, came about without comprehensive economic planning. Rather, it happened in response to the profit stimulus for development strengthened by the right to homestead on public lands, sale of the public domain at low prices, the availability of excellent natural resources in the West, and the policies that hastened rail development, such as free entry until 1920, the right of eminent domain, and Federal land grants and other aids. Thus, last century's predominant transport policy consisted of encouraging development of as many competitive rail routes and lines as would be attractive to private capital, the supply of transport in advance of traffic demand, and a rate structure that would stimulate a maximum flow of commodities and efficient utilization of rail facilities.

As a broad generalization, regulation until the 1930s was basically consistent both with the economic and cost characteristics of the railroads and the requirements of national and regional economic development. The economic development to which the scheme of regulation contributed yielded marked national economic growth, regional specialization and division of labor, the maximum exchange of products between regions, wide markets for large-scale production of industrial products in the Northeast, and a rapidly growing population enjoying ever-increasing per capita real incomes. Ultimately, however, significant development problems emerged, especially as the outlying regions began to engage in manufacturing and to press for government investments and policies designed to promote balanced

375

regional economies. In addition, some of the perplexing and unsolved urban problems of today eventually emerged from the great concentrations of population and industry fostered by efficient transport and the value-of-service rate structure accepted by the ICC.

New Concepts in Transport
Regulation and Rising Criticism

In the 1930s, however, transport regulation took a highly paradoxical direction. Even though transport markets were becoming more competitive and the railroads were experiencing diversion of traffic and revenues to new modes, economic regulation shifted from the task of controlling monopoly power and maintaining competition to that of limiting intramodal and intermodal competition. This was accomplished by extending regulation to new competitive modes and by shifting to the regulatory tools of controlled entry and minimum rate regulation from long-standing dependence on control of discrimination and prescription of maximum rates.

Gradually, the paradox became better understood, of expanding regulation when competition enables transport markets to function as efficiently as in many unregulated industries. Even the railroads, the original sponsors of extended regulation, began to criticize particular regulatory policies as their market shares and profitability declined after World War II. In a series of reports to the Congress, the Executive Branch recommended some relaxation of the new restrictive regulation to permit competition to divide the traffic more efficiently among the modes. Moreover, the long delays in getting any substantial change in regulation and the accumulating evidence that regulation has misallocated resources in intercity freight traffic promoted a widening demand for drastic regulatory policy revision, even including abolition of the ICC[4]. Because the ICC's regulation widely touches the pocketbooks of shippers and influences industrial location and the availability of markets, most criticism of transport regulation has focused on the ICC. Though not free of criticism by any means, the CAB has operated under such favorable conditions of demand growth and aircraft innovations as to escape the harsh criticism leveled against ICC regulation[5].

The earliest criticism of extended ICC regulation came from a few transport economists in the late 1930s[6]. Agricultural industries early opted for the free market in truck and water carriage, strongly preferring exempt to regulated carriers on grounds of more flexible services and competitive rates. Since the 1950s, the railroads have increasingly blamed ICC regulation of minimum rates for their declining market shares. Moreover, many shippers have turned to private trucking and have criticized the deficiencies in regulated trucking service and the generous rate and profit levels allowed by the ICC. The most serious strictures, however, have been those of a number of economists, whose studies have repetitively shown that ICC regulation has been making freight transport inefficient and has been contributing to unnecessary railroad decline[7].

These criticisms have raised the fundamental question whether the benefits of economic regulation are any longer worth the costs

376

imposed on consumers, governments, shippers and carriers. Thus, the basic issue stated in the 1942 report of the National Resources Planning Board on Transportation and National Policy has surfaced for consideration in the 1970s[8]. Should this nation continue to restrict competition in domestic transport by the brand of protective regulation adopted in the heart of the Great Depression, and continue to move in the direction of monopoly organization and cartel pricing in transport? Or should it turn toward increasing the widespread competitive forces that now naturally exist in transport, and toward allowing the market to determine the relative economic roles of the competing modes?

Underlying those critical questions, of course, are the transport requirements for national, regional, urban and rural economic development. Would the national and regional economies be more productive if transport supply and rates were determined more by the forces of a free market? Would urban areas benefit from a more balanced supply of transport?

Specific Effects of the New Regulation after 1935

A staff paper in Transportation and National Policy in 1942 questioned the rationale advanced for extending minimum rate and entry controls to interstate motor and water carriers[9]. The alleged destructiveness of competition, the financial demoralization attributed to competition, competition's supposed contribution to excess capacity and the rate and service instability at the time were traced to the low general level of aggregate demand and employment during the Depression rather than to growing transport competition. Thus, excessive competition could not be a logical basis for restricting transport competition in full-employment economies for modes not evidencing long-run decreasing costs[10].

Structural, rate and service effects in the early years of the new regulation. The 1942 NRPB paper found that entry control and minimum rate regulation were having significant impacts on the market structures of transport and on rates and service. These included strong tendencies toward fewer and larger firms in regulated trucking, attributable to the highly restrictive "Grandfather" and new-service entry policies of the ICC and to the incentives that closed entry gave to mergers[11].

A most important structural change was the rapid organization of many new rate bureaus in trucking. Stimulated by ICC insistence on uniform rates and rate bureau influences, the regulated truckers (except in New England) adopted the rail value-of-service rate structure, adjusted to discourage types of traffic that the truckers could not haul profitably at rates based on low rail costs[12]. Without this institutional structure for rate agreements, discriminating prices had not been viable in trucking because of the atomistic competitive conditions in that field. Hence, the ability of the regulated truckers to establish value-of-service rates revealed that regulation had converted the industry from a highly competitive field into a monopoly cartelized one. This resulted in regulated truck rates at higher levels than rates in unregulated trucking markets.

377

The quality of trucking service was also affected by regulation. Even when regulated truckers held extensive "Grandfather" rights, there was a straight-jacketing of service into rigid molds. Commodity, return-haul, route, point, and service restrictions in certificates and permits reduced the inherent flexibility of trucking services. Denials of entries and division of markets between noncompeting groups by means of service restrictions reduced the number of firms authorized to carry particular commodities between city-pair markets. Back-haul restrictions often reduced shippers' opportunities to utilize private trucking. Regulatory discouragement to carriers offering lower rates for lesser service greatly limited shippers' choice between low rates for inferior service or high rates for superior service. Enhanced service competition under the requirement that all carriers assess the same rates increased the unit costs of regulated service and the level of regulated rates.

Continuing structural, rate and service effects of the new regulation. Subsequent studies of the new protective regulation confirm that the ICC has continued its restrictive entry policies[13]. And the ICC has also continued to authorize many mergers involving large truckers each year, though these have not been supported by evidence of economies of scale in size of firm[14].

Significant structural changes in regulated trucking markets have taken place. The number of ICC-regulated truckers has fallen markedly, in spite of enormous growth in trucking traffic and revenues. Fewer regulated truckers now have like authority to operate in particular city-pair markets. Between specific city-pair markets over particular routes and for particular groups of authorized commodities the typical situation has become one of oligopoly, even of a small number of firms[15].

Evidence has multiplied that regulated trucking rates have been maintained at levels substantially higher than competitive rates[16]. Higher rates can be explained by the higher costs of regulated truckers and by monopoly influences. Regulated carriers bear the costs of attending hearings, of submitting and protesting entry applications, and of giving evidence in regulatory proceedings. Higher cost levels significantly reflect commodity, return-haul, route and service restrictions that bring about poorer utilization and excessive supplies of trucks and labor. The high rates of return of regulated truckers have resulted from the cartel monopoly influences in rate making and regulation.

High rates of return to regulated truckers. Evidence in ICC cases reveals that regulated truckers have earned relatively high rates of return. Class I regulated truckers earned a return on net investment after income taxes averaging 11.78 percent in the 1957-66 decade. The ratio of net income after taxes to equity for Class I carriers was 15.7 percent in 1966, placing regulated trucking among the leading industries in high returns to equity[17]. Regulated truckers would have a case for such high returns if the risk to capital were actually higher because of the low revenue margins or other factors. However, with protection from entries and extensions, legally fixed rates by agreement, and rate cutting limited by minimum

378

rate orders, their rates have most likely exceeded marginal costs, an indication that monopoly explains part of these high returns[18].

Significant misallocation of traffic and revenues away from railways. Misallocation of traffic and resources traces to several factors. Regulation holding truck rates and profits above competitive levels has encouraged private carrier transport, often when common carriers could operate more efficiently. Regulation has encouraged trucker adoption of rail value-of-service rates and rail dependence on restrictive regulation to cure their ills, contributing a false sense of security that the existing rail market share would continue without aggressive rate and service competition. When the railroads later discovered that rate parity with trucking was not dividing the traffic according to relative costs, their attempts to reduce many rates above fully distributed or out-of-pocket costs proved difficult or impossible because of the full-cost and fair-sharing standards of the ICC in intermodal minimum rate cases[19]. Finally, rail technological improvements have been retarded by regulatory processes of disapproval of the necessary rate and service adjustments because of competitive impacts on competing modes[20].

No estimates are available on the economic cost of misallocation of traffic to private carriers. But studies have revealed that common motor carriers operate with a higher percentage of full-load round trips, a lower incidence of empty returns, and higher average loads than private carriers. Consequently, misallocation occurs because common carriers cannot lower their regulated rates to competitive levels, operate efficiently and attract the traffic moved on private carriage[21].

Evidence has multiplied that the static costs of misallocation of road-rail traffic are substantial. The relative outputs of rail and highway freight carriers with equal inputs of labor, fuel, and comparable capital are shown to favor the railroads by ratios of approximately 3 to 1, making the railroads the low-cost mode except for small shipments and short hauls. With truck and rail rates held at the same level in spite of the markedly lower rail costs, changes in the division of traffic do not prove that traffic has moved by the most efficient mode[22].

Taking into account the added costs of rail services to shippers in view of the service advantages of trucks, another study also found road-truck misallocation. For the same social cost of $5.5 billion expended either on intercity rail freight or on intercity truck freight, Meyer and Associates found that railroads would produce 567 billion revenue ton-miles while trucks would produce only 414 billion revenue ton-miles [23].

Regulatory signals toward overinvesment in highways and inland waterways and resource misallocation. Regulation, in shifting freight traffic from low-cost to high-cost modes, leads to higher traffic volumes over the highways, exerting additional demands for highway capacity and for stronger highways and bridges. Diversions of traffic to inland waterways have stimulated greater investments in

379

channels and locks. Thus, the investment signals given in the transport markets call for more highway and inland waterway investment and
less rail investment than otherwise would occur. Hence, the large
misallocations of traffic and revenues resulting from regulation have
also affected resource allocation uneconomically over the long run.

The effects of regulation have made railroads inefficient and
unable to contribute their full role in development. To the extent
that increasing returns exist, the traffic lost to railroads because
of regulation has raised their average costs. The revenues lost on
high-value traffic have lowered rail returns to capital, limiting the
capital railroads could raise for modernization. Regulatory influences impair the railroads' ability to render long-haul service at
low rates, tending to decentralize industry and promote regional
self-sufficiency. And the low profitability of the railroads under
regulation has contributed to declining suburban and intercity passenger train services and thus to air pollution, noise and excessive
congestion, the principal concerns of advocates of regional planning
in transport today[24].

Adjustment of Economic Regulation to an Efficient Role

If regulatory reform is to be effective, changes will have to be
made in the key provisions, standards and policies that have molded
transport regulation into uneconomic channels in the last four decades. Of prime importance is the wording of the National Transportation Policy. While the ICC was directed "to recognize and preserve
the inherent advantages of each" mode, the Policy also called for
ruling out "unfair or destructive competitive practices" and for
fostering "sound economic conditions in transportation and among the
several carriers." The latter standards have been the statutory
basis for the Commission's protective minimum rate and entry control
policies and its full-cost standards in intermodal minimum rate
cases. Even an effort by the Congress to correct the overemphasis on
protecting high-cost modes in the 1958 Act failed because of the
linking of the new rate control standard in Section 15a(3) to those
influential policy standards[25].

The many rate and entry decisions of the ICC which shore up the
value-of-service rate structure have been influential in the misallocation that has taken place and in the decline of the railroads[26].
As most ICC entry policies started before the National Transportation
Policy was enacted in 1940, they must either be traced to standards
in the Motor Carrier Act of 1935 or to deliberate protective standards adopted by the ICC itself[27]. (The ICC clearly could have
adopted policies to avoid uneconomic service restrictions and was
urged to do so by Commissioner William E. Lee, the great dissenter in
motor carrier entry cases.)[28] The ICC also authorized many mergers
creating large-scale trucking firms, even though the Commission was
fully aware that growth traffic and revenue in trucking would have
supported more firms and had testified in Congressional hearings in
1955 that it did not have studies to indicate whether larger trucking
firms would attain significant scale economies[29]. Consequently,
the ICC's large-firm emphasis can be traced largely to its own
policies.

380

The ICC, too, adopted loose standards for determining earnings levels for the regulated truckers. Under carrier pressures, the ICC utilized the operating ratio as a standard for rate-level and profit control despite the fact that regulatory practice and economic theory had long validated rate of return on necessary capital as the appropriate standard for regulated enterprise. Hence, the Commission's own policies must be held accountable for the generous rates of return on depreciated capital investment that many regulated truckers have earned.

Both the Congress, in enacting the 1935, 1940, 1942, and 1958 Acts, and the ICC must therefore be held accountable for the substantial inefficiencies in transport that regulation has produced. Even so, many effects could have been avoided or minimized if the ICC had interpreted the mandates of the Congress differently and had utilized the tools of minimum rate regulation and entry control less restrictively of competition.

Two realistic alternatives exist for modifying ICC regulation. These are (1) change in ICC entry, merger and minimum rate policies to minimize their uneconomic effects, continuing the present structure of regulation largely intact; and (2) partial deregulation by eliminating some important parts of the existing regulatory structure and the questionable mandates in the regulatory statutes.

If politically practicable, the second alternative would be preferable because it would remove the root causes of principal inefficiencies and misallocative effects by abolishing minimum rate regulation and entry control for motor and water carriers and reapplying antitrust laws to common carriers. Such deregulation would eliminate totally the fallacious new concepts in surface transport regulation introduced in 1935; that is, the idea that ordinary competition in the naturally competitive modes requires regulation as much as monopoly power in a monopoly mode and the associated notion that regulation can allocate traffic between the modes more efficiently than competition.

Short of such change, lesser legislative actions could be taken. For example, the "unfair or destructive competition practices" and the "sound economic conditions" standards of the National Transportation Policy could be abandoned. Or a new policy with emphasis on maintaining workable competition within and between modes could be substituted. Either would go a long way to reduce misallocative effects, as the ICC would be constrained to apply the logic of economic theory by utilizing long-run variable or marginal costs as the relevant rate standard.

An obvious step in making existing regulations efficient would be legislative directive to abandon restrictions on commodities, return-hauls, routes and points served, and types of service in motor carrier certificates and permits. Such restrictions result in higher average costs of service and in service less than the flexible capabilities of trucks are capable of rendering. But at least the minimum changes outlined above for the National Transportation Policy are also essential, to redirect the ICC's energies toward implementation

381

of workable competition and efficient divisions of traffic. But if
the ICC should fail to adopt fully economic cost criteria for measuring the low—cost mode and for setting floors on competitive rates,
legislation additionally would be needed to clarify Section 15a(3) by
specifying that the standard of variable or relevant marginal cost
should be used in minimum rate cases[30].

Experience has shown that enactment of even small fundamental
changes in the Interstate Commerce Act has been politically difficult
because of the opposition of the carrier groups benefiting from protective regulation. Thus, the possibility that the ICC might be induced to change its own administrative standards to yield a more
efficient role for regulation might be considered. Obviously, the
Commission cannot abandon minimum rate regulation or entry control
under present law. What the Commission could do is to make far less
use of minimum rate and entry control powers than in the past. The
statute does not require the Commission to utilize its rate control
powers to raise motor carrier profits above competitive or fair—
return levels. The ICC could refuse to allow earnings higher than
necessary to attract capital. Too, the Commission could refuse to
suspend independently-filed rate reductions by carriers whose costs
and service might be more efficient than those of protesting carriers. Also, a greater burden could be placed on protesting carriers
to prove that proposed rate reductions might be unlawful.

Present law requires the elimination of "unfair or destructive
competitive practices," but it does not define those practices. The
Commission has much discretion and could apply economic theory in
determining the cost standards for judging whether competition is
economic or "destructive" in each situation. In the Ingot Molds
case, the Supreme Court held that the determination of cost criteria
in intermodal competitive cases was within the special expertise of
the ICC[31]. Hence, if the Commission resolves this issue by finding
that the variable or long—run marginal cost standard is the relevant
one for establishing limits for minimum competitive rates, the Commission could remove the protective coloring and fair—sharing traffic
allocations that its past full—cost standards have introduced.

Even without legislation the Commission could remove many of the
uneconomic service restrictions in certificates and permits. Shipper
complaints of inadequate through service for less—truckload shipments
and of cost-raising service practices under certificate restrictions
recently prompted the ICC to move modestly toward some liberaliza-
tion. For example, in Removal of Truckload Lot Restrictions, the ICC
in 1968 ordered deletion of truckload restrictions in common carrier
certificates, on a blanket basis as recommended by the BIR[32].
Clearly, the Commission could order additional blanket liberaliza-
tions of certificate restrictions.

Income losses to the protected regulated carriers and some
shippers. A policy of allowing competitive forces more sway would
bring about appreciable income losses to regulated truckers and possibly some adverse income changes for long—distance shippers of agricultural and extractive products. Shippers located in small centers

382

192

might also be affected. Yet adverse income distribution effects can be exaggerated. First, the offsets to income losses would include lessened regulatory expenses and avoidance of the cost-raising effects of restricted operations and service competition. Highly restricted motor carriers would gain new markets and greater revenues. Second, many overextended trucking operations could shift from long-haul and volume transport to short-haul and gathering and distributional services just as automobile truckers shifted to such types of operations after the introduction of efficient rail tri-level rack cars returned medium- and long-haul automobile traffic to the railroads. Third, much traffic now moved by private and exempt carriers could be attracted to the regulated truckers. Even if not avoidable in those ways, the income losses to protected truckers represent monopoly gains from regulation of a type that are not justifiable as economic returns.

Some income losses to long-distance shippers of agricultural and extractive products might occur as relaxed regulation allowed the railroads to raise rates that do not yield revenues sufficient to cover out-of-pocket costs. The railroads, however, are already pressed by their low returns to take such pricing action, and they might take even more drastic action to raise rates if the diversion of profitable high-value traffic to trucking continues. On the other hand, as larger shares of the profitable traffic will increase the profitability of the railroads over the long run, the need for raising rates on agricultural and extractive goods can be limited to avoidance of the real losses from such traffic.

Why should income changes from deregulation or limited regulation be considered a barrier to change at all? Traffic frequently has been diverted from one regulated mode to another in response to technological developments and rate and service changes. The income losses to inefficient carriers in such cases are seldom compensated. In some cases, however, it might be better to compensate some income losses from deregulation than to continue indefinitely the uneconomic effects of regulation restrictive of competition.

Some benefits of regulatory revision in transport. Giving freer rein to competitive forces in transport would both make freight transport more efficient and raise the output of the economy. The lower rates resulting for most firms would extend the market; promote further exploitation of resources; and increase regional specialization. More rapid introduction of technical advances would take place because the associated service and rate designs for making them profitable would not be limited. Efficient intermodal transport combining the economies of large efficient container ships, mass land carriers for long container hauls, and trucks for short gathering and distribution hauls would be encouraged. Finally, the savings in resources of up to several billions of dollars each year from ending misallocations of traffic could be employed to enlarge the output of other goods and services.

Lessened regulation will be conducive to achieving more balanced transport development and greater economic progress in transport. By accurately revealing the true relative economic demands for each

383

mode's services, competitive transport markets will assist planners
to correct the large imbalances in transport investment and development since 1920 in the United States. And by freeing the railroads
to compete, those carriers can earn higher returns with which to
acquire capital for modernization, innovation, and selective expansion of their capacity. Removal of truck regulatory restrictions
will enable the regulated firms to make the adjustments in their
routes, services and rates required for highway transport to perform
its most economic role.

Enlarging the efficient role of rail transport should reduce the
social costs of current transport and assist urban areas to solve
their congestion and passenger transport problems. Minimization of
accidents, congestion, noise, and smog would come from transference
of long-distance freight to the railroads, with fewer large truck
combinations on the highways. Indirectly, by reducing the needs
expressed for additional high-capacity highways, more capital can
become available for investments in socially efficient rapid transit
and intercity high-speed trains in corridors, while remaining sufficient to improve highways for their best uses. Thus, society will
benefit in yet another way.

Promotion of Transport by
Government Investment and Subsidy

Government, as a public entrepreneur in ownership and operation
of transport facilities and in giving financial aids and subsidies,
has become the controlling factor in shaping the development of the
entire transport system. Although many of the basic way, terminal
and navigational facilities for highway, air, and inland water carriers would have been developed either by private enterprise or toll-
financing authorities if they had not been provided directly as
government enterprises, those facilities would have been on a smaller
scale overall and with far less subsidy than has actually been
involved.

National, Regional and Local Emphasis
in Transport Promotional Policy

Regions of the country, states, and municipalities have long
been active in promoting public transport development. As inland
waterways requiring deeper channels, locks and navigation aids to
become navigable are localized where the rivers and lakes happen to
be located, the promotional pressures for public investment usually
come from contiguous or nearby cities, states and regions. Thus,
though most improved inland waterways today are planned and financed
on the Federal level and operated by the Corps of Engineers, regional
and local planning is inherently involved. This is especially true
of marginal or submarginal waterways as they do not necessarily contribute to development of the national economy. As the efficient
central waterways of the Mississippi River System and the Great Lakes
have obviously contributed to national economic development in a
manner much like the railways, they command wider support and are
planned with more attention to national development objectives.
Their role in supplying efficient transport would continue even if

384

194

user fees were assessed. The situation is different with the marginal and submarginal waterways -- full user fees might contract the traffic and raise the question of continued operation considering maintenance and operating costs.

Promotion of modern highways is considerably different from that of waterways, yet it has common features. A major difference is that the states and their subdivisions own and operate the highways and streets, and until recent years, have largely planned and financed them as well. The Federal Bureau of Public Roads has granted matching aid from general funds up to 1956 and from Federal user fees since that time toward financing the construction costs of the state systems having general and interstate, or national, economic significance. State and Federal planning and development has been a cooperative process, but with increasing Federal involvement. Although state user fees were inadequate to cover the entire cost of highway modernization in the early years and a long period existed in which Federal user fees were not assessed, highway users, unlike water users, have had to pay significantly toward costs of highways almost from the beginning.

In addition to being the largest factor in the revolutionary changes in the transport system and in the division of passenger and freight traffic among the modes since 1920, highway development has radically changed the location and style of living of urban populations, the configuration and functions of cities, the role of the small town in rural areas, and the location and relocation of many industries. Unfortunately, it has also produced the lion's share of the most discouraging of the social costs from transport, such as excessive noise, health-damaging smog, and a high accident toll of fatalities, personal injuries and property damage each year. Included also are some social problems associated with central cities; inadequate urban transport alternatives for urban residents and job-seekers; and the decline of the railroads in a situation in which highway transport cannot match the low unit costs of rail transport or entirely substitute for rail service, even in the passenger field.

The current problems that arise from highway development have their most serious impacts in urban communities and densely populated regions. Although significant economic problems have arisen concerning urban goods movements by truck, the most serious problems associated with urban highway development and use have involved personal travel. A key problem is congestion at times of peak use of streets, freeways and parking facilities. Another is the decline of public transit service in recent decades, seriously affecting some classes of urban residents. A third is growing social costs, to which highway solutions for passenger travel definitely contribute.

On the other hand, overdeveloped truck transport of goods has a far more general impact on the nation as a whole. First, if regulatory and promotional policies do not change, and unless the railroads achieve improved management and pricing, the nation will face permanent government ownership of some or all railroads instead of temporary take-overs as during wartime or labor emergencies. This would

385

create widespread demands for the Federal Government to continue payments of the huge local property taxes now paid annually by the railroads in support of schools and local roads. General Federal tax revenues or highway user revenues might also be drawn upon to support the subsidization of some essential rail services and even to raise capital for rail investment. Alternatively, significant restrictions might be placed on the development and use of highways and other public transport facilities. Second, railway passenger services have already been greatly curtailed and even the National Railway Passenger Corporation plan enacted by the Congress in 1970 will save only a moderate mileage and quantity of intercity rail passenger service. Third, low rail profitability will turn the railroads more actively in the direction of abandoning unprofitable lines and freight services, particularly in rural areas. Finally, the higher total cost of overland transport, because of the huge misallocations of traffic between road and rail, already increases the cost of goods for all consumers.

The Federal role in the development of air transport has been predominant, although local authorities have planned, managed and financed airports terminals. Thus, the U.S. Post Office Department started the first commercial airlines and long regulated and subsidized the trunk airlines through its airmail contracts. From the beginning, the Federal Government provided and operated the civil airways. The CAB, guided by promotional guidelines in the 1938 Act, regulated the trunk airlines to promote a rapid development of air transport and aircraft manufacturing[33]. The CAB has also given the smaller cities and towns scheduled air service that would not have developed without continued airmail subsidies, at least until the fairly recent organization of the third-level airlines employing small but speedy and safe aircraft afforded an alternative.

In view of the differential speed of air transport which makes that mode particularly efficient in long-distance travel, national planning for national transport improvement and objectives has always been predominant in air transport. Although large subsidies have been involved in airmail payments, in the long-time lack and present inadequacy of user fees for airways, and in insufficient landing fees, there can be little question about the economic contribution of air transport to development. The only questionable area would concern the economic contribution of the local service airlines which depend on large subsidies in an attempt to equalize the travel opportunities of rural and small communities with those of large cities.

In many ways, the entire nation has been made more productive by the speed and efficiency of air transport, giving travel, educational and recreational opportunities that could not have occurred otherwise. The economic advantages of airline travel, however, probably have gone largely to the huge cities and population clusters, which have been in the best position to generate the traffic volumes required to support frequent, nonstop and competitive services. Because the demand for air cargo of very high-value goods is concentrated on the routes between large centers, most of the air cargo services have been attracted to the large metropolitan areas. Air cargo, however, has yet to attain a significant role in freight

386

transport or in the location of many industries. And though the air services available at rural communities and small towns still receive heavy airmail subsidies, they are distinctly inferior to those available at large cities.

Although most benefits from air travel go to the large metropolises, urban communities also experience the great bulk of its disbenefits in the form of uncompensated social costs. Residents of large cities must necessarily experience the noise of aircraft in terminal operations, the smog contributed by jet planes, and bear much of the tax subsidy costs for local airports that are not self-sustaining. Additionally, they experience street and highway congestion from flows of persons to and from airports.

From this discussion, the following are evident. First, the supply of public transport facilities has been planned to bring about national economic gains and development as well as to satisfy regional development objectives. Necessarily, some transport systems, such as the railroads and the trunk airlines, have been planned primarily with national needs in mind, and others, such as the local service airlines and many inland waterways, have been planned largely to satisfy regional needs. Rail rapid transit systems, such as the ones under construction in San Francisco and Washington, D.C., have been planned to provide improved home-to-work and other travel for the population of localized urban areas. Second, in the highly mobile and integrated American economy, the beneficial and disbeneficial impacts of development of public transport facilities can affect almost all citizens, although their incidence is concentrated in the large urban centers and corridors. Urban and corridor person-transport problems are among the most difficult ones remaining to be solved, and these will very likely command the greatest attention in regional planning of transport development in the future. Third, viable solutions for the inefficiencies and inadequacies of the nation's promotional and regulatory policies will require attention to national, regional and local problems. Planning and action (though not organization for planning) will necesarily have to be as comprehensive as are the elements of the transport problem to be solved.

Deficiencies in Developmental Policies for Transport

In several ways, state and federal promotional policies for transport have been deficient. Investment in highways, airways and airports, and inland waterways have recurrently been undertaken on the basis of political demands as well as on economic demands. Political demands can be congruent with economic demands, but often they are not, reflecting log-rolling, the organized interests of strong pressure groups, and an acquisitive motivation of communities and areas for regional or local development. Moreover, the investment planning process for public transport facilities usually does not consider whether the most productive investment might be in another mode of transport. Instead, emphasis is placed on ascertaining which of the several investments possible in one mode (for example highways) will be given priority. And, public investment decisions are not made under the same economic constraints as railway and

387

pipeline investments. We have no user fees on domestic inland waterways to aid the markets for rail and barge services to ascertain true
economic demands. User fees have only recently been assessed for
airway services and past fees to finance airways and airports have
not covered all the costs[34]. Highway user fees have not been fine-
ly adjusted to the differential investment and maintenance costs of
the demands of the different classes of motor vehicles for special
features and services[35]. The cost-benefit studies made to test
whether public transport projects are economic are often not rigorous
enough to confirm that a proposed investment should be made. In inland waterway projects, overestimation of benefits and underestimation of costs have been chronic[36]. Finally, until recently, none
of the indirect or social costs of a public transport facility investment have been counted, although the indirect or social benefits
have often been taken into account.

The tradition that user fee revenues going into state and federal highway trust funds must be spent on highways is another source of
misallocation of capital in transport. Those funds provide an automatic source of capital for reinvestment and new investment in highways of gigantic magnitude. The necessity of spending almost all
highway user revenues collected from national or statewide levies
only for highway purposes, and the fact that government is in a
monopoly position in imposing such levies, result in over-financing
highways. User charges thus provide no sufficient economic test of
what outlays are justified for specific highway projects or systems.
Overall highway investment has been greater than if each project had
to compete in the capital markets for funds and if user fees or tolls
had been imposed to pay its full long-term costs[37].

In addition to factors that unduly expand public transport investment, railways and pipelines have to bear ordinary property taxes
on their ways, terminal facilities, and equipment. If net income is
earned they must pay state and Federal income taxes. Of course,
carriers in the modes using public facilities pay equivalent property
taxes on their equipment and owned terminals and income taxes on net
income. But the government agencies do not pay property taxes on
their immense fixed facilities, or income taxes on any net income
earned or which could be earned from their operation.

In total, then, public transport investments have probably been
considerably larger than otherwise would be the case. More capacity
has been installed than would be economically justifiable if the same
pricing conditions and criteria of investment applied to both private
and public transport investments. The result is rapid growth of the
newer modes dependent on public facilities, and growth in excess of
the true economic demands for their services.

In sharp contrast, the railroads have been relatively stagnant
in postwar traffic and revenue growth until the 1960s, and their
overall market shares have continued to decline. Overall rates of
capital investment have been low, efficient rail cars and locomotives
have often been in short supply, and their technical innovations and
modernization rates have been slowed by lack of ability to command
capital.

388

While exact impacts cannot be ascertained, there can be little question that government promotional policies have contributed to considerable uneconomic diversion of rail traffic and revenues. Those public policies have worked hand in hand with regulatory policies in lowering the market shares of the railroads, in hastening their retirement from many passenger services, in contributing to their low rates of return, and in bringing about underinvestment and too little modernization.

Moreover, enormous waste in the expenditure of public funds has occurred from overinvestment in transport, such as in marginal inland waterways, the rural Interstate System, county roads and beyond those justified by traffic or the willingness of benefited landowners to support, and airports not justified by prospective traffic. Other sources of waste of public funds are the premature breakup and excessive maintenance of highway surfaces and the premature obsolescence of bridges because of growing volumes of heavy-axle and heavy grossload truck movements over many highway sections not constructed for such vehicles[38]. The application of nonrigorous and nonuniform investment criteria and preferential tax and user fee treatment are factors in overinvestment in those public facilities, specifically by adding to the benefits and the traffic demands advanced to justify public investment and by not counting future social costs from the operation of motor vehicles, aircraft and even subsidized barges. Altogether, those resource wastes could possibly match the huge annual costs from the misallocation of traffic on account of regulatory policy and uneconomic pricing of freight services. But the precise costs of resource misallocation from regulation as distinct from promotion are not known. Additional research to measure them more closely would be well justified. Importantly, however, regulatory reform alone would be incapable of achieving an efficient allocation of resources in transport. Correction of overinvestment in public transport facilities and underinvestment in the railroads will also require major change in the promotional and investment policies of the state and Federal Governments, and substantial adjustment of state and Federal user fee policies toward greater economy.

Crises in Transport Supply
Requiring Transport Policy Change

Several real crisis situations have arisen in transport due to longstanding public transport policies. These suggest drastic changes in both regulatory policy and in transport promotional policies. The first involves the future of private ownership and operation of the American railroads. This is more seriously threatened than ever before. Several large and small railroads are in bankruptcy and a number of other bankruptcies may occur in spite of industry and ICC faith in mergers as a solution to the rail problem. Further, the rates of return of many other railroads have sunk to extremely low levels. The implications of a do-nothing policy with respect to the railroads since World War II have now become visible. They reveal themselves in the Federal Government's decision to share in financing a minimum quantity of intercity rail passenger service; in the threatened abandonment of up to 100,000 miles or more of railway routes for freight traffic; and in the possible nationalization of the Penn-Central and other roads.

389

Second, a crisis has been developing in urban transportation. The mass transit systems of large cities and the bus systems of many small cities typically have deteriorated in equipment and service. And public transit, except for taxicabs, is nonexistent in many American communities. In spite of declining or static patronage of transit systems since 1945, many believe that rail rapid transit (or possibly bus mass transit on separate lanes or ways) is the desirable long-term solution for airport access and airport location problems as well as for home-to-work travel in the great cities. They recognize that capital subsidies and Federal aid will be required to finance rapid transit, but point out that demand has been lower than it would be if satisfactory alternatives to automobiles and ordinary frequent-stop bus services were in existence, and if freeway and expressway users paid peak-use fees and full congestion prices for use of such facilities. They look to rail rapid's capacity to lessen smog and noise levels in addition to its speed of service as unique advantages. Others contend that rail rapid transit will seldom be a viable solution except in the great cities already having such systems. They argue that autos and bus systems serve the decentralizing urban areas better and at lower unit costs, except where traffic densities are extremely high. Before new capital-intense rail systems are undertaken, they argue that vigorous effort should be made to improve the efficiency of bus systems on reserved lanes, to explore new transit technology further and to regulate highway use more effectively[39].

Third, vehicle congestion has limited the speed and increased the cost of transport in the growing corridors of urban communities along the Atlantic Seaboard, the Great Lakes, the coastal area of California between San Diego and San Francisco, and along the Puget Sound to Portland, Oregon. Some of these megalopolises may eventually require high-speed train service similar to that between Tokyo and Osaka in Japan. In the U.S., only a small beginning has been made to test the market for high-speed intercity service, by the Metroliner between New York and Washington, D.C., and the Turbo-Train between New York and Boston. Possibly, a massive capital investment might be desirable to test the market for high-speed train service more definitively and its possibilities for reducing the social costs of excessive congestion.

The effects of not funding better solutions to the urban and megalopolitan passenger transport problems and of not solving the railroad problem are becoming obvious to many. Traffic congestion at peak periods becomes ever more harassing, more costly in time and expense, and always more fraught with noise and air pollution. Numerous classes of urban residents do not have a means of travel alternative to public transit, and some low-income groups find their employment and educational opportunities limited. Thus, many wonder why this country cannot afford at least one high-speed train on the Japanese model and why they cannot travel in passenger trains between cities as easily and comfortably as in Europe.

In truth, the underlying crisis in U.S. transport lies in the automatic investment standards and political motivation that dominate

390

public investment in transport facilities. ,Highway investments automatically reach ever higher levels as users revenues pour into state
and Federal highway trust funds, enlarged partly because of the de-
teriorating alternatives that the unbalanced transport investment
policy makes available. The continuing community and political pressures exerted for development of highly marginal inland waterways for
regional advantage comprise another example of the crisis in public
investment standards for transport development. At a time when the
capacity of alternative highways and railways is ample for additional
freight traffic, marginal but expensive inland waterway projects are
still being promoted and transport projects promising greater social
returns continue to be neglected.

Adjustment of Transport Promotion
to an Efficient Role

The obvious first step toward more efficient investment in public transport facilities is to subject all state and Federal transport projects, whatever the mode, to far more rigorous economic analysis. This requires the uniform and competent application of fully
economic investment criteria to all modes in which public investments
occur in the manner originally contemplated when legislation to create the U.S. Department of Transportation was under consideration.

Priority lists of individual transport projects should be established in such manner as to differentiate those with high net benefits from those with low or negative net benefits. Then, investments
in specific projects should be undertaken in the order that will
bring the largest real net benefits and make the best use of scarce
capital and other resources. To assure that result, it would be
essential that investments in a single mode cannot automatically and
excessively be made just because user funds or other capital have
become available to the authorities. Also essential is insuring that
the best net-benefit producing projects in each mode will be undertaken only to the extent that those projects can meet their opportunity costs by out-producing projects in alternative modes in real net
benefits to society.

If transport development is to be fully efficient, it is necessary to compare the net benefits of particular public transport projects against the benefits to be realized from alternative investment
projects in privately-owned transport facilities. There is a growing
literature on the criteria and procedures for making efficient public
project investments, some of which also examines the problem of evaluating public investments against private investments in terms of
social efficiency[40]. Suffice it to say, the productive public projects must be differentiated from the unproductive ones as expertly
as this is done by private firms having the advantage of operating in
highly developed markets and under complete, though often imperfect,
price systems for final goods, the factors of production, and capital
funds. Already benefit-cost ratios are commonly used in appraising
inland waterway and other public transport investments; for many significant highway projects, revenue-cost or rate-of-return tests similar to those used in private enterprise have been utilized. The urgent need is for more rigor in avoiding double-counting of benefits;

391

in subjecting the indirect or social benefits to tests equivalent to the willingness of particular consumers to pay for project services; in avoidance of underestimation of the future costs of the carriers using public transport facilities and overestimation of the future costs of the closest alternative mode; and the expenditure of more effort to count explicitly all of the social costs of a public transport project as well as the indirect or social benefits. A requirement of special importance is that realistic interest and discount rates be employed to represent the social cost of capital raised from taxpayers. The assumption that such capital is costless or relatively without cost begs the question and often renders public investment analysis incapable of finding truly efficient public investments.

The second step toward improving investment in public transport facilities is for the Congress to act quickly to close the gaps in user charging. Primarily, this means enactment of suitable and sufficient user fees or tolls for the inland waterways. Federal studies have been made of the economic case for and against user charging for waterways and to ascertain the user fee structure best designed for that mode. Only the strong opposition of the barge lines, the large corporate users of barge service at uneconomically low rates, and the nearby communities benefiting from subsidized transport prevent a return to the 19th Century toll-pricing policies for inland waterways. The myth should be ended that inland waterways are free goods to their users and that their services need not be priced as are other transport services.

In addition, however, existing user fees, both state and Federal, for highway services require adjustment to increase the payments from large and heavy vehicles, especially the diesel-powered vehicles, to closer equality with the long-run marginal construction, maintenance and operation costs occasioned. Although finding the differential cost of highway services for each class of motor vehicles is complicated by the existence of fixed and common costs in the highway function, a great deal of Federal-state test-road and other research has been done on that problem. Sufficient information is available and has been reported to the state legislatures and the Congress to enable immediate action to be taken toward eliminating the underpayments of large and heavy vehicles[41].

Much more consideration than in the past should be given to the social costs of highway use. Because of air and noise pollution, displacement of residences and business units, and displacement of alternative forms of travel without substituting for the displaced modes, user prices should raise the social marginal cost of highway use above the highway-service (or private) marginal cost[42]. Hence, user fees should be higher than levels just sufficient to cover the long-run marginal costs of rendering highway services whenever those social costs are tangible and significant, and especially when they can be at least roughly measured. Moreover, when congestion exists the social marginal cost of highway use rises steeply above the levels during uncongested periods (and above private marginal costs). Peak-period user fees or tolls should be high to equate with the social marginal costs occasioned by congestion[43].

392

A third step toward improving transport promotional policy involves some pooling of the trust fund revenues earmarked for highway or airway and airport development with other revenues available for financing public transport investments such as rapid transit. From the pooled financial resources, Federal and state aid would be granted so as to bring about the most efficient investments in whatever mode of transport the high priority projects happened to appear.

It should be recognized that the case for earmarking user funds for expenditure only for the particular facilities desired by those who pay the fees is subject to limitations. First, expending all highway user funds automatically for highway purposes can lead to overinvestment in highways. Second, the need for trust funds to be totally reinvested in a particular mode's basic facilities is greater in the developmental period for a new transport technology than after it has matured. Thus, in the early days of motor transport technology and in view of its evident potential for improving transport service in many ways, it made good economic sense to utilize all revenues collected from highway user fees for investment in the necessary road system to test and improve the new technology and rapidly to establish a new mode of transport. Now that motor transport has become well established and an excellent and extensive highway, road and street network has come into being, the excess user revenues over the annual maintenance and operating costs and the necessary replacements of capital required by continuing traffic flows should be considered as a free pool of capital funds. Capital in such pools should be invested in whatever projects in whatever modes, including highways, happen to have the potential of producing the maximum net benefits to society.

Various objections have been raised to opening highway and other trust funds for investments in other modes. Some fear that lower returns might be realized from alternative modal investments, or that diversion of revenues could make it easier for politically inspired allocations of capital to finance low-productivity investments. The argument is made that benefit-cost studies do not necessarily give assurance that uneconomic investments will not take place, as questionable investments in inland waterways have been made on the basis of extensive benefit-cost justifications that exaggerate the benefits. Additionally, it has been argued that it would be inequitable to ask highway users to subsidize users of rail rapid transit in addition to paying for highways.

The possibility exists that a partial opening of highway trust funds for investment in other modes would occasionally provide funds for investments in transit or in politically-inspired facilities that are not economically justified. The remedy for this, however, is to arrange for an unbiased planning organization to make rigorous analyses for alternative projects. Moreover, there is evidence that the process of automatic reinvestment of highway trust funds has far from eliminated all politically-inspired road investments. And as the social costs from air and noise pollution and relocations are far from being fully counted as highway costs to be covered by user payments, it cannot be assumed that users always fully pay for their

393

highway services. If those social costs were assessed and peak
charges were levied to reduce both congestion and the otherwise required highway expansion, the excess revenues that would accumulate
could more logically be employed to compensate all persons disadvantaged by highways or to provide alternative facilities to lessen the
social costs of highways, than to expand the highway facilities more
or less automatically[44]. With user fees lacking for waterways and
inadequate to cover all relevant public costs of highway use, the
derived demands for waterways and highways can be exaggerated by the
market, and the demand for alternative transport facilities can be
understated. In any case, the problems that have arisen from relying
on highways for urban travel seem so obvious and difficult to solve
by building more freeways that some partial opening of highway user
funds appears to be justified for investment in appropriate transit
systems for which good benefit-cost justifications exist.

   With the allocation of trust fund revenues for investment in
alternative transport limited to the excess user revenues from peak
charges and the user charge increments to cover the social costs of
highways and highway use, highway users would not be subsidizing the
riders of rapid transit systems. Highway users would be paying fully
for the social marginal costs of highways, but they would not be
overpaying as implied in the subsidy argument. These and other excess revenues would be a capital pool, available for investment in
any mode yielding the largest net benefits. To the extent that geographical inequities might arise from diversion of highway trust
funds for rapid transit, these can be mitigated or eliminated by
utilizing the excess user revenues collected from the urban areas
whose rapid transit systems are to receive aids from the trust funds.
Again, the apportionment of state highway user funds among road systems has long created significant inequities, mainly against the
urban populations and in favor of those who live on and use county
roads[45]. In the light of this widespread situation, the complete
avoidance of some inequities can be considered far less important
than financing balanced transport systems in urban areas to avoid
excessive congestion and social costs and the other inadequacies of
highway solutions.

   Since the 1930s, highway and other public transport investments
have at times been justified primarily as a counter-depression device
to increase employment and stimulate business, as the best way to
utilize public expenditures to deal with depressed areas, or as a
fruitful way of insuring real economic growth over the long run. But
experience has indicated that highway programs take too long to plan
and organize to be of much aid in increasing employment during recession periods; that often it takes far more than a program of building
roads in rural areas to stimulate industrial development in a depressed region[46]; and that the 1956 Federal policy of utilizing
highway expenditures to stimulate a rapid rate of real economic
growth has several limitations[47]. One of these drawbacks is the
huge annual cost of misallocation of traffic away from the low-cost
rail mode. Another is the threat of general bankruptcy of the railroads and their nationalization. Hence, the time has come to reeval-
uate the gains of using highway and other public transport development for general economic development purposes, against losses,

394

failures and wastes of public funds that heavy reliance on that expenditure policy occasions.

Implications for National, Regional,
State and Local Planning

In a setting of transport deregulation, the only planning required would be to fix the timing of deregulation actions to minimize the transitional effects of moving toward freer transport markets, and to reexamine the regulatory standards and policies to be changed by regulatory bodies to allow competition to work productively. The U.S. Department of Transportation is the principal agency to plan deregulation and the series of steps to be taken in that direction, although the Antitrust Division of the Department of Justice and other departments also have roles to play. If the regulatory bodies are to be entrusted to relax regulatory policies under minimal statutory changes, they would have the leading planning role. But even here, the Department of Transportation and other agencies would have significant research inputs and would serve as public advocates of desirable changes.

As the important regulatory policies affecting transport are determined at the Federal level and the need is to arrange for transport markets to work more freely, regional planning could contribute little toward adjusting regulation to an efficient role. However, the states that regulate wholly intrastate transportation would have a role to play in planning regulatory reform within their jurisdictions. As some states, for example, New York, have already transferred transport regulation from independent commissions to state departments of transportation in an effort to improve policy and to coordinate regulatory and promotional policies, it can be expected that many states would follow the Federal Government if the latter should substantially deregulate transport. Regulation of carrier rates, services and returns seems an unworkable and blunt tool for promoting regional economic development.

The application of rigorous and more uniform investment criteria for public transport facilities and more efficient user pricing will obviously require centralized planning of the public transport development function at whatever level is appropriate under the circumstances. At the Federal level, the U.S. Department of Transportation already has general jurisdiction over Federal highway investment and aids, civil airway development and operations, and the grant of aids for construction of civil airports. The DOT does not have jurisdiction over inland waterway and merchant marine investments, and the DOT has limited statutory power to coordinate investment planning and project reporting by the action agencies under its general supervision. DOT jurisdiction should at least be extended over the investment planning activities for waterways and the merchant marine; its power to subject Federal investment planning for all modes to common and relevant economic investment criteria and to coordinate the investment recommendations of all action agencies should be increased.

The potential benefits of utilizing the DOT as an effective coordinating body would be considerable over the long run. Congressional Committees and the Congress would then have full knowledge of

395

the benefits and costs of alternative transport development project plans that would come before them for consideration. Overall, this would more surely lead to rejection of the least beneficial projects and to a more balanced development program. Though Congress might still vote to undertake some low-priority transport projects, the number of such cases undoubtedly would fall. Regions and communities would be less able to press successfully for projects that create benefits to them during the construction stage but have no real promise of stimulating economic growth afterwards. More effective means can be found to aid disadvantaged regions and communities without creating an oversupply of expensive fixed transport facilities.

At the state level, too, urgent need exists for state departments of transportation to be established with power to plan and to integrate statewide transport developments for all modes in which state investments are made or state aid given[48]. Like the Federal DOT, those agencies should rigorously apply economic investment standards as uniformly as possible over all modes under their jurisdiction and work out more efficient user fee structures. As in the case of Federal-state cooperation in planning the highway and airport functions, the state DOTs and the Federal DOT would often work closely together in analysis and priority evaluation of public transport investment projects. The process not only would further inject the expertise of the Federal DOT's economists and engineers into state and local planning, but it would reciprocally contribute materially to the knowledge and expertise of Federal planners.

The transport problems of large metropolitan areas are of sufficient magnitude and complexity as to require those urban regions to engage in investment analysis essential to selection of the best projects within their orbits. Those urban regions require organizations for planning, investing in, and operating transport facilities. However, as illustrated by the Port of New York Authority, a compact or other interstate type of regional planning organization will be essential when projects extend into or affect two or more states[49]. This might also be true of regional airports serving two or more states. As both Federal and state aids for metropolitan or corridor transport development will likely be on a vaster scale in the future, cooperative planning and investment analysis between the Federal DOT and metropolitan or urban regional authorities, and between the state DOTs and those authorities, will also become essential.

On the other hand, far less need exists for regional transportation authorities beyond the urban or corridor-type regional organization. An exception might exist with underdeveloped or disadvantaged regions (such as the Appalachian Region), but in such cases there can be considerable doubt that large-scale transport development programs will transform a region into a diversified and growing economy. By cooperative planning efforts the Federal and state DOTs can discover the good cases for transport opportunities that promote regional diversification and development. Only the failure of present agencies would provide a good case for establishing a new set of regional planning organizations intermediate between the states and the Federal Government.

396

Summary and Conclusions

Government in the U.S. has a long history of transport promotion and regulation. Both types of government intervention have powerfully influenced the development of transport systems and the rates and services rendered to national, regional and state economies.

Probably promotional policies have been of greater long-term significance in influencing transport and economic development than regulation. Those policies have involved virtually every major transport mode and level of government.

Government regulation began with the railroads in response to marked monopoly or cartel conditions, and until 1920 sought to limit excessively high and discriminating rates. In general, regulation did not attempt to rationalize transport industries until 1920 and particularly until after passage of the Motor Carrier Act of 1935. Prior to 1935, the principal regulatory tools were the maximum rate power and controls over discrimination. But with extension of regulation to interstate motor and water carrriers in 1935 and 1940, regulation fundamentally changed character to the present-day emphasis on restricting both intramodal and intermodal competition. Under this scheme, primary reliance has been on entry controls and minimum rate regulation to eliminate "destructive" competition. In view of growing competitive areas in transport after 1920 this change was paradoxical, and obviously motivated mostly toward producing benefits for carriers rather than consumers.

To the extent early ICC regulation was effective, it substituted for competitive forces that were not strong enough or sufficiently pervasive to limit rates to cost and prevent uneconomic discrimination. Early ICC regulation eliminated much long-short haul discrimination and often gave relief from rate discriminations to particular shippers, producing areas, and low-grade commodities unable to stand high rates. The ICC basically accepted the value-of-service, or discriminating, rate structure that the railroads had already adopted, finding it well fitted the railroads' economic characteristics and was promotive of national and regional development. Consequently, up to the 1930s, ICC regulation promoted development that was already taking place on the basis of other economic factors.

The new regulation starting in 1935 gradually produced economic effects that have stimulated widespread dissatisfaction and growing demands for a policy of allowing competition to work in transport. Studies have shown that the highly competitive trucking industry has been cartelized under regulation and that the motor carriers adopted the railroad value-of-service rates, with modifications. Restrictive entry control has fragmented trucking markets; reduced the number of competing firms; increased the size of trucking firms far beyond economies of scale; and together with minimum rate regulation has encouraged costly service competition, excess capacity due to certificate restrictions, higher costs and rates, and high rates of return.

397

The new regulation originally designed to assist the continuation of rail common carrier services and rate equalization responsibilities, has turned out to provide incentives for more rapid expansion of truck and barge transport than otherwise would have occurred. Moreover, it stimulated greater investment in public highway and waterway facilities. Thus, the new regulation has gone hand in hand with the promotional policies of government in the last several decades in encouraging overdevelopment of the modes dependent on public facilities and underdevelopment of the rail network. Even airline regulation has increasingly come under attack as restricting rate competition and leading to high rate levels, overencouraging service competition and vast excess seat capacity, and bringing about carriers too large to be efficient and able to adjust profitably to changing market conditions.

Without the vast highway, airway and airport, and inland waterway systems provided by state and Federal investment and subsidies, the great growth of highway, air and barge transport could not have taken place. Beyond doubt, government promotion has expanded those types of public facilities beyond the capacities that the market would have provided. Thus, motor, barge, and air carriers have ample and riskless capacity in ways, channels and locks, and terminals to accommodate rapid expansion. They can more quickly take advantage of technological improvements that lower their costs and make their services faster. Their rates can be lower than otherwise to the extent that user fees are not assessed or are insufficient to cover the long-run public and social costs of use of public transport facilities. The effects on the railroads, however, have been adverse and far from wholly economic. To what extent uneconomic promotional policies for the modes dependent on public facilities have contributed to uneconomic diversion of traffic and revenues from the railroads is unknown. Nevertheless, there can be little question that government promotional policies have contributed to considerable uneconomic diversion and to the economic decline of the railways.

Promotional and regulatory policy have both contributed to the present crises in transport, including the threat of permanent government ownership and operation of the railroads, unbalanced transport supply situations in both large and small cities, and the growing problem of providing access to airports, relief from the social costs of air and highway transport, and adequate person transport in corridor regions. Adjusting government regulatory and promotional policies to more efficient roles will make significant contributions to solving the intercity and urban transport problems.

With respect to regulation, the fact that transport industries, except for the oil pipelines, have become essentially and pervasively competitive should be accepted, and regulatory policy should be made to conform to this market condition. Thus, either the ICC and the CAB should change their entry and exit, minimum rate, and merger policies to allow competition to work more freely, or substantial deregulation by legislative means should take place. In the case of freight transport, control of entry and prescription of minimum rates for truck and barge carriers could desirably be eliminated, although

398

208

some discrimination and maximum rate control of any rail monopoly markets might still be essential. At the minimum, the standards in the National Transportation Policy that provide the legal basis for protective, cartel-like regulation restrictive of competition should be eliminated; a variable cost standard for minimum competitive rates should be adopted; and the wasteful restrictions on commodities, return hauls, routes and points should be removed from certificates and permits. Substantial change in CAB regulation, too, is probably desirable to permit competition to work more fully in determining fare levels, to reduce excess capacity and to eliminate inefficient carriers.

The obvious first step toward more efficient investment in public transport facilities is to subject all state and Federal transport projects to far more rigorous economic analysis. This will require uniform application of fully economic investment criteria to all modes. It will also require drawing up priority lists of individual transport projects to differentiate those with high net benefits from those with low or negative net benefits. Finally, investments in specific transport projects should be undertaken in the order that will bring the largest real net benefits and make the best use of scarce resources. The ability of a proposed transport investment in one mode to meet the full opportunity cost of an alternative project in an alternative mode should be proven.

As it will be difficult to make efficient public transport investments and to avoid some misallocations of traffic without user fees for all modes, the gaps in user fee requirements should be closed. Too, existing user fees for highway, airway and airport services should be more closely adjusted to the long-run marginal costs for each class of user. Thus, user fees or tolls should be enacted for the inland waterways. Diesel differentials in motor fuel taxes should be enacted to raise the user contributions of large and heavy vehicles. Property tax equivalents and increments to compensate for the social costs of smog, noise, relocations, displacement of essential public services, including peak-use charges, should be assessed on motor vehicles, barges and aircraft to the extent feasible.

A final step toward improving transport promotional policy involves opening up earmarked trust fund revenues for financing other public transport investments in cases where good benefit-cost justifications exist for such investments. Excess user revenues over the annual maintenance and operating costs and the necessary replacements of capital required by continuing traffic flows should be considered as a free pool of capital funds for investment in whatever mode the projects of highest net benefit actually occur.

Regional planning could contribute little toward adjusting regulation to an efficient role. This will have to be done either by the regulatory bodies themselves under legislative directive or by specific legislation to deregulate transport. In adjusting transport promotional policy for a more economic role, the principal planning and analytical tasks will be done by the U.S. Department of Transportation, state departments of transportation and municipal or

399

interstate compact authorities. The power of the Federal DOT to coordinate Federal transport investments should be strengthened. More state DOTs should be established to plan and coordinate public transport development within the states. Federal, state and municipal planning groups should cooperate fully and give close attention to regional development needs. A case for special regional authorities may exist in a very few cases where special problems exist such as corridor transport, but not for general establishment of such authorities for transport planning.

NOTES

1. For the history, magnitude, problems and effects of the promotional role of government in transport development, see C.L. Dearing and Wilfred Owen, National Transportation Policy, The Brookings Institution, Washington, 1949, Chaps. I-VIII; James C. Nelson, Railroad Transportation and Public Policy, The Brookings Institution, Washington, 1959, Chaps. 2-4, and "Policy Issues and Economic Effects of Public Aids to Domestic Transport," Law and Contemporary Problems, Autumn 1959, pp. 531-556; and Association of American Railroads, Government Expenditures for Highway, Waterway, and Air Facilities and Private Expenditures for Railroad Facilities, Washington, D.C., April 1970.

2. For example, see Gabriel Kolko, Railroads and Regulation, 1877-1916, Princeton University Press, Princeton, 1965. But see the review article on that book by R.W. Harbeson in The Journal of Economic History, June 1967, pp. 230-242; and C.L. Dearing, "Transportation," in Lyon and Associates, Government and Economic Life, The Brookings Institution, Washington, 1940, Vol. II, Chap. XXII, pp. 753-770.

3. K.T. Healy, The Economics of Transportation in America, The Ronald Press Company, New York, 1940, pp. 202-232, 237, 240-250, 285-286, 462, 464, 488, and 501.

4. The widening public interest in ICC reform or abolition apparently prompted The Ralph Nader Study Group Report on the Interstate Commerce Commission and Transportation, The Interstate Commerce Omission by Robert C. Fellmeth and Associates, Grossman Publishers, Inc., New York, 1970. See pp. 324-325 for the Nader Group's recommendation to abolish the ICC.

5. But see W.A. Jordan, Airline Regulation in America, Effects and Implications, The Johns Hopkins Press, Baltimore, 1970, pp. 13, 53-56. 70-72, 131-133, 143, 155-157, 175-177, and 223-244, criticizing CAB regulation for emphasizing service rather than rate competition.

6. C.L. Dearing, "Transportation," op. cit., pp. 842-853 and 857-863; R.L. Dewey, "Transport Coordination," Transportation and National Policy, National Resources Planning Board, Washington, D.C., May 1942, pp. 154-160; and J.C. Nelson, "The Motor Carrier Act of 1935," The Journal of Political Economy, August 1936, pp. 464-504, especially pp. 497-504, and "New Concepts in Transportation Regulation," Transportation and National Policy, op. cit., pp. 197-237.

7. J.C. Nelson, Railroad Transportation and Public Policy, op. cit., pp. 171-179, 184-186 and 191-192; J.R. Meyer, M.J. Peck, John Stenason and Charles Zwick, The Economics of Competition in the Transportation Industries, Harvard University Press, Cambridge, 1959, pp. 145-167, 184-186 and 189-196; E.W. Williams, Jr., and D.W.

400

Bluestone, Rationale of Federal Transportation Policy, U.S. Department of Commerce, Washington, D.C., April 1960, pp. 4-7; G.W. Hilton, The Transportation Act of 1958, Indiana University Press, Bloomington, 1969, pp. 205-207; R.W. Harbeson, "Toward Better Resource Allocation in Transport," The Journal of Law and Economics, October 1969, pp. 321-338; and A.F. Friedlaender, The Dilemma of Freight Transport Regulation, The Brookings Institution, Washington, D.C., 1969, pp. 65-99.

8. J.C. Nelson, "New Concepts in Transportation Regulation," op. cit., pp. 204 and 232-233.

9. Ibid., pp. 204-216, 230, and 233-237.

10. For an extensive treatment of the economic theory rationale for motor carrier regulation, to the extent one exists, see C.J. Oort, The Economic Regulation of the Road Transport Industry, International Bank for Reconstruction and Development, Washington, D.C., Report No. EC-177, September 1970.

11. J.C. Nelson, "New Concepts in Transportation Regulation," op. cit., pp. 216-219.

12. Ibid., pp. 219-244 and 226-277.

13. Board of Investigation and Research, Federal Regulatory Restrictions upon Motor and Water Carriers, S. Doc. 78, 79th Cong., 1st sess., 1945; ICC Administration of the Motor Carrier Act, Hearings before the Senate Select Committee on Small Business, 84th Cong., 1st sess., 1955; Competition, Regulation and the Public Interest in the Motor Carrier Industry, Report of the Senate Select Committee on Small Business, March 19, 1956; J.C. Nelson, Controls of Entry into Domestic Surface Transportation Under the Interstate Commerce Act, U.S. Department of Commerce (multilithed), October 1959; and J.C. Nelson, "The Effects of Entry Control in Surface Transport," Transportation Economics, National Bureau of Economic Research, New York, distributed by Columbia University Press, 1965, pp. 381-422. See also the Nader Study, The Interstate Commerce Omission, op. cit., pp. 120-131.

14. For a critical review of British studies on economies of scale in trucking, concluding that "no convincing evidence of economies of scale" exist in road haulage, see A.A. Walters, Integration in Freight Transport, The Institute of Economic Affairs, Research Monograph 15, London, England, 1968, pp. 28-33.

15. J.C. Nelson, "The Effects of Entry Control in Surface Transport," op. cit., pp. 401-407, and "Coming Organizational Changes in Transportation," Transportation Problems and Policies in the Trans-Missouri West, University of Nebraska Press, Lincoln, Nebraska, 1967, pp. 319-323; 82nd Annual Report, 1968, ICC, pp. 64-67, 137 and 149; and 81st Annual Report, 1967, pp. 44-46 and 108-110.

16. J.C. Nelson, "The Effects of Entry Control in Surface Transport," op. cit., pp. 414-415; and Walter Miklius, Economic Performance of Motor Carriers Operating Under the Agricultural Exemption in Interstate Trucking, U.S. Department of Agriculture, Marketing Research Project No. 838, Washington, D.C., January 1969, pp. 1, 3-5.

17. Protest and Petition for Suspension of the Department of Transportation against Increased Rates and Charges in Tariffs Published by the Pacific Inland Tariff Bureau, the Middle Atlantic Conference, the New England Motor Rate Bureau, Inc., and the Middlewest Motor Freight Bureau, Cases Nos. 47280, 47374, 47375, 47376 and 47380, ICC Suspension Board, March 20, 1968, pp. 13-16; and 84th Annual Report, 1970, ICC, pp. 67 and

401

142, where Class I intercity motor carriers of property were shown to average 18.4 percent as the return from transportation service and 11.4 percent as the ratio of net income to equity for the 1960s.

18. G.W. Wilson, "The ICC Profit Criteria — Rail vs. Truck," Transportation Journal, Fall 1966, pp. 17-19; and R. Nevel and W. Miklius, "The Operating Ratio as a Regulatory Standard," ibid., Winter 1968, pp. 15-18. Also see Annual Reports of Motor Carriers of Property, 335, ICC 707 (1969).

19. J.R. Rose, "Regulation of Rates and Intermodal Transport Competition," I.C.C. Practitioners' Journal, October 1965, pp. 11-26.

20. E.A. Nightingale, "Some Effects of Recent Changes in the Railway Grain-Rate Structure on Interregional Competition and Regional Development," Transportation Problems and Policies in the Trans-Missouri West, op. cit., pp. 105-168, especially pp. 109-131; and G.E. McCallum, New Techniques in Railroad Ratemaking, Bureau of Economic and Business Research, Washington State University, February 1968, pp. 115-127.

21. A.F. Friedlaender, The Dilemma of Freight Transport Regulation, op. cit., pp. 115-120. The author relied on the findings of W.Y. Oi and A.P. Hurter, Jr., Economics of Private Truck Transportation, William C. Brown Company Publishers (for the Transportation Center at Northwestern University) Dubuque, 1965. See also Meyer and Associates, The Economics of Competition in the Transportation Industries, op. cit., pp. 97-100.

22. Railroad Transportation and Public Policy, op. cit., pp. 171-179, 186-188 and 191-192.

23. The Economics of Competition in the Transportation Industries, op. cit., pp. 159-165. See also Rationale of Federal Transportation Policy, op. cit., pp. 4-7; The Transportation Act of 1958, op. cit., pp. 205-206; "Toward Better Resource Allocation in Transport," op. cit., pp. 332 and 334; The Dilemma of Freight Transport Regulation, pp. 64-99; and "The Social Costs of Regulating the Railroads," presented at the Meetings of the American Economic Association, December 28, 1970, showing deadweight loss from value-of-service pricing of about $300 million in 1969, while costs of excess rail capacity ranged between $2.4 billion and $3.8 billion. This implies relaxation of regulatory restraints on rail abandonments and rate competition might yield considerable social savings. For another estimate of net savings from reduction of inefficiencies and a nominal estimate of the cost of the transport regulatory process, see G.W. Wilson, "Transportation and Price Stability," The American Economic Review, May 1969, pp. 263-265.

24. National Transportation Act, Hearings before the Senate Committee on Commerce, 91st Cong., 2d Sess., on S. 924 and S. 2425, to Develop a Comprehensive National Transportation System, Serial 91-69, February, April and May, 1970.

25. Hilton, The Transportation Act of 1958, op. cit., pp. 28-34, 47-78, and 186-193.

26. M.J. Peck, "Competitive Policy for Transportation?," in The Crisis of the Regulatory Commissions, P.W. MacAvoy (ed.), W.W. Norton & Company, Inc., New York, 1970, pp. 74-78; and E.W. Williams, Jr., The Regulation of Rail-Motor Rate Competition, Harper & Brothers, New York, 1958, pp. 220-222.

27. J.C. Nelson, "The Motor Carrier Act of 1935," op. cit., pp. 471-475, 499-500, and 502-503.

28. Federal Regulatory Restrictions upon Motor and Water Carriers, op. cit., pp. 218–221, 223, 229, and 239.

29. ICC Administration of the Motor Carrier Act, op. cit., pp. 188–195, and 333–334; and Nelson, "The Effects of Entry Control in Surface Transport," op. cit., pp. 406–407 and 409.

30. Hilton, The Transportation Act of 1958, op. cit., pp. 47–48, 186–193 and 204–207; and D.J. Oswald, Cost Standards for Rail–Barge Competition, M.A. Thesis, Washington State University, 1969, pp. 186–189, 191–194, and 208–224.

31. Oswald, ibid., pp. 77–79. See reprint of the Supreme Court decision in American Lines v. L. & N.R. Co.., Nos. 797, 804, 808, and 809, October Term 1967, decided by Mr. Justice Marshall on June 17, 1968, with Mr. Justice Douglas dissenting and Mr. Justice Harland concurring in the result, pp. 13–16 and 18–19, particularly footnote 16. Case cited as 392 U.S. 571 (1968).

32. 106 M.C.C. 455, 490 (1968). But see Motor Common Carriers of Property — Routes and Service, 88 M.C.C. 415 (1961); and Nelson, "The Effects of Entry Control in Surface Transport," op. cit., pp. 408–409.

33. Air Transport and Its Regulators, op. cit., pp. 125–127; and Airline Regulation in America, Effects, and Imperfections, op. cit., pp. 55–56, 224–225, 230–233, and 238–243.

34. Government Expenditures for Highway, Waterway, and Air Facilities and Private Expenditures for Railroad Facilities, op. cit., pp. 4–5; Railroad Transportation and Public Policy, op. cit., pp. 93–107; and the Airport and Airway Development Act of 1970, Public Law 91–258, 91st Cong., approved by the President May 21, 1970. Title II — Airport and Airway Revenue Act of 1970 contains the user charges and provides in Sec. 208 for an Airport and Airway Trust Fund.

35. The Dilemma of Freight Transport Regulation, op. cit., pp. 37–38 and 103–107; and U.S. Bureau of Public Road's report, Supplementary Report of the Highway Cost Allocation Study, Letter from the Secretary of Commerce, H. Doc. 124, 89th Cong., 1st Sess., 1965, Table 2, p. 4.

36. For example, see J.R. Cannon, An Economic Evaluation of the Proposal to Extend Columbia River Navigation from Pasco to Wenatchee, Master's Thesis, Washington State University, 1970, pp. 77–121 and 129–133; and E.P. Renshaw, Toward Responsible Government, Idyia Press, Chicago, 1957.

37. A.F. Friedlaender, The Interstate Highway System, A Study in Public Investment, NorthHolland Publishing Company, Amsterdam, 1965, pp. 2–4, 34–36, 51–55, 73–78, 113–115, 133–134, and especially pp. 136–138. See Shorey Peterson, "The Highway from the Point of View of the Economist," in J. Labatut and W.J. Lane (eds.), Highways in Our National Life, Princeton University Press, Princeton, New Jersey, 1950, p. 165.

38. The Interstate Highway System, pp. 3 and 136–137; Dearing and Owen, National Transportation Policy, op. cit., pp. 86–87, 351, and 353–354; J.C. Nelson, Financing Wasington's Highways, Roads and Streets, Joint Fact-Finding Committee on Highways, Streets and Bridges of the State of Washington, Olympia, 1948, pp. XII and 94–104, and J.C. Nelson, Taxing Washington's Motor Vehicles Equitably for Highway Services, Olympia, September 23, 1950, pp. xxi, and 94–105; and John W. Fuller, Current Issues in the Regulation of Motor Vehicle Sizes and Weights, Congressional Record, Vol. 114, No. 124, 90th Cong., 2d Sess., July 18–29, 1968, pp. H7608–H7617 and H7773–H7774.

403

39. For views recognizing some need for extension of rail rapid transit, see Williams and Bluestone, Rationale of Federal Transportation Policy, op. cit., pp. 52–54; Friedlaender, The Interstate Highway System, op. cit., pp. 137–138; Lyle C. Fitch and Associates, Urban Transportation and Public Policy, Chandler Publishing Company, San Francisco, 1964, pp. 5–6 and 206; G.M. Smerk, Urban Transportation: The Federal Role, Indiana University Press, Bloomington, 1965, pp. 79–81 and 186–193. On the other hand, a very limited role is found for rail rapid transit in J.R. Meyer, J.F. Kain, and M. Wohl, The Urban Transportation Problem, Harvard University Press, Cambridge, 1965, pp. 364–367; and by Wilfred Owen, The Metropolitan Transportation Problem, rev. ed., The Brookings Institution, Washington, 1966, pp. 133–141. See also J.R. Meyer and M.R. Straszheim, Pricing and Project Evaluation, The Brookings Institution, Washington, 1971, pp. 131–133. For a critical analysis of the benefit-cost analysis in support of the proposed rail rapid transit system for Los Angeles, see Alan Carlin and Martin Wohl, An Economic Re-Evaluation of the Proposed Los Angeles Rapid Transit System, The Rand Corporation, Santa Monica, California, P-3918, September 1968.

40. C.D. Foster, "Investment Policy and Pricing in Transport," paper before the International Symposium on Transportation Pricing, The American University, Washington, D.C., June 17, 1969, and The Transportation Problem, Blackie & Son Limited, London, 1963, Chaps. 5, 6, 11, and 13; Meyer and Straszheim, Pricing and Project Evaluation, op. cit., Chaps. 11–16 and Appendix B.

41. The Dilemma of Freight Transport Regulation, op. cit., pp. 37–38. Also see J.C. Nelson and W.H. Dodge, Financing North Dakota's Highways, Roads, and Streets, the Legislative Research Committee, State of North Dakota, Bismarck, N.D., September 15, 1952, pp. XXVI and 243–250.

42. A.A. Walters, The Economics of Road User Charges, International Bank for Reconstruction and Development, Washington, D.C., January 11, 1968.

43. Fitch and Associates, Urban Transportation and Public Policy, op. cit., pp. 122–161; and Meyer, Kain and Wohl, The Urban Transportation Problem, op. cit., pp. 69–74.

44. J.C. Spychalski, "The Diversion of Motor Vehicle-Related Tax Revenues to Urban Mass Transport: A Critique of Its Economic Tenability," Transportation Journal, Spring 1970, pp. 44–50, in particular, pp. 46–48.

45. R.W. Harbeson, "Some Allocational Problems in Highway Finance," in Transportation Economics, National Bureau of Economic Research, New York, 1965, pp. 139–160, especially pp. 144–153.

46. J.M. Munro, "Planning the Appalachian Development Highway System: Some Critical Questions," Land Economics, May 1969, pp. 149–161.

47. Friedlaender, The Interstate Highway System, op. cit., pp. 36, 51–58, 64–67, 113–115, and 136–138.

48. Already at least 13 state DOTs have been established. See "NARUC Eyes Emerging State Departments of Transportation," Transport Topics, September 7, 1970.

49. For the activities of the New York Metropolitan Transportation Authority in comparison with those of the Port of New York Authority, see J.D. Williams, "The People Mover: MTA's Ronan Pushes to Improve Mass Transit," The Wall Street Journal, April 2, 1971, pp. 1 and 29.

404

214

IMPROVING THE EFFICIENCY OF THE TRANSPORTATION AND UTILITIES SYSTEMS

EFFECTS OF PUBLIC REGULATION ON RAILROAD PERFORMANCE

By JAMES C. NELSON
Washington State University

The broad problem, how to improve the performance of the American economy, which President Burns has posed for this year's sessions of the American Economic Association, furnishes an excellent focus for another analysis of the railroad situation. As an industry, the rails have lagged in the postwar economy. What are the fundamental reasons for continued railroad decline in times of general economic growth and high profitability? Do postwar trends mean that the railroads should be encouraged to accept an ever diminishing role in transport? Can the economy attain its maximum growth without greater rail participation in traffic, investment, and employment? If highest attainable performance by the economy requires railway progress, how can a greater contribution by the railroads be assured? Will a fundamental modification of transport regulation contribute to that end?

I

Since the economy attained both high levels of employment and tolerable rates of growth in postwar years during which the railroads stood still or declined, it can be argued plausibly that scant reason exists for public concern over railroad retrogression. According to this view, the best remedy for the economy, if not for the railroads, would be to encourage them to disinvest and to withdraw rapidly from the passenger business and gradually from commodity transport.

For this view to be tenable, several conditions must be met. First, it must be demonstrable that rail service can physically be replaced by alternative transport. Second, it must be shown that other modes cannot only perform the railroads' traffic load but also that they can carry it at lower total costs in resources, or at the same total costs but with improvements in service. Third, it must be likely that future technological change will be limited to modes of transport other than railroading.

None of those conditions is likely to occur in any foreseeable period. With the railroads still handling almost half of the intercity ton-miles by

495

all agencies, it will take a long time before their key transport role is reduced to insignificant proportions. The economy could come much closer to doing without the railroad passenger service, for the rails already have largely been displaced in the passenger market. Air and highway carriers now handle almost 97 per cent of the total intercity passenger-miles. Even so, some rail passenger service will permanently be required in metropolitan transport, on dense routes up to medium length, and for military needs. And with commodity transport so largely carried on the rails, it would seem the counsel of economic nonsense to conclude that railway progress is not still of significance to the economy as a whole.

In comparison with the railroads, tankers and pipelines transport oil at far less cost, integrated barge tows and ships haul bulk traffic more efficiently on some channels, and trucks carry high-value goods at less cost over short hauls. But it cannot be demonstrated today that the vast residual freight traffic handled by the railroads can be carried by alternative agencies at lower total costs, even if it were possible to transfer the entire load to them. Meyer and associates have explored the relative cost question in their recent volume, *The Economics of Competition in the Transportation Industries*.[1] Giving barge lines and motor carriers the benefit of the doubt as to the existence and traffic-diversion effect of subsidies and allowing for growth of efficient transport of solids through pipelines, these authors found that for the same "residual social cost" of 5.5 billion dollars the railroads can haul 37 per cent more ton-miles than could be handled by truck. This was the case even though a low figure of twenty cents per truck-mile was taken as the basis for estimating truck marginal costs and after adjustments were made for the inventory savings that accrue to shippers because truck service is superior to rail service.

It must always be considered that technological change might greatly reduce the cost of alternative transport relative to that by rail. For example, truck trains might achieve this result unless offset by higher incremental highway costs. However, in view of the diesel revolution, electrification and atomic power possibilities, the capital savings from centralized traffic control, the piggyback method, electronic car tracing and other automation possibilities, and the low levels of way investment in recent years, it would not be safe to assume that additional improvements in rail technology will not be made. More rapid technological change in nonrail transport may well reflect the greater national encouragement to investment in public facilities rather than any inevitable

[1] John R. Meyer, Merton J. Peck, John Stenason, and Charles Zwick, *The Economics of Competition in the Transportation Industries* (Harvard Univ. Press, 1959), Chap. VI.

outcome of the relative rates of invention in different fields of transport or of the greater maturity of the railroads.

As transport costs can be minimized only if the railroads operate efficiently, it must be concluded that rail transport is still highly significant to the performance of the entire economy, although not as important as in the last century. Hence a closer look at the declining role of the railroads is desirable.

II

The facts showing retardation in railway growth after 1920 and relative decline within transport as a whole have been documented.[2] Hence only a few pertinent trends need be cited to point up the critical question whether the entire extent of railroad decline can logically be accepted as inevitable and economic or whether institutional factors, including public control, have extended it beyond economic limits.

Compared with the late twenties, postwar rail freight traffic levels have risen about 40 per cent, although the rail share of total intercity ton-miles has fallen from 76 per cent in 1926 to about 45 per cent today while the barge, pipeline, and truck shares have risen rapidly. Rail ton-miles have not risen above their 1947 postwar peak whereas those carried by competing truckers, barge operators, and pipelines have doubled. Hence, while the railroads were standing still, truck traffic rose in excess of 150 billion ton-miles, pipeline traffic by more than 125 billion ton-miles, and barge traffic by 80 billion ton-miles. Rail passenger traffic is now far below 1926-29 levels, the rail share having dropped to barely more than 3 per cent of total intercity passenger-miles, including automobile travel, and to less than one-third of common carrier travel. Most of the vast increase in postwar travel went to the automobiles and the airlines took the rest. Plainly, the railroads did not participate in the traffic growth of the postwar economy.

Failure to share in growth traffic, tremendous losses of high-rated traffic formerly carried, and rate adjustment restrictions combined to produce slippage in the rail share of carrier revenues. Thus the rail share of the total revenues of all federally-regulated carriers dropped from 72 per cent in 1947 to 56 per cent in 1956. And while total motor freight revenues (including those of exempt carriers and the expenses of private truckers) rose from 1.7 billion dollars in 1940 to 13.6 billion in 1955, rail freight revenues increased only from 3.5 billion to 8.5 billion.

Together with the cost effects of inflation and the impact of sub-

---

[2] See Harold Barger, *The Transportation Industries, 1889-1946* (NBER, 1951), Chap. 4; and James C. Nelson, *Railroad Transportation and Public Policy* (Brookings Inst., 1959), Chaps. 2, 3 and Appendix A.

stantial passenger service deficits, these conditions soon returned the railroads to the status of a low-return "sick" industry after wartime prosperity and traffic levels gave promise that a full employment economy might solve major railroad problems. Postwar rates of return on net railway investment, with few individual and regional exceptions, have been at the 3 to 4 per cent level. Returns have been lowest in the Eastern District. Not only has low profitability not been limited to a few marginal roads, but the operating deficits during the 1957-58 recession revealed once again that such low earnings are wholly inadequate for important railroads to establish sufficient reserves to tide them over adverse times without experiencing an almost immediate threat of bankruptcy. In marked contrast, the motor carriers, barge lines, pipelines, and airlines have generally prospered.

Notwithstanding, a strong financial condition at the close of the war, accelerated depreciation, reinvestment of net income, and large issues of equipment obligations enabled the railroads to make gross capital expenditures averaging 1.1 billion dollars yearly during 1946-55. About 60 per cent went to finance dieselization and limited freight car replacement. But government investment in public transport facilities has expanded far more and continues to rise while rail investment has fallen sharply since 1957. Thus the annual capital expenditures by all government units for highways rose from about 5.0 billion dollars in 1956 to 7.1 billion in 1959; and those for the competitive Interstate System rose from 1.3 billion to 2.8 billion, or by 1.5 billion annually. Without access to public capital, it has been impossible for the railroads to keep up in capital investment and in applications of improved technology.

For three decades, the railroads have not attracted capital for making any but the most profitable or needed investments. Often only investments in improvements capable of yielding returns of 25 to 40 per cent a year can be undertaken. A Brookings Institution questionnaire estimated annual railway capital requirements for 1956-65 at 1.4 billion dollars on one set of reasonable assumptions and at almost 1.6 billion on another, or from 30 to 43 per cent higher than actual capital expenditures during 1946-55.[3] John W. Barriger has estimated that rail investment should be doubled, to about 2 billion dollars a year at 1954 prices; and that the greater part should go into roadway improvements to enhance the speed of service and to bring about substantial cost reduction. In any event, recurring freight car shortages, insufficient modern cars for efficient loading and unloading, slow progress in installing roller bearings on freight cars, and the small annual capital funds (only 329 million dollars a year during 1946-55) going into road improvements compared with the twenties suggest that rail capital investment has

[3] Nelson, *op. cit.*, pp. 378-411, Appendix B.

lagged behind the many opportunities for modernization and achievement of higher standards of efficiency and service.

III

Of the numerous reasons given for railroad decline or growth retardation, technological substitution has been in the forefront. Indeed, much of the shift of traffic from the rails can be attributed to the ability of competing agencies either to render more flexible, convenient, and speedy service or to furnish service at lower costs to consumers.

If all displacement of rail transport merely reflected such factors, railroad decline would be of slight concern. However, technological substitution must be rejected as a complete explanation. In the first place, rail freight rates have not been adjusted in close relation to relevant unit costs and in such a manner as to induce achievement of maximum economy and profitability in railway operations. Second, the rates quoted for competitive air, highway, and water services have not included all resource costs essential to their provision. Third, some critical efficiency problems in utilization of labor and freight cars remain to be solved. Fourth, rail investment has been insufficient for attainment of all potential economies. Finally, the effects of public regulation must be taken into account.

The long-standing attempt to maintain a monopoly value-of-service rate structure in what has become an essentially competitive transport market suggests that much of the railroad loss of freight traffic and revenues has been uneconomic. In the areas of greatest profit potential, that is, manufactured goods, rail rates have been maintained at levels far above relevant rail costs. Aggregative pricing through a succession of horizontal rate increases has contributed to that result. Thus the discriminating rate structure has been steadily preventing the railroads from carrying profitable traffic but not from transporting low-rated and even unprofitable traffic. On the other hand, high-cost carriers emphasizing superior services have been able to divert vast portions of the high-rated volume traffic simply by maintaining rate parity with the railroads. The truckers have maintained rate parity despite cost differences by adopting rail rates and by following rail leadership in raising rate levels. Minimum rate orders have also emphasized parity in rates.

Although railroad traffic losses resulted from the exercise of free choice by shippers, this does not necessarily imply that over-all shipper choice has divided the traffic between road and rail in the most efficient way from a resource-use standpoint. Undoubtedly, the shippers usually choose between service and rate offerings so as to maximize their individual gains from transport. But with rail rates frequently far above long-term rail marginal cost, with rail service usually inferior to truck service, and with rail and truck rates in parity relationship at or above the higher truck costs, shipper choice logically has favored the superior but high resource-cost truck service. Notwithstanding, shippers would choose the lower cost but inferior rail service at rates below truck rates in all cases in which the added truck service does not create savings in production or marketing greater than the rate differentials in favor of the rails.[4] Accordingly, there has been no adequate market demonstration that the present traffic distributions would be unchanged were the rates of each agency to reflect its unit costs. Since considerable evidence exists that shippers will shift back to the rails if rail rates reflect the lower rail costs under efficient shipment practices, it cannot be concluded that all past changes in the division of traffic and revenues have been economic because of the force of technological substitution.

In the past, rail pricing has also failed to stimulate the most efficient shipments, loading of freight cars, and railway operations. But as recent rate innovations, such as those in the Paint case, have revealed, incentive rates to induce full loading of cars, multiple-car shipments, regularized rather than sporadic use of rail plant, piggyback and other terminal-simplifying methods of container shipment, and the aggregation of small shipments can bring about substantial unit cost reductions.[5] Thus judgments adverse to rail economy should be deferred until the many opportunities to lower rates to induce lower unit costs have been exhausted.

A thorough analysis of subsidy effects cannot be undertaken here. Logically, however, the costs of air and water carriers, and probably those of long-distance truckers, have been lowered relative to rail costs because user fees have not been charged or have been inadequate to cover the annual costs of public facilities, including proportionate general tax contributions. Until user fees become universal and return such costs, including reasonable social costs, there will be ground for doubt that market divisions of traffic are fully in accord with relative economy. This would still be true were rates made in close relation to carrier costs. But even if subsidies are treated as insignificant in traffic allocation, the greater availability of capital for public transport investment can have, and probably has had, serious effects in weakening the railroad position.

Contrary to a popular view, the rail industry's over-all productivity has continued to increase at rates comparable to or in excess of the productivity gains of other leading industries.[6] This has been accom-

---

[4] Meyer and Associates, *op. cit.*, pp. 189-96 and Appendix D; and J. R. Sargent, *British Transport Policy* (Oxford Univ. Press, 1958), Chap. I.

[5] ICC, I. & S. Docket No. 7027, *Paint and Related Articles—Official Territory*, decided Aug. 27, 1959 (mimeo.).

[6] Barger, *op. cit.*, pp. 52-57, 94-111; and Nelson, *op. cit.*, pp. 235-42.

plished by dieselizing motive power, operating long and faster trains, equipping main lines with heavy rail and ballast, installing CTC, utilizing machine methods in maintenance-of-way operations, and by adopting automation in clerical functions. But there is evidence that the railroads still overemploy labor in relation to traffic. This is particularly true in train and engine service, with firemen on freight diesels an outstanding case. Of comparable importance, efficiency in use of freight cars has lagged far behind motive power and train performance gains. For example, no improvement has been made in the miles per freight car-day since 1947. The achievement of greater efficiency in use of labor and cars, including discouragement of excessive shipper detention, would reduce rail costs and improve service. With appropriate pricing and scheduling, the reasonable result would be more traffic and higher returns for the railroads and rail labor.

Trailers and containers on flat cars comprise a notable service breakthrough. Taking advantage of the low line-haul costs by rail, eliminating much costly terminal handling and switching, giving speedier and more complete service, and reducing loss and damage claims, piggyback transport, with its associated incentive rates encouraging freight forwarders and shippers to ship by rail, appears to be the most significant innovation since dieselization. If it attracts large volumes of traffic from private carriers and co-ordinates rail and highway transport, it may strengthen substantially the traffic role and long-term profitability of the railroads. In addition, when flat cars and trailers are furnished by the users, capital funds are released for other urgently needed investments in modern technology.

In certain cases, some efficiency gains can also be achieved through consolidations, such as the recent merger of the Norfolk and Western and Virginian. By utilizing the best grades, consolidating yards, concentrating traffic on fewer main lines equipped with CTC, and by reducing maintenance of other lines, consolidations can reduce costs.[7] However, because many economies of scale have been attained, consolidation offers more promise where it can increase utilization of excess capacity created by traffic shifts and technological change than where it merely increases the size of railroads.

IV

Several observations can now be made as to the effects of regulation. In the first place, the extension of entry and minimum rate controls to motor and water carriers has obviously not prevented railway decline, nor has it resulted in profitable, energetic, and flexible railroading. In-

[7] ICC, Finance Docket No. 20599, *Norfolk & Western Railway Company—Merger, Etc. —Virginian Railway Company,* decided Oct. 8, 1959 (mimeo.).

deed, with about nine-tenths of the inland waterway services and two-thirds of trucking entirely exempt from such controls, the attempt of regulated common carriers to maintain high rates, with the support of entry and minimum rate limitations on regulated competition, has had the reverse effect of lessening the role of common carriers.

Second, the welcome revitalization of rail management that is now appearing was delayed by the false feeling of market security which the regulatory program of the thirties long engendered among railroads. With motor and water carriers also bearing some regulatory burdens, competing rates published, and rate and service changes subject to protest and regulation, the railroads thought it safe to continue their traditional discriminating rate structure long after its monopoly base had been fatally undermined by rapid growth of air, highway, and waterway facilities. The regulators were equally confused but have been far slower than the railroads to recognize the role of competitive pricing in bringing about an efficient allocation of traffic. Like the regulated common carriers, the Interstate Commerce Commission called for closing the gaps in regulation, tightening restrictions even when plainly creating inefficiencies, and holding to high minimum rates as long as possible. How bankrupt this policy has been is now evident to all except those standing to gain from uneconomic railway decline and a few specialists who still fail to recognize that competitive forces have made the past pattern of discriminating rates unworkable and that cost and institutional conditions have changed in such manner that competition has become tolerably workable in transport.[8]

Third, the decisions interpreting the National Transportation Policy as requiring minimum rate orders allocating traffic so as to enable all regulated modes to remain permanently in the markets presently occupied have been barriers to rail action toward reducing rates to costs and attracting traffic for which rail costs are lower and superior service is not worth a higher charge. Such regulatory interference necessarily injured the market position of the railroads most, for in motor-rail competitive cases the rails generally have been found the low-cost carriers and are fully under regulation. While rail management could have justified their need for competitive rates more adequately, regulatory philosophy and conditions actually discouraged vigorous rate experimentation until the recent desperate position of the railroads demonstrated to Congress and the ICC the serious long-term effects of regulatory "fair-sharing" and other protective regulatory policies.

Fourth, regulatory processes and decisions contributed to weakening the railroads by delaying and limiting the essential rate-level adjust-

[8] For example, see George W. Wilson, "Current Criticisms of the Interstate Commerce Commission," *Current Economic Comment*, Aug., 1959, pp. 3-16.

ments to postwar inflation. Thus the judgments of shippers and regulators were substituted for those of responsible carriers as to the elasticity of demand for rail carriage. In early postwar years, this reduced rail profitability when transport was in short supply. By delaying adjustments to a time when general rate increases diverted much profitable traffic, the final diversionary effects were increased. Had the railroads not been held down in this way and in raising unprofitable rates, their higher profits would have induced additional investment, greater modernization of facilities and services, and lower unit costs than actually occurred.

Fifth, state regulation blocked or delayed the discontinuance of numerous hopelessly unprofitable passenger train services and also many intrastate rate and fare adjustments. Moreover, the ICC found no solution for the passenger-deficit drain upon railroad profitability, although it rendered a real service in the recent Railroad Passenger Train Deficit case by shocking the public into widespread concern over the institutional conditions that may eventually cost the public their long-standing and valued right to turn to the trains when all other transport fails.[9] And after the Transportation Act of 1958 transferred ultimate authority over discontinuance cases to the ICC, encouraging realism has been shown in permitting the dropping of distinctly unprofitable passenger trains and ferries.

Also standing in the way of efficient railroading are the state full-crew laws requiring employment of more train labor than essential for safe operations. Likewise, the collective bargaining procedures under the Railway Labor Act cannot be neglected in a search for factors possibly contributing to the railroads' failure to attain as great advances in efficiency as seems possible with modern technology. Clearly, the railroads have not been adamant enough in insisting on elimination of featherbedding and make-work rules. Labor, too, may have some points requiring consideration. Notwithstanding, the role of public regulation of labor relations in labor productivity should be examined, as in Canada, in an impartial and thoroughgoing way.

Regulatory law has kept the agencies of transport in separate compartments, except for through routes and joint rates and railroad trucking operations in supplementary service along rail routes. Railroad trucking between key rail points has been greatly restricted. Although strongly supported in the past as essential to maintenance of interagency competition, it is entirely possible that this basic policy has been carried so far as to undermine the railroads in a situation in which their competitors enjoy public way and terminal facilities free of charge

---

[9] ICC, No. 31954, *Railroad Passenger Train Deficit*, decided May 18, 1959 (mimeo.); see also the proposed report by Examiner Howard Hosmer, issued Sept. 18, 1958.

or at inadequate user fees and do not contend with their fixed costs. To what extend piggyback transport can overcome the technological inflexibilities of nonintegrated transport cannot be predicted. However, numerous regulatory cases reveal that regulatory restrictions on railroad trucking, like those on certificated motor carriers, create inefficiencies and often deny the public of services that the independent truckers appear unwilling to perform. Here, again, regulation has retarded rather than stimulated service innovations.

V

In conclusion, regulation cannot be blamed for all troubles of the railroads. Management must take far more aggressive and imaginative action with respect to competition, especially in solving its pricing, service, labor, and car-service problems. But regulation has contributed significantly to railway decline in a variety of ways and has demonstrated neither how regulatory allocations of traffic can create more economic divisions of traffic nor why market allocation, with a minimum of regulatory hindrance, cannot accomplish that social purpose. By standing in the way of change rather than by encouraging it, by creating inefficiencies in transport organization, by protecting high-cost modes, and by neglecting the truly important allocative efficiency questions, regulators have placed themselves increasingly on the defensive with not only the railroads but also with growing elements of the public. Clearly, an objective re-examination of public policy is desirable.

Relaxation of regulation in terms of present-day market conditions and needs, especially the urgent need for achieving an economic allocation of resources in transport, can no longer be delayed. The Transportation Act of 1958 provided only a modest start in this direction. Protection of socially inefficient carriers or agencies should be eliminated as a goal or consequence of regulation. The only protection needed is that which will insure the maintenance of competition in the long run, at least until evolving technology makes it clear that another regulated monopoly would bring minimum total costs in transport as a whole. Social objectives that the market cannot assure should be provided by direct means rather than by tampering with transport pricing. Regulation of entry that creates inefficient operations, such as empty return hauls, low utilization of equipment, and circuitous mileage, should be eliminated as speedily as practicable. And if carriers are to price for efficient and profitable transport, minimum rate standards must allow economic rate competition by the low-cost mode. Some long-standing standards of rate equality may have to be sacrificed to the greater but partially conflicting goal of an efficient resource allocation in transport.

Much, but not all, of the railroads' declining role is explainable by technological change and the forces in industry emphasizing short rather than long hauls. But there has been no reliable demonstration that all railroad decline in the freight field has been economic. As the railroads remain one of our largest industries and employers of labor and minimum transport cost is basic to efficient performance of the economy, it is important to adopt public policies that will work toward, and stimulate, the achievement of maximum productivity and efficient traffic performance by the railroads. Allowing the roads to adjust dynamically to the competitive conditions facing them is the best way to assure rapid railway progress, the minimization of transport costs, and the maximum contribution that transport can make to economic growth and prosperity. This will increase rail investment and maintain employment and at the same time will release resources, including labor, used wastefully in high resource-cost transport for more productive employment elsewhere in the economy.

DOES HORIZONTAL PRICE FIXING RAISE PRICE? A LOOK AT THE BAKERS OF WASHINGTON CASE*

CRAIG M. NEWMARK
North Carolina State University

[T]he enforcement agencies should thus concentrate their efforts in areas (like price fixing) where it can be convincingly argued that successful cases generally create net benefits.[1]

The advocates of strong measures against price fixing and information exchanges should no longer be allowed to treat the welfare case for their position as self-evident. . . . My analysis provides ample justification for condemning any use of scarce antitrust enforcement measures to harass small-fry price fixers and low-budget trade associations. Let the local laundries collude in peace.[2]

I. Introduction

How effective are horizontal price-fixing conspiracies? According to some recent studies, very effective. Producers of asphalt, gymnasium bleachers, rock salt, concrete pipe, and circuit breakers all raised prices through conspiracies.[3] One textbook concludes that the average price-fixing agreement increases price by 10–30 percent.[4] Another text as-

---

* I appreciate the helpful comments of Frank Easterbrook, Robert Fearn, David Flath, Stan Liebowitz, Steve Margolis, Douglas Pearce, and Walter Thurman. I am solely responsible for any errors.

[1] Richard Schmalensee, Antitrust and the New Industrial Economics, 72 Am. Econ. Rev. 24, 27 (1982).

[2] Donald Dewey, Information, Entry, and Welfare: The Case for Collusion, 69 Am. Econ. Rev. 587, 594 (1979).

[3] See Dale R. Funderbunk, Price-Fixing in the Liquid Asphalt Industry: Economic Analysis versus the "Hot Document," 7 Antitrust L. & Econ. Rev. 61 (1974): W. Bruce Erickson, Price Fixing Conspiracies: Their Long-Term Impact, 24 J. Indus. Econ. 189 (1976); Alfred L. Parker, Economics in the Courtroom: Proof of Damage in a Price-Fixing Case, 9 Antitrust L. & Econ. Rev. 61 (1977); and David F. Lean, Jonathan D. Ogur, & Robert P. Rogers, Does Collusion Pay . . . Does Antitrust Work? 51 S. Econ. J. 828 (1985).

[4] William G. Shepherd, The Economics of Industrial Organization 245 (1985).

[*Journal of Law & Economics,* vol. XXXI (October 1988)]

469

serts that many conspiracies have increased price by 30–60 percent.[5]

Almost all successful conspiracies shared an important characteristic:
government agencies or utilities were major customers of the price fixers.
But economists have long predicted that conspiracies against these two
types of buyers will be unusually effective.[6] An open question is whether
price fixing succeeds against other buyers. We have a small set of empirical studies that suggests that the answer is no: conspiracies against unregulated, for-profit buyers do not raise prices significantly, if at all.[7]

There is, however, an apparent exception to this finding. The staff of
the Federal Trade Commission (FTC) presented evidence that the Bakers
of Washington conspiracy operated very successfully.[8] The FTC staff
concluded that, from 1955 to 1964, this conspiracy increased the retail
price of bread in Seattle by at least 15 percent.[9] This conclusion has been
widely—and uncritically—cited.[10] Some observers have referred to it

[5] Douglas F. Greer, Industrial Organization and Public Policy 264 (1984).

[6] See Fred M. Westfield, Regulation and Conspiracy, 55 Am. Econ. Rev. 425 (1965);
Armen A. Alchian, Electrical Equipment Collusion: Why and How, in Economic Forces at
Work 259 (Ronald H. Coase ed. 1977); and F. M. Scherer, Industrial Market Structure and
Economic Performance 224 (1980).

[7] For quantitative studies, see George J. Stigler & James K. Kindahl, The Behavior of
Industrial Prices 92–93 (1971); Erickson, *supra* note 3, at 197–200; James E. Duggan & Gorti
V. L. Narasinham, 1981 Proc. Bus. & Econ. Stat. Sec. Am. Stat. A. 241 (1981); Michael O.
Finkelstein & Hans Levenbach, Regression Estimates of Damages in Price-Fixing Cases, 46
L. & Contemp. Probs. 145 (1983); Robert M. Feinberg, The Timing of Antitrust Effects on
Pricing, 16 Applied Econ. 397 (1984); Robert M. Feinberg, Strategic and Deterrent Pricing
Responses to Antitrust Investigations, 2 Int'l J. Indus. Organ. 75 (1984); and Franklin M.
Fisher, Statisticians, Econometricians, and Adversary Proceedings, 81 J. Am. Stat. A. 277
(1986). For a qualitative study of two conspiracies, see Almarin Phillips, Market Structure,
Organization and Performance (1962). These studies found that most conspiracies increased
price by only a small amount: 2 percent or less.

[8] U.S. Federal Trade Comm'n, Economic Report on the Baking Industry, 66–71 (1967).
(Hereinafter cited as FTC Report.)

[9] *Id*. at 52. See also Russell C. Parker, The Baking Industry, 2 Antitrust L. & Econ. Rev.
111 (1969).

[10] Citations in the professional literature are Louis P. Bucklin, Competition and Evolution
in the Distribution Trades 250–52 (1972); Leonard W. Weiss, An Analysis of the Allocation
of Antitrust Division Resources, in The Antitrust Dilemma 39 (James A. Datton & Stanford
L. Levin eds. 1974); Andrew James McLaughlin, An Economic Analysis of Resale Price
Maintenance 60–74 (unpublished Ph.D. dissertation, Univ. Calif. at Los Angeles 1979);
Wesley J. Liebeler, Bureau of Competition: Antitrust Enforcement Activities, in The Fed-
eral Trade Commission since 1970: Economic Regulation and Bureaucratic Behavior 92
(Kenneth W. Clarkson & Timothy J. Muris eds. 1981); Greer, *supra* note 5; and Bruce W.
Marion, The Organization and Performance of the U.S. Food System 380–81 (1986). (Weiss
qualified his acceptance of the FTC's conclusion, saying that the FTC "seemed" to show
that the conspiracy elevated price.) Other citations are William N. Leonard, Business Size,
Market Power, and Public Policy 215–16 (1969); William Robbins, The American Food
Scandal, 133–34 (1974); and Jennifer Cross, The Supermarket Trap 18 (1976).

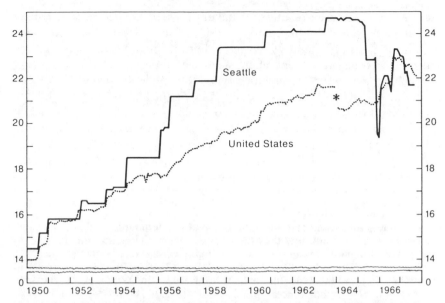

FIGURE 1.—Average retail prices for white bread, Seattle and United States, 1950–67. December 1963 and January 1964 prices for the United States are not comparable because of a revision in sampling procedures. Source.—Federal Trade Comm'n, Economic Report on the Baking Industry 67 (1967).

when arguing for greater antitrust effort against horizontal price fixing. For example, a diagram illustrating the hypothesized effect of the conspiracy on Seattle's bread price (Figure 1) was printed in the *Antitrust Law and Economics Journal* five times in ten years.[11]

This article reexamines the contention that the Bakers of Washington conspiracy raised Seattle's bread price. I present a different explanation of why the Seattle retail price was higher than the U.S. average price during 1955–64 and why the Seattle price fell in 1965. I conclude that the conspiracy did not raise Seattle's price at all.

II. The FTC's Case against Bakers of Washington

On March 7, 1961, the FTC issued a price-fixing complaint against Bakers of Washington (64 F.T.C. 1089). Formed in 1936, Bakers of Wash-

[11] Willard F. Mueller, Effects of Antitrust Enforcement in the Retail Food Industry: Price Fixing and Merger Policy, 2 Antitrust L. & Econ. Rev. 83, 86 (1968–69); Parker, *supra* note 9, at 119; Charles E. Mueller, Lawyer's Guide to the Economic Literature on Competition and Monopoly: An Introduction to the Doctoral Dissertations (I), 5 Antitrust L. & Econ. Rev. 83, 92 (1972); Paul D. Scanlon, Measuring the "Performance" of the FTC: The Wrong Kind of Numbers Game Again, 7 Antitrust L. & Econ. Rev. 15, 23 (1974); and Mayo J. Thompson, The FTC Strikes Again: Rooting Out "Low" Prices in the Bread Industry, 7 Antitrust L. & Econ. Rev. 85, 95 (1974).

ington was a trade association of bakers located in the western half of Washington State. In September 1961 the association had forty-nine members. Both retail and wholesale bakers belonged to the association, but the great majority of members were wholesale bakers.[12]

The hearing examiner concluded that "Respondents, using Bakers as a medium, do two things: one, cooperate in the establishment and announcement of price changes; and two, collectively enforce adherence to prices established and announced."[13] In addition to discussing union contracts and labor grievance problems, firm representatives frequently discussed prices at the trade association meetings. The FTC sarcastically dismissed the firms' defense that they made pricing decisions independently:

Representatives of the larger respondents were something less than persuasive when interrogated about how they happened to have picked a particular date to raise prices and about the reasons for deciding to raise the price by the particular amount chosen. Thus, the 1957 increase had been a 1¢ raise, the 1958 increase had been a 2¢ hike, and the 1960 jump was for only 1¢ again. Why pick 2¢ one year, and 1¢ another? . . . Each time a "price leader" raised his prices, it "stuck." The others followed him up quickly. . . . The figure he selected—whether 1¢ or 2¢— was always just the amount that his major competitors, also exercising their "independent" business judgement, agreed was neither too large nor too small for the state of the market.[14]

The trade association manager threatened firms that cut prices below the agreed level with the prospect of a retaliatory price war. The commission majority concluded that "[some firms] would not have raised their prices had it not been for the urgings, and sometimes the threats, of the association's manager and certain of their competitors."[15]

In its subsequent report, the FTC staff argued that the price-fixing conspiracy significantly affected the Seattle retail bread price. The report noted that from the mid-1950s through 1964, the Seattle price, as measured by the Bureau of Labor Statistics, averaged 15 percent above the U.S. average price (see Figure 1).[16] The conspiracy's effect was also

---

[12] In the Matter of Bakers of Washington, Inc., et al., 64 F.T.C. 1079 (1964).

[13] Id. at 1091.

[14] Id. at 1131.

[15] Id. at 1134–35. In a vigorous dissent, Commissioner Elman argued that these actions "do not permit an inference of a conspiracy or agreement to fix prices; they form no sinister pattern." Id. at 1146.

[16] FTC Report, supra note 8, at 66.

evident, according to the report, in the post-1964 movement of the Seattle retail price.[17] In February 1964 the commission found the trade association and other respondents guilty of price fixing; at the request of a respondent, the commission stayed the effective date of its order and held further hearings. On December 3, 1964, the commission reaffirmed its original judgment and ordered the respondents to cease price fixing. Shortly thereafter, the Seattle retail price began to fall: it fell .3¢ from January to April 1965 and 1.5¢ more in May. While the 1964 Seattle price was 3.9¢ (15.85 percent) above the U.S. average, in 1965 the Seattle price was only .2¢ above the U.S. average; in 1966, .1¢ above; and from 1967 to 1977—when the Bureau of Labor Statistics stopped publishing city food prices—the Seattle price remained below the U.S average. A plausible inference, therefore, is that the commission's action forced Seattle bakers to cut price by approximately 15 percent, a percentage equal to the price-fixing overcharge.

III. A Different Explanation

In this section, I present evidence that the conspiracy had no effect on Seattle's bread price. The evidence is organized around two contentions. First, after allowing for a higher retail markup on bread, higher wage rates, and a higher normal profit rate in the western United States, the Seattle price during 1955–64 was not unusually high. Second, the sharp decline of the Seattle price in 1965 was caused by a change in the structure of Seattle's bread market. Bread imported from Canada probably triggered this change.

A.   The 1955–64 Period

I use 1955 as the starting date of the conspiracy, following other authors.[18] My explanation for the difference between Seattle's price and the average U.S. price during 1955–64 builds on the observation that retail bread prices were high all over the West Coast during this period. Prices in San Francisco and Los Angeles were higher than in Seattle, and the Portland price was nearly as high (see Table 1).[19] The average price in these other three West Coast cities was 19 percent higher than the average

---

[17] *Id.* at 69–70.

[18] W. Mueller, *supra* note 11, at 86–87; and McLaughlin, *supra* note 10, at 67.

[19] The twenty cities listed in Table 1 are all the cities for which the Bureau of Labor Statistics (BLS) published bread prices. The year 1964 is not included in the averages because BLS published prices for only twelve of these twenty cities for that year.

TABLE 1

1955–63 AVERAGE REAL RETAIL PRICES OF WHITE BREAD

City	Average Price (¢/Pound)
San Francisco	18.9
Los Angeles	18.4
New York City	17.7
Seattle	17.7
Portland, Oreg.	17.6
Philadelphia	17.1
Scranton, Pa.	17.0
Pittsburgh	15.8
Cleveland	15.8
Baltimore	15.4
Boston	15.4
Washington, D.C.	15.2
Atlanta	15.1
Kansas City	15.1
St. Louis	14.9
Detroit	14.7
Cincinnati	14.7
Minneapolis	14.3
Chicago	14.3
Houston	13.1
West Coast average price	18.15
Nonwestern average price	15.35

Sources.—Nominal bread prices from U.S. Dep't of Labor, Bur. of Labor Statistics, Bulletin Numbers 1217, 1254, 1301, and 1446. City Consumer Price Index data from U.S. Dep't of Labor, Bur. of Labor Statistics, Bulletin Number 1256 (Table C-2) and Bulletin Number 1554 (table A).

Note.—The nominal price in each city in each year, 1955–63, is deflated by the city Consumer Price Index for that year (1947–49 = 100) before averaging.

price in sixteen nonwestern cities. Other data show that bread prices were higher all throughout the West.[20]

What was different about bread markets in the West? One difference was that retail markups on bread were larger. When asked why bread prices were higher on the West Coast than in Washington, D.C., the president of the Continental Baking Company testified, "I might add that on the west coast the grocers themselves take a larger margin of profit than they do in Washington. In Washington your grocers take approxi-

[20] In 1960 in the three West Coast states, the average retail price paid by farmers was 24.0 cents/pound; in the eight Mountain states, 22.0 cents/pound; and in the thirty-seven nonwestern states, 19.5 cents/pound. Prices were therefore 23 percent higher on the West Coast than in the nonwestern United States and nearly 16 percent higher in the West as a whole. See U.S. Dep't of Agriculture, Statistical Reporting Service, Crop Reporting Board, Agricultural Prices: 1960 Annual Summary, June 1961.

TABLE 2

REGIONAL PRICE-COST MARGINS FOR BAKERS, 1947–72

Year	Washington Margin	Western Region Margin	Rest of United States Margin (Excluding Western Region)
1947	.1663	.1993	.1817
1954	.1802	.2113	.1946
1958	.2324	.2552	.2300
1963	.2546	.2593	.2452
1967	.2853	.2828	.2618
1972	n.a.	.3002	.2992

SOURCE.—U.S. Dep't of Commerce, Bur. of the Census, Census of Manufactures, various years.
NOTE.—The price-cost margins equal value added minus payroll divided by value of shipments for industry SIC nos. 2051–12, "Bread and Related Products—Wholesale Bakeries" (Industry SIC no. 2051 was used for Washington in 1967); n.a. = not available.

mately 2 cents profit. Out there they take 4 and sometimes as much as 5 cents profit. This makes a difference because you are talking retail prices."[21]

A 1960 Senate report supports the executive's claim. The report lists wholesale prices of major brands of bread in 127 cities. For twenty-one western cities the average wholesale price was less than 9 percent above the nonwestern average price.[22] Thus, approximately half of the difference in retail price between the West and the rest of the country was created by grocery retailers, not by bakers.[23]

Another difference in western markets was that wage rates were higher. Higher labor costs accounted for one quarter of the regional difference in retail prices.[24]

[21] U.S. Senate, Committee on the Judiciary, Subcommittee on Antitrust and Monopoly, Hearings on Administered Prices, Part 12, 6125 (1959).

[22] U.S. Senate, Committee on the Judiciary, Subcommittee on Antitrust and Monopoly, Administered Prices: Bread (Report No. 1923) 183–86 (1960). I used a median price for cities that had more than one major brand.

[23] Why western grocery retailers obtained larger markups on bread is unclear. Company strategies may have played a role in creating the regional difference. Consider A & P, Kroger, and Winn Dixie, the first-, third-, and seventh-largest supermarket chains in 1958. These three chains used their store brands of bread as loss leaders more extensively than other chains. See Richard G. Walsh & Bert M. Evans, Economics of Change in Market Structure, Conduct, and Performance: The Baking Industry, 1947–58, at 106 (1963). But Kroger and Winn Dixie did not operate west of the Rockies, and A & P had only a tiny presence of thirty-seven stores in the West. (See Business Guides, Inc., 1958 Directory of Supermarket and Grocery Chain Stores.) Another factor that may have contributed to the difference was that the Teamsters Union tried to restrict the sale of "cheap" bread, and the Teamsters Union was stronger in the West. See Section IIIB infra.

[24] Hourly earnings of factory production workers were 14 percent greater on the West Coast than in the rest of the country in 1958. Per capita income in 1957 was 19 percent higher

The remaining one quarter of the retail price difference was reflected in larger accounting profits for the western bakers. In 1960 western bakers earned .7 cents/pound more in pretax profit than bakers in the rest of the country; in 1964, .4 cents/pound more, according to a survey done for the National Commission on Food Marketing.[25]

Western bakers earned higher profit margins for at least twenty years, 1947–67 (see Table 2). Their margins ranged from 6 to 11 percent higher than elsewhere.[26] (Note, though, that until 1967 the margin for Washington State was lower than for the western region as a whole.)

Are these higher margins rates evidence that bakers colluded, either explicitly or implicitly, all throughout the West? Available information provides scant support for a regional collusion hypothesis. Explicit price fixing of bread was detected infrequently in the West.[27] Seller concentration in western markets was not much greater than in other markets. And regression analysis indicates that seller concentration does not explain the western bakers' higher price-cost margin.[28]

---

on the West Coast. See M. W. Reder, Trends in Wages, Savings, and Per Capita Income, 82 Monthly Lab. Rev. 524, 526–27 (1959). Payroll per employee in wholesale baking firms was 20 percent higher in the West in 1958 and 26 percent higher in 1963 according to Census of Manufactures data. My contention that higher wages accounted for about 25 percent of the retail price difference is based on survey information; see note 25 *infra*.

[25] Nat'l Comm'n on Food Marketing, Organization and Competition in the Milling and Baking Industries, Technical Study No. 5, 128–31 (1965). The average wholesale price for bakery products in the nonwestern United States was 18 cents/pound according to this survey. The extra .7 cents/pound in pretax profit earned by western bakers is equal to 4 percent of that price. Since retail bread prices in the West were either 16 percent higher (using state price data, note 20 *supra*) or 18 percent higher (using city price data, Table 1 *supra*), this 4 percent is equal to about one quarter of the retail price difference.

[26] U.S. Dep't of Commerce, Bur. Census, Census of Manufactures, various years.

[27] The Department of Justice filed three price-fixing cases involving western markets during 1955–85. One conspiracy involved firms in Las Vegas and lasted from 1953 to early 1957. Two of the five firms indicted were acquitted. Another conspiracy occurred in Arizona, beginning "sometime before 1963" and lasting until 1974. And a third case was brought against six firms operating in San Diego, but all six firms were acquitted. East of the Rockies, the Justice Department brought six cases from 1955 to 1964 and ten cases from 1965 through 1985. See Block, Nold, & Sidak, The Deterrent Effect of Antitrust Enforcement, 89 J. Pol. Econ. 429 (1981); Clabault & Block, Sherman Act Indictments, 1955–80 (1981); and Commerce Clearing House, Trade Regulation Reporter, various issues (1981–85). I could not find any other price-fixing cases filed against bakers by the FTC. One authority notes that FTC price-fixing cases in *any* industry were rare. See Alan Stone, Economic Regulation and the Public Interest: The Theory and Practice 90 (1977).

[28] Due to its perishability, the relevant geographic market for bread was generally local (FTC Report, *supra* note 8, at 42–44). A special tabulation of Census of Manufactures data lists 1963 seller concentration ratios for eleven metropolitan areas. Los Angeles and San Francisco both had four-firm ratios of .56; the average of the nine nonwestern areas was .51 with a standard derivation of .11. See U.S. Senate Committee on the Judiciary, Concentration Ratios in Manufacturing Industry: 1963, Part II, 338–39 (1963). The FTC staff estimated

This higher margin is better explained by its similarity to the higher margins earned by other manufacturers in the West. Using a list compiled by William Shepherd, I identified sixty-nine four-digit Standard Industrial Classification (SIC) industries as having either local or regional markets.[29] For each of these industries I compared the 1958 price-cost margin in the West to the margin in the nonwestern United States. The western margin was larger for forty-five of the sixty-nine industries. According to the nonparametric sign test,[30] we can reject the null hypothesis that margins were equal in the two regions at the .02 confidence level (two-tailed test). Further, the western margins exceeded the nonwestern margins by an average of 8.4 percent. This average difference is significantly larger than zero, and it explains most of the 11-percent higher margin that western bakers earned in 1958.[31]

Data on regional interest rates also indicate that a higher rate of return on capital prevailed in the West. Interest rates on short-term business

---

1963 concentration in seventeen cities (FTC Report, *supra* note 8, at 44). Four western cities—Denver, Long Beach, Portland, and Phoenix—had four-firm ratios of .46, .59, .58, and .78, respectively. Thirteen nonwestern cities averaged .64. Senate hearings (*supra* note 21, at 6146) contain a bar chart from which lower bounds for four-firm concentration can be estimated for twenty-seven cities for 1957. Five of ten western cities had ratios equal to at least .50, while nine of seventeen nonwestern cities had ratios at least that large. The available data do not show higher local concentration in the West. The Nat'l Comm'n on Food Marketing (*supra* note 25, at 52–53) reported 1958 four-firm concentration ratios for states. The eleven western states had an average value of .61, while the thirty-seven other states had an average value of .51 with a standard derivation of .18. These state concentration data can be combined with data from the 1958 Census of Manufactures to crudely test the tacit collusion hypothesis. The dependent variable is the 1958 price-cost margin (in percentages) for each state, for industry SIC no. 2051, "Bread and Related Products." The results (*t*-statistics are in parentheses):

$$\text{price-cost margin} = 21.9 + .02 \text{ concentration ratio} + 3.2 \text{ western region dummy,}$$
$$(15.3) \quad (.81) \quad\quad\quad (3.0)$$

$$\text{mean of dependent variable} = 23.79.$$

The higher seller concentration of the western states accounts for little, if any, of western bakers' higher margins.

[29] William G. Shepherd, Market Power and Economic Welfare: An Introduction 263–67 (1970). Shepherd identified a total of eighty-eight industries, other than bread, as having local or regional markets. For nineteen of these industries I could not compute a western margin because of missing data in the Census of Manufactures, so sixty-nine industries were used for the two tests. I also performed the tests for a set of sixty industries identified by Schwartzman & Bodoff as sold in local or regional markets (David Schwartzman & Joan Bodoff, Concentration in Regional and Local Industries, 37 S. Econ. J. 343–48 (1971)). The results were qualitatively the same as those reported in the text.

[30] Lothar Sachs, Applied Statistics: A Handbook of Techniques 316–18 (2d ed. 1984).

[31] The average difference is significantly different from zero using both a nonparametric test and a parametric *t*-test (*t*-value = 3.8).

loans in the Southwest and West ranged from 4 to 9 percent higher (twenty to thirty-three basis points) than elsewhere in the United States during 1954–64.[32]

B.   The 1965–66 Period

The retail price of bread in Seattle dropped from December 1964 to January 1966, while the U.S. average price rose. Both the unusual size of Seattle's decline, 3.2 cents/pound, and the timing of the decline suggest that a successful price-fixing conspiracy among bakers collapsed in 1965 following the FTC's final judgment in *Bakers of Washington*.[33]

But contrary to what should have occurred had a price-fixing agreement collapsed, the wholesale prices of Seattle's leading brands did *not* fall during 1965–66. By August 1966, the wholesale prices of these leading brands—all produced by alleged conspirators—were 2.3 cents/pound higher than they were in December 1964.[34] This increase was almost identical to the price increases that occurred in other major cities.[35]

Seattle's average bread price fell not because collusion ceased but because several inexpensive, lower-quality brands of bread began selling in Seattle during 1964–66. Principal among these new brands was one manu-

[32] U.S. Federal Reserve System, Board of Governors, Banking and Monetary Statistics, 1941–1970, at 708 (1976). This publication lists two rates for years before 1967: one rate is the average rate for "7 large northern and eastern cities," and the other rate is an average rate for "11 large southern and western cities." For 1967, the publication breaks out the "southern and western" rate into values for the Southeast, Southwest, and West Coast. The Southeast rate is lower than both the Southwest and West Coast rates, suggesting that 4–9 percent is a lower bound for how much higher western rates were during 1955–64.

[33] The coincidental timing of the FTC's final decision on December 3, 1964, and the beginning of Seattle's price fall in May 1965 is less suspicious than it appears because the decision did not end legal action on the case. The major wholesale bakers appealed the decision to the U.S. Circuit Court; on losing in 1966, they appealed for review by the U.S. Supreme Court. That request was denied (386 U.S. 932), but not until February 20, 1967.

[34] During 1964 and 1965, the wholesale price of the advertised-label brands was 28¢/loaf, based on a conventional discount of 20 percent from the retail price of 35¢/loaf. See In the Matter of International Telephone and Telegraph Corp., *et. al.*, 104 F.T.C. 280, at 327 (1984). (Hereinafter cited as IT&T Case. IT&T owned Continental Baking Co., a large wholesale baker.) The FTC Report, *supra* note 8, at 61–62, based on a survey of Seattle grocers, stated that grocers' markups on advertised-label brands were still exactly 20 percent in January and August 1966 and that this markup resulted in retail gross margins of 7.4¢/loaf and 7.8¢/loaf. These amounts imply wholesale prices of 29.6¢ and 31.2¢/loaf in these two months. Since the standard loaf weight in Seattle was 22.5 ounces (ITT Case, at 326), the increase of 3.2 cents per loaf from 1964–65 to August 1966 equaled 2.3 cents/pound.

[35] Wholesale prices in New York City and Chicago increased 2.4¢/pound over this period. See U.S. Dep't of Labor, Bur. Labor Statistics, Wholesale Prices and Price Indexes, January 1965 and September 1966. The U.S. national average wholesale price increased 1.8¢/pound over the period (FTC Report, *supra* note 8, at 117–19).

factured in Canada by Granddad Baking Company. Granddad's bread sold at wholesale for seven cents per pound (nearly 30 percent) less than the leading brands. The other new brands were priced similarly.[36]

I now discuss the reasons why the new brands sold at such a significant discount to the leading brands and why these new brands appeared in Seattle when they did.

The new brands of bread were not identical to the leading brands. The leading brands in Seattle, as in other U.S. cities, were advertised-label brands. Advertised-label bread was sold under the principal trade names of wholesale bakers. Competing against advertised-label bread were private-label brands. Grocery retailers and some wholesale bakers manufactured private-label bread; in either case, grocery retailers sold this type of bread under their own trade names. Private-label bread was generally made from a leaner formula than advertised-label bread, containing less milk, shortening, and sugar.[37] Private-label brands were advertised less intensively than the leading brands.[38]

The two types of bread also were distributed differently.[39] Wholesale bakers employed "driver-salesmen" to distribute their products. Driver-salesmen spent considerable time restocking bread shelves, removing stale loaves, and performing bookkeeping services for retailers. The driver-salesman system was well-suited for deliveries to small, nonchain stores. Large grocery chains employed a less costly method of distribution. The chains' contracts with the Teamsters Union, which represented driver-salesmen as well as chain-store drivers, permitted the chains to pay their drivers a flat hourly wage; in contrast, the union contracts stipulated that driver-salesmen receive a guaranteed hourly wage plus a commission on route sales. The chains also distributed their bread in larger, more efficient lots and relied on cheaper in-store labor for stocking of shelves and removal of stales. Two studies concluded that the large chains could distribute bread for as little as one quarter the cost of wholesale bakers using driver-salesmen.[40]

---

[36] IT&T Case, *supra* note 34, at 327; and FTC Report, *supra* note 8, at 72–73.

[37] See the testimony of R. N. Laughlin, president of Continental Baking Co., and R. A. Jackson, president of Ward Baking Co., in U.S. Senate, *supra* note 21, at 6154 and 6253. And see In the Matter of ITT Continental Baking Co., 84 F.T.C. 1349, at 1370 (1974).

[38] FTC Report, *supra* note 8, at 30–31; and U.S. Council of Wage and Price Stability, A Study of Bread Prices 21 (1977). Consumers probably inferred from the heavier advertising of the advertised-label brands that these brands were qualitatively different from private-label brands; see Benjamin Klein & Keith B. Leffler, The Role of Market Process in Assuring Contractual Performance, 89 J. Pol. Econ. 615 (1981).

[39] FTC Report, *supra* note 8, at 29–30 and IT&T Case, *supra* note 34, at 302.

[40] Walsh & Evans, *supra* note 23, at 79; and FTC Report, *supra* note 8, at 30.

, Because of these differences, grocery retailers priced private-label brands below advertised-label brands. In 1958 the U.S. average retail price for private-label bread was 17 percent below the average price of advertised-label brands.[41] In most areas of the country, retailers occasionally used private-label brands as "loss leaders" by cutting prices to ten cents per pound or less.[42] Retailers increased the discount on private-label brands during the 1960s and 1970s.[43] The discount helped raise private-label brands' share of the national bread market. In 1960 their share was 18 percent; in 1971, 36 percent; and by 1977, approximately 50 percent.[44]

Wholesale bakers recognized early that the chains' less expensive distribution method and lower private-label prices threatened their advertised-label business. The bakers tried to respond by lowering the cost of the driver-salesman system. But the Teamsters Union vigorously resisted any change to this system.[45]

Western Teamsters made a particularly strong effort to maintain the incomes and jobs of driver-salesmen. The union in the West was unusual in its number of members, its leadership, and its activities. The number of Teamsters per capita in the West was nearly twice the national average.[46] This organizational success has been credited to Dave Beck.[47] Beck was president of a Seattle Teamsters local and organizer of the Western Conference of Teamsters. He believed that the key to maintaining the incomes of his members was to insure that Teamsters' employers were profitable. Toward that end, the Western Teamsters tried to restrict entry of firms into many local industries. They refused to serve new firms in "overcrowded" industries. They also, particularly in Seattle, tried to discourage firms from cutting prices.[48] Beck argued, "If [railroad] fares between Seattle and Spokane can be stabilized, why can't we apply the same principle to the prices charged for rye bread and chocolate pies?"[49]

[41] Walsh & Evans, at 127.

[42] Id. at 106.

[43] In the Matter of ITT Continental Baking Co., supra note 37, at 1371.

[44] IT&T Case, supra note 34, at 304.

[45] FTC Report, supra note 8, at 29–30. See also In the Matter of ITT Continental Baking Co., supra note 37, at 1369.

[46] Robert D. Leiter, The Teamsters Union: A Study of Its Economic Impact 51 (1957).

[47] Beck's influence and activities are described in Murray Morgan, Skid Road: An Informal Portrait of Seattle 256–63 (1982); Donald Garnel, The Rise of Teamster Power in the West 67–77 (1972); Leiter, supra note 46, at 49–51; David Bell, Labor's New Men of Power, 47 Fortune 148, 156 (1953); Robert Laughlin, The Boss of the Teamsters Rides High, 36 Life 122 (1954); and Richard A. Lester, Labor and Industrial Relations: A General Analysis 127 (1957).

[48] Morgan, supra note 47, at 259. See also Garnel, supra note 47, at 68–70; and Laughlin, supra note 47, at 130.

[49] Bell, supra note 47, at 156.

In 1963 a Seattle firm challenged the Teamsters' support of the driver-salesmen. Granddad Baking Company bought bread from a wholesale baker and distributed it to retailers using nonunion drivers.[50] The following year Granddad's supplier stopped selling to Granddad because of "certain pressures" applied by the Teamsters.[51] Because other Seattle wholesale bakers refused to sell to Granddad and because the Canadian dollar had recently fallen against the U.S. dollar, Granddad began importing bread from Canada.[52]

Granddad priced its bread well below the wholesale prices of the advertised-label brands. Retailers typically sold Granddad's bread for more than ten cents per pound (nearly 50 percent) less than the advertised-label brands.[53] This discount was especially attention getting because in Seattle—as all throughout the West—grocers had maintained unusually low discounts on private-label brands.[54]

Although the Teamsters pressured retailers not to sell Granddad's bread, Granddad sold 40,000 loaves a week in 1964 and early 1965.[55] I

[50] IT&T Case, *supra* note 34, at 326–27. Granddad may have been encouraged by the example of Ashbrook Bakeries. In 1960 Ashbrook sold bread to a grocer under an arrangement by which the grocer's drivers picked up the bread at Ashbrook's plant. Ashbrook thereby avoided using driver-salesmen. The arrangement was the key issue in collective bargaining between the Seattle Teamsters and the bakers' organization in 1962. The Teamsters won a contract provision forbidding this practice, but the provision permitted bakers already using the arrangement to continue. When Granddad entered the market in 1963, it for a short time purchased bread from Ashbrook. See Granddad Bread v. Continental Baking Co., 612 F.2d 1105 (9th Cir. 1979).

[51] See Granddad Bread, note 50 *supra*.

[52] *Id*. The Canadian dollar fell 11 percent against the U.S. dollar from 1960 to 1963. International Monetary Fund, Bur. of Statistics, International Financial Statistics Yearbook 222–23 (1985). If the exchange rate movement prompted Granddad's importing, then when the Canadian dollar rose in the 1970s to nearly its 1960 level, Granddad should have stopped importing. And it did: see IT&T Case, *supra* note 34, at 329.

[53] IT&T Case, *supra* note 34, at 327. Granddad's low-priced bread was sold in 1964, but Seattle's average retail price, as measured by the BLS, did not decline until 1965. Why? I suspect that the answer lies in BLS's sampling method. At each retail outlet sampled, only the best-selling brand in that outlet was priced. (See Frederick E. Geithman & Bruce W. Marion, A Critique of the Use of BLS Data for Market Structure-Price Analysis, 60 Am. J. Agric. Econ. 701, 702 (1978).) It is reasonable, therefore, that a new brand did not affect the BLS-measured price immediately. In this case, not until other Seattle bakers began making cheap bread and Seattle retailers began discounting private-label brands more did the BLS price fall. See text accompanying notes 60–65 *infra*.

[54] In 1958 the average retail price difference in the West between advertised-label and private-label brands was just one cent per pound (4 percent). This contrasted with an average 3.3 cents per pound discount (17 percent) nationwide. Walsh & Evans, *supra* note 23, at 127.

[55] IT&T Case, *supra* note 34, at 327–30. The initial decision in the IT&T Case concludes discussion of the Seattle market with the finding, "Moreover, it appears that Granddad's principal adversaries in Seattle were Local 227 of the Teamsters Union, Hansen [a wholesale baker], and the driver-salesmen of all the wholesale bakers." I do not think that

estimate that this volume equaled a market share of more than 3 percent, probably 5 percent.[56,57] Several Seattle bakers told the FTC Staff that Canadian bread was cutting into their business.[58] And over the period 1966–68, Granddad's volume grew.[59]

The entry of Granddad's Canadian bread apparently prompted Seattle's wholesale bakers and grocery retailers to change their bread-marketing strategies. Both groups spent less effort selling advertised-label brands. In early 1965, Continental Baking Company, the largest wholesale baker in Seattle, introduced a "secondary-label" brand.[60] (Secondary-label brands were similar to private-label brands in that they were advertised little, if at all, and they were made from leaner recipes.) This brand sold at retail for about seven cents per pound less than Continental's advertised-label brand and just three and a half cents per pound more than Granddad's bread.[61] Continental announced that its secondary brand was intended "to meet the competition of Canadian bread."[62] Two other leading

the Teamsters were acting simply as a tool of the Bakers of Washington. Just the opposite was probably true. Beck urged businessmen to form trade associations, and in some industries association staffers were former union officials friendly with Beck (Garnel, *supra* note 47, at 70). Beck and the Seattle Teamsters had been working with trade associations to "stabilize" prices since 1927, which predates the formation of the bakers' organization (Laughlin, *supra* note 47, at 130).

[56] I estimate a lower bound for Granddad's market share as follows. In 1963 $37,226,000 worth of "bread and bread-type rolls" were manufactured in Washington State (source: 1963 Census of Manufactures, at 20E-20). This value is multiplied by the ratio of the wholesale value of "white pan bread" to the wholesale value of "bread and bread-type rolls" sold in the United States, .58812. Dividing by the wholesale price per loaf in Seattle in 1964, $.28 (IT&T Case, *supra* note 34, at 327), I estimate that 78,190,554 loaves of bread were produced in the state. Granddad's sales of 40,000 loaves a week thus constitute a market share of 2.66 percent for the *entire state*. But the whole state was larger than the relevant market. Most bread markets consisted of a metropolitan area and an urban-rural fringe (FTC Report, *supra* note 8, at 42). The population of the Seattle area on July 1, 1965, was 1.179 million (U.S. Statistical Abstract). According to the FTC Report, *supra* note 8, at 39, the per capita shipment of white bread in the United States in 1963 equaled 52 pounds. Straightforward computations, given a loaf weight of 22.5 ounces (IT&T Case, *supra* note 34, at 326), yield an estimate of Granddad's share of the Seattle market of 4.77 percent.

[57] Three factors restricted Granddad's sales despite its low price. The Teamsters successfully pressured some retailers not to carry Granddad's bread. For example, K-Mart stopped buying 13,000 loaves per week as a result of Teamster pressure (IT&T Case, *supra* note 34, at 329). The efforts of the Teamsters could account for Granddad's use of two nontraditional distribution channels: service stations and roadside fruit stands (FTC Report, *supra* note 8, at 71). Second, Granddad did not advertise (FTC Report, at 71). Finally, beginning in 1965, Granddad's bread had to compete with other new brands (see text accompanying notes 60–64 *infra*).

[58] FTC Report, *supra* note 8, at 71.

[59] IT&T Case, *supra* note 34, at 328.

[60] *Id*. at 327.

[61] *Id*.

[62] *Id*. Continental's reaction to Granddad's entry was similar to Continental's competitive reactions in other cities. For instance, in Denver in August 1964, Continental began supply-

wholesale bakers subsequently introduced secondary-label brands.[63] The number of retailers selling private-label brands increased.[64] Retailers also cut prices on private-label bread. In contrast to their practice prior to 1965, Seattle grocers began sharply discounting private-label brands.[65] By 1974 the market share of private-label brands in Seattle had increased so much that in a sample of eighteen large U.S. cities, the city in which private-label brands held the largest market share was Seattle.[66]

That Canadian bread was responsible for the Seattle price decline is also indicated by the movement of bread prices in Detroit. Two Michigan bakers complained during Senate hearings in 1959 that Canadian bread was threatening their business even though Canadian bread held just 2 percent of the Detroit market at that time.[67] The Canadian bread carried a wholesale price of about six cents per pound less than the Detroit bakers' price. From 1959 to 1966, while the U.S. average retail price rose 2.5 cents/pound, the Detroit price rose only .3 cents/pound. (The prices in three other midwestern cities, Chicago, Cleveland, and St. Louis, all rose over two cents/pound.)[68] Among the thirty-two nonwestern cities for

---

ing a private-label brand to a grocery-retailing cooperative to preempt another baker from doing so. The cooperative accounted for only 4 percent of Denver's grocery sales (IT&T Case, *supra* note 34, at 311). In Minneapolis, Los Angeles, San Francisco, and Cleveland, Continental was charged with predatory pricing by several small firms, as well as by the FTC (IT&T Case, *supra* note 34, at 291, 317–25, and 330–65). In most of the instances complained of, Continental chose to fight cheaper bread by producing private and secondary-label brands, *not* by cutting the price of its advertised-label brand. Other U.S. wholesale bakers made this same choice, even at the cost of a significant loss in market share for their advertised-label brands. See text accompanying note 44 *supra* and In the Matter of ITT Continental Baking Co., *supra* note 37, at 1371. The bakers may have maintained high prices on advertised-label brands because they feared that price cuts would undermine their investment in brand-name capital; see Joseph E. Stiglitz, The Causes and Consequences of the Dependence of Quality on Price, 25 J. Econ. Literature 1, 23, 38 (1987).

[63] IT&T Case, *supra* note 34, at 327–28.

[64] IT&T Case, *supra* note 34, at 328. Private-label brands of large grocery chains held a 21 percent share of the market in 1966, compared to just 4 percent in 1956. See FTC Report, *supra* note 8, at 71.

[65] The typical discount in early 1966 was 8.5 cents/pound, compared to 1.0 cent/pound or less during the conspiracy. FTC Report, *supra* note 8, at 72–73. That the retailers' introduction of new brands and their increased discounting was a response to Granddad's and Continental's new brands is suggested by analogy to other cities. For example, the opening of a single store selling inexpensive private-label bread in Minneapolis in 1966 prompted major chains there to cut private label prices by 27.6 percent. IT&T Case, *supra* note 34, at 320. A discount grocery chain's entry into Denver triggered a 25 percent drop in price in 1965. FTC Report, *supra* note 8, at 73–74.

[66] U.S. Senate, Select Committee on Nutrition and Human Needs, 1975 Food Price Study, Part 4, 45–145 (1975).

[67] U.S. Senate, *supra* note 21, at 6369, 6408, and 6415.

[68] U.S. prices are reported in the FTC Report, *supra* note 8, at 103. City prices are reported in U.S. Dep't of Labor, Bur. of Labor Statistics, Estimated Retail Food Prices by City, various annual summary issues.

which the Bureau of Labor Statistics published 1966 bread prices, Detroit's was third lowest, 3.9 cents/pound (17 percent) below the U.S. average.[69]

IV. Conclusion

A comparison of Seattle's retail bread price to the U.S. average retail bread price over the years 1955–66, as shown in Figure 1, appears to illustrate dramatically the effect of a successful price-fixing conspiracy. I have argued in this article that neither Seattle's high price during the conspiracy period of 1955–64 nor Seattle's lower price after the conspiracy ended should be interpreted as evidence of an effective price-fixing agreement. Seattle's high price during 1955–64 was matched, even exceeded, in other cities in the western United States. The three reasons why prices were higher in the West were higher retail markups, higher labor costs, and a higher normal rate of return. Given these three regional factors, well beyond the control of Seattle bakers, Seattle's retail price during the conspiracy is seen to be nothing more than the competitive price.

Despite the competitive pricing of Seattle's bakers, new brands of bread entered the market during 1964–66. The first new brand was sold by a firm that imported bread from Canada. This bread carried a much lower price than Seattle's leading brands primarily because of the seller's lower-cost distribution system. After Seattle's wholesale bakers introduced lower-quality brands and grocery retailers slashed the prices on these brands, Seattle's average price fell. Neither group's action could have been, logically, a response to the prosecution of an ineffective conspiracy. And information from several sources indicates that the Seattle bakers' failure to adopt a lower-cost distribution system and their delay in introducing inexpensive brands resulted from extraordinary pressure applied by the Seattle local of the Teamsters Union. The Teamsters' inability, despite considerable effort, to keep out the Canadian bread should be viewed as the probable cause for Seattle's price fall in 1965.

[69] U.S. Dep't of Labor, Bureau of Labor Statistics, City Worker's Family Budget, Autumn 1966 (Bulletin 1570-3). I have no indication that Canadian bread was exported to any of the other thirty-one nonwestern cities in the sample. Bread's perishability would have made it economically infeasible to transport bread far from the Canadian border. The city among the other thirty-one closest to Canada was Buffalo. Interestingly, Buffalo's bread price was also well below the U.S. average (by 13 percent).

By Joseph A. Pratt

ASSISTANT PROFESSOR OF BUSINESS ADMINISTRATION
UNIVERSITY OF CALIFORNIA, BERKELEY

Growth or a Clean Environment? Responses to Petroleum-related Pollution in the Gulf Coast Refining Region*

❡ *The power of history to instruct policy makers and enforcers is demonstrated in this study of the seventy-five-year effort to control pollution by the petroleum industry of the upper Texas Gulf coast. Dividing his subject into three time periods, Professor Pratt shows that the goal of economic growth, even with highly inefficient and polluting production methods, ruled until about 1914; from 1914 to 1940, progress in pollution control resulted primarily from less wasteful refining technology; and in the most recent era pollution, having become critical, is finally being controlled insofar as industry cooperation and national regulation can achieve it. But, he warns, the problem has now attained international proportions, and he asks where the social institutions to effect regulation are to be found on that plane.*

Along the Gulf coast from Port Arthur, Texas, to the Houston Ship Channel stands the largest concentration of petroleum refineries and petrochemical plants in the world. For most of the twentieth century, as much as 20 per cent of the nation's production of refined petroleum products has come from this approximately 100-mile-long area.[1] Inevitably, the region has also been plagued by a corresponding share of the nation's refinery-related pollution. For half a century before the national government began to respond to pollution in the 1960s and 1970s, local and state governments and the owners of the larger refineries along the upper Texas

Business History Review, Vol. LII, No. 1 (Spring, 1978). Copyright © The President and Fellows of Harvard College.

* The author acknowledges with thanks the suggestions of Louis P. Galambos and his economic history seminar at Johns Hopkins University and the Political, Social, and Legal Environment of Business seminar at the School of Business Administration, University of California, Berkeley; and the Institute of Business and Economic Research at Berkeley for clerical services in the preparation of this article.

[1] Throughout this paper, "upper Texas Gulf coast" refers to the region from around Lake Sabine (near the Texas-Louisiana border) to Galveston Bay. More specifically, the refining and petrochemical complex that is the center of my study is in the four northernmost counties on the Texas coast (Jefferson, Chambers, Harris, and Galveston). For a history of this region, see Joe Pratt, "The Growth of a Refining Region" (doctoral dissertation, Johns Hopkins University, 1976).

Gulf coast had attempted to contain the mounting problem. These earlier efforts proved unsuccessful, for reasons which this article will explore, and which can help to understand the evolution of the institutional framework within which present and future solutions to the problems of pollution control must be sought.

Petroleum-related pollution was a by-product of the rapid, sustained expansion of the region's production and refining of crude oil and the transportation of petroleum products. Discovery of the famous Spindletop oil field near Beaumont, Texas, in 1901 temporarily made the area the center of national crude oil production. Two companies founded in response to the discovery of the field, Gulf and Texaco, first built major refineries at nearby Port Arthur in 1902 and 1903. Even after the initial importance of the Spindletop field as a source of crude had waned with the subsequent discovery of larger new fields throughout the Southwest, the Beaumont-Port Arthur area continued to prosper as a refining center. In 1914, the opening of the Houston Ship Channel less than 100 miles west of Port Arthur encouraged the growth of a second large cluster of refineries south of Houston. The capacity of the plants throughout the region increased steadily thereafter because of their closeness to the rapidly expanding Southwestern oil fields and their convenience as a shipping point for the large markets in the urban centers of the Northeast. This growing refining complex then helped to attract petrochemical plants to the region in the post-World War II era. Many areas near the sea throughout Texas and Louisiana shared in the resulting growth, but the benefits — and the costs — were concentrated in the historical and geographical center of the Gulf coast refining region, the upper Texas Gulf coast.[2]

The environmental impact of the growth of refining is best studied as one part of the broader history of the region's oil-related economic development, which falls into three eras: (1) the early years (1901–1914) of unrestrained production that resulted in localized pollution in the Port Arthur area; (2) a middle period (from about 1914 to the late 1930s) in which the geographical spread

[2] For the story of the development of these oil fields, see Carl Coke Rister, *Oil! Titan of the Southwest* (Norman, Oklahoma, 1949). See, also, Arthur Johnson, "The Early Texas Oil Industry — Pipelines and the Growth of an Integrated Oil Industry, 1901–1911," *Journal of Southern History* 32 (November 1966), 516–528. One of the best sources for regional information is a history of the parent company of the largest of these refineries: Henrietta Larson and Kenneth Porter, *History of Humble Oil and Refining Company* (New York, 1959). For a history of Houston, see David McComb, *Houston: The Bayou City* (Austin, 1969). For an excellent survey of development on the Texas Gulf coast, see Joseph L. Clark, *The Texas Gulf Coast: Its History and Development*, 4 vols. (New York, 1955). See, also, Marilyn Sibley, *The Port of Houston: A History* (Austin, 1968).

of refining and the introduction of new production techniques designed to increase the yield of gasoline brought more severe problems; and (3) a modern era (1940 to the 1960s) marked by the diversification of the sources of pollution with expansion of other major industries and growing use of the automobile. In all three periods, petroleum-related pollution was substantial. Despite improved efficiency of the refineries, the absolute quantity of pollutants increased as the refining complex continued to expand, while new production techniques brought pollutants of greater chemical complexity.

Each of the three eras saw a fairly distinct pattern of response to pollution. During the early years, neither the state nor the oil companies made serious attempts to control the escape of oil into the region's air and water. In the middle period, however, the companies and their primary trade association, the American Petroleum Institute (API), took the lead in responding to petroleum-related pollution. They did this by closing up the production process to eliminate waste and by attempting to control the political process to forestall public intervention. These voluntary efforts ultimately failed, and in the modern era, first state and local governments and then the federal government gradually took greater control in attempting to deal with the environmental problems brought about by the cumulative impact of more than fifty years of refining. Several significant changes in the response to pollution over time are thus evident: both the private and public institutions most directly concerned with petroleum-related pollution became increasingly national rather than regional, and leadership in defining solutions shifted gradually from private to public institutions.

The Era of the Gusher, 1901–1914

Pollution was a problem on the upper Texas Gulf coast before oil was discovered. Coal-burning trains had brought unsightly and unhealthy smoke, a hazard that was especially bad in rail centers like Houston. The rapid cutting of timber had stripped the soil of its protective covering in parts of east Texas and the milling of this lumber in coastal towns like Beaumont had resulted in contamination of the air. Cotton and timber production had been rapidly expanded without regard to the effects on the soil or the forests. Municipal waste disposal was also a major problem; in 1913 — before the construction of large refineries in the Houston area — the mayor of Houston acknowledged that sewage disposal

GULF COAST POLLUTION   3

had caused local pollution that was "little less than disgraceful." [3] In the long run, the combined influence of such abuses would have led to extensive damage to the region's land, air, and water systems, even without the intrusion of the oil industry.

Nevertheless, the discovery of oil brought an era of much more rapid exploitation and a new and more troublesome source of pollution. In the rush for instant wealth, oil was seen as black gold, not black sludge. The gusher was the ecological symbol for this early period — photographs of the Lucas gusher went out across the world, showing the magnificent spectacle of a six-inch stream of oil rising more than 100 feet above the top of the derrick. So powerful was this image that wise well owners arranged to turn on similar gushers for the entertainment and persuasion of potential investors. [4] In this atmosphere of uncontrolled exploitation, few cameras recorded what happened to the gushing oil after it splashed to earth.

The gushers were only the most visible sources of pollution. In this formative period, a regional oil industry was constructed from scratch. In an all-out race to beat competitors to market, new facilities were generally hastily built, emphasizing speed and quantity of production, not efficiency and the prevention of waste. As a result, the race to market was run over a very slick track. Flush production led to often massive drain-offs of crude that soaked the ground, while the rapid removal of oil from the wells meant the introduction of salt water into the underground reservoirs of oil and into the region's water system. For lack of better storage, producers often used open earthen pits and wooden tanks. Adequate transportation and loading facilities did not exist, so large quantities of oil were lost between pumping stations and the tankers that carried much of the crude to the East coast. At least as much oil probably found its way into the region's ground, water, and air in this period as found its way to market.

Inside the early refineries, all aspects of the operations reflected a general lack of regard for the environmental consequences of unrestricted exploitation. Throughout much of the period up to 1914, numerous topping plants attempted to survive by distilling off only the most valuable products, like kerosene and gasoline, and disposing of the remainder of the crude. The large plants owned

[3] Mayor Ben Campbell to Judge James Autry, letter dated August 12, 1913, in Box 30, Personal Correspondence (1913), papers of James L. Autry, Rice University, Houston, Texas. For a good summary of regional and state development prior to 1901, see John Spratt, *The Road to Spindletop* (Dallas, 1955).

[4] James Clark and Michel Halbouty, *Spindletop* (New York, 1952), 52–94, 105.

by Gulf, Texaco, and Magnolia (now Mobil) recovered a greater portion of the total amount of crude they processed, but they, too, relied on the simple technology of straight distillation in stills heated by burners fueled by crude oil. Such open flames were economically and ecologically inefficient, using large amounts of oil while producing a heavy smoke. Sulphur fumes created during refining escaped into the air, as did hydrocarbon vapors from poorly constructed storage and transportation equipment. Widespread water pollution resulted from frequent oil spills at the plants and at refinery shipping terminals. Flood control equipment was inadequate, and periodic floods in the coastal region washed much of the spilled oil into rivers and streams. Methods for separating oil out of the water used in refining operations were rudimentary and did not prevent the return of much oil-polluted water to the regional water system. Oil particles thus entered the region's lakes and, ultimately, the Gulf of Mexico. Here they joined large amounts of oil lost during the loading of tankers and contaminated ballast dumped at sea by the oil-burning tankers that were replacing coal-burners. By any measure, past or present, these rudimentary refineries and their supporting distribution systems were major sources of water and air contamination.

In the early period, oil pollution of air and water was both extensive and obvious in the Port Arthur-Beaumont area. Although the exact levels can only be roughly estimated, it is clear that air pollution was a problem at a very early date.[5] Several days after Spindletop blew in, a thick, yellow, sulphur-laden fog began periodically to discolor Beaumont houses. Similar fumes threatened the lives of some of the drillers. With the decline of crude production, the region's air quality improved (or, more precisely, the level of visible air contamination decreased), and the large refineries then became the primary source of air pollution in the Jefferson County area. Because of the distance between them and the surrounding cities, and because of prevailing ocean breezes that removed contaminated air, they did not at first cause a major air pollution problem.[6]

Such was not the case for water pollution, however. Fourteen years of increasing discharge led to serious levels of contamination in the regional waterways. Like refinery-related air pollution, this

[5] The lack of reliable, systematic sources of information on the extent of pollution in this early period forces the historian to rely, perhaps excessively, on descriptive information — read in the context of recent advances in the understanding of pollution — in reconstructing conditions.

[6] *Oil Investors' Journal*, July 5, 1902, p. 5; September 1, 1902, 8.

problem was concentrated in the Port Arthur area. But it also spread outward along the paths taken by the oil-carrying and oil-burning tankers, and conditions in the shipping lanes and at the loading and unloading terminals on both ends of the voyage reflected those around Port Arthur. Both water and air pollution, however, went largely unnoticed for most of the early period.

Blatant disregard for the waste of large quantities of oil during the era of the gusher seems very remote now that energy shortages are the rule. Nevertheless, many of the attitudes toward pollution formed during the era of unrestrained expansion were remarkably durable, and many of the institutional problems continued to hamper the search for solutions for much of the remainder of the century.

ATTITUDES AND INSTITUTIONS, 1901–1914

In this early period, the major large-scale organizations in the region, the oil companies, had no incentive to recognize and respond to the pollution problems caused by their operations. Crude prices dipped to as low as three cents a barrel, making the spillage of a few barrels, or even a few hundred barrels, of minor importance. A highly competitive market structure made short-run survival more crucial than long-run planning, and the low level of available technology led to the recovery for sale of only a small portion of each barrel of crude. Because of the small size and limited resources of many companies, expenditures for control of pollution were an unaffordable luxury, especially in the context of a larger society that made few demands for the control of pollution but on the contrary, encouraged speed and quantity of production, not efficiency and the lack of waste. The oil companies did as the market they faced dictated: they chose rapid, unrestrained production with minimal concern for the escape into the air and water of large quantities of their cheap raw material.[7]

The dominant values of the region and of the larger society of which it was a part further discouraged concern about pollution. Growth was the primary economic goal shared by most segments of society. Restraints on rapid growth and impingements on the rights of property owners were necessary to deal with the oil-related damage to the environment, but neither was likely to be tolerated until oil pollution should begin to threaten other industries

[7] For the classic statement of the long-run costs of such attitudes, see K. William Kapp, *The Social Costs of Private Enterprise* (New York, 1950). See, also, Matthew Edel, *Economics and the Environment* (Englewood Cliffs, N.J., 1973) and Joseph Petulla, *American Environmental History* (San Francisco, 1977).

or the health of the population. In the absence of such a crisis, the oil companies enjoyed great leeway in determining what was best for their own well-being and, by extension, for that of the region.

This early period of nearly unchallenged oil industry dominance had a long-lasting influence on government-business relations. Through an ideological lens of "free competition," oil executives in the Spindletop era viewed government suspiciously, as a potential usurper of corporate power and a threat to corporate autonomy. Politicians were usually seen as meddlers who were both opportunistic and incompetent. The legislation they produced was, almost by definition, confusing and wrong-headed. Extremely threatening campaign rhetoric by office seekers and periodic antitrust assaults on the oil companies reinforced these perceptions. The resulting distrust of government and disdain for it did not disappear. Of course, such attitudes did not prevent business from cooperating with government on measures that were beneficial to it. But when government attempted to assert power in areas previously controlled solely by the corporation, cooperation became most difficult. Pollution control was one of the most volatile of such issues.[8]

The oil companies' ideological devotion to free enterprise thus reinforced a very practical aversion to sharing power. But the oil executives' mistrust of government officials was not simply the result of their own particularly strong ideological and practical disdain for government. Businessmen often perceived much government activity as incompetent and misguided because it was, in fact, incompetent and misguided. In the early period and throughout much of the century, various levels of government were often simply not capable of governing; they could not respond effectively to the wide variety of demands placed on them by rapid growth.[9] Such deficiencies in the public sector did not arise entirely because politicians were opportunistic or poorly suited to their offices. In-

[8] Texaco's first attorney reflected a general attitude when he wrote to the company's president: "The oil business is young in Texas. Its operations are to a degree spectacular and attractive to public attention.... It is the kind of shining mark which attracts the attention of the average politician." Attorney James Autry to President Joseph Cullinan, letter dated May 12, 1904, "Business Correspondence, 1901–1912," in Folder 1904, Box 27, Papers of James Lockhart Autry, Rice University, Houston, Texas. For Autry's view of antitrust, see Autry to Cullinan, letter dated May 28, 1904, ibid. For a very different view of antitrust, that of the Texas Attorney General, see Jewel Lightfoot, *Antitrust Laws of the State of Texas* (Austin, 1907), 51.

[9] Wallace Farnham, "The Weakened Spring of Government: A Study of Nineteenth-Century American History," in Stanley Katz and Stanley Kutler, eds., *New Perspectives in the American Past* (Boston, 1972), 28–44, provides insights into the inadequacies of late-nineteenth-century government. His general approach is also useful in understanding important shortcomings of the public sector in the twentieth century. See, also, Thomas Cochran, *Business in American Life: A History* (New York, 1972), chapters 12, 13, and 20.

deed, enough structural problems existed within the public sector to account for many of its shortcomings.

In the absence of better solutions, several state agencies became the focus of pollution-control efforts for almost sixty years. From the beginning of the region's oil-induced development, these agencies were ill-equipped to deal with the problems that accompanied the sudden intrusion of the industry. The state government lacked the money, personnel, expertise, or institutional arrangements to do much more than acknowledge that pollution existed. In 1901, the budget for the entire Texas state executive office was only an estimated $23,150. At that time, the attorney general's office, which would come to carry the brunt of the legal fight against pollution, consisted of the attorney general, three assistants, and two clerks and had a budget of $17,600. The Fish and Oyster Commission, which became one of the agencies responsible for controlling water pollution, consisted of just one man with annual expenses of $2,400. The State Board of Health, which later took on an important role in pollution control, had substantially greater resources, but most of its expenditures involved the inspection of incoming ships.[10] The resources of state agencies expanded gradually throughout the century, but they were still meager weapons with which to combat the pollution caused by one of the world's largest refining complexes. From 1901 until the 1960s, these underfunded, understaffed state agencies were the center of public initiatives to control oil pollution.[11]

Perhaps even more significant than the general lack of resources was the absence in the early years, as throughout most of the century, of even an underfunded public body with a specific and overriding institutional mandate to control pollution. Instead, each of the existing agencies reacted to pollution as a minor problem that was largely incidental to its central duties. Thus, the Attorney General's office prosecuted nuisance cases against polluters, but it focused most of its energies elsewhere. Similarly, although pollution sometimes became a threat to public health, local and state public health departments had many more pressing demands on

[10] Even these figures are deceptively high, since these funds were used for various purposes throughout the state, not just in the refining region. See *Annual Report of the Comptroller of Public Accounts of the State of Texas, Year Ending August 31, 1900* (Austin, 1901), 107–124. For purposes of comparison, it is useful to note that about $40,000,000 was invested by private companies in the Southeast Texas oil industry from 1901 to September 1904. See *Oil Investors' Journal*, September 1, 1904, 1–3.

[11] For a brief sketch of the histories of national pollution control and conservation agencies, see Cynthia Enloe, *The Politics of Pollution in a Comparative Perspective: Ecology and Power in Four Nations* (New York, 1975), 178–189. For the Texas state agencies, see John T. Thompson, *Public Administration of Water Resources in Texas* (Austin, 1960), 14–60.

their resources. As the scale and complexity of petroleum-related pollution mounted, such inadequacies in the existing institutional arrangements in the public sector became increasingly evident.

Such problems were to be expected when a political structure inherited from a much simpler age attempted to respond to difficult problems brought about by the very large production of a relatively new product by corporations operating on a scale previously unknown to the region. The growing oil industry and the general regional development induced by oil created pressures for new public services and regulations. In this sense, the rapidly expanding industry pulled the public sector into the twentieth century, encouraging the modernization of government at many levels.[12]

In the early period, the public sector lacked both the experience and resources of the dynamic private corporations. The evolution of an efficient and independent public sector capable of responding to the demands created by sustained industrial growth was a lengthy and often painful historical process. As the oil companies that controlled most of the region's refining capacity continued to expand, they remained more highly organized — geographically, technologically, and administratively — than the various levels of government under which they operated. This continuing lag in capabilities resulted in part from the public sector's late start and its confusion as to purpose and authority. But it also reflected the scale and complexity of the problems that accompanied growth and the variety of difficult demands that were thus made on the public sector.

A lack of efficiency went hand-in-hand with a lack of independence. The companies quickly realized that in areas as diverse as social overhead expenditures, tax policies, and especially antitrust, the state offered important benefits while, at the same time, posing substantial threats to corporate well-being.[13] They thus moved quickly into the political arena to secure their needs and to control uncertainty. In a political system that responded to organized, sustained, interest-group pressure, the large oil companies were in an excellent position to acquire government favors and to resist government challenges.

[12] For a pathbreaking treatment of conservation policy in the context of the evolving national political structure, see Samuel Hays, *Conservation and the Gospel of Efficiency* (New York, 1975). See, especially, the author's preface to the 1975 edition (Atheneum) of the book, which was originally published in 1959.

[13] The largest regional companies spent considerable effort in attempting to push through the Texas legislature corporation laws that would allow vertically integrated operations, thereby removing the threat of prosecution for violation of existing, highly restrictive corporation laws. See John O. King, *Joseph Stephen Cullinan* (Nashville, 1970), 168–175.

Their adeptness at political maneuvering reflected both the oil companies' organizational strengths and structural characteristics of the political system that made public responses to problems like pollution most difficult. The twin pillars around which the system was built — federalism and checks and balances — insured that political power would be dispersed. Existing political boundaries did not match the boundaries of the region's growing pollution problem. Political units at the local, county, state, and national levels were, at least theoretically, capable of exerting control over portions of the problem. In practice, however, an often debilitating confusion of authority resulted, especially in dealing with a pollution problem that resolutely refused to be turned back at the county or state line and, instead, continued to grow across political boundaries. Even when authority over a portion of the problem could be asserted by an existing agency, its limited resources and concentration on short-run solutions generally prevented a wide-scale, systematic response. Thus, amid an overabundance of potential public authority, there was a paucity of institutions capable of exerting real power to control pollution.

In the early period, those agencies that might have attempted to do so lacked more than resources; they did not even possess the clear legal authority to forbid the dumping of pollutants into the air and water. During the first twenty years of regional development, no local or state laws prohibited such discharge. The existing national law, the Rivers and Harbors Act of 1899, also provided little practical means for the control of oil pollution. The law had been framed to meet conditions prevalent when "the production and use of petroleum oil was insignificant," and it was "not considered broad enough in its meaning or character" to include most petroleum-related pollution.[14] Such limited authority combined with equally limited incentives for action, debilitating structural problems in the public sector, and a societal commitment to rapid growth meant that little would be done about regional pollution until it reached crisis proportions.

THE ERA OF INDUSTRY LEADERSHIP, 1914–1940

Such a crisis came in the early years of the 1920s, when the extraordinary water contamination that accompanied the rapid expan-

[14] Department of the Interior, U.S. Bureau of Mines, *Pollution of the Coast Waters of the United States* (Washington, 1923), 538. A copy is in the API library in Washington, D.C. See also Lynn M. Alperin, *Custodians of the Coast: History of the United States Army Engineers at Galveston* (Galveston, 1977), 267–281.

sion of the oil industry during and immediately after World War I focused regional and national attention on water pollution. During the 1920s and 1930s there were several significant departures in public regulation by the state and national governments. These public initiatives were constrained, however, by many of the same attitudinal and institutional problems that had previously blocked government action. In this middle period the oil industry, not public agencies, generally played the dominant role by implementing private pollution control measures while striving to avert public measures that threatened corporate control of environmental affairs. A close examination of the responses of the oil companies and of the state to the water pollution crisis of the early 1920s reveals much about the relative power of each. Indeed, as the first major response to water pollution by oil in the twentieth century, the events leading up to the passage of several oil pollution laws in the 1920s set the tone for much of the period until the 1960s.

Before the crisis of the early 1920s could be treated, it had to be identified and measured. In response to public outcries and to complaints by other industries affected by petroleum pollution, the API, the American Steamship Owners' Association, and the U.S. Bureau of Mines cooperated in completing a comprehensive investigation of national conditions. Compiled by representatives of the government and of the large oil companies and published in 1923, *Pollution by Oil of the Coast Waters of the United States* painted a bleak portrait of a nation whose coastal waters were covered with oil. This descriptive report provided the first general survey of regional pollution, and it serves as a convenient benchmark for discussion of the levels of regional water pollution after 1923.[15]

After studying ports along the East and Gulf coasts, the investigators concluded that Port Arthur, "with its exceedingly heavy oil commerce, represents one of the worst, if not the worst, condition of oil pollution witnessed by the Committee." So bad were the spillages in transferring oil to ships and the run-offs from refinery operations that "the large refiners maintain crews of men and equipment for skimming the surface of the harbor waters." Their efforts were not very successful, however: "they appear to be doing little more than holding their own." Beaumont and Galveston were somewhat cleaner. But the Houston Ship Channel "undoubtedly represents one of the worst oil polluted localities seen by the Committee," and was surpassed in this regard only by the channel at

[15] *Ibid.*, 1–10.

Port Arthur. Since the Houston waterway had been in use by oil companies for only seven years at the time of the investigation, its contamination had been extremely rapid and thorough. The survey cited various sources of regional oil pollution, including dumping of oil at sea, run-offs from one oil field near Houston, and the careless handling of fuel oil by railroads and other industries. But in the Houston-Port Arthur areas, the primary sources were industrial waste and the escape of oil during transfer from refining docks to seagoing vessels.[16]

The 1923 investigation suggests that the region experienced perhaps its worst surface water pollution of the twentieth century in the early 1920s. This contamination drove the lumber industry, whose product was ruined by oil, away from Port Arthur to Orange and Beaumont. Gulf coast fishing and oyster dredging suffered, and the wildlife that had initially helped to attract hunters and fishermen to the area in the 1890s became less plentiful. The region's beaches became nearly unfit for recreational use. At Galveston, where tourism was the major business, oil pollution in the water and on the beaches became "extremely bad," so bad, in fact, that cans of gasoline were placed along the beach so that bathers could remove the oil accumulated while swimming.[17]

Such conditions focused public attention on the inadequacies of the existing laws and several new laws resulted. In 1918, the Port of Houston passed a harbor regulation that prohibited the dumping of untreated oil products into the Houston Ship Channel. In 1924, the federal government passed a Federal Oil Pollution Act, which regulated the dumping of fuel at sea by oil-burning vessels.[18] These statutes were among the first aimed specifically at water pollution by oil, and they were important in establishing the legal basis for the control of all types of pollution.[19]

Significant as they were, these laws had only limited impact because of the way they were passed and enforced. The Port of Houston regulation explicitly prohibited the discharge of harmful oil products. But when the new port director, B. C. Allin, who had been recommended for the job by a former president of Humble Oil, attempted to enforce the law as he interpreted it, he faced heated opposition from various refiners. After failing to obtain court convictions in cases against numerous polluters, despite what

[16] *Ibid.*, 434, 440, 64.
[17] *Ibid.*, 435, 461, 462
[18] *Ibid.*, 577–578.
[19] J. Clarence Davies III and Barbara Davies, *The Politics of Pollution*, 2nd ed. (Indianapolis, 1975), 38.

he viewed as ample evidence, Allin called for city council measures to assure that "proper convictions" could be obtained. This action, and the belief that the director was harassing the industries along the ship channel while attempting to usurp jurisdiction that was not his, gave the companies an opening; the attorney for the Galena-Signal Oil Company demanded that the mayor of Houston replace the port director. Allin had antagonized influential oil men like the president of Galena-Signal, Joseph Cullinan, who had been president of Texaco until 1913. Cullinan, along with other founders of the regional oil industry, had given much of his time and a considerable amount of his own money to advancing the interests of Houston and its waterway before Congress. In fact, it had been Cullinan who had originally suggested that the city of Houston exercise police powers along the ship channel, but he was now angered when these powers were used against his own firm and others in that area. Important oil men considered Allin's actions as a way of using "trifling matters to harass companies which had invested millions in plants along the waterway." They were utilizing, they felt, "the most modern appliances to prevent the escape of oil." Against such opposition, an appointed public official, whose primary duty was to oversee the rapid development of the port, was not in a good position to demand further water treatment equipment. Subsequent actions aimed at curbing oil pollution were more restrained.[20]

The oil companies exerted similar influence on the national law passed in 1924, although in this case their efforts were less direct. Protests by other industries adversely affected by petroleum pollution and by sportsmen created much of the demand for legislation, but the oil industry proved very adept at controlling the actual content of the Act that was finally passed. The API-Bureau of Mines report discussed above served as an important source of information for those who framed the Federal Oil Pollution Act of 1924. After providing much of the information available to Congress, the API and the large oil companies that were its major members used their political power to constrain the scope of the law. In the end, oil industry interests succeeded in limiting the law to coverage of oil discharged by vessels at sea, despite the fact that

[20] Benjamin Allin, *Reaching for the Sea* (Boston, 1956), 80–103; B. C. Allin to Mayor of Houston, letter dated December 10, 1922, in "Houston Ship Channel" folder, papers of Joseph Stephen Cullinan, University of Houston, Houston, Texas; W. W. Moore to Mayor Amerman, letter dated December 11, 1922, in "Houston Ship Channel" folder, Cullinan papers; memo to Joseph Cullinan, dated December 27, 1922, in "Houston Ship Channel" folder, Cullinan papers. The Houston *Chronicle*, July 12, 1925, p. 8, records citizens' protests of continuing discharges of waste oil into the ship channel.

even the API-Bureau of Mines report had also cited refineries and oil field run-offs as important sources of pollution.[21]

A similar political strategy of containment also succeeded in the late 1930s, when water pollution control measures received an unprecedented amount of attention in the national legislature, and, for a time, a national stream pollution control Act seemed probable.[22] A study prepared for the API on the bills pending before Congress was unusually explicit in suggesting how such bills could be influenced. The study's recommendations to the API were in the form of a comprehensive strategy for controlling the fate of pollution legislation. It stressed that the Texas delegation in Congress, which included the chairmen of several important committees, was of "the greatest possible strategic value." Thus, in the Texas delegation and in those of other southern and southwestern states, the oil industry's "not inconsiderable influence can be exerted quietly in any number of ways . . . setting in motion throughout the Southern States those forces of opinion to which members of Congress are especially sensitive." Special news features could be used to educate the polity, but "public statements should be confined to groups of producers — preferably independent organizations which are free of the political liabilities that some of the industry's major units have inherited from a fairly recent past." The report suggested that industrywide lobbying and possibly the cooperation of other affected industries should be mobilized in support of state and interstate action on water pollution in order to decrease pressures for federal legislation. Above all, the industry should not compromise by recognizing the principle of federal regulation, since "the only thing which practical politicians . . . recognize is an organized opposition capable of influencing votes. If the industry proceeds on that basis — plays poker rather than throwing down its cards in advance — it may again, as it did in 1924, postpone drastic anti-pollution legislation." [23]

This assessment proved unduly pessimistic; almost thirty more years were to pass before the enactment of a strong national water pollution control law in 1965. The key to the oil industry's ability to control the political environment was its access to the decision

---

[21] Bronson Batchelor, *Stream Pollution: A Study of Proposed Federal Legislation and Its Effect on the Oil Industry*, 51, manuscript dated February 1937, in the API library, Washington, D.C.; and Bureau of Mines, *Pollution of the Coast Waters of the United States*, 1–44.

[22] W. B. Hart, "Controlled Disposal of Wastes Versus Pollution," *Oil and Gas Journal*, May 14, 1936, p. 234. For a general discussion of these bills, see Herman Baity, "Aspects of Governmental Policy on Stream Pollution Abatement," *American Journal of Public Health* (December 1939), 1297–1307.

[23] Bronson Batchelor, *Stream Pollution*, 45–51.

makers in Congress and the lack of equal access by those with different interests. The relative balance of political power between polluters and those affected by pollution was correctly perceived in industry discussions regarding the possibility of legislation: "Action is likely, not to appease sportsmen or Walton leagues (which are largely without political influence), but because of purely political factors." [24] In a political system characterized by dispersed power, those who could identify the crucial centers of power and bring political pressures to bear on those centers could generally succeed in attaining their political interests. The individual oil companies and the oil industry in general were well-equipped to succeed in a broker-state political bargaining process; those groups that gradually emerged to challenge industry lobbying efforts in the area of pollution control were not so well-equipped. They lacked the clarity of purpose, the unity of goals, the scale of political resources, and the political experience of the oil industry interest groups. As a result, in the 1930s, and for several decades thereafter, effective national legislation aimed at curbing petroleum-related pollution never quite made it through Congress, despite wide-scale rhetorical support for such a measure.

Water pollution thus remained primarily a matter for state concern. The experience of Jefferson County (Beaumont and Port Arthur) with oil pollution in 1939 provides a good example of the difficulties of handling such problems at the state level. When salt water from producing wells in east Texas flowed down the Neches River and threatened Jefferson County's fresh water supply for domestic and industrial use, local authorities had no established means to remedy the situation. There was still no single state agency whose primary task it was to deal with such matters. Given this institutional-jurisdictional void, four agencies that were peripherally concerned with such problems issued a joint warning; the action was taken by the Texas Railroad Commission, which regulated oil production, the Attorney General's office, the State Board of Health, and the Game, Fish, and Oyster Commission. The threat of legal action led "several of the larger oil operators" to make improvements. But substantial pollution continued, and it led to a suit seeking an injunction against the producers who were allegedly causing "irreparable injury to property rights and civil rights, for

[24] *Ibid.*, 34. A broad study of the oil industry's experience with such "political factors" is Robert Engler, *The Politics of Oil* (New York, 1961). For a general review of national oil policy, see Gerald Nash, *United States Oil Policy, 1890–1964* (Pittsburgh, 1968). For a general review of air and water pollution legislation, see Clarence Davies III and Barbara Davies, *The Politics of Pollution.* Also, see Frank Smith, *The Politics of Conservation* (New York, 1966).

which no adequate remedy at law exists." Although hailed as a pioneer case, the suit was compromised by the Texas attorney general. The Beaumont city attorney and the Jefferson County group that had pursued the matter for over a year and a half objected, but to no avail. In return for dropping the suit, the oil companies involved promised to stop polluting. They paid no penalties, however, for past abuses. Since the state attorney general was serving out a two-year term, his acceptance of "full responsibility" for enforcement was unconvincing to Beaumonters, who feared that the oil companies would not respect the agreement.[25]

Reliance on the promise of an elected official to enforce a voluntary agreement pointed up the absence of an adequate institutional framework for dealing with the external, environmental costs of economic growth. Several state agencies had limited authority over aspects of pollution-related problems. In each case, however, pollution control was a peripheral concern of an organization whose primary functions, allocated resources, and trained personnel dictated greater concern for other tasks. Lacking the administrative machinery to handle even the Jefferson County case, which involved obviously harmful pollution clearly traceable to a known source, the state of Texas was ill-equipped indeed to control the more complex air and water pollution that accompanied the subsequent development of the refining region.

Private Responses in the Middle Period

During this middle period, only limited political initiatives were taken at either the national or state level, but the public debates over control seem to have had some impact on the search for private solutions. Throughout this period, the large refiners and the API pursued private measures aimed at ameliorating pollution. The incentive for such actions was primarily economic; efficiency meant higher profits. But political factors undoubtedly reinforced these economic considerations. The desire to contain and ultimately to control politically imposed solutions accelerated the pace of the oil companies' search for cleaner methods of production. An oil industry spokesman summarized this attitude in 1936. He noted that, in the past, "as a rule, it has been only under threats from authorities that action has been taken." This had resulted in much ill-will while increasing the demand for new laws. To be in a posi-

---

[25] *Beaumont Enterprise*, March 26, 1939, p. 1; November 11, 1939, p. 4; January 24, 1940, p. 9; January 26, 1940, p. 16.

tion to "demand a voice in creating the rules under which it must play," however, the industry must have "clean hands" and "a clean house."[26] The fear of government intervention was a strong secondary motive behind private responses to pollution in the 1920s and 1930s.

The API was in the forefront of these efforts. After aiding the Bureau of Mines in the investigation of oil pollution in 1923, the API conducted its own follow-up survey in 1927. Its report cited a marked improvement in oil pollution conditions in support of its contention that "existing legislation is adequate" and "that better results can be obtained by voluntary effort and cooperation than by further legislation." This survey was at once a public relations measure aimed at soothing public concern and a serious report on private initiatives in the area of pollution control. Subsequent efforts of the API also had this dual nature, but they should not therefore be categorized as merely "P.R." and dismissed as meaningless. The public relations value of such activity was grounded in the specific, industry-sponsored research programs that laid a foundation for understanding the impact and treatment of oil pollution. An industry spokesman in a later period aptly summarized the API's attitude in the middle period when he said that "the best defense the industry has against unnecessary corrective measures and an out-of-proportion control effort is a heavy backlog of definitive information." Beginning in the 1920s, the API's research made it a primary source of such information for the oil industry, for political institutions involved in regulating the industry, and for the general public.[27]

The API's first discovery was the void of knowledge concerning petroleum pollution, and it set out to begin to fill this void.[28] Its environmental research aimed at accumulating and compiling practical knowledge useful in building and operating cleaner refineries. One of the earliest results was the three-part *Manual of Disposal of Refinery Wastes*, which outlined the best methods for the disposal of waste waters containing oil, waste gases and vapors, and waste waters containing solutes.[29] The API's applied research focused on the development of a modern, efficient separator. The

[26] W. B. Hart, "Controlled Disposal of Wastes Versus Pollution," 237.
[27] API, "Report Covering Survey of Oil Conditions in the United States," 1927, p. 1. Report on file in API library, Washington, D.C.; API, *Proceedings of the 17th Mid-Year Meeting, Division of Refining*, San Francisco, May 12–15, 1955, 299–300.
[28] W. B. Hart, "Disposal of Refinery Waste Waters," *Industrial and Engineering Chemistry* 26, no. 9 (September 1934), 965.
[29] API, *Manual of the Disposal of Refinery Wastes, Section I: Waste Water Containing Oil* (New York, 1941); *Section II: Waste Gases and Vapors* (New York, 1931); *Section III: Waste Waters Containing Solutes* (New York, 1935).

specifications and standards that the association established were accepted and used throughout the industry in coping with two related problems: the separation of oil from water prior to its discharge from the refinery and the treatment of trapped wastes.

Environmental research within the individual oil companies also helped to fill gaps in the understanding of waste disposal. Atlantic Refining Company led the way with a "Division of Waste Control" that had its own separate laboratory by 1933.[30] This commitment of resources to environmental research marked a significant departure by establishing both research programs and research institutions that could be expanded in later years.

Unfortunately, such potentially significant initiatives had little impact on pollution control during the middle period. For while a small group of industry researchers found answers to the most basic questions involving the treatment of water discharge, a much greater industry-wide research effort developed new techniques of production. Indeed, a defining characteristic of the middle period was the introduction of a series of important technological breakthroughs that resulted in increased yields of improved gasoline from each barrel of crude refined. Such advances, however, also brought increased yields of "improved" — that is, more chemically complex — types of pollution. Thus, while a few researchers developed an efficient separator to control water pollution, many more introduced changes in production technology that only much later would be recognized as important departures in the production of pollution.

This lag between implementation of production technology and the introduction of control technology can be seen most clearly in the case of tetraethyl lead. As refiners searched for ways to improve the quality of gasoline in the 1920s, the laboratories of General Motors made a major breakthrough by adding tetraethyl lead to gasoline. Thirty years later, researchers were still unraveling the basic chemistry of air pollution and were only beginning to understand the general nature of this phenomenon. Responses to the specific atmospheric effect of lead additives did not come until nearly forty years after their introduction. A similar lag in understanding was apparent, at least in retrospect, in the development of fluid cracking units in the late 1930s and the 1940s. At that time, refiners hailed the new unit as a major breakthrough in gasoline production. Not until thirty years later, however, did environmental researchers begin to recognize and react to the fact that it

[30] W. B. Hart, "The Waste Control Laboratory of the Atlantic Refining Company," *Water Works and Sewerage* 88 (January 1941), 30–31.

also represented a major breakthrough in the production of air and water pollution. Other similar advances in production technology generally had long-run environmental implications that were not recognized, much less planned for, in the rush to produce more and better refined products. As a result, despite the industry's pioneering research efforts in pollution control in the middle period, the imbalance between production and control techniques increased as the refineries became more technologically advanced.[31]

Although the oil companies did not fare very well in anticipating the environmental consequences of new technologies, they proved much more successful at eliminating the older problems of waste. The most significant antipollution measures taken by the individual refineries in the middle period were those directed at increased efficiency, which were greatly encouraged by the rising value of petroleum. The *Oil and Gas Journal* cited the main rationale behind such measures in an article in 1926: "Reduction of waste is nothing more or less than increased efficiency in the management of the various departments of an oil company." The goal of waste reduction was increased profits, but an indirect and usually unnoticed consequence was often pollution reduction. In the early 1920s, for example, Texaco's Port Arthur works "undertook a campaign of fuel efficiency in order to reduce, if possible, the enormous quantity of fuel oil consumed under stills and boilers." "A very noticeable" reduction in fuel waste resulted, conserving oil and eliminating excessive smoke as well. Even greater economic and environmental benefits accompanied a more radical change in fuel use, the substitution of natural gas and refinery gases for oil fuels in the 1920s and 1930s. Another important aspect of the campaign for increased efficiency involved the prevention of excessive evaporation from storage tanks; the construction and sale of improved tanks designed to cut down evaporation losses proliferated in the 1920s. While saving valuable oil, such tanks also prevented the discharge of potentially harmful hydrocarbon vapors.[32]

[31] For a brief discussion of tetraethyl lead, see *Oil and Gas Journal — Oil City Derrick*, Diamond Jubilee Issue, August 27, 1934, p. 199. For a general discussion of the cumulative effects of such lags, see Barry Commoner, *The Closing Circle: Nature, Man and Technology* (New York, 1971). See, also, W. B. Hart, *Industrial Waste Disposal for Petroleum Refineries and Allied Plants* (Cleveland, 1947); W. B. Hart, "Disposal of Refinery Waste Waters," 967; C. G. Rebman, "Elimination of Waste in Refining," *Oil and Gas Journal*, November 4, 1926, pp. 126–130. The general advances in refining technology are discussed in Johns Enos, *Petroleum Progress and Profit: A History of Process Innovation* (Cambridge, Mass., 1962).

[32] *Oil and Gas Journal*, November 4, 1926, p. 126; *The Look Box* 3, no. 8 (August 1921), 6; *Oil and Gas Journal*, January 13, 1922, pp. 25 and 27. See, also, James H. Wescott, *Oil: Its Conservation and Waste* (New York, 1930); Clifford Russell, *Residuals Management in Industry: A Case Study of Petroleum Refining* (Baltimore, 1973).

The rising cost of oil was incentive enough for increased efficiency, but other, noneconomic factors often entered into such considerations:

> The installation of suitable drainage systems and separators in refineries is primarily a measure to prevent industrial waste, although it seems probable that, in order to comply with the laws against oil pollution, many refineries have installed equipment much more extensive than the mere prevention of industrial wastes would appear to warrant.[33]

In such cases, the desire to save oil was reinforced by the desire to avoid intervention by the public sector; the results were a reduction in waste and a decline in water pollution.

Substantial long-run decrease in the volume of refinery discharges also resulted from the often ingenious transformation of waste materials into useful products. In the early period of regional development, most firms sold only one or two primary refined products and disposed of the remaining by-products. Gasoline, natural gas, sulphur, sludge, coke, and a variety of other commodities once discarded as waste later became important products. Beginning in 1932, for instance, the petroleum coke that had long accumulated at Port Arthur area refineries was sold to Great Lakes Carbon Company, which manufactured pure carbon from it. Later, recovery units began to convert sulphur fumes that once had been released into the air, and spent acid once dumped into rivers, into marketable sulphur and fertilizer. After treatment, sludge acid and other residues became fuel, as did the carbon dioxide derived from the carbon monoxide fumes created in the recovery of catalyst material. As a result of such efforts, the level of pollutants released in refining declined as those who could afford new processes, primarily the large oil companies, found ways to salvage useful products out of wastes.[34]

These measures were part of a continuing search for methods to extract greater value from each barrel of crude refined. The firm tried to minimize losses of oil during processing, increase the yield of the most desirable end products through sophisticated cracking techniques, and find markets or industrial uses within the refineries for as many by-products as possible. These trends characterized regional refining throughout its history, but economic, competitive

---

[33] Bureau of Mines, *Pollution of the Coast Waters*, 42–43. Of course, "noneconomic" factors — a court case, political lobbying, public relations — could represent substantial "economic" costs to the firm.

[34] See "Port Arthur Scrapbooks," vol. II, index number 18, at Gates Memorial Library, Port Arthur, Texas; C. G. Rebman, "Elimination of Waste in Refining," 130; Texaco, *Protecting the Environment*, 1973, 7.

pressures among large refiners accelerated the drive for efficiency during the middle period, just as political pressures to control environmental contamination were to do in the 1960s. The companies profited from the expansion of their marketable goods; the regional society profited from the reduction of discarded pollutants.

Such on-going reductions in the amount of pollutants discharged per barrel at least partially offset the increased absolute level of pollution caused by the sustained growth of refining throughout the upper Texas Gulf coast. Although still a regional problem, the severe surface water pollution of the early 1920s probably declined in the next two decades.[35] New, more difficult problems accumulated, however, as a result of the introduction of new production technologies. In particular, there was little awareness of the coming problems with air pollution. Thus, while the oil industry took the lead during the middle years in combating the most flagrant forms of water pollution, other more complex environmental problems that were largely ignored in this period would later call forth stronger public initiatives.

THE EMERGENCE OF PUBLIC LEADERSHIP, 1940–1960s

World War II and its aftermath brought a period of extraordinary expansion to the upper Texas Gulf coast. The continued growth of the petroleum industry and the rapid rise of several major new regional industries, notably petrochemicals and primary metals production, fed a postwar surge of economic development. The resulting industrial waste, combined with the added municipal waste caused by a growing population and the increased air pollution that accompanied the expanding use of the automobile, created major new environmental problems.[36] In the 1950s and 1960s, in the face of increasing air and water contamination from the cumulative impact of a half century of growth in population and industry, those in the refining region sought a better understanding of the causes of pollution and more forceful means of implementing solutions. The means chosen were usually in the public, not the private, sector. The large refiners' historical role as the primary source of much of the area's pollution meant that, no matter how

[35] W. B. Hart and B. F. Weston, "The Water Pollution Abatement Problems of the Petroleum Industry," *Water Works and Sewerage* 88, no. 5 (May 1941), 217, suggests that improvement occurred throughout the nation in waters affected by the oil industry in the decade before 1941. For a general survey of national conditions in the 1930s, see U.S. Natural Resources Committee, Special Advisory Committee on Water Pollution, *Report on Water Pollution* (Washington, 1935).

[36] Texas Highway Department statistics record an increase of more than 500 per cent in automobile registrations in Harris County (Houston) from 1947 to 1970.

well their record compared to that of other industries, they faced stricter public scrutiny in these years.

The post-World War II era witnessed continued problems with oil-related water pollution, but the "new" problems associated with air pollution absorbed much of the region's control efforts. By the mid-1950s, air contamination could simply no longer be ignored. The smog problem of Los Angeles had captured the nation's attention in the late 1940s. In its sprawling size and dependence upon its freeway system, Houston resembled Los Angeles, and it developed a similar air pollution problem. One response was a survey of air pollution in the years 1956–1958. The study's conclusions suggested the intensity of the problem. It recorded "localized," not "community-wide," air pollution. Although the photochemical reactions that contributed to Los Angeles' smog were not in evidence, the survey reported a variety of chemical pollutants from automobiles and from industry, including hydrocarbons in the ship channel area, where "approximately equal concentrations result from oil refining and other industrial operations."

The Beaumont-Port Arthur area, which had far fewer automobiles, did not experience such serious air contamination. Beginning in the late 1940s and 1950s, however, it did confront air pollution problems of primarily industrial origin. Oil and chemical fumes, believed to be potentially hazardous sulphur compounds, caused great discomfort, discoloration of houses, and bad odors. No survey equivalent to Houston's report in the 1950s recorded the precise level of air pollution in the Beaumont-Port Arthur area. But there and throughout the refining region, in the 1950s, widespread air contamination joined the water pollution inherited from an earlier era to create often severe problems for many in the refining region.[37]

Those most apt to seek new public controls over this pollution were those most directly exposed to it. In the early 1950s, a group of citizens from the Houston Ship Channel area began a private campaign to reduce pollution through meetings with local industries. They sought to extract voluntary promises under the threat of court action; there was no public agency other than the courts to which they could turn. Their protests generated pressure for the creation of such an agency and encouraged the formation of an air and water pollution control section in the Harris County Health

[37] Southwest Research Institute, "Project 566–1: Air Pollution Survey of the Houston Area," dated July 1, 1958, pp. ii–x, on file at Houston Chamber of Commerce, Houston, Texas; *Beaumont Enterprise*, July 25, 1952, p. 10; September 6, 1962, p. 9; September 26, 1952, 1; September 22, 1955, 11.

Department (1953). Despite limited resources and its status as a secondary group within a larger organization with diverse functions, the new section utilized publicity, private conferences, and court action to make some progress in controlling water pollution. In the late 1950s, however, two developments limited its power to force reductions in discharges. First, a series of state court decisions made it much more difficult to prosecute offending corporations. Then, in 1961, the state of Texas established a state Water Pollution Control Board, whose jurisdiction conflicted with that of the Harris County agency.[38]

The organization of the state board shifted the focus of political action from a highly industrial, highly polluted region to the state legislature of a large, relatively unpolluted state — thereby undermining the campaign to achieve more effective governmental solutions. The traditional apportionment of state representation meant that agricultural sections held greater political power than the rapidly-growing urban-industrial centers. In addition, the support of powerful oil producers from throughout the state could be mobilized to block moves against the coastal refiners. The evolution of the state board and its policies showed the effects of these political factors. Its program included the use of "grandfather clauses" that permitted continued pollution by existing industries, and it freely used its power to grant waste disposal permits. Even the charter of this first state pollution control agency reflected its weakness; included was a clause requiring behavior consistent with the "industrial development of the state." All in all, in its early years, the board did not hamper the growth of industry or of pollution.[39]

By the mid-1960s, such inaction was a luxury the region could no longer afford. In 1965, a follow-up survey to the Houston air pollution investigation of 1956–1958 revealed how quickly the limits to natural pollution dispersal could be reached in a period of rapid growth: "The most significant change which has taken place is the occurrence of the type of chemical reactions in the atmosphere which are characteristic of the well-known Los Angeles smog situation."[40] Water pollution also demanded attention. In 1967, federal investigators found that "the Houston Ship Channel was by far the worst example of water pollution observed by the board

[38] Edward B. Williams, Jr., "Pollution Control: A Houston Ship Channel Issue" (Master's thesis, Texas A&M University, 1972), 34–47.
[39] *Ibid.*, 48.
[40] Southwest Research Institute, "Project 21–1587: Air Pollution Survey of the Houston Area, 1964–1966," dated October 1966, vi, on file at Houston Chamber of Commerce, Houston, Texas.

on its Texas tour." The problem was "overwhelming," and local officials were reported to feel that "it's so bad already, we don't need to worry about adding more pollution." [41] The investigators cited industry as the biggest polluter, with municipal sewage as a major secondary source. Despite forty-four years of gradual experimentation with water pollution control devices and laws, the 1967 report thus sounded disturbingly similar to that in 1923. Such conditions generated strong pressures for solutions, and Texas state authorities were soon forced to respond.

A newly activist national government further encouraged state action; under the threat of national legislation (in the absence of stronger state antipollution efforts), Texas passed a clean air act in 1965, followed by a water quality act in 1967.[42] These two measures gave public institutions at the state level the potential to exercise much stricter control of air and water pollution. For oil-related problems, this potential could be realized only when the agencies matured into regulatory bodies independent of oil industry control, but now, at least, the potential and the necessary institutions for implementing effective government control existed.

The early history of the implementation of these acts did not indicate that the agencies involved were going to take strong, independent action. Both laws called for programs that were consistent with "the operation of existing industries and the economic development of the state." Most of the original nine members named to the board established for the enforcement of the clean air act seemed to be citizens who would take this admonition seriously. Public protests followed the nomination of the president of a chemical company that had been cited earlier as a polluter of the Houston Ship Channel, and the appointment failed, primarily due to the efforts of citizens' groups concerned about the environment. But this powerful, unified political pressure from those affected by pollution was called forth only when such a clear choice was involved and public enthusiasm was aroused by the drama of a highly charged issue. On more routine matters, the board in its formative period weighed industry needs more heavily than those of less organized groups.[43]

Part of the problems involved in enforcing the new laws resulted from the weaknesses of the young agencies themselves. The air

---

[41] Houston *Post*, September 13, 1967, p. 1.
[42] G. Todd Norvell and Alexander Bell, "Air Pollution Control in Texas," in *Legal Control of the Environment* (New York, 1970), 337–376.
[43] *Ibid.*, 355; Edward Williams, "Pollution Control," 71–76, argues that "the official composition and actual membership on the Board made its position inevitably pro-industry" (71).

board's members served without salary, and salaries for staff positions were insufficient to attract highly qualified personnel. In general, these regulatory bodies had budgets that were far below the amount required to fulfill their stated purposes. In the crucial matter of establishing enforceable norms, they lacked the expert personnel to establish and defend standards upon which the board members could agree.

Some of these difficulties were eased by the increasing federal role in pollution enforcement. In the late 1960s federal air and water pollution laws required states to reduce pollution to federally established levels or face intervention by the U.S. government. The national government had greater resources with which to establish effective standards. It also made financial assistance available to state agencies. Finally, it helped develop a "public" body of knowledge and a new pool of experts. As a result, the public sector could, for the first time, deal critically and forcefully with the information and expertise made available to it by the more experienced, more highly specialized private sector.[44]

In addition to such federal leadership, pressures for improved state enforcement also came from the regional level, where pollution problems were still more easily identified. Harris County officials helped to force the Texas Air Quality Board into action against flagrant violators by bringing suit against regional polluters. Jefferson County citizens' groups organized to protest the granting of air pollution variances to numerous local refineries and petro-chemical plants. With the creation of regional air pollution control districts under federal authority, local initiative became more systematic and more powerful. As public institutions at all levels gained experience, jurisdictional confusion decreased, and the public agencies could turn more of their resources to the problems of enforcing their regulations.[45]

Private organizations like the API and the large oil companies retained a strong interest in imposing their own standards on these public institutions, and the oil firms did not easily surrender their traditional autonomy in this area. In the 1970s, the emerging public regulatory bodies sought to establish their power to enforce com-

[44] G. Todd Norvell and Alexander Bell, "Air Pollution Control in Texas," 373. For a detailed account of another state's difficulties in passing and enforcing environmental protection legislation, see Marc Landy, The Politics of Environmental Reform: Controlling Kentucky Strip Mining (Baltimore, 1976).

[45] G. Todd Norvell and Alexander Bell, "Air Pollution Control in Texas," 368–373; Beaumont Enterprise, November 5, 1969, p. 1. The Harris County Air Pollution Control District was created in 1967; a Beaumont-Port Arthur-Orange District in 1969.

pliance, and a series of major disputes resulted. Texaco and Gulf's Port Arthur refineries and Mobil's Beaumont plant were charged with violations of the clean air act. Responding to the pressure of federal deadlines, the state agency levied fines that were substantial in comparison to anything levied previously, if not in comparison to the companies' ability to pay. Unfavorable publicity seemed to bother the companies involved more than the fines, and they sought to counteract government charges by appealing to the public's desire for continued growth and for adequate supplies of gasoline. In their on-going struggle over the definition and implementation of new standards, the oil companies' record of sustained growth in both quantity and quality of refined products was a politically potent and frequently cited argument.[46]

Despite this record, however, by the 1970s the balance between public and private control of the environment had begun to shift toward the public sector. The sustained growth of manufacturing and the increasing complexity and diversity of pollution had led to a series of crises that called forth demands for solutions. Reliance on private control of industrial pollution had proven inadequate; the resulting rise of public environmental planning bodies represented the most significant rearrangement during this century of the institutional framework within which responses to pollution took place.

Along with this shift came a new level of public interest in environmental problems. In 1922, water pollution in the Houston Ship Channel had been labeled a "trifling matter" by a prominent oil industry spokesman, and the large oil firms subsequently had beaten back most political efforts to impose controls. But in 1971, the head of Texaco's Port Arthur refinery voiced a far different attitude: "Our objective is to keep well within government air and water quality standards, and we will continue to correct any adverse conditions which may be attributable to our operations."[47] At about the same time, the president of Texaco cited the government's "major responsibility" of "setting standards based on realistic goals that have proved necessary to protect the nation's health and welfare."[48] Such statements were supported by substantial invest-

---

[46] For such offenses, the possible fines were $1,000 per day per offense. In 1972, Texaco's Port Arthur refinery was fined $6,000 by the Texas Air Control Board. Great Lakes Carbon in Port Arthur paid a $25,000 fine for more severe violations in the same year. See *Beaumont Journal*, July 4, 1972, p. 1; April 4, 1972, p. 1; *Beaumont Enterprise*, July 27, 1973, p. 1.

[47] Press release to the Port Arthur *News*, CavOilcade edition, 1971, p. 3. Xerox copy from the Refining Department of the Texaco Archives.

[48] Texaco, *Protecting the Environment*, 3.

TEXACO'S PORT ARTHUR PLANT IN 1976.

GULF COAST POLLUTION 27

ments in antipollution equipment.[49] Pollution control was no longer primarily the private concern of those who produced refined goods. Rather, maturing national public institutions had taken the initiative in establishing and enforcing standards of allowable discharge.

The tension between compliance with these standards and unrestrained expansion of productive capacities remained strong in this refining region, since any threat to the continued growth of the refineries was also a threat to the health of the entire regional economy and most of its population. The potential impact of strict pollution control on regional growth was evident in 1971, when the Texas Air Control Board shut down a small chemical plant in Port Arthur for failure to meet discharge standards. This order starkly contradicted the traditional commitment to growth regardless of costs. It was hardly a fair test of the depth of the public sector's resolve to control pollution, however, since the plant affected was a relatively small operation and a blatant polluter. Indeed, when Texaco faced a similarly stringent state ruling, local public officials appealed to the governor of Texas in support of the company's successful bid for a variance.[50]

CONCLUSION

Such compromises between the corporate autonomy of the not-so-distant past and demands for immediate solutions from the youthfully belligerent public agencies seem likely to characterize future pollution control efforts. Having recognized the government's authority to set and enforce standards, the private concerns nonetheless retain a substantial measure of influence, especially in establishing what level of pollution control is economically feasible.[51] For their part, public planning bodies continue to operate under several constraints inherited from an earlier period that will probably keep them from increasing to a significant degree their newly attained power. First, the tasks that they must perform continue to mount, while their resources are still very limited. More importantly, environmental planning is a volatile political issue that

[49] API estimates of oil industry environmental expenditures suggest an increase of nearly 500 per cent between 1966 and 1974, with the total of such spending in the nine-year period surpassing $7 billion. See API, *Environmental Expenditures of the United States Petroleum Industry, 1966–1974* (Washington, 1975). See, also, Council on Economic Priorities, *Cleaning Up: The Cost of Refinery Pollution Control* (New York, 1975).

[50] *Beaumont Enterprise,* July 29, 1971, 2A; Gregg Kerlin and Daniel Rabovsky (Council on Economic Priorities), *Cracking Down: Oil Refining and Pollution Control* (New York, 1975), 394–395.

[51] For example, see Earl Oliver, Robert Muller, and F. Alan Ferguson, *The Economic Impact of Environmental Regulations on the Petroleum Industry* (Menlo Park, Ca., 1974). This is a report prepared for the API by the Stanford Research Institute.

28   BUSINESS HISTORY REVIEW

directly affects numerous powerful economic interest groups. Past performances suggest that in the broker-state political system of the United States, these groups will, in the long run, prove capable of a large measure of control over policy. Finally, the environmental agencies appear to be vulnerable to a form of political emaciation. Support for their efforts could wane if they prove unable, even in the short-run, to define and implement equitable programs of resource allocation and conservation.

No matter how well conceived, planning that is perceived by the polity as a threat to sustained growth faces severe difficulties. The public planning institutions became strong by responding to crises caused by the cumulative effects of a long-standing lack of adequate controls on pollution. While easing the problems that they were created to deal with, however, these agencies may undermine their own position, because once the short-run crises are "solved" society might well revert to its traditional stance of disregarding long-run environmental problems. In that case, a paradoxical deadlock could result: several decades of experience will have prepared public institutions for environmental planning tasks in a political economy that is unwilling to utilize them.

Even if the long-standing devotion to unrestrained growth has been permanently tempered in the United States by the events of the last decade, a critical institutional barrier to pollution control remains. The growth of petroleum pollution has continued to mirror that of the oil industry. Local government could not respond to the new conditions created by the initial development of Spindletop. After several decades of growth, the state government no longer had the jurisdiction or power to deal with many of the problems associated with the giant refining complex and the expanding national petroleum industry of which it was an integrated part. Currently, the national government is powerless to control many of the *international* environmental consequences of the growing petroleum industry. The lag between public and private capacities remains; mounting pollution of the oceans and the atmosphere, as increasing amounts of petroleum products are shipped over long distances, could well lead to demands for stronger controls in a world without the institutional means to impose and enforce them.

The Texas Railroad Commission and the Elimination of the Flaring of Natural Gas, 1930–1949

DAVID F. PRINDLE*

ROM THE 1930S TO THE 1970S, THE RAILROAD COMMISSION OF TEXAS was one of the most important regulatory bodies in the United States. Its decisions determined how many oil and gas wells could be drilled, where they might be located, and the quantity of petroleum that they might produce. By regulating the drilling, operation, and plugging of wells, and the transportation and storage of both oil and gas, it protected the ecological environment of Texas and the safety and health of the state's citizens. By suppressing ("prorating") the rate of production of the state's oil, it placed a floor under the price of that commodity. Because Texas looms so large in the nation's domestic petroleum picture, the Railroad Commission's control over the oil and gas industry within the state's boundaries had a decisive effect on that industry in the rest of the country, and, as a consequence, on the supply and price of petroleum to consumers in every other state.[1]

One of the most animated and important episodes in the history of the Commission involved its successful attempt, in the 1930s and 1940s, to prevent the destruction of the state's natural gas reserves. An account of this episode illustrates both the historical importance of the Commission, and the interaction of technology, economics, and politics in twentieth-century Texas history.

From the earliest days of oil production, the industry had problems with natural gas. The difficulties all rested, at bottom, on a fact that seems incredible to our gas-hungry age: the stuff was practically worth-

---

*David F. Prindle is an assistant professor of government at the University of Texas at Austin.

[1]Erich W. Zimmermann, *Conservation in the Production of Petroleum: A Study in Industrial Control* (New Haven, 1957), 142–159; John M. Blair, *The Control of Oil* (New York, 1976), 159–169; James P. Hart, "Oil, the Courts, and the Railroad Commission," *Southwestern Historical Quarterly*, XLIV (Jan., 1941), 314–315; Morris A. Adelman, "Efficiency of Resource Use in Crude Petroleum," *Southern Economic Journal*, XXXI (Oct., 1964), 103–109; J. C. Rothwell, Jr., "The Conservation Program of the Railroad Commission and the Structure of Crude Oil Prices in Texas" (Ph.D. diss., University of Texas, 1958).

less. Unlike oil, which can be temporarily stored and easily transported, gas is a difficult substance to handle. It is hard to store and transport, dissipates quickly, and is likely to ignite and explode.[2] Moreover, although both oil and gas can be used for heating, gas is useless as a lubricant and auto fuel.

Because of these problems, there was in the 1930s very little market for natural gas. The lack of a market made the monetary value of gas quite low by today's standards. In 1930, when oil sold for almost a dollar a barrel, the price of natural gas was 3.6 cents for a thousand cubic feet ("MCF"). At a heat equivalency of six MCF of gas to one barrel of oil, this meant that oil was five times more valuable than gas in terms of its available energy.[3]

As a result, gas fields were not then considered by most citizens to be the great natural resources that they would be today. When Amarillo, situated near an ocean of gas in the Panhandle, spent $60,000 advertising its abundance nationally, it found not a single buyer. The city administration then offered free gas for five years to any industry that would move to Amarillo and employ fifty or more people, but still found no takers.[4] This example illustrates the situation of the petroleum industry in general for its first eighty years. Most producers regarded oil as the only hydrocarbon worth searching for.

For the leaseholder who owned a well over the 70 percent or so of natural gas that occurs "unassociated" with oil, the low price was at worst an annoyance. In the early days of the industry, discovery wells in gas fields were often simply capped and forgotten.[5]

There were, however, a few uses for gas. A small number of industrial concerns burned it for boiler fuel, and a few cities (such as Amarillo) used gas in public utilities. Gas could be burned to produce the "carbon black" that was employed by the rubber industry, and, as the

---

[2]John R. Stockton, Richard C. Henshaw, Jr., and Richard W. Graves, *Economics of Natural Gas In Texas*, University of Texas, Bureau of Business Research, Monograph no. 15 (Austin, 1952), 152–189, 228–246; Zimmermann, *Conservation*, 237–238.

[3]*Texas Almanac and State Industrial Guide, 1978–1979* (Dallas, 1977), 410; Zimmermann, *Conservation*, 238.

[4]Ernest O. Thompson, "Flare Gas Wastage in Texas: Steps Taken to Utilize," speech to American Gas Association, May 1, 1947, pp. 1–2, Railroad Commission Collection (Archives Division, Texas State Library, Austin).

[5]Interviews. (Some of the information on which this article is based came from interviews conducted by the author. Because it proved impossible to secure informants unless complete anonymity was promised, these interviews cannot be further identified.)

1930s progressed, some companies learned to use it to make other chemicals.[6] During the 1930s, however, the major conservation problem caused by the exploitation of unassociated gas arose from the fact that it was used to produce a liquid known as "condensate" gasoline.

When natural gas is allowed to expand suddenly, as it does when let out of a well-bore, somewhat less than 10 percent of its contents will condense into a liquid almost indistinguishable from refined gasoline. This process is called "stripping" gas. Condensate gasoline could be used like the refined variety to power automobiles. Companies could make a profit by setting up over a gas field, marketing the stripped condensate, and simply releasing ("venting") the nine-tenths remainder into the atmosphere.[7]

As it was soon discovered that natural gas in the air poses a deadly hazard, producers began to run it up pipes and burn it at the top. The flames from these pipes are known as "flares." The practice of retrieving the 10 percent of stripped condensate and flaring the rest became the object of a legal and political struggle in Texas that lasted for the first five years of the 1930s.[8]

Stripping-and-flaring of unassociated gas clearly presents a waste of natural resources. For a second type of gas production, however, the conservation problem is more complex. This type of production involves what is known as "casinghead gas."

While gas may be found without oil, the reverse is not true. Oil-bearing rock formations often contain a "gas-cap" at the top, and oil in underground reservoirs always contains dissolved gas. When the oil is extracted, the dissolved gas is an inevitable by-product. There is no known method of producing oil without simultaneously bringing up large quantities of gas. About 30 percent of the gas that is produced is of this "associated" type.[9]

Within the well, the petroleum travels to the surface inside a metal

---

[6]Interviews; Stockton, *Gas in Texas*, 17, 27–35, 72–75; Kendall Beaton, *Enterprise in Oil: A History of Shell in the United States* (New York, 1957), 502.

[7]Efforts have been made to quantify the amount of gas used as a proportion of that produced, but unreliable records make all such results extremely imprecise. See Stockton, *Gas in Texas*, 24, 58, 99, 107; for a discussion of the technology and economics of natural gas liquids, see ibid., 55–88.

[8]Interviews; Maurice Cheek, "Legal History of Conservation of Gas in Texas," American Bar Association, Section of Mineral and Natural Resources Law, *Legal History of Conservation of Oil and Gas: A Symposium* (Chicago, 1938), 269–285.

[9]Stockton, *Gas in Texas*, 5.

tubing. The tubing is held in another set of pipes called the "casing." At the top of the well, a metal device called the "casinghead" connects the casing and the tubing. When oil arrives at the mouth of the well, the associated gas dissolved in it escapes into the casing and out of the casinghead. It is therefore called "casinghead gas."[10]

For the casinghead gas that was extracted with oil in the 1930s, the prospects for productive employment were even less than for unassociated gas. Its rate of production could not be controlled, for it was an inescapable by-product of oil extraction. Because its supply was dependent on the demand for oil, it was unattractive to industrial customers, who preferred to contract for a steady, predictable supply of unassociated gas. The market, which was weak for unassociated gas, was thus practically nonexistent for casinghead gas. To put it back into the ground was expensive. As a result, casinghead gas was almost invariably flared.[11]

The combination of low gas prices, the technology of condensation, and the uncontrollable nature of casinghead gas production caused a waste that staggers today's imagination. There are no reliable figures on the total volume of gas dissipation in the industry's first seven decades after 1859, but it must have amounted to dozens of trillions of cubic feet, as drillers in oil field after oil field vented or flared the entire accumulation of casinghead gas, and as stripping plants in unassociated gas fields utilized only a tiny proportion of the resource.[12]

The waste in the nation's petroleum fields in the 1930s and 1940s continued apace, especially in regard to casinghead gas. As Texas produced the most oil and gas, it was the scene of the greatest despoliation. According to many accounts, motorists could drive for hours at night in parts of the state in those years and never have to turn on their automobile lights, because the casinghead flares illuminated the countryside. Miles away from any major oil field, newspapers could be read easily at night by the light of these flares.[13]

Historian Maurice Cheek estimated that in 1934 roughly a billion cubic feet of unassociated gas was stripped and flared daily in the Pan-

10Zimmermann, *Conservation*, 56–57.

11Ibid., 244; Stockton, *Gas in Texas*, 231–236.

12Gerald Forbes, *Flush Production: The Epic of Oil in the Gulf-Southwest* (Norman, 1942), 140–148; Beaton, *Shell*, 131; Stockton, *Gas in Texas*, 233–235.

13Interviews.

handle. Assuming that this total was matched by casinghead flares from oil fields then in production (especially East Texas), then roughly three-quarters of a trillion cubic feet were lost that year. The best estimate from the early 1940s is that one and a half billion cubic feet of casinghead gas was flared each day from Texas's larger fields; that would make the state total for all fields about two and a half billion a day, or over nine-tenths of a trillion a year. As the yearly consumption of natural gas in the entire United States was only about twenty trillion cubic feet a year in the mid-1970s, this means that a sizable proportion of the nation's potential energy supply vanished in a glow of prosperity in Texas in the two decades before 1949.[14]

The magnitude of this devastation was not lost on observers of the time. But, as might be expected, the effort to stop it was met with determined resistance from oil producers, who did not wish to lower their profits by spending money to preserve a substance that they considered valueless.[15]

The engineering staff of the Railroad Commission, however, joined by others of scientific training, argued that the waste of natural gas must stop. They made this argument for two reasons. First, they believed simply that gas-flaring was an unforgivable destruction of natural resources. Second, they wanted to save casinghead gas in order to increase the state's recoverable oil reserves.[16]

In most reservoirs, the propulsive force that moves the oil to the wellbore is provided by gas pressure. The higher the pressure, and the longer it lasts, the more the oil that is ultimately recoverable. The faster the pressure is depleted, the smaller the proportion of the oil-in-place that can be brought to the surface, without using sophisticated (and expensive) recovery techniques.[17]

When a method of returning the gas to the producing rock formation ("pressure maintenance") was invented in the early 1930s, it meant that the life of oil fields could be greatly extended. But pressure maintenance was costly. Although in the long run it might quadruple the

---

[14]Cheek, "Conservation of Gas," 279; Ernest O. Thompson, "Natural Gas in the State of Texas," in Miscellaneous Political File, 1942, Railroad Commission Collection; *Energy Information Digest*, Subcommittee Print, 95th Congress, 1st Session, Committee Print 95–17, Stock #052-070-04305-9 (Washington, D.C., 1977), 33.

[15]Interviews.

[16]Ibid.

[17]Ibid.

amount of oil extractable from a field, in the short run it cost producers money to no obvious advantage. Their perspectives dominated by short-run profit considerations, oil producers resisted suggestions that they should take the necessary steps to preserve gas pressure.[18]

As the agency charged with conserving the state's oil and gas resources, the Railroad Commission was at the center of the controversy over gas flaring. Throughout the 1930s and 1940s, the three commissioners and their engineering staff attempted to deal with the technological and political problems of gas conservation. This conflict placed the commissioners in a difficult political position. To have forced "uneconomical" conservation on the industry would have incited it to strong opposition. As politicians subject to electoral defeat, commissioners were not eager to provoke hostility from this, their basic constituency. Until 1947, consequently, the various commissioners treated the problem of gas gingerly. The Commission's engineers, however, worked for two decades to eliminate the waste of gas, and finally created a political momentum that succeeded in making the Commission move decisively to stop the flaring.[19]

In the 1930s, the Railroad Commission employed less than twenty engineers to oversee Texas's 75,000 wells in more than 500 fields. These men had many jobs relating to oil; in regard to gas, their chief task lay in trying to enforce the Commission's rules about "gas/oil ratios."[20]

In 1899, the state legislature had passed a comprehensive conservation law, later amended several times, in which the flaring of unassociated gas from a gas well was prohibited. In 1925 the legislature passed another law permitting the flaring of associated (casinghead) gas from an oil well. In theory, the Railroad Commission's task in enforcing these statutes was easy: it should prohibit the flaring of gas from gas wells but not from oil wells. In practice, however, the two laws created a regulatory nightmare.[21]

18Ibid.

19Ibid. For the principal statutes empowering the Railroad Commission to conserve the state's petroleum resources, see Tex. Rev. Civ. Stat. Ann. art. 6008–6008b, 6014–6014a, 6015, 6016, 6017, 6018, 6029–6029a, 6049–6049e (Vernon).

20Interviews; Ernest O. Thompson, "Texas Resources," speech to State Convention, Texas Real Estate Boards, Oct. 7, 1937, Railroad Commission Collection.

211899 Tex. Gen. Laws ch. 49, § 3; Tex. Rev. Civ. Stat. 6008, 6014 (1925); 1933 Tex. Gen. Laws ch. 100, § 1; Barth P. Walker, "What Is an Oil Well? What Is a Gas Well? What Difference Does It Make?" Southwestern Legal Foundation, *Proceedings of the Fourteenth Annual Institute on Oil and Gas Law and Taxation* (Albany, 1963), 175–232;

Even in a gas field, there may be traces of oil. Gas that is "unassociated" with oil in a practical sense may be "associated" with minute quantities in a literal sense. Furthermore, the amount of oil found in a "gas" field may vary widely, which must bring up the question: how much oil can be found in a well before that well stops being a "gas" well and becomes an "oil" well? With producers permitted to flare gas from one kind of well but not another, this technical problem of differentiating gas from oil wells became a political problem.

Moreover, gas expands, contracts, and changes its physical composition under differing pressures and temperatures; under some conditions gas will change to a liquid, and vice-versa. These circumstances combine to create an uncertainty as to whether it is a "gas" or "oil" well that is under consideration. The task of regulating gas production is therefore subject to many technical ambiguities. Producers attempted to use these ambiguities to evade Commission regulations.

The statutory definition of a "gas well" was one that produced 100,000 or more cubic feet of gas for every barrel of oil. If the ratio was less than 100,000 to one, the well was classified as "oil," the gas was "casinghead," and could be flared. If the ratio was higher, the well was classified as "gas," and its product could not be flared. It was thus in the interest of operators who owned wells that produced both gas and oil to have as many of them as possible classified as "oil," producing at less than a 100,000-to-one ratio, so that they could flare unmolested. They played cat-and-mouse with the Commission's undermanned inspection staff to attain that goal.[22]

One of the critical junctures in this struggle occurred in 1934. A number of the fields of the time produced large quantites of a clear petroleum liquid known as "water-white oil," along with conventional oil and gas. Their operators treated this liquid as though it were oil. By doing so, they made the gas/oil ratios of their wells 40,000 or 50,000 to one, thereby causing them to be categorized as "oil" wells. This permitted the operators to flare a large amount of gas after they had retrieved a small amount of oil. If the water-white oil were to be classified as "gas," however, the ratio of the wells in question would rise above 100,000-to-one, the wells would be reclassified as "gas," and the flaring could be halted. The Railroad Commission hired Dr. Eugene P.

---

interviews.
    [22]Interviews; Tex. Rev. Civ. Stat. Ann. art. 6008, § d, e (Vernon).

Schoch, a chemist at the University of Texas, to investigate this water-white oil.[23]

Schoch instructed one of his students, Jack K. Baumel—later to be chief engineer for the Commission—to take samples of water-white oil from the Agua Dulce field near Corpus Christi. Back at the University of Texas laboratory, Schoch and Baumel put this liquid into a "high-pressure separator," which allowed them to recreate reservoir conditions by raising the temperature to 247 degrees and the pressure to 3,700 pounds per square inch. When they did this, the water-white oil turned into a gas. The substance had been gas in the reservoir, but had turned into liquid upon reaching the surface.[24]

With this evidence, the Commission's engineering staff recommended that hundreds of "oil" wells be reclassified as "gas" and ordered to stop flaring. The operators naturally objected to this order, but in a series of judicial opinions known collectively as "the Clymore case," the Texas courts backed the Commission to the hilt.[25]

Now the operators were in difficult circumstances, for they had to find something to do with the gas produced with the oil, or shut in their wells. The Commission engineers suggested to them that they could both keep their oil wells flowing, and make further revenues from gas, by making use of a process called "cycling."

The Schoch-Baumel experiments had demonstrated that the gas in many fields like Agua Dulce was rich in condensable liquids. Why not, suggested the engineers, collect the ("wet") gas on the surface, extract the liquids, return the remainder of the gas (now "dry") to the reservoir, where its added pressure could aid in the production of more oil and wet gas, and so on? The condensate from the gas could be marketed, as could, of course, the oil.[26]

If they wanted to continue production, the operators had no choice but to begin cycling. The first commercial cycling plant began operating in the Cayuga field of Northeast Texas in March, 1938. To everyone's relief, it proved profitable. By 1942 there were over twenty-nine cycling plants in Texas, processing over forty-four billion cubic feet of

---

[23]Interviews.

[24]Ibid.

[25]Clymore Production Co. v. Thompson, 11 F. Supp. 791 (W. D. Tex. 1935); Clymore Production Co. v. Thompson, 13 F. Supp. 469 (W.D. Tex. 1936).

[26]Interviews.

gas a year.[27] By losing a technical battle to the Railroad Commission, petroleum producers had improved their economic position.

One of the conflicts over gas-flaring thus ended happily for all concerned. With superior technical imagination and a determination to take the long view, the Railroad Commission had finessed one of the problems of gas conservation. Other struggles, however, were more complicated.

One of the more difficult challenges concerned the flaring of unassociated gas in the enormous Panhandle field. One hundred twenty-five miles in length and an average of twenty-five miles wide, when discovered in 1918 it is estimated to have contained between fifteen and twenty-five trillion cubic feet of natural gas. Beginning in 1930, some operators began to attempt to acquire the right to strip and flare this gas. This desire brought them into conflict, however, with pipeline interests, who were simultaneously beginning to develop markets in northern cities. By 1933 there was a serious political struggle between strippers and pipeliners over the use of the Panhandle's resources. At the same time, the Texas public was becoming more conscious of conservation, largely due to the conflict over oil prorationing in the East Texas field that was occurring during the same years.[28] The fight between pipeline and stripping interests over gas, therefore, took on the mantle of an argument over the public interest, with the public at large and the Railroad Commission as interested spectators.

In 1933, under lobbying pressure from stripping interests, the legislature passed a law specifically permitting Panhandle operators to strip and flare gas under certain conditions. The same year, in the Canadian River case, a federal court placed severe restrictions on the Railroad Commission's authority to regulate gas. In combination, the 1933 law and court decision had the effect of repealing the 1899 conservation statute and freeing strippers from any restraints.[29]

The enormous volume of gas burned and vented under these conditions—over a billion cubic feet a day—caused both a public outcry and a lobbying campaign by pipeline companies to persuade the legislature

---

[27]*History of Petroleum Engineering* (Dallas, 1961), 862; Texas, Railroad Commission, *Annual Report of the Oil and Gas Division, 1942* (Austin, 1942), 49.

[28]Cheek, "Conservation of Gas," 269–273, 276–278; Zimmermann, *Conservation*, 252; James A. Clark and Michel Halbouty, *The Last Boom* (New York, 1972), 144–237.

[29]Interviews; Canadian River Gas Co. v. Terrell, 4 F. Supp. 222 (W.D. Tex. 1933); 1933 Tex. Gen. Laws ch. 100, § 1; Cheek, "Conservation of Gas," 278.

to adopt a more satisfactory conservation policy. This effort succeeded in 1935 when house bill 266 forbade the production of gas in any manner so as to cause underground waste (e.g. the stripping and flaring of unassociated gas). The Railroad Commission was empowered to enforce the act.[30]

Most portions of HB 266 were upheld in the courts, and the Commission swiftly put an end to stripping-and-flaring operations, in the Panhandle and elsewhere.[31] Since 1935, therefore, there has been no problem in Texas with the destruction of unassociated gas reserves.

The waste of casinghead gas, however, increased during this period. Throughout the decade, the Texas industry continued to discover giant fields: Conroe in 1931, Tom O'Connor in 1934, Wasson in 1936, Levelland in 1938, Hawkins in 1940, and so on.[32] Every new field opened to development meant another great volume of casinghead gas doomed to vanish unproductively.

Without actually forbidding the flaring of such gas, commissioners of the late 1930s and early 1940s attempted to encourage its conservation. For example, they issued a statewide order establishing a permissible gas/oil ratio of 2,000 feet per barrel. If the flared gas amounted to more than 2,000 feet for every barrel of oil produced, the well was subject to having its oil allowable reduced.[33]

This and other Commission efforts at conservation were well-intended, but they made little impact on the problem of casinghead gas, for two reasons.

First, the Commission had such a small staff that it could not enforce the order. In the case of oil regulation, there was an actual substance flowing in commerce, which could be monitored. In the case of gas, however, the substance in question was destroyed as soon as it was produced; there was no commerce to monitor. The only way to enforce the order was to keep testing the gas/oil ratios of many thousands of wells. The commissioners did not have anything like a staff adequate

---

[30]1935 Tex. Gen. Laws ch. 120; Cheek, "Conservation of Gas," 281–284.

[31]Interviews.

[32]George H. Fancher, Robert L. Whiting, and James H. Cretsinger, *The Oil Resources of Texas: A Reconnaissance Survey of Primary and Secondary Reserves of Oil*, Texas Petroleum Research Committee (Austin, 1954), 70, 112, 210, 289, 310.

[33]Jack K. Baumel, "The Feasibility and Possibility of a Statewide Plan of Gas Proration and Ratable Take," paper presented at meeting of Interstate Compact Commission, Dec. 9–11, 1946, p. 8 (copy in possession of the author).

to this task, although they did what they could with the staff at their disposal.[34]

Second, even if there had been some means of ensuring that all oil wells were kept within the 2,000-to-one boundary, that would have eliminated only the most wasteful wells. The basic problem of the wanton flaring of "useless" gas was not touched by creating "acceptable" levels of destruction. Within the prescribed limit or not, the flared gas was gone forever. The only way to save this resource was to outlaw the flaring completely.

Fearing to provoke opposition from the industry, and reluctant to impose economic hardship on it, the commissioners of the 1930s and early '40s refused to take this step. They were happy to encourage conservation by approving schemes for repressuring fields with gas, but they would not consider compelling the industry to act responsibly. It would take the elevation of a petroleum engineer to the Commission to change this attitude.[35]

The engineer fated to play the role of effective conservationist was William J. Murray. Graduating with many honors from the University of Texas in 1936, he was employed for two years in private industry, then hired by the Railroad Commission. In 1939 he took a crew to South and West Texas, testing gas/oil ratios for the Commission. In the course of observing thousands of wells, and testing several hundred, he became appalled at the tremendous volume of gas that was being lost through casinghead flares. Most of this flared gas did not show up on Commission reports, for the operators were lax about keeping records, and the Commission did not have the staff to police them effectively. There was little that Murray could do to stop the waste, since most of the ratios were within the acceptable limit, but he nevertheless resolved to do something about it in the unlikely event that he ever got the chance.[36]

Murray worked for the Commission another two years, then left and was employed by the Federal Petroleum Administration for War until 1943. He then resigned and returned to Texas, where he again went to work for private industry.[37]

---

[34]Interviews.

[35]Ibid.; Baumel, "Feasibility," 9.

[36]*TIPRO Reporter* (Feb.–Mar., 1963), 9–10; interviews.

[37]Interviews; Austin *American*, Dec. 7, 1946.

During this period, events were pushing Texans into a confrontation with the federal government. Some federal officials were concerned that the waste of casinghead gas in Texas was damaging potential oil recovery. Additionally, for several years some members of the Federal Power Commission had been contemplating an attempt to extend federal regulatory authority over the gas industry; the evident waste in Texas provided them with an excuse to move in that direction.[38]

Sitting on the Railroad Commission in the mid-1940s were Ernest O. Thompson, Olin W. Culberson, and Beauford H. Jester, all of them vociferous advocates of states' rights. They attempted to forestall federal meddling in Texas conservation policy by convincing the FPC that the state had the gas problem under control.[39]

In December of 1944 the Commission scheduled a special hearing to discuss the gas-flare problem, among other topics. The official figures showed that over four hundred billion cubic feet of casinghead gas had been produced in the state in 1943, of which only 3,690,787,000 cubic feet, or less than 1 percent, had been flared. Ernest Thompson argued that this volume was reasonable and posed no threat to conservation. But William Murray, attending the hearing as a private citizen, stood up and stated that he knew from personal experience that the received figures were gross underestimations, that from ten to twenty-five times the official estimates were being lost, and that this was indeed a serious conservation problem.[40]

This accusation drew some press coverage, and embarrassed the commissioners.[41] Gas flaring is the sort of dramatic issue that is "news," for the unproductive burning of a natural resource is easily understood by a mass audience. In addition, of course, to refuse to take Murray's charges seriously would have looked bad in Washington. So the Commission was forced to make at least symbolic gestures to solve the problem.

---

[38]*Oil Weekly* (Apr. 16, 1945), 25. A discussion of the national political struggle over the jurisdiction of the Federal Power Commission is beyond the scope of this article, but see Joseph P. Harris, "The Senatorial Rejection of Leland Olds: A Case Study," *American Political Science Review*, XLV (Sept., 1951), 674–692; Anne H. Morgan, *Robert S. Kerr: The Senate Years* (Norman, 1977), 56–102.

[39]Interviews.

[40]Ibid.; Texas Railroad Commission, *Annual Report of the Oil and Gas Division, 1943–44* (n.p., n.d), 41; Fort Worth *Star-Telegram*, Dec. 22, 1944; George O. Ives, "Many Phases of Gas Conservation Discussed by Texans at Austin Meet," *Oil Weekly* (Dec. 25, 1944), 30; Dallas *Morning News*, Dec. 21, 1944.

[41]Fort Worth *Star-Telegram*, Dec. 22, 1944.

The commissioners appointed an industry-wide committee to "look into" the flaring problem, and asked Murray to chair it. But since Murray knew that some of the worst offenders were on the committee, he declined, and asked instead to chair a smaller group, composed only of engineers, that would report to the larger body.[42]

The "Murray Committee Report," released in November of 1945, pulled no punches and caused a furor in the industry. Many of the most important members of the state oil industry—which included, of course, some of the most prominent citizens of Texas—were seen to be contributing to a waste of casinghead gas of almost a billion and a half cubic feet a day, or 57 percent of the state's total production.[43]

The big producers complained vigorously in private about this engineers' committee to their friends on the Commission. Publicly, they argued that an order to stop flaring the gas would ruin them. But because of the publicity created by the report, it would have been dangerous for the commissioners to ignore it. Instead, they stalled.[44]

Meanwhile, some members of the industry were awakening to the magnitude of the problem. The Murray Committee report, by compiling accurate figures on the volume of lost gas, forced the industry to confront its own profligacy, and those producers who were more far-seeing became convinced that this resource must be conserved. In particular, Dan Moran, president of the Continental Oil Company and an active member of the industry committee, concluded that the flaring had to be stopped. Moran vigorously supported Murray and his fellow engineers within the industry.[45]

While the struggle over flaring was taking place, the petroleum industry was evolving in a direction that favored the conservationists. During the war, technical advances had been made in the process of cycling, and it became more feasible to employ that process with casinghead gas. Also during the war, the Big Inch and Little Inch oil pipelines had been built from Texas to the Northeast, to avoid the attacks of German submarines on tankers. With the war over and oil moving

[42]Interviews (quotation); *Oil and Gas Journal* (Nov. 10, 1945), 56.

[43]Internal Railroad Commission memo (no date; copy in possession of the author); Austin *American*, Dec. 19, 1945; Corpus Christi *Caller*, Dec. 19, 1945; *Oil Weekly* (Dec. 24, 1945), 32.

[44]Interviews; *Oil Weekly* (Mar. 5, 1945), 30; ibid. (Apr. 16, 1945), 25; Charles J. Deegan, "Proper Price Incentive Would Do Much to Further Gas Conservation," *Oil and Gas Journal* (Feb. 9, 1946), 56–58.

[45]Interviews; *Oil and Gas Journal* (Nov. 10, 1945), 56.

again by sea, the pipelines were capable of carrying gas, and people in the industry were discovering that they could sell it, once they had the means to move it. Finally, the war had given a great boost to the petrochemical industry, to which natural gas was becoming important.[46]

As a result of all these changes, the price of natural gas began to rise. Through the 1930s, the price had deteriorated, so that in 1940 it was only 1.8 cents per MCF. By 1947, however, it had more than doubled to 3.7 cents.[47] This was not enough to make gas conservation profitable for most operators, but it did tend to forestall panic in the industry at the thought of having to eliminate flaring.

Moreover, federal control threatened to overtake the industry if something was not done about the gas situation. In 1946 the Federal Power Commission held a series of hearings on gas waste; the obvious implication was that the FPC might resolve to extend its regulations over the state industry for reasons of conservation. At a hearing in February in Houston, six Texas officials, including two railroad commissioners, told the FPC that they were making great progress in eliminating waste, and that they did not need federal help. If the Murray Committee report was to be believed, however, they *were not* making progress, and that knowledge made figures in both public and private life in Texas nervous.[48]

All of these forces would have combined, sooner or later, to stop the flaring. But in January of 1947 a political act occurred that made it sooner. Commissioner Jester had been elected governor in 1946. One of his first acts as chief executive was to appoint William Murray, the crusading engineer, to serve out his own unexpired term on the Commission.[49]

As Murray had spent the previous two years disrupting the most im-

---

[46]Robert E. Hardwicke, "Texas, 1938–1948," Blakely M. Murphy (ed.), *Conservation of Oil and Gas: A Legal History, 1948* (Chicago, 1949), 457–458; *Oil and Gas Journal* (Aug. 18, 1945), 109; ibid. (Jan. 5, 1946), 45–46; ibid. (Feb. 2, 1946), 99; R. B. Tuttle, "Natural Gas and Cycling Industry Operating at 91 Per Cent of Capacity," ibid. (Apr. 26, 1947), 140–148; C. O. Willson, "5,000,000-Bbl. Production Rate Needed, Economists Report," ibid. (May 3, 1947), 36–37, 145; ibid. (Aug. 4, 1945), 117.

[47]*Texas Almanac . . . 1978–1979*, p. 410.

[48]*Oil and Gas Journal* (June 16, 1945), 76; ibid. (Feb. 16, 1946), 76; *Oil Weekly* (Apr. 16, 1945), 25; testimony by Ernest Thompson, "Progress in Oil and Gas Conservation by the Texas Railroad Commission," Federal Power Commission Docket no. G-580, In the Matter of Natural Gas Investigation, Proceedings at Houston, Texas, Feb., 1946 (copy in possession of the author).

[49]Austin *American,* Dec. 7, 1946.

portant industry in Texas, the governor's choice of him as a successor may seem surprising. But Jester stated at the time that he thought the most important problem facing the industry was gas flaring, and that Murray was the best man to handle the problem; there is no reason to disbelieve him.[50] Jester must be given credit for possessing considerable political courage.

The confirmation of the appointment might have been stopped in the state senate, for in fact there was considerable opposition to Murray within the industry. But that opposition could only have succeeded in blocking the appointment if it had represented the unanimous sentiment of Texas producers. A small group of very active, influential independents, including Robert L. Foree and Glenn H. McCarthy, backed Murray vigorously, and prevented any movement to contest the appointment. He was confirmed easily.[51]

With Murray's ascension, the tone of Railroad Commission activity altered abruptly. Because they had been worried about imposing economic burdens on the industry and political burdens on themselves, Culberson and Thompson had been halfhearted in their efforts to stop flaring. The arrival of a colleague committed to eliminating the waste, however, coinciding with rising gas prices and a nosy FPC, made it clear that they would have to move, or lose their positions as leaders. The course of political expediency suddenly coincided with the path of political virtue. And so, faced with the inevitable, Thompson and Culberson jumped on the bandwagon with vigor.[52] The Railroad Commission became a conservation tiger.

On April 1, 1947, the Commission issued an order shutting in all 615 oil wells in the new Seeligson field in South Texas until a cycling and compression plant was completed, and the flaring of casinghead gas eliminated. To say the least, this order shocked the industry. Shell, Sun, and Magnolia (Mobil), big operators in the field, immediately filed suit. Former governor Daniel J. Moody was the attorney for Shell, and was confident of victory.[53]

---

[50]Austin *Statesman*, Dec. 8, 1946.

[51]Interviews.

[52]Ibid.

[53]Ibid.; Railroad Commission Oil and Gas Docket #129, Order #4-10,351, Mar. 17, 1947 (Records Department of the Railroad Commission, Austin); *History of Petroleum Engineering*, 914; *Oil and Gas Journal* (June 28, 1947), 91.

But the Texas Supreme Court upheld the order.[54]

Having won its test case, the Commission proceeded to issue a series of orders shutting down seventeen fields for flaring.[55] These orders were also appealed to the courts. Despite the fact that for several decades the Commission had been accumulating constitutional and statutory power to compel the conservation of oil and gas, industry lawyers tried to convince the judges that the Commission did not have the authority to force operators to save gas if such savings were uneconomical.[56] The state supreme court, however, unambiguously endorsed the Commission's authority. In the Flour Bluff case, the court made it clear that it would do the industry no good to plead that saving gas was unprofitable:

If the prevention of waste of natural resources such as gas is to await the time when direct and immediate profits can be realized from the operation, there would have been little need for the people of Texas to have amended their Constitution by declaring that the preservation and conservation of natural resources of the state are public rights and duties and directing that the Legislature pass such laws as may be appropriate thereto . . . for private enterprise would not need the compulsion of law to conserve these resources if the practice were financially profitable.[57]

More legal and political maneuvering followed, but it was only skirmishing.[58] The war had been won by 1949, with the Railroad Commission the unquestioned victor. Henceforward, with relatively insignificant exceptions, casinghead gas would go into a pipeline or back into the ground.

---

[54]Railroad Commission v. Shell Oil Co., 206 S.W.2d 235 (1947).

[55]These orders are in Oil and Gas Docket #129 (Records Department of Railroad Commission, Austin). See, for example, for Flour Bluff field, Order #4-13,551, Nov. 22, 1948; for Tijerina-Canales field, Order #4-13,554, Nov. 22, 1948; for La Gloria field, Order #4-13-555, Nov. 22, 1948.

[56]For historical summaries of the accumulating authority of the Railroad Commission over conservation, see Cheek, "Conservation of Gas," 271–286, and Robert E. Hardwicke, "Legal History of Conservation of Oil in Texas," American Bar Association, Section of Mineral and Natural Resources Law, *Legal History*, 214–269.

[57]Railroad Commission v. Flour Bluff Oil Co., 219 S.W.2d 506 (Tex. Civ. App. 1949) error ref'd p. 508.

[58]The major controversy after 1949 was over the Spraberry field. See Railroad Commission v. Rowan Oil Co., 259 S.W.2d 173 (1953), and Nelson Jones, "The Spraberry Decision," *Oil and Gas Law: With Articles Pertaining to Sulphur, Taxation, Tidelands and Other Related Subjects* (2 vols.; Austin, 1954), II, 2,093.

ADMINISTRATIVE TRUSTIFICATION

Elma M. Saletan*

New School for Social Research

THE VAST EXPANSION of the field of government activity during our century has profoundly enhanced administrative power. In exercising this augmented power, administrators have turned with increasing frequency to private groups for information and advice on how to construe and implement legislative decisions. These groups have included professional societies, trade associations, prominent industrialists and financiers, and technical consultants. An appropriations act of 1902, for instance, authorized the Secretary of Agriculture to consult with members of the Association of Official Agricultural Chemists in determining standards of purity for food products, and the Transportation of Explosives Act of 1908 authorized the Interstate Commerce Commission to consult with the American Railway Association in formulating its regulations.[1]

After World War I, the use of advisory groups by government came to be viewed by public administration experts as the preferred method of democratizing administration and combatting bureaucratic rigidity.[2] In its most radical formulation, the theory took on syndicalist overtones, and it was argued by Harold Laski, for instance, that group autonomy, operating through the mechanism of interest-group organizations, was both necessary and desirable in the pluralist society.[3] More moderate formulations saw group participation in government as a means of bringing administration into closer contact with the private interests it regulated, the private groups functioning as a check against administrative power.[4] And late in the thirties, it was argued that self-government furnished a solution to the problem of the political alienation of the masses.[5] The practical consummation of this body of theory is to be found in the "self-regulation" program of the New Deal, which was written into the National Industrial Recovery Act.

---

* This article grew out of a seminar paper prepared at the New School for Social Research under the guidance of Dr. Francis D. Wormuth. I take this opportunity to express my thanks for his interest and valuable advice.

[1] *Final Report of the Attorney General's Committee on Administrative Procedure* (Washington, 1941), p. 103.

[2] W. F. Willoughby, *Principles of Public Administration* (Washington: The Brookings Institution, 1927), p. 171; see also Arthur W. Macmahon, "Advisory Boards," *Encyclopedia of the Social Sciences* (New York: Macmillan, 1930), II, 610–11. Norman F. Keiser, "Public Responsibility and Federal Advisory Groups," *Western Political Quarterly*, XI (June, 1958), 251.

[3] Harold Laski, *Foundations of Sovereignty* (New York: Harcourt-Brace, 1921), *passim.*

[4] This is the basic theme of E. Pendleton Herring, *Public Administration and the Public Interest* (New York: McGraw-Hill, 1936), and is also reflected in the *Final Report of the Attorney General's Committee . . . , op. cit.*

[5] Louis L. Jaffe, "Law Making by Private Groups," 51 *Harv. L. Rev.* 201–53 (1937).

Previous to 1932, however, private groups were often invited to participate in the administrative rule-making process, although few of these groups
were more than *ad hoc* committees formed by one or another executive
agency. The Revenue Act of 1918, for instance, provided for a temporary
Advisory Tax Board, and an Advisory Statistical Council was created in the
same year to advise the Commerce Department on census compilation.[6]
Important exceptions to this pattern of *ad hoc* organization occurred during the twenties in the fields of conservation and commerce. The National
Petroleum War Service Committee, organized in 1918, functioned as an
operating group and was authorized to co-ordinate wartime oil operations
for the entire industry. The same group, reorganized after the war as the
American Petroleum Institute, worked with the Oil Conservation Board
until 1929 on the elaboration of an oil conservation program.[7] Other exceptions occurred in the Department of Commerce, which had created 343
permanent advisory committees, and in 1926 alone held over 1,200 conferences with leading industrial and commercial organizations.[8]

The most controversial use made of advisory groups during the interwar
period was that of the Trade Practices Conferences initiated by the Federal
Trade Commission in 1919. The Federal Trade Commission Act of 1914
had charged this agency with application of the "unfair competitive trade
practices" prohibitions of the Clayton Act. Although Congress had deliberately denied the Commission the authority to underwrite or give advance
approval of any business practice, it early assumed the role of informal
adviser.[9] The program involved the promulgation of rules of fair competition, which the Commission formulated by consultation with the affected
private groups. One part of these rules (Group I) was mandatory and
expressive of the legal requirements of the various acts of Congress; the
other part (Group II) included those recommended practices which, although not compulsory, were considered to promote conditions of fair
competition.[10]

Between 1919 and 1929, eighty-three Trade Practices Conferences were
held and, although in some instances the work of the Commission was
thwarted by the Courts, by 1941 it had held more than two hundred trade
conferences.[11] These proceedings covered a wide section of American in-

---

[6] *Final Report of the Attorney General's Committee . . . , op. cit.*, p. 103.

[7] "National Petroleum Council," quoted in *WOC's and Government Advisory Groups,*
Hearings, Part III, 84th Cong., 1st Sess. 2220–26 (1955).

[8] Willoughby, *op. cit.*, p. 176.

[9] Robert E. Cushman, *The Independent Regulatory Commissions* (New York: Oxford University Press, 1941), 220–22.

[10] Federal Trade Commission. *Control of Unfair Competitive Practices through Trade Practice Conference Procedure of the Federal Trade Commission,* TNEC Monograph No. 34
(Washington, 1941), pp. 4–5.

[11] Thomas C. Blaisdell, Jr., *The Federal Trade Commission, An Experiment in the Control
of Business* (New York: Columbia University Press, 1932), p. 93.

dustry and by 1935 the rules prohibited or enjoined roughly three hundred different trade practices including sales below cost, tie-in sales, discriminatory pricing techniques, accurate cost accounting, etc.[12] Both in scope and purpose, therefore, the Trade Conferences procedure of the FTC anticipated the more ambitious program enacted by the New Deal.

In 1933 a grand-scale experiment in business self-regulation was launched. It was argued by the theorists that the great good of economic stability could be achieved only by eliminating some of the extreme effects of free competition, and to this end the National Recovery Administration encouraged the adoption of codes of "fair competition." The codes were drafted by industry itself; and to facilitate this, trade associations were organized in those industries where they did not already exist. For the duration of the NIRA, the code-making participants enjoyed antitrust immunity, whereas violators of the codes were liable to legal sanctions.

The Schechter decision in 1935 closed this chapter of self-regulation, holding that the NIRA constituted an unlawful delegation of authority.[13] The experiment was consequently short lived, but nevertheless furnished ample proof that American business had rather thoroughly abandoned its free-enterprise premises.

During these two years the NRA approved 874 codes, and almost all contained provisions which were more or less collusive in intent. Production quotas were established in a variety of ways: 4 codes fixed inventory limits, compelling manufacturers to hold their transactions to the level of current sales; 77 codes limited construction, relocation and conversion of productive capacity; 60 codes placed time limits on allowed working hours; and 5 codes assigned outright production and sales quotas.[14] Price controls were adopted by 560 of the early 677 codes: price reporting systems were included in 422; standard costing systems were required by 361; and 403 codes prohibited sales below cost.[15]

In practice the codes represented the most drastic departure of antitrust policy ever embarked on by the United States, and their nullification in 1935 left behind a complete network of centralized trade associations which had learned the essential techniques of collective market control.

Since the NRA, the number of advisory groups has multiplied in response to the continued growth of government control of business and in response to wartime mobilization needs. Their number now exceeds 1,000 and they may properly be considered a permanent feature of the contemporary administrative system. Theoretically, they are authorized by

---

[12] Federal Trade Commission. TNEC Monograph No. 34, pp. 6–9.

[13] *Schechter Poultry Corp. v. United States*, 295 U.S. 495.

[14] David Lynch, *The Concentration of Economic Power* (New York: Columbia University Press, 1946), p. 152.

[15] *Ibid.*

statute or administrative finding.[16] The Defense Production Act of 1950 authorized the formation of business or industry advisory committees to advise government officials in the formulation of economic controls, and most of the current advisory committees attached to defense agencies are based on this authorization. The National Petroleum Council as now organized was created by executive order and statute in 1946.[17] The majority of advisory groups, however, are created by administrative findings and except for those authorized by specific statute, Congress has retained little control of their organization and use.

In structure and function advisory groups vary widely. They exist as both standing and *ad hoc* groups, and are subdivided into committees, task groups, subcommittees, conferences, etc. The National Petroleum Council, for example, has committees dealing with the special problems of the domestic industry as well as questions of foreign supply and tanker capacity, and the Business Advisory Council has more than a dozen standing committees covering foreign economic policy, industrial uses of atomic energy, Latin-American policy, etc. Task groups are organizational units set up for a specific study (often of a highly technical nature), although in practice the main distinction between a task group and other groups appears to be size.

In addition to the permanent advisory groups, *ad hoc* groups are often established, many of them under the provisions of the voluntary agreements program of the Defense Production Act. The Foreign Petroleum Supply Committee, which handled the Iranian oil crisis in 1951, was organized under the voluntary agreement relating to foreign petroleum supply in June, 1951.[18] The Suez oil crisis was handled by the Middle East Emergency Committee, which was formed under an agreement of August 1956.[19] Committees formed under these agreements are unique in the important respect that they are granted antitrust immunity for the duration of their activities.

As suggested above, congressional control of advisory groups is minimal, even over those created by the authority of statute, although the Defense Production Act attempted to place several restrictions on the use and composition on the groups it authorized. Section 709 of the Act requires that each rule, regulation, or order issued with the participation of an advisory committee be accompanied by a statement that such consultation had taken

---

[16] The Business Advisory Council (BAC) of the Commerce Department, however, would seem to have been autogeneric. No administrative finding or statute authorized its formation, which would seem to have rested on the "implied powers" of the Secretary of Commerce.

[17] "National Petroleum Council," *loc. cit.*

[18] "Voluntary Agreement Relating to Foreign Supply of Petroleum to Friendly Foreign Nations," 16 F.R. 8375; and 16 F.R. 8377.

[19] "Plan of Action Under Voluntary Agreement Relating to Foreign Petroleum Supply," August 10, 1956.

place, and Section 701 requires that membership be properly representative of the affected industry. The first requirement has been evaded by some agencies through the simple method of literal interpretation — the ill-defined but useful distinction between advisory groups and task groups has been used to exempt the latter from all procedural rules.[20] And the problem of representative membership is sufficiently difficult to offer convenient justification for failure to solve it.

The main problems which have arisen from the use of advisory groups are related to the antitrust laws, and this fact has caused the Justice Department to assume some degree of supervision over them since early in the 1940's. This authority is not based on explicit delegation, however, except in a few specific cases. The Defense Production Act of 1950 gave the Attorney General a veto power over the voluntary agreements program, but otherwise authority rests on the implied powers of the Justice Department to prosecute individuals whose activities are in violation of the antitrust laws.

In 1941, the Attorney General recommended a number of procedural rules to guide advisory group meetings. Although adherence to these rules does not grant immunity per se, the Attorney General has maintained that they are designed so as to minimize possible violations. In general, therefore, antitrust immunity has been withheld, and in fact a group of cases has been initiated because of antitrust violations transacted during meetings.[21]

The rules recommended by the Justice Department, unchanged since 1941, are:[22]

1. There should be statutory authority for the employment of such committees or an administrative finding that it is necessary to utilize such committees to perform certain statutory duties.
2. The agenda for such committees and their meetings should be initiated and formulated by the Government.
3. The meetings to be held should be at the call of and under the chairmanship of a full-time Government official.
4. Full and complete minutes of each meeting should be kept.
5. The functions of such committees should be purely advisory and any determination of action to be taken should be made solely by Government representatives.

There have been some slight refinements of these rules made in the past few years (e.g., in regard to the advisability of using without-compensation

---

[20] The Defense Transport Administration has used task groups in preference to advisory groups as a matter of policy, according to the testimony of Asst. Attorney General Morison, Hearings on *The Mobilization Program*, Part 4, H.R. Subcommittee on Study of Monopoly Power, 82d Cong., 1st Sess., 219–20 (1951).

[21] These cases are: *United States* v. *Socony Oil Co.*, 310 U.S. 150 (1940); *United States* v. *National Fertilizer Assn.*, Cr. 1167, M.D.N.C. (1941); *United States* v. *Libby-Owens-Ford Glass Co.*, Civil 5239, N.D. Ohio (1945); CCH 1946–47 Trade Cases Para. 27489; CCH 1948–49 Trade Cases Para. 62323; and *United States* v. *Standard Oil Co. (N.J.), et al.*, Civil 86–27 S.D.N.Y. (1953).

[22] Letter of Attorney General Jackson to John Lord O'Brian of April 29, 1941. Quoted in full in *WOC's and Government Advisory Groups*, Part I, pp. 584–85.

personnel [WOC's] and trade executives as government chairmen), and some new questions have arisen in conjunction with the voluntary agreements program, but the broad areas involving the public interest remain as defined by Attorney General Jackson: that the groups be representative, that they not be used to achieve collusive purposes, and that administrative decisions remain the exclusive prerogative of the government.[23]

These issues all pose difficult problems in public administration, which are further complicated by the ambiguities of our antitrust laws, and it is the purpose of the present analysis to measure the extent to which industry groups have actually been used in the public interest.

The Membership of Advisory Groups

The Defense Production Act of 1950 delegated special powers to the President to handle the mobilization requirements of the Korean crisis. Section 701, authorizing the formation of business advisory groups, provides that "fair representation be given to independent, small, medium and large business enterprises, for different geographical areas, for trade association members and nonmembers, and for different segments of the industry."[24] This statutory requirement grew out of the experiences of World War II, during which the large corporate interests managed to dominate advisory groups despite protests of the Justice Department, and received an increasingly larger share of the government procurement dollar.

The lack of standardized ideas on what constitutes a fair share of defense contracts for small business has resulted, according to the House Select Committee on Small Business, in a steadily increasing inequity. The share of small business dwindled from 24.5 per cent of the total dollar value in 1950, to 17.6 per cent in 1952, despite the provisions of the 1950 Defense Production Act.[25]

While a variety of factors must be adduced to explain this development (notably, the near-complete absence of small business enterprises in some of the heavy defense materials industries), the strong numerical position of the large corporate interests on virtually all advisory groups suggests some relation between the procurement and representation problems.

Logically, there are two methods for determining fair representation. Membership can be weighted according to the relative *share* each size of enterprise contributes to the total industry product, or it can be weighted according to the *number* of enterprises of each size. In other words, representation can be apportioned so as to merely reflect the market positions of the producers, or it can attempt to equalize these positions. It seems obvious

---

[23] *Ibid.*

[24] Testimony of Asst. Attorney General Morison, *The Mobilization Program*, Part 4, p. 181.

[25] *Final Report of the House of Representatives Select Committee on Small Business*, 82d Cong., 2d Sess. 163–66 (1952).

that a rigorous antitrust policy would lean towards equalization, but in general representation has followed the alternative pattern.

Analysis of the membership of the Department of Commerce advisory committees reveals a consistent pattern.[26] Characteristically competitive industries simply reflect their market structure. Of the twenty members of the Cotton Textile Industry Committee of 1954 only one represents a company listed among the five hundred largest industrial corporations.[27] The remainder can properly be considered representative of small, medium and independent firms. Similarly, only four of the thirty members of the Precision Instruments Committee, and two of the fifteen of the Bicycle Industry Conference group represented the largest industrial corporations.

Committees of industries with a mixed structure (i.e., in which industrial concentration has not yet eliminated effective competition from independents) have a balanced membership. Nine of the twenty members of the Automotive Parts Industry Conference of 1954 represented the industrial giants. Eleven of the twenty-three members of the Motor Vehicle Industry Conference of the same year, and twelve of the nineteen members of the Chemical and Rubber Industry Advisory Committee of 1953, were drawn from that group.

Industries with a definitely oligopolistic structure are represented almost entirely by the corporate giants: twenty of the twenty-six of the Steel Products Committee, and all eleven of the Aluminum Producers Committee, represent companies among the five hundred largest.

The National Petroleum Council of the Interior Department also reflects the integrated structure of the industry. A large majority of its membership is composed of executives from the major oil companies, and its subcommittees are likewise dominated by the majors: seven of the nine members of the strategic Agenda Committee for 1946, for example, represented the major oil producers.

The Business Advisory Council of the Department of Commerce, which is one of the oldest advisory groups, and distinctive in that it is a horizontal rather than a vertical organization, largely represents the large corporate interests: one-third of its active and graduate members were drawn from the five hundred largest industrial corporations, and a substantial portion of the remainder represents the largest commercial, utility, insurance, and investment firms.[28] In 1955, its chairman was the president of Owens-Corning, and its three vice-chairmen were officers of Standard Oil, du Pont, and

---

[26] In 1955, the Commerce Department had 576 committees, active and inactive, according to a Justice Department survey. *WOC's and Government Advisory Groups,* Part III, pp. 1816–17.

[27] Unless otherwise cited, reference is made to *WOC's and Government Advisory Groups,* Part III, in which these Minutes are quoted in full.

[28] Interim Report of the Antitrust Subcommittee of the House of Representatives, 84th Cong., 1st Sess., on *The Business Advisory Council* (Washington, 1955), pp. 2-6.

Goldman, Sachs. Its executive committee is almost wholly staffed by the large corporate enterprises, and only one of its thirteen members is from the small business category.[29]

Numerical considerations do not make up the entire membership problem, however, since regional, as well as segmental representation of an industry can vitally affect the welfare of nonmembers. For instance, the Aluminum Producers Advisory Committe in 1955 was composed of the only three producers in the industry, who are also fabricators. At a meeting called to discuss revisions of the defense "set-aside" for independent fabricators, the three producers were requested to offer their definition of "independent fabricator." The members gave their definition, and further offered to supply a list of their customers whom they deemed covered by this definition.[30] Although the government was in no way obliged to accept these recommendations, and might well submit the same questions to the fabricators for counterrecommendations, this added exercise of administrative discretion would be unnecessary if the committee were initially organized to represent the various segments of the industry. In the absence of such representation, fair material allocation to fabricators rested only upon the conscientious discretion of the administrator.

A large measure of administrative discretion is also involved in the determination of what constitutes "small business." The Selective Service Act of 1948 defined small business according to three criteria: its position in the industry is not dominant, the number of employees does not exceed five hundred, and it is independently owned and operated.[31] More realistically, the Small Defense Plants Administration Act of 1951 made no attempt at precise definition. Instead, it provides that "the Administration, in making a detailed definition, may use these criteria, among others: independency of ownership and operation, number of employees, dollar volume of business and non-dominance in its field." [32] The House Committee on Small Business itself has concluded that the concept of small business must be flexible, vary from industry to industry, and be subject to the trends of public policy.[33]

In practice, then, small business representation on advisory committees has necessarily been left to the discretion of the administrator. Some industries, such as textiles, lend themselves to the rigid five hundred employees definition; others, including most of heavy industry, must be classified in a more relative manner. In the steel and aircraft industries, five

---

[29] Ibid.

[30] Hearings on The Mobilization Program, Part 4, p. 730.

[31] Pub. L. No. 759, 80th Cong., 2d Sess. (1948).

[32] Pub. L. No. 96, 82d Cong., 1st Sess. (1951).

[33] Final Report of the House Select Committee on Small Business, 82d Cong., 2d Sess. 4–5 (1952).

thousand employees may place a company in the small business category, and firms with a monthly net of one million dollars may still be considered small business.[34]

One other controversial problem concerning the composition of advisory groups involves the advisability of granting membership to trade association executives. The position of the Justice Department on this question has been that full-time, paid association officials should not be included on advisory groups, although individuals who are primarily working in industry and only incidentally associated with these organizations, are acceptable if their experience is such as to make them valuable advisers.[35] This opinion stems from the important role trade associations have played in the history of antitrust violations, and the experiences resulting from their inclusion during World War II.[36] During the war the Office of Price Administration attempted to exclude trade association officials from membership and from advisory group meetings, but this policy proved to be ineffective. Association officials caucused before meetings and managed to exert their influence through the association membership.[37]

Administrative practice has varied greatly on this question. The National Petroleum Council, as constituted in 1946, included twenty-five trade association officials among its membership, and in 1955 the Council had over twenty. On the other hand, the National Production Authority rigorously discouraged the practice. Its position was based on the conclusion that trade associations tend to represent only the special interests of their members, rather than the industry as a whole, and that inclusion thus introduces the factor of competition between the various trade associations in a given industry.[38]

In general, then, it appears that except for characteristically competitive industries, the membership of advisory groups largely represents the big business interests. The favored market positions of these interests are reflected in numerical superiority on the committees, and to the extent that advisory groups influence policy, the large corporate interests dominate that policy.

---

[34] Testimony of John D. Small, Chairman of the Munitions Board, Hearings on *The Mobilization Program*, Part 4, p. 325; and E. H. Lane's testimony, *loc. cit.*, p. 596.

[35] Testimony of Asst. Attorney General Morison, Hearings on *The Mobilization Program*, Part 4, p. 183.

[36] According to Asst. Attorney General Morison, 30 per cent of antitrust cases and complaints involve trade association activities. *Ibid.*, p. 209.

[37] Emmette S. Redford, *Administration of National Economic Control* (New York: Macmillan, 1952), p. 261.

[38] Testimony of Manly Fleishmann, Hearings on *The Mobilization Program*, Part 4, p. 743.

The Collusive Potential of Advisory Groups

Fundamentally, most questions relating to the use of advisory groups must be viewed against the background of their collusive potential. The main concern of the Department of Justice has thus been to control industry participation in the administrative process so that it should not lead to further concentrations of American industry. The procedural rules it recommends to guide advisory group meetings are the primary safeguards against collusion, and it is therefore not without interest to examine them more closely.

These recommendations require that the agenda for all meetings be formulated by the government, that the meetings be called and chaired by a government representative, and that full and complete minutes of each meeting be kept. Compliance with these requirements varies widely. Many groups strictly adhere to the rules, while others regularly disregard one or more of them.[39] The list of violations is long and varied, and includes relatively trivial violations such as the use of industry representatives, rather than government personnel, as chairmen, as well as more serious infractions such as the submission of committee minutes to trade associations and other groups for deletions and changes.[40]

The Celler Committee investigations of 1951 and 1955 cited numerous instances of noncompliance, and found that responsibility for procedural violations was not always that of the industry membership. The Committee discovered, for example, that the Business Advisory Council of the Commerce Department consistently violates all of the formal rules, and in fact had been advised by the General Counsel of Commerce that the rules were inapplicable to its operations.[41]

Other practices uncovered by the investigations indicate how widely an advisory group can depart from its proper functions when it is not limited by strong controls. It appears, for instance, that the tax-deductible funds of the Business Advisory Council are not always used for clearly admissible purposes, as is suggested by the fact that the greater part of its labor research fund (which amounted to $41,550 in 1950) has been used as pay-

---

[39] A survey undertaken by the Justice Department in 1954 disclosed that of the more than 1000 advisory groups it had examined, 250 were operating without regulations conforming to the recommended standards. Most of these were attached to the independent agencies. All of the Defense committees, and all but eight of the Commerce committees, conform to the standards. Testimony of Asst. Attorney General Stanley N. Barnes, *WOC's and Government Advisory Groups*, Part I, p. 552.

[40] See the letter of Asst. Attorney General Morison to the Secretary of Defense of October 8, 1951, which lists the more usual types of violations. Quoted in full in *WOC's and Government Advisory Groups*, Part I, pp. 591–92.

[41] This position rests on the distinction drawn by the Commerce Department between "vertical" and "horizontal" groups. The Department has assumed that the Attorney General's rules do not apply to horizontal groups. See the testimony of Walter White, *WOC's and Government Advisory Groups*, Part II, p. 991.

ment for the services of a registered lobbyist.[42] Actually, the financial records of the Business Advisory Council are generally somewhat irregular, since they are used for a variety of purposes unrelated to the Council's legal function.[43]

Beyond the question of actual compliance, however, is that of the usefulness of the standards recommended if adopted. It is obvious that full, if not verbatim, minutes are an absolute minimum for effective control of advisory group meetings, but it is questionable if the other standards can really contribute much in the way of control. The agenda may be formulated by the government, and the meetings be called and chaired by government officials, and still a group may contravene the purposes of the antitrust laws. The primary reasons why this can happen are that members are effectively free to consult with each other outside of the official meetings, and because much of the government-supervised activity of advisory groups is per se collusive in nature.

That such consultation does occur is established fact, and the Celler Committee hearings have furnished additional information on the extent to which it occurs and the extent to which it is condoned and encouraged by government officials. The following paragraph, taken from the minutes of the Copper Wire and Cable Industry meeting of February, 1955, is typical:

It was pointed out that informal task-group meetings could be held by the members themselves at any location they choose and without the necessity of Government participation.[44]

Similarly, the minutes of the March, 1951, meeting of the Contract Motor Carriers group open with the remark that discussion of the agenda was unnecessary:

The Chairman stated that the prepared agenda, which had been submitted in advance, had been quite fully discussed at a previous informal meeting of the group which was held in Chicago, Ill., March 5, 1951, attended by all except one of the members of the formal committee. Committee members agreed that there was no need to repeat in detail what had taken place at the informal meeting.[45]

In other groups, even the pretense of government initiative has been abandoned, and the committee functions with the autonomy of a shadow government, choosing the topics it will introduce for discussion and inde-

---

[42] Officially, he serves as legal consultant to the Council's Labor Policy Committee.

[43] The tax-deductible funds of the BAC have financed social gatherings at resorts, gifts to Secretary Sawyer and others of jewelry and silver trays, prizes for golf and tennis tournaments, and the payment of the legal fees for the wife of an ex-employee. See the Monthly Statements of Receipts and Disbursements, WOC's and Government Advisory Groups, Part II, pp. 1148–78.

[44] When questioned about the propriety of this advice, Asst. Attorney General Barnes replied: "When you say informal meetings, what do you mean? Two of them meet for lunch, and discuss it? Is that a task force informal group meeting? I don't know." WOC's and Government Advisory Groups, Part I, p. 602.

[45] The Mobilization Program, Report of the Subcommittee on Study of Monopoly Power of the Committee on the Judiciary, H.R., 82d Cong., 1st Sess. 32–33 (1951).

pendently defining its own functions. The Business Advisory Council in particular would seem to merit this characterization, as instanced by its activities in 1951 when, during a Wage Stabilization Board dispute, it wilfully forced its unwanted advice on the Administrator.[46]

The second point suggested above, involving "government-sponsored collusion" is more complex and raises some basic issues of public policy. To the extent that government intervention in business is not compatible with the antitrust laws and free competition, the inroads made on the competitive system must be justified in terms of the public interest. For example, the adoption of an oil conservation policy which significantly limits competition may well be in the public interest, but if the policy is administered so as to unnecessarily strengthen the monopolistic structure of the industry, then public authority will merely have subserved private gain.

To permit industry participation in policy formulation is to expose policy to incalculable pressures. Theoretically at least, these pressures can be controlled if they can be traced exclusively to private interest groups, but it is increasingly evident that pressures exist *within* administration itself which challenge the primacy of the public interest. It has been observed that there is a strong tendency for administrators to identify their own interests, if not the public's with those of the group they regulate.[47] Then given a sympathetic administrator who is sensitive to the problems of his clientele, regulation can easily pass into accommodation.[48]

This identity of interests, coupled with the growing independence of bureau chiefs from the higher executive echelons, enhances the potential power of advisory groups and magnifies the possibility that what is forbidden under the antitrust laws may well be achieved under the guise of regulation. That this is no mere chimera can be plausibly demonstrated, and the activities of the Middle East Emergency Committee, which are discussed below, provide strong support for the argument.

This entire problem of government-industry co-operation has been brought into sharper focus by the voluntary agreements program authorized by the 1950 Defense Production Act. This Act gave the President broad powers to channel materials into defense production, to requisition materials and facilities necessary for national defense, and to stabilize prices and wages through regulation. The Act required that whenever possible,

---

[46] *WOC's and Government Advisory Groups*, Part II, pp. 1019–24.

[47] There is a brief discussion of this problem in Melvin Anshen and Francis Wormuth, *Private Enterprise and Public Policy* (New York: Macmillan, 1954), pp. 75–76.

[48] An instance illustrating this attitude, concerning the Business and Defense Services Administration of the Commerce Department, was reported by a New York trade journal: "The agency's enthusiasms sometimes carry it into apparent conflict with Eisenhower administration aims. The President is an outspoken proponent of freer trade abroad, but BDSA has gone to bat more than once for United States firms that want tighter trade restraints to shut out foreign competitors." *Wall Street Journal*, April 15, 1954.

these objectives were to be accomplished by the voluntary action of business and labor, and to protect such co-operative efforts, Section 708 provided for grants of immunity from antitrust prosecution.

This Act was based on the belief that the needs of national defense might require concerted action by industry that would be in positive violation of the antitrust laws. The Act made no attempt, however, to define or limit such action beyond stating that the President must request the exemption and approve the program only if he deemed it in the public interest and in furtherance of the objectives of the Act. If the request for immunity was to come from officials acting under delegated authority, prior approval of the Attorney General was required.[49]

Application of these broad criteria for antitrust exemptions necessarily calls for cautious discrimination. The long-run effects of departures from established antitrust policy must be balanced against the manifest value of such departures to the defense effort. There is good reason to conclude, however, that as the program has been implemented, defense needs have consistently been accorded a high priority over antitrust considerations.

In 1951 more than twelve voluntary agreements were approved, and of these at least half involved industries with highly integrated structures. There were three agreements concerning the petroleum industry, one agreement with the iron and steel industries, one with the aircraft industry, and one in the field of credit and finance.[50] The activities accorded antitrust immunity through these agreements included the adoption of maximum prices on iron and steel products, integration of production facilities, and co-operative action by American companies in the production and foreign distribution of Mid-East oil.

All of these activities have serious long-term implications since it is axiomatic in economic theory that cartellized patterns, once established, are self-perpetuating and can be dislodged, if at all, only by the most drastic means. If the antitrust laws are to be violated, therefore, government regulation and stringent control is a technique better adapted to minimizing concentration than is the use of voluntary co-operative action.

THE ADVISORY FUNCTION

The third area with which the Justice Department has been concerned involves the limitations of private groups to purely advisory functions. The inherent danger here is that the policy-making prerogative will be exercised by nongovernment groups. That there have been such delegations of ad-

---

[49] Presidential delegations made under the immunity section were restricted to officials who had been appointed by the President with the advice and consent of the Senate.

[50] The full list of the 1951 voluntary agreements is presented in the House Report on *The Mobilization Program*, pp. 8–10.

ministrative authority is well known, and the record of World War II abounds with examples.

In many instances this delegation has been the result of deliberate policy, as is clear from the following quotation regarding the use of the Petroleum Industry War Council:

> While it was the original intention that the Council's activities should be of an advisory nature only, subsequent developments have convinced him [the Secretary of the Interior] that there were many national problems and activities that the Council could well administer.[51]

Actually, this delegation went far beyond "national problems and activities," since by administrative directive a foreign operations committee of the Council was empowered to co-ordinate its activities with the British Ministry of War.

A postwar instance, also involving a petroleum group, sheds considerable light on the manner in which federal oil policy has been formed. In 1949, the House Committee on Interstate Commerce requested advice from the Secretary of the Interior on a proposed bill, which called for clarification and co-ordination of national petroleum policies. The Secretary referred the request to the National Petroleum Council, which unanimously expressed its opposition to the bill.[52] That the oil industry has an abiding interest in decentralized governmental control is commonly recognized, and its advice in this instance thoroughly predictable.

The problem of limiting industry committees to purely advisory functions is a complicated one since the distinctions between advice, consent, and delegation are not easily drawn. It is not immediately apparent, for instance, which of the three characterizes the following account of a meeting concerned with the rotation of the government's stockpile of sisalana:

> Discussion concerning the amount of the fee resulted in agreement among the members on three-eighths cents per pound on all the sisalana rotated. Members wished it understood that this figure represented their best guess as the amount which would be high enough to induce general participation and low enough not to demoralize the market.[53]

The language of the minutes is ambiguous enough to make it difficult to decide whether the government is making the decision, or is quite simply trying to determine the "asking price" for the industry's co-operation.

Similar ambiguities are often found in the minutes of meetings in which discussion has centered about price regulations, production allocation, export quotas, etc., and the question remains whether "agreement" in these cases is advice, or is consent to the proposed regulation. The fact-finding and statistical activities of many advisory groups are often patent substitutes

---

[51] From a speech given by the Deputy Co-ordinator of the PIWC, quoted in a report by the Antitrust Division of the Justice Department, "The National Petroleum Council," in *WOC's and Government Advisory Groups*, Part III, pp. 2220–26.

[52] *Ibid.*

[53] Minutes quoted in *WOC's and Government Advisory Groups*, Part I, p. 607.

for comparable government activity. The National Petroleum Council and the Business Advisory Council, in particular, make lavish expenditures on research, much of which is not duplicated by government agencies. Situations occur, therefore, in which proffered "advice" based on this research merely bridges the gaps in official policy. In view of the weighted membership of many groups, policies based on the results of such research will thus tend to reflect the special interests of the dominant companies in the industry.

Since the demise of the NRA there have been few explicit delegations of power as broad as those made during the New Deal. At the time of the Suez crisis, however, the American oil cartel members were given nearly complete administrative power to divert the world's oil supplies to shortage areas in western Europe, and their operations during this period present an interesting study of the use of delegated authority.

The basic legislative authority for the oil-lift program was the Defense Production Act of 1950. Section 708 of this Act, the immunity section, authorizes the President to encourage the formation of voluntary agreements with industry to further national defense objectives, and grants these agreements antitrust immunity. The first voluntary agreement on oil was reached in 1951, and the Iranian crisis was handled under it. A new agreement was enacted in 1953 providing for possible future emergencies, and authorizing two types of activity: co-operative action by suppliers in the event of oil shortages in friendly nations, and the gathering of information and statistics on production, supply, and demand. The first activity was authorized only in the event that an emergency actually existed, but the second was to be a continuing function of the Committee set up under the agreement.

From June, 1953, until late in 1956 the Committee performed its statistical functions with an industry staff and chairman, despite objections by the Attorney General. Under the then current arrangements, the Committee members, representing competing oil companies, were reading each others' production estimates, and the Attorney General was concerned that these estimates would in fact become production quotas.[54] He therefore proposed that the production figures of the individual companies be funneled through the government so that the information passed along to the Committee could not be used by the participating companies to deduce each others' production figures.

In 1956, the Committee was finally forced into making concessions on this point, and they were written into a new agreement. This agreement required that the Committee staff and chairman be government employees, which in practice meant that WOC's on loan from the companies replaced

[54] See the testimony of Asst. Attorney General Barnes, *WOC's and Government Advisory Groups*, Part III, p. 2217.

the personnel directly employed by the companies.[55] According to testimony collected by the Senate investigation of the oil lift program, however, these minor concessions were not intended to apply in the event of actual operations. When the Suez crisis developed in the summer of 1956, therefore, these safeguards were eliminated from the plans.[56]

The Committee was activated in August, 1956, and the Secretary of the Interior requested it to prepare plans to meet the emergency. The government itself appears to have resigned all responsibility for the actual drafting of the plans, for on the day Interior announced its emergency finding, a draft was being prepared in New York by the legal staff of the member companies.[57]

The plan as finally adopted created the Middle East Emergency Committee (MEEC), which was authorized to make estimates of the petroleum needs of each of the countries to be supplied, to draft supply schedules, and to pool transportation facilities. Its statistical functions were to continue.

This broad delegation of power was accompanied by none of the usual antitrust safeguards written into the various voluntary agreements, and included no stipulations regarding price.[58] As might have been expected, the venture was highly profitable for the participants,[59] but far more significant are the long-run effects the program will have on the international and domestic distribution patterns of the industry.

While the MEEC had no over-all allocation powers (that is, the Committee did not make decisions concerning the country-by-country allocation of available oil), it was entrusted with implementing the allocation decisions reached by the intergovernmental Organization for European Economic Co-operation. The companies themselves were left free to decide which of them would supply the designated quota, and how the total would be apportioned amongst them. These arrangements were made so as to minimize disruptions in the established supply patterns, and notwithstanding the tremendous impact of the emergency, no significant shifts occurred in the relative market positions of the participating companies. According to the

---

[55] *Emergency Oil Lift Program and Related Oil Problems,* Joint Hearings before Subcommittees of the Committee on the Judiciary and Committee on Interior and Insular Affairs, U.S. Senate, 85th Cong., 1st Sess., Part 3, p. 1990 (1957).

[56] *Ibid.,* p. 1052.

[57] *Ibid.,* Part 1, p. 66.

[58] According to the testimony of Secretary of the Interior Seaton before the O'Mahoney Committee, there is no authoization in law for any agreement on price. Such an agreement, furthermore, would violate the provisions of the Defense Production Act, and the antitrust laws generally. Hearings on the *Emergency Oil Lift Program,* Part 1, pp. 551-63.

[59] Earnings of the five major participants increased substantially during the period, and profits increased between 13 and 32 per cent over those of the pre-emergency period. *Petroleum, The Antitrust Laws and Government Policies,* Sen. Rep. No. 1147, 85th Cong., 1st Sess. 62 (1957).

report made by the Senate investigating committee, these historical patterns of distribution are those which the Justice Department has charged illegal in its oil cartel suit.[60]

The arguments usually made in support of such a delegation as that made to the MEEC are that the superior efficiency of private industry and the need for prompt action militate against leaving the job to be done by government. The inadequacies and insufficiency of government personnel are contrasted with the dynamic qualities of private management and its large reservoir of specialized skills. The implication is thus made that private planning is in some crucial way superior to its public counterpart. While there is surely an element of truth in this argument, the case for delegation, even with adequate safeguards, must take account of the intense conflict of interests which is likely to arise. Charges have been made against the members of the MEEC, for example, that its failure to divert Venezuelan oil shipments to Europe resulted from such a conflict of interests. Whether these charges are true or not is immaterial in view of the more crucial charges of cartellization, but they illustrate nicely the complex of competing interests which may be created by any such delegations of public power.

In 1957, following the Cellar Committee investigations, an amendment to the Clayton Act was introduced with the avowed purpose of establishing standards for the organization and operation of government advisory groups.[61] In effect, the bill called for legislative endorsement of the procedural rules recommended by the Attorney General to guide advisory group meetings. As of this writing, the bill has yet to emerge from committee, and it is generally thought that its chances for survival are slight, but it is questionable if this legislation, if enacted, could achieve any substantial reforms of existing practice.

The use of advisory groups is only a part of the larger problem of concentration in American industry; as such, effective control is dependent on factors which reach far beyond their institutionalization. The consultative technique, however, provided one more lever made available to pressure groups to influence policy, and it provides it at an especially vulnerable point in the governmental process. An aggressive control of advisory groups will not in itself solve the problem of monopoly power, but it is a primary requisite for checking administrative intensification of this power.

An early commentator on the growing use of advisory groups cautioned:

It daily sharpens the need for administrative authorities who are skilled in consultation, vigilant in arranging representation that is reasonably comprehensive, sympathetic but wary,

---

[60] See the testimony of Edwin G. Moline, Hearings on the *Emergency Oil Lift Program*, Part 1, pp. 122-24.

[61] H.R. 2144, 85th Cong., 1st Sess. (January 7, 1957).

and above all independent. Only by the careful use of advisory boards will the danger of compromising administration at its core be avoided.[62]

The above observations were written before the NRA, and before the sustained mobilization efforts of the forties and fifties had produced the additional concentrations of industry which exist today, but the problem raised remains unsolved.

If the proper use of advisory groups requires an independent administration, then no procedural techniques can effectively compensate for the lack of one. The weaknesses of the group participation theory follow from this. It places a total reliance on the vagaries of administrative discretion, and assumes a psychology of dedicated public service which is at tension with its own underlying concepts of the function of government. The "broker" theory of government, conceiving of government as arbiter or referee, reduces the public-private interests dichotomy of classical political economy to an irrelevancy. For this reason, the theory is incapable of coming to grips with the new relations which have emerged between these two great sectors. This failure has led to attempts to merge the sectors by reducing one to the other, and to a view of the public interest as a mere *additive* expression of private interests. Public policy is accordingly seen as a resultant of the free interplay of competing forces, and the function of government becomes one of enforcing the rules of fair play.[63]

The fallacy here is obvious, and derives from the easy assumption that all groups have the resources and the organization necessary to formulate and energetically promote their own interests. The most superficial examination of the contemporary American scene contradicts this assumption, and thereby denies the validity of the broker theory.

It follows from the above that questions concerning the relation of government and business permit of only two alternative formulations: government is either the means of actuating and protecting the common good, or it is the tool of private ends. The discredited self-regulation experiment of the New Deal, as well as subsequent experience with advisory groups and delegations of public authority, indicate the need for a forceful redefinition of the boundaries between the public and private sectors. To be compatible with traditional antitrust policy, such a redefinition must exclude the possibility of administrative trustification. It must be grounded in an awareness that what is good for General Motors is not necessarily good for the nation.

---

[62] Arthur W. Macmahon, "Advisory Boards," *loc. cit.*, p. 611.

[63] The presidential veto of the Harris-Fulbright natural gas bill was inspired by this philosophy. Although the President was in substantial agreement with the obectives of the bill, he thought that the activities of the oil lobby were "so arrogant and so much in defiance of acceptable standards of propriety as to risk creating doubts among the American people concerning the integrity of governmental processes." From a White House Press Release, February 17, 1956.

Cycles of Illegality: Antitrust Violations in Corporate America*

SALLY S. SIMPSON, *University of Oregon*

Abstract

This paper explores the relations between antitrust behavior and variations in macroeconomic conditions and Republican–Democratic administrations. Its major premise is that corporate antitrust criminality results when business conditions deteriorate (i.e., during recessionary periods) and corporate profits are squeezed. This hypothesis is tested using longidutinal data from 1927 through 1981 and OLS time series analysis. Fifty-two "survivor" firms are tracked as to their patterns of antitrust criminality across these sample years. Interpretation of the findings suggests that both economic and political variables are directly related to the criminal behavior of these firms. Antitrust behavior increases as unemployment rates climb and aggregate stock prices drop. It is also apt to occur during Republican administrations. The implications of these findings, as well as how they integrate into the extant literature, are discussed.

Corporate crime is perhaps the most enigmatic of all the possible areas of research in criminology. Originally conceptualized by Sutherland (1949) as white-collar crime, in recent years corporate misbehavior has·been defined and dissected by sociologists and criminologists (Clinard et al. 1979; Coleman 1985; Geis & Meier 1977; Shapiro 1985; Simon & Eitzen 1982; Vaughan 1983), lawyers (Clark 1983; Hay & Kelley 1974; Posner 1970), and business/organization scholars (Staw & Szwajkowski 1975; Strachan, Smith & Beedles 1983; Walton & Cleveland 1964).

 Within this growing literature, there has been very little hypothesis-testing research. Indeed, most studies of corporate crime are descriptive and/or theoretical; they focus on particular corporations, industries, or "cases" of misbehavior. Therefore, findings may not be generalizable. An-

*This is a revised version of a paper presented at the annual meetings of the Society for the Study of Social Problems. I thank Andy B. Anderson and Alan Lizotte for advice on statistical techniques, appropriate methods, and logical data base construction. Also, I acknowledge the contributions of my friends and colleagues, Robert Faulkner, Anthony Harris, Lawrence Zacharias, Victoria Swigert, Steven Ainley, Royce Singleton, Rhys Williams, and two anonymous referees. Address correspondence to the author, Department of Sociology, University of Oregon, Eugene, OR 97403.

943

other problem with the literature is a conceptual tendency to subsume a variety of violations—labor, trade, manufacturing—under the rubric "corporate crime" (e.g., Kramer 1982). This conceptual monolith passively encourages scholars to view all corporate crime as having the same etiology. The present paper addresses these problems by isolating one type of corporate illegality (antitrust violations) and testing for its occurrence using economic and political variables.

Theoretical Framework

Many scholars implicate corporate financial difficulty as a source of intraorganizational pressure which culminates in illegal actions (Barnett 1981; Conklin 1977; Finney & Lesieur 1982). When corporate profit goals are not achieved, severe organizational strain is likely. "Performance pressures mount because of reduced salaries and dividends, declining stock values, and shrinking market shares" (Finney & Lesieur 1982, p. 270).

A firm's reaction to profit-squeeze typically involves ways of reducing costs and increasing revenues. Firms may engage in strategic interaction with competitors, potential industry competitors, and producers of substitute products as well as negotiate with labor and/or governmental regulators—all without making significant changes in the legitimate behavior of the corporation (Porter 1980). Yet, there are reasons to suspect that when "legitimate" market manipulation fails, illegitimate behaviors may substitute.

Theoretically, the literature does not distinguish which types of illegality are likely to occur during profit-squeeze periods. Empirically, however, certain types of corporate crime are more apt to occur than others. One such illegality is antitrust (e.g., Asch & Seneca 1975; Staw & Szwajkowski 1975).[1] Low or declining profits may stimulate interfirm conspiracy with subsequent high prices (improved profitability) and strong demand causing conspirators to persist (Lean, Ogru & Rogers 1982; Sultan 1975). Sharply declining profits and performance pressure may trigger attempts to forcefully increase the dependence of purchasers on the firm's products, to heighten entry barriers, and/or to pass profit constraints on to others within a transaction network. Opportunism and self-interest in the search for comparative advantage encourages the cultivation and continuation of transactions through which buyers are moved into weaker bargaining positions. Vehicles for that movement may be illegal tying agreements, selective price negotiation and price discrimination, refusals to deal, and other strategies designed to secure structural leverage and market control (Denzin 1977; Farberman 1975). Finally, large firms may resort to predatory pricing as a means to undermine the market share of weaker competitors.

The profit-squeeze–antitrust thesis has been tested empirically with poorly performing firms (Clinard et al. 1979; Staw & Szwajkowski 1975) and/or industries (Bain 1951; Hay & Kelley 1974). Certainly, firm-level decision-making and product market scarcity or munificence have an impact on a company's ability to operate profitably. Yet, other environmental factors also may impose constraints on the firm. Those scholars who acknowledge the role of market in affecting firm action effectively ignore the plausible influence of macroeconomic fluctuations on these same processes. This oversight is troublesome as firms often plot strategy and action based on trends in the economy as a whole, rather than relying solely on industry movements. Gordon (1961) points out that downswings in the business cycle are carefully monitored by firms for forecasting purposes. Companies will isolate some systematic relations between sales of their products and variability in macro indicators (such as GNP, stock price, or industrial production) and adjust their activities accordingly. Thus, the primary goal of this research is to isolate the macroeconomic factors and circumstances which produce antitrust behavior by corporations. The relation between changes in economic conditions and antitrust criminality is traced longitudinally, across all business cycle phases (depression, recession, recovery, and growth).

This paper differs substantively from earlier works in that it addresses crime causation issues (corporate action) as well as variations in government prosecution/regulatory activity (government action). Several researchers (Moe 1980; Neuman 1983; Posner 1970) hypothesize that antitrust will vary by administrative policy, that is, certain political administrations are more likely to pursue corporate violators than others. From this perspective, criminality may be viewed as a consequence of the political labeling process, typically produced through regulator edict. This argument is examined in conjunction with the economic "profit-squeeze" model where the state plays a secondary, albeit important, role. Given these concerns, it is important to expand upon the idea of business cycle activities.

The Business Cycle

A common definition of business cycles (and that employed by the National Bureau of Economic Research) originates with Burns and Mitchell.

Business cycles are a type of fluctuation found in the aggregate economic activity of nations that organize their work mainly in business enterprises: a cycle consists of expansions occurring at about the same time in many economic activities, followed by similarly general recessions, contractions and revivals which merge into the expansion phase of the next cycle, this sequence of changes is recurrent but not periodic; in duration business cycles vary from more than one year to ten or twelve years; they are not divisible into shorter cycles of similar characteristics with amplitudes approximately their own (1946, p. 3).

Thus, business cycles are defined and identified when an expansion period has ended and contraction has begun. Although this definitional procedure is too complex to fully document here, cycles are often determined through historical comparison of changes in various economic indicators. These indicators vary over the years, but the most consistent are fluctuations in GNP, manufacturing output (Industrial Production Indices), average workweek, new orders, stock prices, wholesale prices, housing, and new business starts (Moore 1980).

Although all phases of the cycle are important for this analysis, contraction periods are of particular interest because of the relations between recessions and declines in corporate profit. There have been fourteen contraction periods in the U.S. economy since 1920 (Moore 1980; Silk 1982). These contractions vary in depth and duration; therefore, it is unlikely that all contraction periods will affect businesses similarly. Further, although the point is not made explicitly in the literature, it seems that certain characteristics of a downturn are more important indicators of severity than others (e.g., depth as opposed to duration, declining demand rather than "inventory recessions" [Gordon 1961; Moore 1980]). Thus, measures of the business cycle should be sensitive to these variations.

If we assume that there is a link between corporate profit-squeeze and corporate crime, it is necessary to model the macroeconomic conditions under which this relation will occur. Sherman (1968) discusses how aggregate profit rates are very sensitive to "the tides in general business activity." Thus, one can expect corporate profit-squeeze to occur during economic contractions, causing a higher incidence of illegal antitrust activity. Moreover, the more severe the contraction period, the greater the "squeeze," increasing the likelihood of crime. These general expectations are tested using time series data analysis.

Data and Methods

In order to test the anticipated relations between macroeconomic change and corporate illegality, data are analyzed for odd-numbered years from 1927 through 1981.[2] Ordinary least-squares regression was used to estimate a two-equation macrodynamic structural equation model of economic profit-squeeze, cycle phase and severity, political administration (regime), and alleged antitrust criminality (Kmenta 1971; Ostrom 1978). Data sources and measurement were as follows:

CORPORATE CRIME

Antitrust and trade violations were tracked each year, from 1927 through 1981, for 52 survivor firms in 7 basic manufacturing industries. (See Appendix A for the sample of corporations and their industries.) Primary sources included the FTC Case Decisions and Commerce Clearing House Trade Cases (*The Blue Book*). The crime variable represents the sum total of alleged yearly violations for all corporations in the sample, values range from 0 to 32.

These data document alleged civil, criminal, and administrative antitrust cases tapping such acts as false advertising; combining or conspiring to fix prices, allocate territories, exchange price information; tying arrangements; exclusive dealing; vertical and horizontal mergers; and interlocks (among others). Whenever possible, the cases were coded *according to the year the alleged criminality occurred*, rather than when a complaint was issued or a case processed. While it is possible that one highly criminal corporation is capable of biasing the findings, comparing the most criminogenic company within an industry with the total amount of yearly corporate criminality, it is unlikely that this will be a problem. (See Appendix B for comparisons of the most and least criminal companies within each product market and their criminality relative to the yearly totals.)

Because there is a lack of systematically recorded data in the corporate crime area (as opposed to, say, the *Uniform Crime Reports* which officially document more traditional crime types on a yearly basis), these data provide us with crude approximations of corporate antitrust behavior. As such, they underrepresent "true" amounts of antitrust and are subject to bias. Thus, the discussion of findings must be filtered through a screen of caution. A further problem exists with the high business failure rate and structural reorganization of both firms and industries. However, because the primary focus of this study is to examine the ways in which certain firms, over time, react to changes in macroeconomic conditions, only those firms that are relatively constant in their economic activity within a particular industry during these years were included in the sample.

ECONOMIC VARIABLES

Changes in the macroeconomy were measured with several variables: manufacturers' total year-end inventories (in millions of dollars), Standard and Poor's Industrial Stock prices (1941–43 = 10), unemployment rates, and manufacturing output (Industrial Production Index, value transformed; 1957–59 = 100). These variables were selected because of their theoretical relevance and consistency across time. All measures are drawn from official government statistics listed in *Historical Statistics of the United States* (1975) and *The Statistical Abstract of the United States* (1975, 1977, 1982–83).

CYCLE PHASE AND SEVERITY

Three measures are created to control for the different phases of the business cycle and its severity. The simplest coding scheme is to assign a cycle phase value to each year within the sample. This was done using information from the Bureau of Economic Research, so that all years are defined as depression (1), recession (2), recovery (3), or growth (4). Although this scheme allows for either dummy coding (e.g., recession vs. all other phases) or a simple index variable (business cycle=1 to 4), it cannot control for variations in cycle severity. In sum, this coding scheme does not differentiate between cycles. In order to overcome this problem, a variable which combines measures of cycle duration and depth was created. All identified cycles between 1927 and 1981 were ordinally ranked by duration and depth. A monotonic index was constructed, weighting cycle depth as twice the importance of duration (Moore 1980). The numeric value obtained for each cycle was then assigned to its corresponding year. Thus, the Great Depression downturn was coded as the most severe of cycles (value=28) and the moderate decline in 1927 (value=6) as the least severe. Clearly this index is somewhat crude in that it is based on the rank order of variables. However, it is theoretically appealing to distinguish the effects of the different cycles.

POLITICAL VARIABLES

It is plausible that criminality varies substantially from one political administration to another (Moe 1980; Neuman 1983; Posner 1970). Based on party ideology, companies may perceive certain political administrations to be more lenient in policy toward antitrust behavior than others. To control for this effect, the sample years are coded as either Republican or Democratic. Still, systematic bias is likely to result from several events which occurred during the Roosevelt/World War II years. Roosevelt created legislation (the National Recovery Act) which not only stimulated government intervention in the market, but encouraged industry trade associations—later during his administration deemed illegal. The Robinson–Patman Act, passed in 1936, protected small business from the predatory pricing policies of larger corporations. After an initial rush of cases (the first 15 years or so), prosecution of Robinson–Patman violations declined in popularity and frequency. World War II also may be a source of systematic bias for two reasons: companies that participated in the "war effort" were sometimes immune from prosecution;[3] and the economy was more "controlled" during the war. Thus the opportunities to violate the law during this time differ substantially from other periods. These biases were controlled in the analysis by dummy coding years 1932–46 as 1 and the remaining years as 0.

Zero-order correlations among the variables of interest are listed in Table 1. Any interpretations of these correlations are clearly problematic, especially given the inherent secular trends in the data. They are given here because time series structural equations may contain multicollinearity among the independent variables.[4] Close examination of the correlation coefficients indicated that this may be a problem. Therefore, the effects of certain independent variables are modeled separately.

ANTICIPATED RELATIONS

The main theoretical argument of this paper, that economic pressures are likely to result in corporate illegality, can be tested in several ways. First, it is assumed that recession—particularly those downturns defined as severe—is more likely to signal potential or real profit losses than other cycle phases. Thus, the criminal *behavior* of corporations should be greatest during these periods. On the other hand, corporate criminal response is apt to be negated by the state's need to protect business interests during particularly severe downturns. Consequently, the needs of the state and of business are likely to be reflected through regulatory *inaction* during threatening recession/depressions. Additionally, although many other factors are involved in economic declines, certain features of a downturn may have a greater impact on corporate profits than others. Perhaps the best indicator of corporate profitability across time is stock price. Unlike officially reported firm balances which are based on accounting sheets and suffer many biases, stock prices, or firm values, respond immediately to business activity. "The fact that investors adjust firm value based on their assessment of the most recent information permits analysis of the effect of individual events . . . on firm value" (McGuire & Schneewies 1982, p. 7). Firm value is a direct reflection of a company's ability, either potential or demonstrated, to perform successfully and competitively (i.e., profitably). Thus, for these purposes, decreases in aggregate stock price suggest a lack of confidence in business, a likely economic decline, and subsequently, higher levels of corporate crime.

Manufacturing output (as measured by the Industrial Production Index) is a particularly effective tool for distinguishing business revivals from recessions and the early stages of expansion. Therefore, extreme fluctuations in the economy which may negatively affect corporate profitability can be identified. Corporate profitability per unit of output declines throughout recessionary periods, but rises promptly when a recovery begins. This suggests that downward trends in the production index will predict higher levels of corporate crime.[5]

Unemployment rates are also included in the analysis as they are likely to be positively related to corporate illegality. As a measure of business activity, unemployment is strongly correlated with upward and

313

Table 1. ZERO-ORDER CORRELATIONS BETWEEN MEASURES OF ANTITRUST CRIMINALITY, BUSINESS CYCLE VARIABLES, AND POLITICAL ADMINISTRATION*

	Inventory	Unemployment	Industrial Production	Stock Price	Cycle Phase	Severity	Regime	Roosevelt WWII	Violations
Inventory	1.0000								
Unemployment	-.230 (.124)	1.0000							
Industrial production	-.932 (.001)	-.428 (.013)	1.0000						
Stock price	.871 (.001)	-.305 (.057)	.949 (.001)	1.0000					
Cycle phase	.088 (.332)	-.275 (.079)	.237 (.117)	.205 (.147)	1.0000				
Severity	-.200 (.158)	.699 (.001)	-.417 (.015)	-.459 (.007)	-.250 (.033)	1.0000			
Regime	-.295 (.068)	.145 (.231)	-.300 (.064)	-.339 (.039)	.177 (.183)	.331 (.043)	1.0000		
Roosevelt WWII	-.458 (.008)	.554 (.001)	-.539 (.002)	-.554 (.001)	.065 (.319)	.638 (.001)	.430 (.011)	1.0000	
Violations	-.079 (.347)	-.012 (.475)	.304 (.061)	.465 (.006)	.120 (.191)	-.433 (.001)	-.264 (.087)	-.250 (.033)	1.0000

*Maximum number of cases=55.

314

downward swings in the economy. A low rate of unemployment indicates an economy that is prosperous and profitable for business, while high unemployment suggests just the opposite. Further, labor layoffs are viable options for firms experiencing profit constraints. Thus, "squeezes" may produce both criminality and layoffs.

Finally, it is anticipated that there will be more antitrust crime during Republican administrations than during Democratic. Republican ideology and dogma is traditionally more supportive of business interests and, in practice, Republican administrations are often hostile to corporate regulation. Since the crime variable is coded by the *year of infraction* and not the year of prosecution, the political regime variable must be seen as a measure of perceived "liberalness" in regulatory climate on the part of business.

Using these anticipated relations as guides, several path models were estimated for the relations between changes in the macroeconomy and illegal corporate behaviors. As noted earlier, stock price and industrial production are highly correlated, indicating that multicollinearity within the equations is a problem. Therefore, their effects are modeled separately. Figures 1 and 2 show the final estimated models.[6] These models are not interpreted as causal, but rather are used as heuristic devices from which a general discussion of the structural equations can be launched. The paths within the figures model a one-year lag or less between the independent variables and alleged criminality.[7] Secular trends in the data are controlled within the analysis by inserting a time variable (year) into each regression equation. This variable may also lessen the effects of autoregressive disturbances over time. While it cannot eliminate the initial source of autocorrelation, it can negate that part of the disturbance which is secular. Variables that are insignificant are dropped from the models unless theoretically relevant.[8]

Findings and Discussion

ECONOMIC VARIABLES

The proxy measures of profit-squeeze (stock price and industrial production) have the anticipated negative relations with alleged trade violations, although only stock price is significant. As the general economy improves, and corporations improve their positions, antitrust violations decline. Further support for a profit-squeeze argument comes from the strong, positive relations between unemployment and criminal behavior. Clearly, high rates of unemployment (as a measure of business recession and corporate troubles) predict increased levels of criminal activity.

Thus, during periods of macro decline, it appears that corporations

315

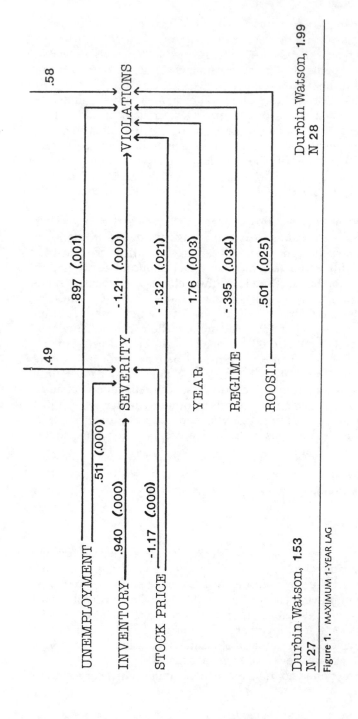

Figure 1. MAXIMUM 1-YEAR LAG

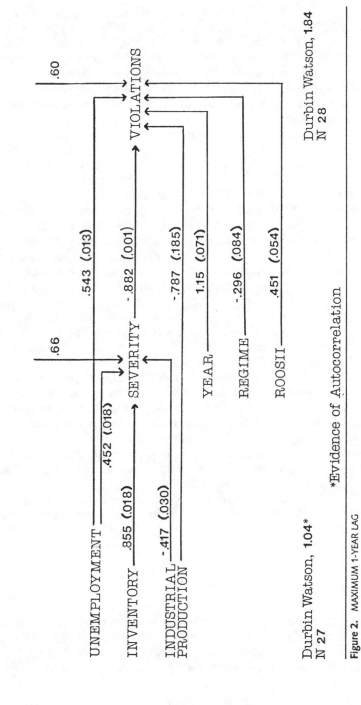

Figure 2. MAXIMUM 1-YEAR LAG

attempt to stabilize potentially profit-threatening situations through anti-competitive responses (e.g., price-fixing, illegal mergers and tying agreements, allocation of territories, and so forth). Industry leaders might engage in these behaviors to prevent price cutting which, if ignored, can further propel prices and profits downward—disrupting any semblance of environmental certainty. In these cases, the negative effects of a recession on firm profitability are exacerbated. Profit rebound becomes more attenuated.

These generally supportive findings are tempered by the strong negative effect of cycle severity on crime. As cycle severity increases, criminal behavior decreases. While counter-intuitive to the economic argument, this relationship makes sense from a political-economy perspective. Corporate criminal activity is *officially* defined and prosecuted. Unless the state chooses to pursue antitrust violators, illegal activities will not be recorded and thus do not appear as crime.[9] Because the special focus of antitrust law is to maintain a healthy and competitive economy, one would expect less government inclination to pursue and punish violators during a severe economic decline. A second possibility for this finding is tied to the coding of the severity variable. The effects of a severe recessionary period may be mitigated by assigning the same severity ranking to the entire cycle of recession, recovery, and growth. Thus, cycle severity does not appear to be measuring the effects of severe recessions on antitrust crime only, but rather the effects of an entire *cycle* on criminal activity. Although the coding of the severity variable is problematic, as one can see in Figures 1 and 2, its relation to other business cycle variables (e.g., unemployment, year end inventories, stock price, and industrial production) is predictable and well-behaved, suggesting that the variable is valid. Finally, cycle severity is inversely related to industry concentration patterns. It is easier for firms to negotiate and enforce certain types of anti-competitive acts as the market becomes more concentrated. Consequently, one can expect that as cycle severity decreases, the opportunities to violate the law will increase (Table 2).[10]

At this point, a profit-squeeze explanation for antitrust crime seems plausible. Yet, macroeconomic trends, in isolation, are not the only relevant factors which produce antitrust behaviors. Political decisions, variations in administration prosecutions, new laws and so forth, also may have important effects on corporate illegality.

POLITICAL VARIABLES

Most scholars who investigate the relations between political regime and antitrust criminality are concerned with the issue of how administrations vary in their selection and prosecution of cases. From this perspective antitrust crime is viewed as state produced. Posner (1970) finds no system-

Table 2. TIME-SERIES REGRESSION EQUATIONS OF BUSINESS CYCLE AND ALLEGED ANTITRUST VIOLATIONS ON ECONOMIC AND POLITICAL VARIABLES

Explanatory Variables*	Dependent Variables						
	Severity	Severity	1-Yr. Lag Violations	1-Yr. Lag Violations	1-Yr. Lag Violations	1-Yr. Lag Violations	1-Yr. Lag Violations
Inventory	.096 (.02015)	$.9 \times 10^{-1}$ (.04952)					.210 (.23815)
Unemployment	.639 (.12909)	.565 (.22154)	.955 (.27347)	.729 (.23197)	1.02 (.24806)	.607 (.22240)	
Stock price	-.196 (.03386)		$-.1 \times 10^{-1}$ (.074113)		-.198 (.07944)		
Industrial production		-.111 (.05185)		$-.3 \times 10^{-1}$ (.05577)		$-.8 \times 10^{-1}$ (.05580)	-.100 (.07218)
Year			.451 (.19616)	.249 (.24942)	.718 (.21136)	.481 (.25222)	.602 (.32166)
Recession							-4.59 (8.8047)
Recession-severity Interaction							.090 (.45717)
Severity			-.836 (.22135)	-.735 (.19696)	-1.08 (.21990)	-.787 (.20280)	
Regime					-5.43 (6.23898)	-4.08 (2.2467)	
Roosevelt WWII					7.63 (3.1618)	6.64 (3.2752)	
Intercept	15.22	18.11	-2.65	.962	8.82	-.150	-14.19
R^2	.79	.57	.53	.53	.66	.63	.27
Adjusted R^2	.76	.51	.45	.44	.56	.52	.10
Durbin-Watson	1.53	1.04**	1.33	1.33	1.99	1.84	1.55
N	27	27	28	27	28	27	27

*Unstandardized betas are reported; standard errors are in parentheses.

**The Durbin-Watson statistic indicates positive autocorrelation, 5% significance.

atic effects of political regime on antitrust cases; neither Democratic nor Republican administrations differ significantly in their pursuit and prosecution patterns. Other scholars, however, find moderate positive relations between antitrust activity (both FTC orders and cases) and Republican administrations (Moe 1980; Neuman 1983). These findings seem counter-intuitive given the ideological stances of both parties. Moe's interpretation is that such results are due to Republican sympathy for small business. However, there is another interpretation.

Isolating the effects of political regime in Figures 1 and 2, this variable (dummy coded with Democrat = 1, Republican = 0) is consistent in its negative relations with antitrust activity. Like Neuman (1983) and Moe's (1980) findings, Republican administrations consistently "produce" more antitrust criminality. (In some instances as many as 26 more cases per 2-year period.) Yet, because of the coding differences between this work and those that focus on government activity,[11] higher levels of criminality during Republican administrations may indicate that the Republicans have a deterrence problem. If corporations perceive the political climate to be conducive to criminal activities, particularly when their profitability is threatened by macro declines, then they are apt to consider violating the law to enhance their competitive advantage. In light of these consistent findings, Neuman and Moe's observations may be a function of higher rates of crime during Republican regimes. In any case, political variables do appear to be related to antitrust crime.[12]

One additional control variable deserves mention. The Roosevelt/ World War II variable (testing for the effects of Roosevelt's policies and World War II on the regulatory and economic climate during years 1932–45) does show the anticipated positive effects on crime—suggesting that there may be some systematic bias associated with these years. New laws and economic controls introduced during these years increase the opportunity to commit violations. Moreover, two of the nation's deepest recessions correspond to these years; thus, a profit-squeeze argument is also a plausible explanation for these findings.

Summary and Conclusions

The relations between declining macroeconomic conditions, political variations, and corporate antitrust behavior are the focus of this paper. While the results of this analysis are not always robust, the data lend plausibility to a profit-squeeze–corporate-crime argument. High levels of unemployment, downturns in stock price and manufacturing output are directly related to criminality. The political economy of antitrust regulation may be indicated by the strong negative effect of cycle severity on violations. While theoretically one would expect a positive relation between severity of business recessions and criminality (i.e., the greater the profit pressures on firms, the more likely their criminality), if the business community is in crisis, the state may passively acquiesce to corporate needs, ignoring illegality when it occurs.

The effects of political regime within this analysis duplicate the findings of other studies; Republicans produce more antitrust criminality during their administrations than Democrats. Yet, rather than implying that Republican administrations issue more complaints or orders, my data indicate the possibility that *criminality* is greater during these regimes. Republicans generate more crime; hence, they issue more complaints and orders. While these findings differ depending on which economic indicator is included in the equations, they nonetheless suggest that antitrust criminality cannot be separated from political considerations.

The current findings contribute to our knowledge about corporate illegality in several ways. By isolating corporate crime according to crime type (i.e., antitrust) and time of infraction, the relations between changes in economic and political climate over time and antitrust criminality are highlighted. As a consequence, different explanations of corporate antitrust criminality can be tested and evaluated. When the effects of political regime and changes in law and opportunity are controlled, indicators of aggregate economic declines are significantly related to the anticompetitive behavior of the 52 firms in the sample. Thus, at least for these companies, during periods of economic decline, corporate antitrust criminality increases.

Notes

1. Additionally, Clinard et al. (1979) find specific environmental, labor, and manufacturing violations to be associated with poor financial performance. Manufacturing violations were the most highly correlated, followed by environmental and labor respectively.
2. This odd-year pattern is selected for two important reasons: (1) this paper and data are drawn from a larger, pooled cross-sectional time-series analysis in which relevant data systematically are missing for odd years. In an effort to maintain continuity, this pattern is duplicated for most of the time-series variables. (2) The likelihood of autocorrelation (usually associated with time-series equations) is reduced as the time between subsequent points (t_1 and t_2) is increased. I do not suggest that this is a solution to the problem of autocorrelated residuals; rather it is a pragmatic step to circumvent a loss of efficiency or biases in the estimated variances that might be confounded over time.
3. For example, a case against GMC and A.C. Spark Plug (FTC 1948), charging exclusive dealing, price discrimination, and price fixing in 1936, was overlooked by the government because of the firms' "patriotic contribution to the war effort." This type of discriminatory justice is also likely to emerge during periods of severe economic decline as the government is hesitant to pursue violators if the economy is truly floundering.
4. Multicollinearity in longitudinal structural equation modeling can be flagged by several factors: (1) an R^2 greater than 1.00; (2) sign changes in zero-order correlations and correlation coefficients; (3) standardized Betas greater than 1.00; and (4) zero-order coefficients greater than .9.
5. It is crucial to note, however, that changes in manufacturing output arise from a variety of

causes, only some of which are associated with the business cycle (Moore 1980). Keeping this in mind, the possibility exists that fluctuations in the levels of productivity, separate from the mediating effects of a business cycle, may affect corporate criminality. For example, increases in production may indicate greater competition between established firms for market dominance or market share creating the potential for more, rather than less, crime. Moreover, more firms may be moving into a particular market, thereby extending the opportunity to commit violations against competitors (Porter 1980). Consequently, changes in industrial production over time may have simultaneous positive and negative effects on antitrust violations and a clear trend may be difficult to ascertain.

6. The Durbin–Watson test for autocorrelation indicates only one case of positive serial correlation. These equations are viewed with appropriate care. It is important to note that these questionable equations are not crucial to the analysis of criminal behavior but rather test the validity of a new variable included in the analysis (i.e., cycle severity).

7. Two- and three-year lags were also estimated, but variable relations were weakened as the length of lags increased.

8. The relative effects of these excluded variables can be examined in Table 2. Because the Durbin–Watson statistic suggests only one incidence of positively correlated residuals, the various techniques which are commonly employed to reestimate the equations are eschewed.

9. All crime, whether it is street or white collar, is subject to underreporting and differential processing. In both situations, we can interpret recorded violations as some fraction of a total "real" amount of crime. Corporate crime reporting is perhaps most similar to rape or drug statistics where changes in law and interpretation occur over time, waxing and waning as public interest and government enforcement practices shift. Further, like UCR statistics, some antitrust measures are more reliable than others. Unfair advertising violations are often caught because of FTC screening procedures. Price-fixing, on the other hand, is usually brought to the attention of regulators by competitors. In these situations, business norms interact with the number of cases brought.

I recognize that the problem of underreporting (a problem in all criminal statistics), once political party is controlled, may not be randomly distributed across the corporations within my sample. But, this is an unfortunate source of error in all analyses of crime.

10. Equations are estimated that include both a recession dummy variable *and* a recession-severity interaction variable in order to isolate (a) recessionary periods from other cycle phases, and (b) severe recessions from more mild downturns. Neither variable is significant in the equations (see Table 2). However, further clarification of this negative severity effect is found through subsequent data analysis. When dummy variables are created for industry-cycle severity interactions, this variable reverses its sign but loses significance. The interaction patterns indicate that it is only within the motor vehicle and oil refining industries that cycle severity has negative and significant effects (industries that are crucial to the economic health of the U.S.). While this is an important finding, industry level analysis is not the primary focus of this research. I cite these additional findings to explicate and inform the reader about this effect.

11. While some FTC and Justice Departments complaints are issued and civil complaints brought during the year of criminal activity, there is often a one- to three-year gap between crime and complaint. If one measures corporate criminality from the time a complaint is issued or a case settled as opposed to when the company actually committed the violations, then certainly enough time has passed for an administration to change from Republican to Democrat and vice versa. Conceptually, the variable becomes one of variations in government enforcement practice or variations in whistle-blowing activities, as many complaints are initiated by competitors—not a proactive government agency. Conversely, the dependent variable in this study (total FTC, Department of Justice, and civil antitrust cases) is coded according to when the alleged activity took place. For example, in 1959 a complaint was issued against Dayton Rubber Company by the FTC. Dayton was charged with price discrimination and price fixing. After a lengthy investigation, in 1964 Dayton was ordered to

cease and desist on both counts. The company sought an appeal which culminated in a dismissal of the price discrimination charge but an affirmation of the FTC ruling regarding price fixing. The criminal activities in question *occurred* in 1958 (coded as such in my sample); a year passed before a complaint was issued (some scholars would code criminality as occurring at this time); and 6 years elapsed before the case was finally settled (others suggest that 1964 is the correct coding scheme). This study addresses *crime etiology*; thus, the effects of political administration in this analysis are interpreted as qualitatively distinct from Moe (1980) and Neuman's (1983) findings.

12. Government processing of cases, once initiated, is a complicated affair, as is the effect this decision-making apparatus has on future corporate criminality. Cases are developed by the Bureau of Competition. If a case is brought by some division and it is successful, the FTC and/or the Justice Department will be "on the back" of the violator to ensure compliance for the length of the order. Meanwhile, the rest of the bureau will be looking for other violators, often within the same industry or those companies within other markets, who follow similar practices. Factors which complicate this process include changes in personnel (if one individual leaves, cases often disappear) and administration turnover. Priorities and foci often change from one administration to another. An informant from the 1980 Reagan administration summed up the situation, "There's no such thing as antitrust in the Reagan Administration."

References

Asch, Peter, and Joseph J. Seneca. 1975. "Characteristics of Collusive Firms." *Journal of Industrial Economics* 23:223–47.

Bain, Joe S. 1951. "Relation of Profit Rate to Industry Concentration: American Manufacturing, 1936–1940." *Quarterly Journal of Economics* 65:293–324.

Barnett, Harold C. 1981. "Corporate Capitalism, Corporate Crime." *Crime and Delinquency* 27:4–23.

Burns, Arthur F., and Wesley C. Mitchell. 1946. *Measuring Business Cycles*. National Bureau of Economic Research.

Clark, Donald S. 1983. "Price Fixing without Collusion: An Antitrust Analysis of Facilitating Practices After Ethyl Corp." *Wisconsin Law Review* 4:887–952.

Clinard, Marshall B., and Peter Yeager. 1980. *Corporate Crime*. Free Press.

Clinard, M., P. C. Yeager, J. Brissette, D. Petrashek, and E. Harries. 1979. *Illegal Corporate Behavior*. Department of Justice.

Coleman, James W. 1985. *The Criminal Elite*. St. Martin's.

Conklin, John E. 1977. *Illegal But Not Criminal: Business Crime in America*. Prentice-Hall.

Denzin, Norman. 1977. "Notes on a Criminogenic Hypothesis: A Case Study of the American Liquor Industry." *American Sociological Review* 42:905–20.

Farberman, Harvey A. 1975. "A Criminogenic Market Structure: The Automobile Industry." *Social Science Quarterly* 16:438–57.

Federal Trade Commission (FTC). 1927–1981. *Case Decisions*. GPO.

Federal Trade Commission v. General Motors Corp. and A.C. Spark Plug. 1948. Federal Trade Commission Case Decisions (Docket #3886). GPO.

Federal Trade Commission v. Dayton Rubber Co. 1959. Federal Trade Commission Case Decisions (Docket #7604). GPO.

Finney, Henry C., and Henry R. Lesieur. 1982. "A Contingency Theory of Organizational Crime." Pp. 255–99 in *Research in the Sociology of Organizations*, edited by Samuel B. Bacharach. JAI Press.

Geis, Gilbert, and Robert Meier. 1977. *White Collar Crime: Offenses in Business, Politics, and the Professions*. Free Press.

Gordon, Robert Aaron. 1961. *Business Fluctuations*. 2d ed. Harper & Row.

Hay, George A., and Daniel Kelly. 1974. "An Empirical Survey of Price Fixing Conspiracies." *Journal of Law and Economics* 13:13–38.
Historical Statistics of the U.S. 1975. GPO.
Kmenta, Jan. 1971. *Elements of Econometrics*. Macmillan.
Kramer, Ronald C. 1982. "Corporate Crime: An Organizational Perspective." Pp. 79–94 in *White-Collar and Economic Crime*, edited by Peter Wickman and Timothy Dailey. Heath.
Lean, David F., Jonathan D. Ogru, and Robert P. Rogers. 1982. *Competition and Collusion in Electrical Equipment Markets: An Economic Assessment Bureau of the Economics Staff Report to the FTC.*
McGuire, Jean, and Thomas Schneeweis. 1982. "Management Change and Corporate Performance: A Market Evaluation." Unpublished manuscript, School of Management, University of Massachusetts, Amherst.
Moe, Terry M. 1980. "Regulatory Performance and Presidential Administration." Paper presented at the annual meeting of the American Political Science Association.
Moore, Geoffrey A. 1980. *Business Cycles, Inflation, and Forecasting*. Ballinger.
Neuman, W. Lawrence. 1983. "Determinants of Historical Variation in Antimonopoly Reform Activism: Changes in U.S. Federal Trade Commission Policy Activity, 1915–1970." Paper presented at the annual meeting of the American Sociological Association.
Ostrom, Charles. 1978. *Time Series Analysis: Regression Techniques*. Sage.
Porter, Michael E. 1980. *Competitive Strategy: Techniques for Analyzing Industries and Competitors.* Free Press.
Posner, Richard A. 1970. "A Statistical Study of Antitrust Enforcement." *Journal of Law and Economics* 13:365–419.
Shapiro, Susan. 1985. *Wayward Capitalists*. Yale University Press.
Sherman, Howard J. 1968. *Profits in the United States*. Cornell University Press.
Silk, Leonard. 1982. "Blame for Economic Trouble as Key Question in Elections." *New York Times* (October 29): A1, A24.
Simon, David R., and D. Stanley Eitzen. 1982. *Elite Deviance*. Allyn & Bacon.
Statistical Abstract of the U.S. 1975. 1977. 1982/3. GPO.
Staw, Barry N., and Eugene Szwajkowski. 1975. "The Scarcity-Munificence Component of Organizational Acts." *Administrative Science Quarterly* 20:345–54.
Strachan, James L., David B. Smith, and William Beedles. 1983. "The Price Reaction to (Alleged) Corporate Crime." *Financial Review:* 121–32.
Sultan, R. G. M. 1975. *Pricing in the Electrical Oligopoly*. Vols. 1, 2. Harvard University Press.
Sutherland, Edwin H. 1949. *White-Collar Crime*. Holt, Rinehart & Winston.
Trade Cases. 1927–81. Commerce Clearing House.
Vaughan, Diane. 1983. *Controlling Organizational Behavior*. University of Chicago Press.
Walton, Clarence C., and Frederick W. Cleveland, Jr. 1964. *Corporations on Trial: The Electric Cases*. Wadsworth.

Appendix A. CORPORATIONS AND INDUSTRIES INCLUDED IN THE SAMPLE

Companies*

Allied Corporation	Keystone
Amerada Hess	Lockheed
American Can	Lukens
American Cynamid	McDonnell Aircraft
American Motors	McDonnell-Douglas
Armstrong Rubber	National Can
Atlantic Richfield	National Steel
Bethlehem Steel	Ormand Industries
Boeing	Owens-Illinois
Celanese	Packard
Cessna Aircraft	Phillips Petroleum
Checker Motors	Rockwell International
Chrysler	Standard Oil (Calif.)
Colorado Fuel and Iron Steel	Standard Oil (Indiana)
Continental Can	Studebaker
Crown Central Petroleum	Studebaker-Packard
Crown Cork and Seal	Sun Oil
Dayco	Union Carbide
Douglas Aircraft	Uniroyal Inc
Dow Chemical	U.S. Hoffman Machinery
DuPont (E.I.) de Nemours	White Motor
Fairchild Industries	
Firestone Tire	Industries**
Ford Motor	
General Motors	Aircraft and Parts
General Tire and Rubber	Inorganic Chemicals
Goodrich (B.F.)	Petroleum Refining
Goodyear Tire	Metal Can Manufacturing
Hercules Inc	Motor Vehicles and Parts
Inland Steel	Steel
Interlake Inc	Tire and Inner Tube

*The selection of firms for this study is a complicated process. First, it is important to include firms that span the time framework selected (1927-81). This requirement alone eliminates a significant number of corporations. Second, in order to achieve and maintain continuity in data sources, corporations large enough to be listed on the New York and/or American Stock Exchanges were chosen as the sample universe. These firms are listed in two main sources: (1) Moodys Industrial Manual and (2) Standard and Poors. Moodys is used because it has a more legible format. Corporate data are also available from Standard and Poor's Compustat tape. This source includes a limited number of years (1961-81) and contains the same economic information as Moodys but is already in machine-readable form. Therefore, this data file was merged with one containing information gathered from Moodys.

**Each firm is classified according to its particular industrial product line. Firms were selected from 7 basic manufacturing industries that exhibited the greatest firm continuity across time. In certain product markets (e.g., aircraft, motor vehicle, tire and inner tube), only 7 corporations or less remain constant throughout the years. Therefore, all remain in the final sample. Industries with more than 7 firms had random numbers assigned each corporation. Seven were then selected for the final sample. If an industry has fewer than 7 continuous firms across the time frame, corporations that come closest to the entire span are included. Moreover, if a firm merged with another company during the years (e.g., McDonnell-Douglas), each firm is tracked separately until the merger and then followed as a single entity postmerger. Thus, the total number of firms in the final sample is 52.

Appendix B. A COMPARISON OF THE ALLEGED CIVIL, ADMINISTRATIVE, AND CRIMINAL ANTITRUST ACTIVITY AMONG THE MOST AND LEAST CRIMINAL COMPANIES WITHIN EACH PRODUCT MARKET, BY YEAR

Year	Aircraft Most	Aircraft Least	Inorganic Chemicals Most	Inorganic Chemicals Least	Metal Can Most	Metal Can Least	Motor Vehicle Most	Motor Vehicle Least	Steel Most	Steel Least	Tire and Tube Most	Tire and Tube Least	Petroleum Most	Petroleum Least	Total
1981															0
1980														1	5
1979	1						2						1		4
1978							1						1		10
1977							2								7
1976							2						1		10
1975							2								12
1974							6					1	1		18
1973	1		1			1	3		1		1		1		27
1972			2						1		1				21
1971			1				4								19
1970			2				2		1		1			2	32
1969	1						2								19
1968							1							3	14
1967							4						1		9
1966							1		1		1		1		20
1965															12
1964							1						1		3
1963			1												11
1962															4
1961							1								13
1960	1						3	1							14
1959			1								2				14
1958											1				17
1957							1				2				12
1956			1		2		4		1				1		21
1955			2				2		1				1		14
1954															7
1953															5
1952							1						1		5

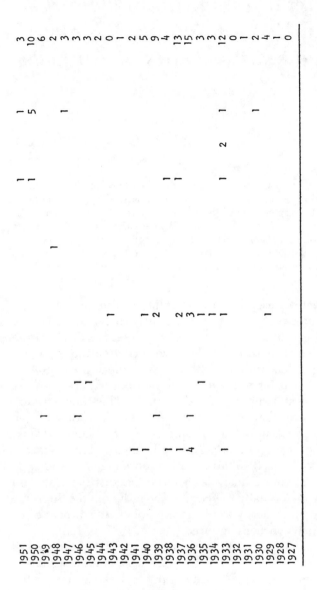

The Impact of the Supreme Court on Trends in Economic Policy Making in the United States Courts of Appeals

Donald R. Songer

University of South Carolina

Previous impact research has primarily investigated controversial civil liberties decisions. The present study examines the response of the United States Courts of Appeals to changes in the labor and antitrust policies announced by the Supreme Court between 1950 and 1977. Significant impact was discovered. In each policy area, the decisional trends of the courts of appeals underwent a significant change after each of two policy shifts on the Supreme Court. Changes in the decisional trends of the courts of appeal were in the predicted direction even after controls were introduced for judges' party and holdover effects.

In a recent assessment of research to date in judicial impact, Johnson and Canon (1984) suggest that too much attention has been given to following up a very few dramatic Supreme Court decisions. They argue that "in focusing on the extraordinary, we have forgotten the ordinary. We believe a complete understanding of the process in the implementation and impact of judicial policies must also include data about cases less heralded but nonetheless still important" (1984, p. ix). This concentration on the dramatic has meant that most empirical research dealt with the impact of a highly biased sample of Supreme Court policies: mainly controversial civil liberties decisions—especially those of the Warren Court (Baum, 1978). Wasby's (1970) admonition more than a decade ago that there was a need for more analysis of the impact of the Court on economic policy has gone virtually unheeded. Even though the Supreme Court devotes considerable energy to economic policy, the impact of its work in this field has been virtually ignored (Baum, 1977, p. 132).

A potential danger of such a limited research focus is that the overall impact of the Supreme Court may be seriously underestimated. Controversial policies may be precisely those in which the impact of the Supreme Court on lower courts is at its minimum (Baum, 1978, p. 210; Johnson and Canon, 1984, pp. 58-60). Shifting the focus of analysis to the Court's economic policy-making may contribute to a more balanced assessment of its overall impact on lower courts. While substantively important, the Court's economic decisions have rarely generated the

*The author wishes to express his appreciation for the Project '87 grant which partially funded the research reported in this paper.

degree of passion and controversy that have followed some of its decisions on race relations and criminal procedure. Consequently, their impact may be greater. For example, Wasby (1970, p. 103) suggests that "an area of law in which it is often speculated that considerable impact has occurred is antitrust, but much of what has been written is speculation; we are without studies to match the speculation."

The present study attempts to redress partially the balance in impact studies with an analysis of the impact of the Supreme Court on economic policy-making in the United States Courts of Appeals. The focus is on the labor and antitrust decisions of the courts of appeals from 1950 through 1977.

Much of the literature on the impact of the Supreme Court on lower courts has dealt with their compliance with specific decisions of the Supreme Court. Although such studies have illuminated some significant problems, a compliance focus inevitably misses much of the dynamics of the relationships between courts in our federal system. Lower courts may fail to support the basic policy of the Supreme Court without being overtly noncompliant with any specific decision (see Wasby, 1970, ch. 2 for a discussion of the problem). As Beatty (1972, p. 261) puts it, there are many ways for courts to "avoid, mitigate or nullify the ruling or advice of the Court" which stop short of overt defiance or noncompliance. Therefore, to gain a more complete understanding of the significance of the constitutional rules announced by the Supreme Court, a broader concept of impact needs to be used. A further problem with the use of a compliance model is that the focus on a few selected decisions is too narrow to gauge the impact of the Court on a given policy area. Canon (1973) maintains that the central significance of the Court for constitutional development is not the specific decisions it makes but the broad policies it fashions from a series of decisions. Baum (1977) expands on this idea to argue that much of an appellate court's policy leadership is exercised through the establishment of decisional trends that signal its inclination without creating a complete set of explicit rules of law. He suggests that there is a great need for research designed to measure the response of lower courts to these more general "decisional trends" of appellate courts in a wide variety of policy areas.

The analysis reported below examines the policy leadership exerted by the Supreme Court on the labor and antitrust decisional trends in the United States Courts of Appeals. It is generally believed that judicial decisions which lack clarity because of their complexity are less likely to have positive impact on the courts below (Johnson and Canon, 1984, p. 49). Since labor and antitrust policies are by nature complex (Johnson and Canon, 1984, p. 32), it might be speculated that the impact of the Supreme Court in these policy areas will be relatively modest. However, if the direction of Supreme Court policy is substantially altered through a series of decisions, the overall change in the decisional trends of the Court should be quite clear even if the details of some specific decisions remain somewhat ambiguous. Therefore, the capability of the Supreme Court to influence the decisional trends of lower courts should not be hampered by the complexity of its decisions. Since labor and antitrust decisions of the Supreme Court have not generally stimulated widespread intense controversy and since there are no other obvious environmental pressures on the lower courts to disregard Supreme Court policy leadership, it is expected that the Court will have a substantial impact on the labor and antitrust decisions of the courts of appeals. Specifically, it is hypothesized that after any statistically significant change in the percentage of liberal decisions announced by the Supreme Court in either of the policy areas under investigation, there will be a statistically significant change in the same direction in the percentage of liberal decisions announced by the United States Courts of Appeals.

DATA AND METHODS

The initial analysis of the impact of the Supreme Court was based on all of the labor and antitrust decisions of both the Supreme Court and the United States Courts of Appeals that were published with full opinions (including per curiam opinions) from 1950 through 1977.[1] The sample of antitrust decisions of the courts of appeals was extended backwards in time to 1947 after a preliminary examination suggested that there were too few cases in the earlier period studied to permit adequate analysis.[2] During this period there were a total of 160 such Supreme Court and 1153 appeals court decisions in the area of antitrust policy and 221 Supreme Court and 4454 appeals court labor decisions. Decisions were classified as liberal or conservative following the widely used definition of liberalism most fully described by Goldman (1966).

The first step in analysis was to compute the percentage of liberal decisions made by the Supreme Court in each calendar year for each

---

[1] Labor cases consisted of all cases which involved the resolution of a significant issue included in the "labor relations" topic of the West Key Number System, except those in which an individual as plaintiff raised an equal protection claim against a union or corporation. Suits between unions were also excluded. Most labor cases therefore involved disputes between a union and a company or between employees and their employer. Antitrust cases involved all civil suits in which the plaintiff alleged violation of an antitrust law (primarily the Sherman or Clayton Acts) or in which the defendant raised a counter claim based on the antitrust laws to resist a patent infringement or breach of contract claim. Included in both the labor and antitrust categories were appeals from federal regulatory agencies (e.g., the National Labor Relations Board) and the Federal district courts.

[2] A list of the citations of the cases used in analysis may be obtained from the author.

policy area (see appendix).[3] It was next necessary to determine precisely when and to what extent the decisional trends in Supreme Court labor and antitrust policy-making actually did change. An examination of the data suggests that there were two dramatic changes in the decisional trends of the Supreme Court in each policy area. In labor policy, the Supreme Court became significantly more liberal after 1958 and then took a decisive turn back to the right after 1969. Overall, the Supreme Court announced liberal decisions in 54.3% of its opinions in the period 1950-1958; 79.8% were liberal in 1959-1969, and 43.0% were liberal in 1970-77. A difference of proportions test (Z) demonstrates that both of these changes are statistically significant at the .001 level.

More traditional analyses also suggest that significant changes in Supreme Court policy occurred at approximately the same time. For example, Theodore J. St. Antoine states that the Warren Court's "main achievement in the labor field involved a simple but fundamental restructuring of intergovernmental relations. What the court did . . . was to nationalize the regulation of labor relations in industries affecting interstate commerce" (1968, p. 126). The first definitive statement of this new policy came in the 1959 case of San Diego Building Trades Council v. Garmon, 359 U.S. 236 (St. Antoine, 1968, p. 128; Shapiro, 1964, p. 85). The shift back to a more conservative interpretation of labor policy began in 1970 when the Burger Court announced its decision in Boys Markets Inc. v. Retail Clerk Local 770, 398 U.S. 235, the first of several decisions which expressly overruled two of the Warren Court's prounion decisions and undermined three others (St. Antoine, 1983, p. 166).

In antitrust policy the Supreme Court decisional trends became decidely more liberal after 1956 and then turned back in a conservative direction after 1973. During the 1950-1956 period, 40.6% of all Supreme Court decisions were liberal. The liberal proportion jumped to 79.5% for the 1957-1973 period and then fell back to 37.0% for the 1974-1977 period. Both changes in the proportion of liberal decisions are significant at the .001 level.

Traditional analyses also lead to the conclusion that the Warren and Burger Courts presided over significant shifts in Supreme Court antitrust policy. Kauper writes that "no one could quarrel with the simple assertion that the so-called 'Warren Court' has had a significant, if indeed not extraordinary, impact on the development of antitrust laws" (1968, p. 134). The first of the Warren Court's major antitrust decisions, which marked the first time that the Court has applied the Clayton Act to vertical mergers, occurred in 1957 in the case of United States v. DuPont, 353 U.S. 586 (Shapiro, 1964, pp. 276-77). The DuPont case was quickly followed

---

[3] Each decision of either the Supreme Court or the courts of appeals which affirmed in part and reversed in part the decision below was scored as half liberal and half conservative.

by a number of cases, such as the 1958 decision in Northern Pacific Ry. Co. v. United States, 356 U.S. 1, in which the Warren Court declared a wide variety of vertical restraints to be illegal and systematically began to resolve apparent conflicts between patent and antitrust laws in favor of the latter (Kauper, 1968, p. 136). The swing back to the right began with two key decisions in 1974. Markovits argues that the 1974 decision in United States v. Marine Bancorporation, 418 U.S. 602, was the first of several in which the Burger Court "indicated that the test of antitrust legality is the effect of the acts in question on competition rather than their impact on populist democracy or the independence and survival of small businessmen" (1983, p. 180). Also in 1974, the Burger Court announced its decision in United States v. General Dynamics Corporation, 415 U.S. 486, which was the key case on horizontal mergers which repudiated the "Warren Court's apparent conclusion that virtually all horizontal mergers are anticompetitive and hence unlawful" (Markovits, 1983, p. 186).

After determining that Supreme Court policy did, in fact, change significantly in each policy area, decisional trends on the courts of appeals were examined to determine whether they changed in the same direction in the period immediately following the change in Supreme Court policy. The basic unit of analysis was the percentage of liberal decisions announced by the courts of appeals in each policy area for each calendar year (a listing of the results by year is provided in the appendix). The periods used to analyze appeals court decisions are lagged one year to assure that appeals court judges had time to become familiar with changes in Supreme Court policy. The basic test of the hypothesis was to determine whether the proportion of liberal decisions on the courts of appeals changed to a statistically significant degree after the policy change on the Supreme Court. Since it is predicted that the decisional trends of the Supreme Court and the courts of appeals will change in the same direction, a one-tailed difference of proportions test is utilized.

FINDINGS AND DISCUSSIONS

The data in table 1 demonstrate that with a one-year time lag, the labor decisional trends on the courts of appeals followed the change in Supreme Court policy as predicted by the hypothesis. After the dramatic increase in Supreme Court liberalism, the percentage of liberal decisions in the courts of appeals increased by 9.1%, a difference that is significant at the .001 level. However, the response by the courts of appeals following the Supreme Court's return to a more conservative orientation is somewhat ambiguous. Although the courts of appeals also became more conservative, the magnitude of the change was much more modest, and the difference failed to reach the .05 level of significance.

TABLE 1

PROPORTION OF LIBERAL DECISIONS IN THE UNITED STATES COURTS OF APPEALS
DURING PERIODS OF CHANGING SUPREME COURT POLICY: LABOR CASES

PERIOD	% LIBERAL	(N)	Z	
1950-59	51.0%	(1113)	5.06	p<.001
1960-70	60.1	(2194)		
1971-77	58.1	(1147)	1.11	p=.1

The data in table 2 also support the hypothesis. Following the Warren Court's adoption of a decidedly more liberal antitrust policy, the output of the courts of appeals also became more liberal. The increase of 8.5% is significant at the .02 level. The response of the courts of appeals following the turn back to the right by the Supreme Court was also decisive. For the period 1974-1977, the proportion of liberal decisions rendered by the courts of appeals fell 8.6% from its previous level, a difference that is significant at the .02 level.

TABLE 2

PROPORTION OF LIBERAL DECISIONS IN THE UNITED STATES COURTS OF APPEALS
DURING PERIODS OF CHANGING SUPREME COURT POLICY: ANTITRUST CASES

PERIOD	% LIBERAL	(N)	Z	
1947-57	34.2%	(199)	2.18	p<.02
1958-74	42.7	(731)		
1975-77	34.1	(223)	2.26	p<.02

Although the findings are not without some ambiguity, they do provide considerable support for the hypothesis. Following each of the four changes in the decisional trends of the Supreme Court, the trends in the courts of appeals moved in the same direction. In three of the cases the differences were statistically significant and in the remaining case the differences were only moderately less than that required for statistical significance.

Although these changes in the decisional trends on the courts of appeals are consistent with the hypothesis of Supreme Court impact, alternative explanations are possible. It is well established that there are frequently partisan differences in the voting behavior of appeals court judges (Goldman, 1966, 1975), and in fact, party differences are evident in the data analyzed above. In labor cases, 57.0% of the votes cast by Democratic judges were liberal compared to 52.0% for Republican judges—a difference which is significant at the .001 level. In antitrust policy Democrats also cast liberal votes more frequently than their Republican counterparts: 42.7% compared to 38.5%. These differences are significant at the .01 level. The existence of such partisan differences raises the possibility that the changes in the decisional trends of the courts of appeals may be due to changes in the partisan composition of the lower courts rather than to any Supreme Court influence.

In order to assess this alternative explanation, the votes of individual judges are analyzed in each time period with a control for the party of the appointing president. The data are displayed in tables 3 and 4. The

TABLE 3

CHANGES OVER TIME IN THE PROPORTION OF LIBERAL VOTES CAST BY DEMOCRATIC AND REPUBLICAN JUDGES ON THE U.S. COURTS OF APPEALS: LABOR CASES

REPUBLICANS	PERIOD	% LIBERAL	(N)	Z	
	1950-59	46.4%	(1245)		
				4.82	p<.001
	1960-70	54.6	(2780)		
				1.69	p<.05
	1971-77	51.9	(1529)		
DEMOCRATS	PERIOD	% LIBERAL	(N)	Z	
	1950-59	52.0%	(1688)		
				4.87	p<.001
	1960-70	59.8	(2959)		
				1.41	p=.08
	1971-77	57.4	(1167)		

changes in the voting patterns of Republican judges are consistent with the hypothesis of Supreme Court impact. For both labor and antitrust policy, the proportion of liberal Republican votes increased to a statistically significant degree after the Warren Court policies became established and then decreased to a statistically significant extent after the policy changes adopted by the Burger Court. Democratic judges also followed the trends set by the Supreme Court in both labor and antitrust policy, and the magnitude of the changes was significant at the .01 level in three of the four cases. Although the proportion of the liberal votes cast by Democratic judges is higher than the corresponding figure for Republican judges in each of the three time periods for both policy areas, it is significant that the trends over time for both parties follow the direction of the changes enacted by the Supreme Court.

TABLE 4

CHANGES OVER TIME IN THE PROPORTION OF LIBERAL VOTES CAST BY
DEMOCRATIC AND REPUBLICAN JUDGES ON THE U.S. COURTS OF APPEALS:
ANTITRUST CASES

REPUBLICANS	PERIOD	% LIBERAL	(N)	Z	
	1947-57	30.1%	(186)		
				2.92	p<.01
	1958-74	41.5	(1023)		
				2.43	p<.01
	1975-77	34.2	(360)		
DEMOCRATS	PERIOD	% LIBERAL	(N)	Z	
	1947-57	37.5%	(371)		
				2.93	p<.01
	1958-74	46.3	(961)		
				2.77	p<.01
	1975-77	36.6	(262)		

This finding that the voting patterns in both parties followed Supreme Court trends strengthens the support for the proposition that the court has had a significant impact on the decisional trends of the courts of appeals and that the observed changes in the courts of appeals were not due to personnel turnover. However, the use of a party control is only a partial test of turnover effects. Since significant presidential appointment effects have been noted even within parties for federal judges (Carp and Rowland, 1983), the possibility remains that the observed changes were produced by the appointment of judges after the Supreme Court policy shift who were ideologically more in tune with the new policy than were previously appointed judges. Although no independent measure of judges' ideologies was available, this alternative was explored by comparing the voting tendencies of holdover judges before and after the changes in Supreme Court policy.[4] Such an analysis, however, supports the original hypothesis rather than the alternative explanation that new judges were responsible for changes in the decisional trends of the courts of appeals. In labor policy, the proportion of liberal votes cast by holdover judges increased from 49.6% prior to 1960 to 57.3% in the middle period and then decreased to 55.9% after 1970.[5] In antitrust policy, the proportion of liberal votes cast by holdover judges increased from 37.8% to 46.8%. The holdovers from the period 1958 to 1974 decreased their support for liberal outcomes from 43.9% to 35.2% after 1974.[6]

If the Supreme Court does have a significant effect on the decisions of appeals courts judges, then policy changes adopted by the Court should create new precedents which authoritatively settle some previously unsettled questions and/or which require that previously settled questions now be decided in a different manner. Songer (1982) has argued that a significant proportion of the cases decided by the courts of appeals should be classified as "consensual" cases because the precedents relevant to the decision are so clear and so generally perceived to be binding that all judges, regardless of their ideology, will feel constrained to decide them in the same way. His findings suggested that unanimous affirmances by the courts of appeals are almost always such consensual cases. But if Supreme Court policy change results in new, clear, binding precedents, the cases which would be consensual in one time period might not be consensual in the next period. Therefore, the decisional trends even among these "consensual" cases in the courts of appeals should follow changes in the decisional trends of the Supreme Court if the thesis of the present study is correct. To test this proposition, the decisional trends in the courts of appeals for unanimous affirmances of the district court or regulatory agency decision below were analyzed.

The results support the original hypothesis. For both labor and antitrust cases, the proportion of liberal decisions consistently moves in the

[4] A judge was classified as a "holdover" or a "new" judge on the basis of their appointing president rather than their individual date of appointment. Although such a convention, necessitated by the way in which the data were coded, may introduce some inaccuracies (e.g., for labor policy, those few Eisenhower judges appointed in 1960 were classified as holdovers), it does not seem likely that it would significantly affect the results. The only break point between time periods located in the middle of a presidential administration is the division of the first two periods for antitrust policy. Consequently a separate analysis was performed on all Eisenhower appointees, and none were classified as holdover judges. Eisenhower judges increased their proportion of liberal antitrust votes from 30.6% to 41.3% after 1957, a change significant at the .05 level.

[5] For the first change, the combined N=6601, Z=6.42, P<.001. The second change does not reach the .05 level of significance (Z=1.05).

[6] For the first change, the combined N=848, Z=2.73, P<.001. For the second change, the combined N=2571, Z=3.78, P<.001.

expected direction. For antitrust policy both changes are statistically significant, while for labor policy only the first change reaches at least the .05 level of significance.[7]

In summary, the analysis reported above suggests that the Supreme Court exercises considerable impact on the general trends in economic policy-making in the United States Courts of Appeals. Even when analysis was confined to judges of a single party, holdover judges, or consensual cases, the trends in the courts of appeals followed the changes in decisional trends of the Supreme Court. The findings reported above of shifts in the decisional trends of the courts of appeals following policy changes in the output of the Supreme Court do not provide definitive proof of causation. It remains possible, for example, that statutory changes or changes in Justice Department prosecution policy were responsible for the shifts on both courts. However, in the absence of any direct evidence to support these alternative explanations, they appear less plausible than the hypothesis of Supreme Court impact.

The major unexplained finding was the failure of the change in the labor decisions of the courts of appeals after 1970 to reach normal standards of statistical significance. The data displayed in table 3 suggest that this failure was due solely to the response of Democratic judges. Although their voting decisions moved in the expected direction, the magnitude of the change was quite modest. A tentative explanation of these results might be found in the suggestion of Carp and Rowland (1983) that the guidelines coming from the Burger Court were more ambiguous than those emanating from the Warren Court. Consequently, judges may have gained relatively more freedom to take their decision-making cues from personal and partisan values after 1970 rather than from guidelines set forth by the High Court.

---

[7] For antitrust policy, the proportion of liberal decisions increased from 22.3% (N=121) to 30.0% (N=417) in the middle period and then falls to 18.9%. For the first change, Z=1.67, P<.05. For the second change, Z=2.27, P<.02. For labor policy the proportion of liberal decisions for each period is 66.6% (N=598), 73.0% (N=1187), and 70.2% (N=662). For the first change, Z=2.78, P<.01. For the second change, Z=1.27, P=.10.

APPENDIX

PERCENTAGE OF LIBERAL DECISIONS IN THE SUPREME COURT AND THE
UNITED STATES COURTS OF APPEALS BY YEAR AND POLICY AREA

| | Labor Cases | | | | Antitrust Cases | | | |
| | Supreme Court | | Appeals Court | | Supreme Court | | Appeals Court | |
Year	% Liberal	N	% Liberal	N	% Liberal	N	% Liberal	N
1950	29%	7	33%	63	33%	6	36%	22
1951	16	3	40	85	33	6	33	9
1952	33	9	58	92	0	2	55	11
1953	67	12	52	150	16	6	31	18
1954	100	3	55	166	57	7	29	29
1955	50	5	57	122	100	3	37	19
1956	64	14	48	128	50	2	40	29
1957	62	13	47	94	80	5	32	25
1958	50	4	59	99	40	5	46	26
1959	67	9	48	121	83	6	39	32
1960	85	13	51	154	100	4	43	28
1961	83	3	56	150	50	4	35	24
1962	81	13	61	167	89	9	38	33
1963	67	9	60	249	57	7	43	35
1964	100	13	57	189	100	8	53	44
1965	64	11	58	160	60	5	43	38
1966	50	6	60	199	100	6	45	47
1967	100	8	63	326	100	10	51	40
1968	75	4	57	153	75	8	30	42
1969	100	5	63	216	89	9	44	40
1970	60	5	66	230	100	1	51	59
1971	42	7	56	250	70	5	42	53
1972	44	8	64	155	67	6	48	53
1973	60	5	59	143	71	7	43	62
1974	29	12	62	150	50	8	29	75
1975	50	7	57	149	20	5	30	85
1976	43	7			12	4		
1977	33	6			50	6		

REFERENCES

Beatty, Jerry K. 1972. State Court Evasion of United States Supreme Court Mandates During the Last Decade of the Warren Court. *Valparaiso Law Review*, 6:260-85.

Baum, Lawrence. 1977. Judicial Impact as a Form of Policy Implementation. In John A. Gardiner, ed., *Public Law and Public Policy*. New York: Praeger.

_____ . 1978. Lower Court Responses to Supreme Court Decisions—Reconsidering a Negative Picture. *The Justice System Journal*, 3:208-19.

_____ . 1980. Responses of Federal District Judges to Court of Appeals Policies: An Exploration. *Western Political Quarterly*, 33:217-24.

Canon, Bradley C. 1973. Reactions of State Supreme Courts to a U.S. Supreme Court Civil Liberties Decision. *Law and Society Review*, 8:109-34.

Carp, Robert A., and C. K. Rowland. 1983. *Policymaking and Politics in Federal District Courts.* Knoxville: University of Tennessee Press.

Goldman, Sheldon. 1966. Voting Behavior on the United States Courts of Appeals, 1961-1964. *American Political Science Review*, 60:370-85.

———. 1975. Voting Behavior on the United States Courts of Appeals Revisited. *American Political Science Review*, 69:491-506.

Johnson, Charles A., and Bradley C. Canon. 1984. *Judicial Policies: Implementation and Impact.* Washington, DC: Congressional Quarterly Press.

Kauper, Thomas E. 1968. The Warren Court and the Antitrust Laws: Of Economics, Populism, and Cynicism. In Richard H. Sayler, Barry B. Boyer, and Robert E. Gooding, Jr., *The Warren Court: A Critical Analysis.* New York: Chelsea House.

Markovits, R. S. 1983. The Burger Court, Antitrust, and Economic Analysis. In Vincent Blasi, *The Burger Court: The Counter Revolution That Wasn't.* New Haven: Yale University Press.

St. Antoine, Theodore J. 1968. Judicial Valour and the Warren Court's Labor Decisions. In *The Warren Court: A Critical Analysis. See* Kauper, 1968.

———. 1983. Individual Rights in the Workplace: The Burger Court and Labor Law. In *The Burger Court. See* Markovits, 1983.

Shapiro, Martin. 1964. *Law and Politics in the Supreme Court.* Glencoe, IL: Free Press.

Songer, Donald R. 1982. Consensual and Nonconsensual Decisions in Unanimous Opinions of the United States Courts of Appeals. *American Journal of Political Science*, 26:225-39.

Wasby, Stephen L. 1970. *The Impact of the United States Supreme Court: Some Perspectives.* Homewood, IL: Dorsey.

VIRGINIA LAW REVIEW

VOLUME 44	MAY 1958	No. 4

ECONOMIC CHANGE AND THE SHERMAN ACT: SOME REFLECTIONS ON "WORKABLE COMPETITION"

GEORGE W. STOCKING[*]

IN *Appalachian Coals, Inc.,*[1] Chief Justice Hughes characterized the Sherman Act as a "charter of freedom" with "a generality and adaptability comparable to that found to be desirable in constitutional provisions."[2] In making this pronouncement the Chief Justice was laying the basis for a decision more consistent with the temper of the times than with legal precedent. The Great Depression had laid low the national economy. Millions were unemployed, national income had shrunk, corporate profits had disappeared, labor unions had disintegrated, farmers were losing their farms, business firms faced bankruptcy, competition had become cutthroat, confidence in private enterprise had waned, fear and even hunger stalked the land. Businessmen, labor leaders, and politicians were insisting that competition must give way to cooperation if a business system was to be salvaged. A sick economy had aggravated the sickness of an industry. The Supreme Court in 1933 found Appalachian Coals, Inc. to be a cooperative sales agency designed to "foster fair competitive opportunities" and "thus to aid in relieving a depressed industry and in reviving commerce by placing competition upon a sounder basis."[3]

Seven years later, with the unlamented National Recovery Administration a matter of history, with New Dealers and the public losing

---

* Professor of Economics and Director of Institute of Research in the Social Sciences, Vanderbilt University. B.A., 1918, University of Texas; M.A., 1921, Ph.D., 1925, Columbia University. The writer wishes to express his appreciation for the assistance in this article of Elizabeth R. Post, LL.B., 1948, Yale University, and member of the Tennessee Bar.

1. Appalachian Coals, Inc. v. United States, 288 U.S. 344 (1933).
2. *Id.* at 359-60.
3. *Id.* at 374.

confidence in "industrial self-government," with politicians and students of industrial structure disturbed by "the concentration of economic power," the Court condemned as unlawful a cooperative gasoline-buying program by the leading oil companies designed to raise and stabilize gasoline prices by insuring an orderly marketing of "distress" gasoline[4]—an experiment that had won the unofficial blessing of NRA administrators at the time it was inaugurated. While any competent law student might differentiate these two cases on the basis of their facts, the opinions reflect less the logic of the law than the temper of the times.

Judges, like other people, cannot dissociate themselves from the institutional matrix in which they have their being. This sociological principle is illustrated by a line of decisions handed down by the Supreme Court during the next decade. The climate of public opinion in which these decisions were formulated had its origin during the post-NRA and early World War II years. It was characterized by an increasing fear of industrial concentration. Berle and Means in 1932 had dramatized the extent of and trends toward industrial concentration in this country in their provocative and discerning analysis of *The Modern Corporation and Private Property*. They found that the 200 largest nonfinancial corporations, representing less than one-tenth of 1 per cent of all nonfinancial corporations, controlled approximately 50 per cent of all corporate wealth in the United States, 38 per cent of all business wealth, and 22 per cent of all national wealth.[5] They found that in the period studied the percentage of corporate wealth owned by the 200 largest corporations had increased significantly, and they estimated that by 1950, at the 1909-29 rate of increase, the 200 largest corporations would own more than 70 per cent of all corporate wealth; at the more rapid rate of increase of the six years ending in 1929, the 200 largest corporations would own 85 per cent of all corporate assets by 1950.[6]

The New Deal, which initially made economic planning a governmental responsibility, had at the same time nourished suspicion if not hostility toward big business. The New Deal's failure through political management to solve the problems of unemployment and to raise national income to economical levels ultimately raised doubts among its leaders about the adequacy of centralized controls to make an economic

---

4. United States v. Socony-Vacuum Oil Co., 310 U.S. 150 (1940).
5. BERLE AND MEANS, THE MODERN CORPORATION AND PRIVATE PROPERTY 32 (1932).
6. *Id.* at 40.

system work. President Roosevelt, in campaigning for re-election in 1936, had noted the improved economic outlook by boasting, "We planned it that way." Only two years later, after the economic setback of 1937-1938, in recommending to Congress the authorization of the Temporary National Economic Committee, Roosevelt expressed his skepticism of centralized control of industry in these words:

> Private enterprise is ceasing to be free enterprise and is becoming a cluster of private collectivisms;
> . . . .
> No one suggests that we return to the hand loom or hand forge. . . . But modern efficient mass production is not furthered by a central control which destroys competition between industrial plants each capable of efficient mass production while operating as separate units.
> . . . .
> The power of a few to manage the economic life of the Nation must be diffused among the many or be transferred to the public and its democratically responsible government.[7]

But to the President governmental control was not an attractive alternative. About it he said:

> Those people, in and out of the halls of government, who encourage the growing restriction of competition either by active efforts or by passive resistance to sincere attempts to change the trend, are shouldering a terrific responsibility. Consciously or unconsciously they are . . . either working for control of the Government itself by business and finance or . . . a growing concentration of public power in the Government. . . .[8]

As a first step in coping with what he regarded as a dangerous concentration of economic power, the President proposed to establish a temporary national economic committee to investigate its extent and causes and to propose remedies. The TNEC, whose investigations extended over a three-year period, reflected not merely Presidential but a national concern about the decline of competition. Congress appropriated $1,070,000 for its activities and voted larger appropriations for the Antitrust Division of the Department of Justice. Under Thur-

---

7. *Message from the President of the United States*, S. Doc. No. 173, 75th Cong., 3d Sess. 3, 6 (1938).
   8. *Id.* at 6.

man Arnold's leadership the division undertook its most aggressive campaign against conspiracies, combinations in restraint of trade, and unlawful monopolies.

Oligopoly in Theory and in Antitrust

Meanwhile economic theory had laid a logical basis for political concern about the concentration of economic power. According to the teachings of neoclassical theory a competitive industrial structure insures an economical allocation of resources and a distribution of income in accordance with the principle of marginal productivity. The forces of a free market—Adam Smith's "invisible hand"—economists had said would harness the selfish interests of businessmen and so guide them as to promote the public welfare. But the theory of monopolistic or imperfect competition as presented in this country by Edward Chamberlin[9] and in England by Joan Robinson[10] in the early 1930's challenged the adequacy of market forces to protect the public welfare in industries where sellers are few and products standardized. Chamberlin in his discussion of oligopolistic pricing concluded on a basis of his rigid assumptions that if informed and rational oligopolists take account of the indirect as well as the direct consequences of their decisions, they will without conspiring behave like monopolists.[11] Other things equal, in oligopolistic markets consumers will pay more and get less than under competition. This disquieting conclusion and the doctrine that supported it quickly got into the textbooks and eventually had an impact on the law.

The leading cases that reflect the widespread fear of industrial concentration and monopoly during this era are *United States v. Aluminum Company of America*[12] and *American Tobacco Company v. United States*.[13] Judge Learned Hand, in deciding that Alcoa possessed an

---

9. The Theory of Monopolistic Competition (1933).

10. The Economics of Imperfect Competition (1933).

11. Chamberlin in recent years has protested against the identification of oligopoly theory with "the" monopoly solution, saying this is only one among other possible solutions and that the theory "yields no certain conclusion as to what will happen, given the bare minimum of information that the number of sellers is small." *Une Formulation Nouvelle de la Théorie de la Concurrence Monopolistique*, in Economie Appliquée, Archives de L'Institut de Science Economique Appliquée, V. (1952), 192, quoted in Arant, *Competition of the Few Among the Many*, 70 Q.J. Econ. 327, 343 (1956).

12. 148 F.2d 416 (2d Cir. 1945), *new petitions considered*, 91 F. Supp. 333 (S.D.N.Y. 1950).

13. 328 U.S. 781 (1946).

unlawful monopoly, rejected the defenses which more recent decisions have found alluring. He was unimpressed by the fact that substitutes might serve as a check on Alcoa's power to exploit the market. "There are indeed limits to [a monopolist's] power; substitutes are available for almost all commodities, and to raise the price enough is to evoke them." [14] He found unconvincing the argument that imports, actual and potential, insured adequate consumer protection.

> It is entirely consistent with the evidence that it was the threat of greater foreign imports which kept "Alcoa's" prices where they were, and prevented it from exploiting its advantage as sole domestic producer; indeed, it is hard to resist the conclusion that potential imports did put a "ceiling" upon those prices. Nevertheless, within the limits afforded by the tariff and the cost of transportation, "Alcoa" was free to raise its prices as it chose, since it was free from domestic competition, save as it drew other metals into the market as substitutes.[15]

Judge Hand rejected good performance as a justification for monopoly under the Sherman Act. As he put it, "it is no excuse for 'monopolizing' a market that the monopoly has not been used to extract from the consumer more than a 'fair' profit." [16] He rejected the doctrine of specific intent as essential to a finding of monopoly. Monoplists ordinarily are not sleepwalkers; they know where they are going. Unless they have monopoly thrust upon them, they have monopolized within the meaning of section 2 of the Sherman Act. Judge Hand brought section 2 of the act into harmony with section 1 by recognizing that "the vice of restrictive contracts and of monopoly is really one, it is the denial to commerce of the supposed protection of competition";[17] and he promulgated the doctrine that it was the existence of monopoly, when achieved by deliberate business policies, not the abuse of monopoly, that the law forbade. Rejecting the rule of reason of the 1911 *Standard Oil* and *American Tobacco* cases,[18] he declared that Congress "did not condone 'good trusts' and condemn 'bad' ones; it forbad all." [19]

The *Aluminum* decision was a vigorous affirmation of the public's

---

14. United States v. Aluminum Co., 148 F.2d 416, 425-26 (2d Cir. 1945).

15. *Id.* at 426.

16. *Id.* at 427.

17. *Id.* at 428.

18. Standard Oil Co. v. United States, 221 U.S. 1 (1911); United States v. American Tobacco Co., 221 U.S. 106 (1911).

19. United States v. Aluminum Co., 148 F.2d 416, 427 (2d Cir. 1945).

distrust of the concentration of economic power as such; but it was the second *American Tobacco* decision that in addition to reflecting community hostility toward industrial concentration seemed to bring the law on monopoly into harmony with the Chamberlinian doctrine of oligopolistic pricing. A federal jury had convicted the "Big Three" cigarette makers—the American Tobacco Company, Liggett & Myers Tobacco Company, and R. J. Reynolds Tobacco Company—of having violated sections 1 and 2 of the Sherman Act. The issue on appeal to the Supreme Court was the meaning of "monopolize" as used in section 2 of the Act. In reviewing the evidence the Court was impressed by the combined size of the defendants. Together they had continuously accounted for more than 68 per cent and usually for more than 75 per cent of the national production of cigarettes. In the production of burley blend cigarettes their dominance was even more marked. Clearly the defendants had earned "the title of the 'Big Three.' . . . the smallest of them at all times showed over twice the production of the largest outsider. . . . [C]omparative size on this great scale inevitably increased the power of these three to dominate all phases of their industry." [20] Quoting *United States v. Swift & Company* the Court said, " 'Size carries with it an opportunity for abuse that is not to be ignored when the opportunity is proved to have been utilized in the past.' " [21]

Nor was the size of the Big Three reflected solely in production figures. Their combined net worth had risen from $277,000,000 in 1912 to over $551,000,000 in 1939. In each of the years 1937, 1938, and 1939 American, Liggett & Myers, and Reynolds had together spent over $40,000,000 for advertising. Tremendous expenditures for advertising and the large sums required for inventories and federal taxes tended to prevent the rise of potential competition. The power of the Big Three was reflected in buying tobacco as well as in selling cigarettes. Together they bought from 50 to 80 per cent of the domestic flue-cured tobacco, and in the burley belt of Kentucky and Tennessee their percentage of total purchases was even larger. The record produced no evidence of a written agreement among the defendants, but it indicated that in both buying tobacco and selling cigarettes they followed a common course of action. They all paid the same price for their preferred tobacco grades, and each adjusted its cigarette prices to that of the price leader's price. When, after having raised cigarette

---

20. American Tobacco Co. v. United States, 328 U.S. 781, 796 (1946). Statements of fact about the tobacco companies are taken from the opinion.

21. 286 U.S. 106, 116 (1932), quoted *ibid*.

prices while the prices of raw tobacco were steadily declining, they lost ground to the so-called economy brand cigarettes, they began a tobacco-buying program that forced up the price of cheaper tobacco used in economy brands, and they cut the price of their own standard brand cigarettes. The Supreme Court concluded that the Big Three had both the power to exclude competitors and the power to control prices, and it confirmed the jury's finding of a criminal conspiracy to monopolize the sale of cigarettes.

Because the Court recognized a common course of action as sufficient evidence of conspiracy, some discriminating students of the law concluded that the Court had brought the law on monopoly into harmony with the theory of oligopolistic pricing. On the significance of the *Tobacco* decision Eugene V. Rostow, a distinguished professor of law, trained also in economics, concluded:

> When three companies produce so large a percentage of market supply, that fact alone is almost sufficient evidence that the statute is violated. Ruthless and predatory behavior need not be shown. The actual elimination of small competitors is unnecessary. . . . Parallel action, price leadership, a reliance on advertising rather than price competition as a means of inducing changes in each seller's share of the market, and, above all, size—the market advantage of a small number of large sellers or buyers—these are now key points to be proved in a case of monopoly, or of combination in restraint of trade. . . . Painstaking search for scraps of evidence with a conspiratorial atmosphere are [*sic*] no longer necessary. . . .[D]ecisive elements are the power to assert a degree of control over price and output *in the market as a whole*. . . .[22]

An equally discerning economist, William H. Nicholls, saw the *Tobacco* decision as

> a legal milestone in the social control of oligopoly. By permitting the inference of illegal conspiracy from detailed similarity of behavior and by shifting attention from the abuse of power to its mere existence (as indicated by degree of market control), the courts have at last brought oligopolistic industries within reach of successful prosecution under the antitrust laws.[23]

---

22. Rostow, *The New Sherman Act: A Positive Instrument of Progress*, 14 U. Chi. L. Rev. 567, 585 (1947). (Emphasis added.)
23. Nicholls, *The Tobacco Case of 1946*, 39 Am. Econ. Rev. 284, 296 (1949).

The Federal Trade Commission and Oligopoly

While judges and economists, both influenced by and influencing the temper of the times, were thus beginning to conceive the monopoly problem in similar terms, administrators, too, reflected the prevailing skepticism about the compatibility of a market of few sellers with effective competition. During the late 1930's and early 1940's the Federal Trade Commission inaugurated a number of proceedings against associated activities by trade rivals designed to lessen the severity of competition among themselves.[24] Frequently the evidence of conspiracy was circumstantial. Business rivals followed common patterns of behavior without written agreements to do so and sometimes without a well-defined mechanism for insuring that they would. A common experience with the untoward consequences of price cutting where sellers were few contributed to behavior patterns calculated to insure identical pricing at stabilized levels. The Federal Trade Commission sought to ban such vaguely defined collective action among trade rivals, which it regarded as not consistent with effective competition, by broad and similarly vaguely defined orders.

In 1941 the Commission found that the market analysis and business counselling program of the Salt Producers Association not only had a dangerous tendency to hinder competition but had prevented effective competition in selling salt.[25] It accordingly ordered association members to cease and desist from "entering into, continuing, or carrying out, or directing, instigating, or cooperating in, any *common course of action*, mutual agreement, combination, or conspiracy, to fix or maintain the prices of salt" or regulate its production.[26] On appeal by respondents and objection to the Commission's banning a "common course of action" by the salt producers, the appellate court modified the Commission's order to prohibit "any *planned* common course of action" by the de-

---

24. Crown Mfrs. Ass'n, 45 F.T.C. 89 (1948), *aff'd*, 176 F.2d 974 (4th Cir. 1949); Rigid Steel Conduit Ass'n, 38 F.T.C. 534 (1944), *aff'd sub nom.* Triangle Conduit & Cable Co. v. FTC, 168 F.2d 175 (7th Cir. 1948), *aff'd per curiam sub nom.* Clayton Mark & Co. v. FTC, 336 U.S. 956 (1949); National Crepe Paper Ass'n, 38 F.T.C. 282 (1944), *aff'd sub nom.* Ft. Howard Paper Co. v. FTC, 156 F.2d 899 (7th Cir. 1946); Milk and Ice Cream Can Institute, 37 F.T.C. 419 (1943), *aff'd*, 152 F.2d 478 (7th Cir. 1946); Cement Institute, 37 F.T.C. 87 (1943), *order set aside*, 157 F.2d 533 (7th Cir. 1946), *rev'd*, 333 U.S. 683 (1948); United States Maltsters Ass'n, 35 F.T.C. 797 (1942), *modified*, 37 F.T.C. 342 (1943), *aff'd*, 152 F.2d 161 (7th Cir. 1945); Salt Producers Ass'n, 34 F.T.C. 38 (1941), *modified and aff'd*, 134 F.2d 354 (7th Cir. 1943).

25. Salt Producers Ass'n, 34 F.T.C. 38 (1941), *modified and aff'd*, 134 F.2d 354 (7th Cir. 1943).

26. *Id*. at 55. (Emphasis added.)

fendants with respect to the matters specified in the Commission's orders.[27] Similarly in the *Cement Institute* case[28] the Commission ordered the respondents to refrain from any "planned common course of action" to sell cement according to the multiple basing point delivered-price system or to follow the practices with which the industry had implemented it. In the *Rigid Steel Conduit* case[29] the Commission developed further its doctrine of implied conspiracy or conscious parallelism of action. It charged that the makers of rigid steel conduit had conspired to use the basing point system, that each respondent had used it knowing that his rivals did so, and that such practices "have a dangerous tendency to, and have actually, hindered . . . and prevented competition in price in the sale of 'conduit.'"[30] The Commission not only ordered the respondents to quit conspiring or following a "planned common course of action," but ordered each respondent individually to quit quoting or selling rigid steel conduit at prices calculated on a basing point system "for the purpose or with the effect of systematically matching delivered-price quotations. . . ."[31]

The Federal Trade Commission, whether deliberately or not, was thus bringing its findings and orders into closer accord with the theory of oligopolistic pricing. It aimed at banning monopolistic behavior that apparently resulted from sellers' recognition of their mutual inter-dependence in markets where they were few in number.

Although these decisions brought legal doctrine somewhat closer to contemporary economic logic, they did not solve the basic problem with which the judges and administrators were concerned: how to make competition effective in markets of few sellers. The decisions banned the monopolistic practices but left unmodified the structure of industry which may have shaped practices. If the pricing practices of American Tobacco, Reynolds, and Liggett & Myers were consistent with independent nonconspiratorial decision-making in a market domi-nated by three companies; if a price cut by one necessarily engendered a price cut by all without any significant redistribution of or increase in the sale of cigarettes; if the business interests of each were served by following a price increase inaugurated by any one—price leadership

---

27. Salt Producers Ass'n v. FTC, 134 F.2d 354, 357 (7th Cir. 1943). (Emphasis added.)

28. Cement Institute, 37 F.T.C. 87, 260 (1943), *aff'd*, 333 U.S. 683 (1948).

29. Rigid Steel Conduit Ass'n, 38 F.T.C. 534 (1944), *aff'd sub nom.* Triangle Conduit & Cable Co. v. FTC, 168 F.2d 175 (7th Cir. 1948), *aff'd per curiam sub nom.* Clayton Mark & Co. v. FTC, 336 U.S. 956 (1949).

30. 38 F.T.C. at 550.

31. *Id.* at 595.

was almost an inevitable business practice, and the finding of criminal conspiracy followed by nominal fines was mild punishment, not a basic remedy. Moreover, it left the executives of the several tobacco companies puzzled and disturbed—puzzled because they did not know just how to protect their separate business interests without following common pricing policies, disturbed by a realization that if they did so they would again run afoul of the law.[32] Conspiracy, they feared, was being identified with sound business practice. Nor was uneasiness confined to tobacco executives. When the Supreme Court sustained the Federal Trade Commission's finding that basing point pricing as practiced in the cement industry was unlawful, the chairman of the board of directors of the United States Steel Corporation announced that businessmen must educate the Court or persuade Congress to change the law.[33]

The Concept of Workable Competition

Meanwhile the economists had become concerned about the political implications of the Chamberlinian logic. If, as Arthur R. Burns[34] and other economists contended, it was the businessman's search for the economies of mass production that had shaped the structure of the contemporary economy, a rigorous enforcement of the antitrust statutes designed to insure competitive pricing could be had only at the expense of industrial efficiency. Burns believed this, but he did not believe that the nation could rely on oligopolistic markets to insure an economical allocation of resources and an equitable distribution of income; and he proposed a system of governmental controls so comprehensive that one of his critics characterized his book as "planning for totalitarian monopoly."[35] Socialists saw in industrial concentration an inevitable

---

32. Counsel for Liggett & Myers expressed the dilemma the "Big Three" faced: "[P]resumably, the appellants were convicted of agreement, not of the particular operations alleged to constitute agreement. Yet, on the Government's theory, continuation by more than one of the appellants of the operations alleged is evidence of a further Sherman Act agreement. . . . If this is so, how is Liggett & Myers to carry on? . . . Is everything that appellants do illegal, or evidence of illegality, if done by more than one of them?" Brief for Liggett & Myers, p. 27, American Tobacco Co. v. United States, 328 U.S. 781 (1946).

33. Irving S. Olds anticipated success in trying to educate the justices or to revise the statute. "I can't believe," he said, "that the country is going to let industry be disrupted by a theory that was developed many years ago by a Princeton professor." New York Journal of Commerce, April 28, 1948, p. 1. The reference is to the late Professor Frank A. Fetter.

34. The Decline of Competition cc. 11-12 (1936).

35. Fetter, *Planning for Totalitarian Monopoly*, 45 J. Pol. Econ. 95 (1937).

trend that would eventually necessitate a choice between private monopoly and the nationalization of industry.

This institutional drift was the occasion for, if not the cause of, a re-examination of the Chamberlinian logic and the implications of industrial structure to public policy. John M. Clark, a pioneer in the new thinking, in 1939 read his now famous paper on the concept of workable competition before the American Economic Association.[36] Clark, like Chamberlin, recognized that pure or perfect competition was an abstraction, a theoretical ideal realized in few if any markets. The actual markets of contemporary industry were compounded of elements of competition and monopoly, only some of which were controllable. To rid a market of some oligopolistic elements without ridding it of all might do more harm than good; and since all were not subject to control, controllable factors if left alone might exert a constructive influence. Clark conceived workable competition to be the best attainable functioning of markets under existing institutional arrangements, and he thought that it was good enough. Substitutes and potential competition, he argued, tended to insure consumers adequate protection from oligopolistic exploitation; rivalry among firms producing differentiated products might insure them a variety of alternatives at reasonable prices.

Clark's ideas on the significance of industrial structure to economic behavior were projected in a fertile economic and social environment, and his concept of workable competition has proved quite as revolutionary to economic thinking and economic policy as Chamberlin's earlier work. The environment that has nourished Clark's ideas is the environment with which all students of contemporary affairs are familiar. World War II inaugurated a prolonged period of deficit financing. The war was a total war, demanding the utmost endeavor of all nationals, civilian and combatant alike. It put a part-time American industry on an overtime basis. It eliminated unemployment. It raised price levels and the national income. By converting a buyers' into a sellers' market it made goods easy to sell and hard to get. It brought a business boom only temporarily interrupted by the cessation of hostilities. The postwar period found a pent-up demand for goods previously in shortage and an accumulated purchasing power with which to buy them. The cold war sustained a prosperity en-

---

36. *Toward a Concept of Workable Competition*, 30 Am. Econ. Rev. 241 (1940), reprinted in American Economic Ass'n, Readings in the Social Control of Industry 452 (1942).

gendered by the hot one. It brought a prolonged expansion in gross national product and national income. It brought a level of employment earlier conceived as an admirable but remote ideal. It brought a stock market rise, lacking perhaps in the dramatic qualities of the 1928-1929 boom but equally persistent in its upward pressure on the prices of stocks of America's leading corporations. It revived the confidence of businessmen in a private enterprise economy and brought a tremendous expansion in industrial facilities financed in large part out of current earnings. It developed an entrepreneurial interest in industrial research hitherto lacking. In short, it brought to this country a level of material welfare and abundance that excited the admiration and envy of the rest of the world. And the business executives were not slow to claim credit for it. Through a spate of institutional advertising they identified corporate welfare with national welfare, economic prosperity with business efficiency, competition with private enterprise. The American economic system worked; competition must therefore have been workable.

Small wonder that businessmen, economists, administrators, and the courts have accepted the logic of the concept of workable competition with its reassuring political and economic implications, while rejecting the Chamberlinian logic at once pessimistic and disturbing. Economists, administrators, and judges are alike in their desire to make peace with their environment. Thus the concept of workable competition is on its way to becoming a standard in antitrust proceedings.

As the concept has gained general acceptance it has undergone clarification and modification. Although economists might differ in their judgments as to the workability of any particular industrial arrangement, they are pretty well agreed on what to look for in reaching a judgment. While differing in the weight they would attach to the several criteria, they would look to an industry's structure, the conduct of the firms that comprise it, and to its performance. By structure is meant the way in which the industry is made up. Relevant questions are: How many sellers comprise it? What is their relative size? Is entry easy or difficult? Determining the boundary of an industry or the relevant market for its products is not easy because rivalry of substitutes may be so vigorous as to justify their inclusion in it. But having defined the boundaries of an industry, economists are pretty well agreed that the number of firms comprising it and their relative size may influence the effectiveness of competition. Where firms are few, in continuing close contact, and operating under similar conditions, other things equal, they may—in accordance with Chamberlinian doctrine—tend to behave like monopolists even without overtly conspiring to do so. The greater the number of firms, other things equal, the greater the likelihood of their behaving like competitors.

Conduct describes the practices and strategies which firms resort to in their dealings with each other and with the market. Trade association activities designed to lessen the severity of competition, price leadership, and basing point pricing are illustrations of the sort of practices that may reflect an absence of effective competition. Do the firms possess market advantages gained through patents or otherwise which they try to protect? Does their conduct reflect the uninhibited forces of a free market or associated activities designed to control market forces? These are relevant questions in determining the significance of conduct to the competitive workability of any industrial pattern.

By performance is meant the manner in which an industry fulfills the functions which a market economy imposes on it. Relevant questions include: What is the course of prices? of profits? of cost-price relationships? of expenditures on advertising? of technological innovation? In general, does the industry reflect the dynamic forces of competitive rivalry or the dead hand of monopoly?

Before economists had precisely defined the concept, some saw in workable competition an appropriate standard by which to judge the legality of alleged antitrust violations. Clark cautiously concluded his initial essay with the hope "that [the] government need not assume the burden of doing something about every departure from the model of perfect competition." [37] Later he urged that "where impairment of competition is an issue, there should be a showing of how competition is impaired, by comparison with an identifiable concept of what would constitute unimpaired competition in an industry having the unavoidable physical and economic characteristics of the one whose practices are being adjudicated." [38] At an earlier date Mason[39] had indicated the usefulness of performance in drawing the line between socially acceptable and unacceptable departures from perfect competition. Markham[40] later defined workable competition in terms of alternatives. According to Markham, when account is taken of its structure and the

---

37. *Id.* at 256, READINGS 475.

38. Clark, *The Orientation of Antitrust Policy*, 40 AM. ECON. REV. 93, 98 (1950).

39. *Monopoly in Law and Economics*, 47 YALE L.J. 34 (1937).

40. *An Alternative Approach to the Concept of Workable Competition*, 40 AM. ECON. REV. 349 (1950).

forces that shaped it, an industry is workably competitive if no change "can be effected through public policy measures that would result in greater social gains than social losses." [41] Griffin,[42] more than any other economist, has emphasized performance as a test of workable competition, and in applying the test he would take account of political as well as economic benefits.

The Lawyers and Workable Competition

Although economists have developed a logic that some think may be of use in antitrust proceedings, it is the lawyers who have been the most unrestrained in urging that the concept of workable competition be utilized as a practical standard in the adjudication of antitrust cases. The most articulate and vigorous of these are S. Chesterfield Oppenheim and Blackwell Smith. Blackwell Smith in an article on *Effective Competition: Hypothesis for Modernizing the Antitrust Laws*,[43] published in 1951, proposed twelve criteria[44] for determining good industrial performance, all of them somewhat vague and difficult to apply. He advocated their application under a rule of reason in determining the legality of alleged violations of the antitrust statutes. The Business Advisory Committee of the Department of Commerce, accepting Smith's ideas virtually unchanged, in 1952 recommended drastic modifications in administrative standards and procedures under the antitrust statutes.[45] The recommended changes were designed to adjust the law to industrial structure and business practice rather than to make in-

---

41. *Id.* at 361.

42. An Economic Approach to Antitrust Problems, American Enterprise Association, xiii (1951); *Needed: A Realistic Antitrust Policy*, Harv. Bus. Rev., Nov.-Dec. 1956, p. 76.

43. 26 N.Y.U.L. Rev. 405.

44. *"Procedure Under the Rule of Reason.* In determining whether any commercial practices or courses of conduct promote Effective Competition or are unreasonably injurious thereto, all relevant circumstances shall be considered, including such actual or probable results of the conduct, under like circumstances in the market, as the increase or decrease of: (1) Alternatives available to customers or sellers; (2) Volume of production or services; (3) Quality of the services or goods; (4) Number of people benefited; (5) Incentives to entrepreneurs; (6) Efficiency and economy in manufacturing or distribution; (7) The welfare of employees; (8) The tendency to progress in technical development; (9) Prices to customers; (10) Conditions favorable to the public interest in defending the country from aggression; (11) The tendency to conserve the country's natural resources; (12) Benefits to the public interest assuming the relief requested by the government in the proceedings." *Id.* at 441.

45. U.S. Dep't of Commerce, Effective Competition: A Report to the Secretary of Commerce by His Business Advisory Council (1952).

dustrial structure and business practice conform to the law. The council identified the performance of the national economy with the performance of big firms and lamented a tendency to confuse bigness with monopoly. To temper the administration of the antitrust laws, the council recommended the creation of a review board consisting of businessmen, engineers, economists, and lawyers to pass on governmental proposals to investigate or proceed against alleged antitrust violations.

Oppenheim, in a more elaborate analysis of trends in the administration of the antitrust statutes,[46] like Smith, saw a need to bring antitrust laws into harmony with the facts of industrial life. Like Smith he vigorously advocated the utilization of the concept of workable competition under a rule of reason in administering the statutes. Like Smith he lamented tendencies in court and administrative decisions to outlaw per se certain business practices which on their face might suggest noncompetitive behavior or monopoly power, without first making a detailed analysis of their economic implications in the light of the whole industrial pattern in which they had developed. Like Smith he emphasized the importance of performance in determining the social acceptability of industrial patterns and structures, and like Smith he seemed to believe in a broad social rather than a narrow economic test of performance. Oppenheim's ideas also caught the attention of administrators and, largely in response to his pleas for new standards in antitrust administration, the Attorney General in 1953 created a national committee to study the antitrust laws[47] and appointed Oppenheim and Judge Barnes, Assistant Attorney General in charge of antitrust, as co-chairmen.

Although it might reasonably have been expected from the committee's make-up and from the forces that created it that the committee would recommend an amendment to the antitrust laws to provide for their administration in accordance with the concept of workable competition under a rule of reason, actually the committee specifically rejected such standards. But there is evidence that the committee tried to achieve by indirection what it did not openly advocate. Smith, a committee member, has revealed something of the committee's internal conflict on the issue of workable competition. The academic economists were skeptical, but their skepticism was matched by the determination

---

46. *Federal Antitrust Legislation: Guideposts to a Revised National Antitrust Policy*, 50 Mich. L. Rev. 1139 (1952).

47. The Committee's report appeared on March 31, 1955. Report of the Attorney General's National Committee To Study the Antitrust Laws (1955).

of the "real-life practitioners."[48] The give and take of democratic discussion "did much to reduce the disparity among groups."[49] Smith concluded that out of the committee's deliberations has come

> the most realistic set of standards for legal and socially acceptable competition since the Business Advisory Council Report on Effective Competition published by Secretary of Commerce Sawyer. The present report makes more official a great deal of what was then and there recommended.[50]

In preference to making basic recommendations for a revision of antitrust policy and standards the committee chose to analyze the decisions of administrative agencies and the opinions of the courts in their interpretation and application of the antitrust statutes, and it sought thereby to shape policy by providing "future guides to enforcement agencies, Congress, and the courts."[51] In its analysis and evaluation the committee commended the courts and administrative agencies when they apparently looked to all economic factors in trying to determine the significance to public welfare of the arrangements complained against, and it criticized decisions that condemned business practices in and of themselves without an examination of their full economic implications in their industrial setting. In evaluating the committee's report Smith has said:

> [The report] should be a bench mark for a long time to come against which to make comparisons of decisions, administrative actions, and legislation to see how far they drift from true readings.[52]

To insure that the courts might have at hand the committee's report as a ready guide, copies were sent to all federal judges. Oppenheim has since expressed the opinion that "the report is commanding the respect and serious consideration of the bar and Government officials."[53]

---

48. Smith, *Antitrust Report To Narrow Gap Between Law and Economics*, Trade Practice Bulletin, May 1955, p. 4.

49. *Ibid.*

50. *Ibid.*

51. Report of the Attorney General's National Committee To Study the Antitrust Laws 3 (1955).

52. Smith, *supra* note 48, at 1.

53. Letter dated August 1, 1955, to an unidentified addressee, *Hearings on Price Discrimination before House Select Committee on Small Business*, 84th Cong., 1st Sess. 194 (1955).

Thurman Arnold, former Assistant Attorney General in charge of antitrust, has corroborated this opinion in testimony before a congressional committee, saying, "[T]he effect of the report is unquestionably very significant when you are arguing a case in court. . . . After all, a large committee of supposedly expert people will inevitably have an effect upon the courts." [54]

Workable Competition in Antitrust Decisions

As previously suggested, without benefit of the committee's work the courts were already manifesting a disposition to judge alleged violations of the Sherman Act by the concept of workable competition. Smith noted this in saying,

> Legal opinions and decisions have been based progressively more and more on the concepts of effective competition. The outstanding opinion was that of Judge Knox in the Aluminum case where full play was given to the tests of effective competition, including inter-industry competition, and increasing ability of competitors to cope with the erstwhile dominant concern. Then Judge Wyzanski in the Shoe Machinery case, Mr. Justice Reed in the Columbia Steel case, and Judge Leahy in the Dupont Cellophane case have further elaborated these standards. [55]

In analyzing the effect on these or other important antitrust decisions of the economists' concept of workable competition, it is important to remember that the concept is vague, economists are not agreed on the relative importance of structure, conduct, and performance in evaluating the workability of any particular market situation, and the judgments of both economists and jurists are influenced not only by their own preconceptions but especially by attitudes currently prevailing on the significance of big business. With such wide discretion as the application of the concept necessarily involves, decisions are likely to give approval to business arrangements acceptable to the general culture within which they have developed.

The National Lead Case

In this case the government charged that the two major producers of titanium compounds in the United States, the National Lead Com-

---

54. *Id.* at 5, 6.
55. Smith, *supra* note 48, at 4.

pany and E. I. du Pont de Nemours & Company, had conspired and combined to restrain and monopolize trade in titanium in violation of sections 1 and 2 of the Sherman Act. The evidence established that National Lead together with du Pont and the leading foreign producers of titanium through a series of patent exchange agreements and inter-corporate arrangements had cartelized world trade in titanium. About these arrangements the district court said:

> In detail, the elapsed quarter century is crowded with negotiations, conferences, correspondence and agreements. The men who partici-pated in these were all articulate, literate and . . . recorded what they saw, heard, said and thought with Boswellian fidelity. When the story is seen as a whole, there is no blinking the fact that there is no free commerce in titanium. Every pound of it is tramelled by privately imposed regulation. The channels of this commerce have not been formed by the winds and currents of competition. They are, in large measure, artificial canals privately constructed. The borders of the private domain in titanium are guarded by hundreds of patents, pro-cured without opposition, and maintained without litigation. The ac-cumulated power of this private empire, at the outbreak of World War II, was tremendous. It was more difficult for the independent outsider to enter this business than for the camel to make its proverbial passage through the eye of a needle.[56]

In the United States, du Pont, National Lead, and two small producers, American Zirconium Corporation and Virginia Chemical Corporation, controlled titanium production—and each of the small producers was tied to National Lead or du Pont through corporate ties and patent licensing agreements. The Supreme Court upheld the district court's finding that the arrangements by which titanium producers had cartel-ized the trade in titanium would tend to violate both sections 1 and 2 of the Sherman Act, and it upheld the district court's injunction against a continuance or revival of such agreements.[57] But the Court denied the Government's request that National Lead and du Pont each be re-quired to dispose of one of its two titanium plants, thereby increasing the number of firms from four to six. In rejecting divestiture the Court apparently attached greater weight to the industry's performance than to its structure in determining the effectiveness or workability of com-petition in the industry. The Court concluded:

---

56. United States v. National Lead Co., 63 F. Supp. 513, 521 (S.D.N.Y. 1945).
57. United States v. National Lead Co., 332 U.S. 319 (1947).

There is no showing that four major competing units would be preferable to two, or, including American Zirconium and Virginia Chemical, that six would be better than four. Likewise, there is no showing of the necessity for this divestiture of plants or its practicality and fairness.[58]

The district court had found that "during the regime of the combination, the art has rapidly advanced, production has increased enormously and prices have sharply declined." [59] Fine performance of course did not justify unlawful conduct, and the Supreme Court did not hesitate to affirm an injunction against the various restrictive agreements by which titanium producers had divided world markets. It apparently believed that the industry, regardless of its structure, if rid of restrictive agreements would prove workably competitive.

THE 1950 ALUMINUM DECISION

Judge Hand in finding that the Aluminum Company of America was an unlawful monopoly decided that nothing should be done to disturb its industrial structure pending the outcome of the Government's disposal of surplus aluminum plants. At the close of the war the Government owned most of the capacity for producing aluminum, and it had been directed under the Surplus Property Act of 1944[60] to dispose of its vast properties in this and other industries so as "to give maximum aid in the reestablishment of a peacetime economy of free independent private enterprise, . . . to discourage monopolistic practices and to strengthen and preserve the competitive position of small business concerns . . . [and] to foster the development of new independent enterprise . . . without fostering monopoly or restraint of trade. . . ." [61] From the Government's disposal program Kaiser Aluminum and Chemical Corporation and Reynolds Metals Company emerged as full-fledged large-scale integrated companies with facilities acquired at only a fraction of their original cost. Accordingly in March, 1947, Alcoa petitioned the District Court for the Southern District of New York to declare that it no longer had a monopoly of the ingot market. The Government filed a counterpetition alleging that competition had not been established in the aluminum industry, that Alcoa continued to dominate

---

58. *Id.* at 352.
59. 63 F. Supp. at 525.
60. 58 STAT. 765.
61. *Id.* at 766.

and control the aluminum ingot market, and that only by divestiture of certain of its plants and properties could competition be established. The Government requested the establishment of an additional fully integrated producer in the industry.

On June 2, 1950, Judge Knox handed down a carefully reasoned opinion running through eighty printed pages.[62] At the outset he observed that "notwithstanding the antiquity of the action, the issues involved must be determined in accordance with the more recently established anti-trust principles, and not by those that were well recognized in an earlier day." [63] Just as the relevant legal principles had changed in the unfolding of the law, so had the relevant economic principles. Judge Knox noted that "the precise ingredients of 'effective competition' cannot be said to have been a static concept under the Sherman Act. Their applications, as well as their implications, have varied with changes in judicial thought with respect to economic and legal philosophies." [64] But Judge Knox lamented that "recent precedents . . . have fallen short of definite specifications as to the requirements of 'effective competition.' " [65] Nevertheless he was hopeful that it would be "possible to formulate a more or less concrete delineation of the standards that should be met in seeking a just decision upon the complicated facts of this case." [66]

To determine "the extent of permissible power that is consistent with the anti-trust laws in a particular industry" [67] Judge Knox applied a broad conception of the principle of workable competition, in which performance plays a relatively important role. He enunciated the following factors as relevant: "the number and strength of the firms in the market; their effective size from the standpoint of technological development, and from the standpoint of competition with substitute materials and foreign trade; national security interests in the maintenance of strong productive facilities, and maximum scientific research and development; together with the public interest in lowered costs and uninterrupted production." [68] To Judge Knox the industry's structure, although not to be ignored, was relatively unimportant to the effectiveness of competition. "Commercial competition . . . is the independent

---

62. United States v. Aluminum Co., 91 F. Supp. 333 (S.D.N.Y. 1950).
63. *Id.* at 339.
64. *Id.* at 340.
65. *Ibid.*
66. *Ibid.*
67. *Id.* at 347.
68. *Ibid.*

endeavour of *two* or more persons or organizations within the realm of a chosen market place, to obtain the business patronage of others by means of various appeals, including the offer of more attractive terms or superior merchandise." [69]

Judge Knox did not find in recent precedents a precise specification for effective competition, but he did find a precise conception of monopoly. Monopoly is the power to fix prices and the power to exclude rivals from the market. Investigating these two determinants of power, Judge Knox quickly disposed of the Government's contention that Alcoa's monopolistic power was manifested in its control over the price of aluminum pig and ingots. As the only producer selling these in substantial quantities to fabricators, Alcoa had "prime responsibility for prices." [70] However, the potential competition of Reynolds and Kaiser (who elected to fabricate virtually all the ingots and pig they produced) effectively limited Alcoa's power over prices. "The Government has not demonstrated that Alcoa enjoys price leadership with regard to fabricated products, a matter which would have to be included if a true representation of the industry were sought." [71] Accordingly Judge Knox held that "price domination on the part of Alcoa has not been established. . . ." [72]

Judge Knox examined more thoroughly the issue of Alcoa's power to exclude rivals from the market. He reviewed meticulously the physical resources of both Kaiser and Reynolds at the several stages of production, their comparative costs, financial resources, and control of patents. In all respects he found that Alcoa had a substantial advantage over either of its rivals. Alcoa's financial strength enabled it to take advantage of trade opportunities and to stifle Kaiser's and Reynolds' growth whenever it wished. The evidence before it, the court said, was insufficient to assure that in the future competitive conditions of

---

69. *Id.* at 355. (Emphasis added.) Compare Judge Knox's conception with that of J. M. Clark. Clark said: "Competition is rivalry in selling goods, in which each selling unit normally seeks maximum net revenue, under conditions such that the price or prices each seller can charge are effectively limited by free option of the buyer to buy from a rival seller or sellers of what we think of as 'the same' product, necessitating an effort by each seller to equal or exceed the attractiveness of the others' offerings to a sufficient number of buyers to accomplish the end in view." *Toward a Concept of Workable Competition*, 30 Am. Econ. Rev. 241, 243 (1940), reprinted in AMERICAN ECONOMICS ASS'N, READINGS IN THE SOCIAL CONTROL OF INDUSTRY 452, 455 (1942).

70. United States v. Aluminum Co., 91 F. Supp. 333, 365 (S.D.N.Y. 1950).

71. *Ibid.*

72. *Ibid.*

an "effective and lawful nature" [73] would prevail in the aluminum industry. But the court did not find in Alcoa's recent behavior an intent to monopolize, and it could not bring itself to disturb the organization of Alcoa's physical properties. A "strong and resourceful domestic aluminum industry" *was* essential to "national security" and "the peacetime welfare of the general public." [74] The development of the industry depended upon its being composed of "financially sound and well-integrated organizations." [75] Aluminum competed with other products and had not only to hold its own against them but to enlarge its acceptance as a substitute for them. This required encroaching on the fields of "strongly entrenched" competitors, and "the weakening of any aluminum producer would lessen the buoyancy of the industry as a whole." [76] Big business is "an actuality" and if it is to meet effective competition its trade rivals must be "of somewhat comparable strength." [77] The court was unwilling "to tamper unnecessarily with economic and industrial forces from which the public has reaped substantial benefits." [78]

In thus giving its blessing to Alcoa and the industry's structure the court warned that if Alcoa should use the power which its lower production costs and its financial and physical resources gave it to injure or weaken Reynolds and Kaiser, the court would have to take another look at the matter. "If, for any reason, it should appear that their competition with Alcoa is feeble, uncertain and ineffective, appropriate action . . . will be in order." [79] The court in effect gave official sanction to Alcoa's holding an umbrella over the industry and encouragement to a pricing policy calculated to profit the industry rather than benefit the consumer of aluminum products. Because, in responding to the temper of the times, it confused a giant firm with a dynamic industry, the court lost the opportunity it had been given by the peculiar circumstances of the *Aluminum* case to "foster independent private enterprise."

THE UNITED SHOE MACHINERY CASE

On December 15, 1947, the Government filed a complaint against the

---

73. *Id*. at 416.
74. *Ibid*.
75. *Ibid*.
76. *Ibid*.
77. *Ibid*.
78. *Ibid*.
79. *Id*. at 418.

United Shoe Machinery Corporation alleging that it was monopolizing interstate commerce in the shoe machinery industry of the United States in violation of section 2 of the Sherman Act. On February 18, 1953, Judge Wyzanski of the District Court for the District of Massachusetts handed down a decision finding the corporation guilty.[80] The defendants appealed, and on May 17, 1954, the Supreme Court upheld the lower court without writing an opinion.[81] Judge Wyzanski's opinion is important for two reasons. It clarifies the doctrine laid down by Judge Hand in the *Aluminum* case that a monopoly is guilty of monopolizing if it does not have monopoly thrust upon it; and it reflects a characteristic timidity of the courts in determining the remedies to be applied in antitrust cases.

Judge Wyzanski recognized three main sources of United's power in the shoe machinery market: (1) the original organization of the company in 1899, which combined the leading manufacturers of shoe machinery; (2) the superiority of its products and services; and (3) the business practices it had pursued, especially its system of leasing rather than selling shoe machinery. The original combination had brought under a single control the two largest producers of shoe machinery, themselves the product of previous mergers, and a number of small but important producers.[82] In the language of the new cor-

---

80. United States v. United Shoe Mach. Corp., 110 F. Supp. 295 (D. Mass. 1953), *aff'd*, 347 U.S. 521 (1954).

81. In a *per curiam* statement the Court found the decree supported by the findings and the findings justified by the evidence. 347 U.S. 521 (1954).

82. The United Shoe Machinery Co. was the subject of both criminal and civil actions under the Sherman Act, and the several court opinions give varying accounts of the number and size of the firms that made up the original combination. Justice Clarke in dissenting from the Supreme Court's 1918 opinion holding that the combination did not violate the Sherman Act undertook to give a "plain history" of the company's formation and later acquisitions, and Justice Holmes speaking for a unanimous Court in the 1913 criminal case stated the percentages of domestic production that were controlled by the larger units that made up the combination. S. W. Winslow, the controlling spirit of the Consolidated and McKay Lasting Machine Co., with 60 per cent of the country's lasting machines, and E. P. Howe, the controlling spirit of the Goodyear Shoe Machinery Co., with 30 per cent of the country's welt-sewing machines and outsole-stitching machines—both companies being the products of earlier consolidations—organized the United Shoe Machinery Co., a New Jersey corporation, in February 1899. United by an exchange of stock acquired the Goodyear and International Goodyear Shoe Machinery Cos., and in 1900 it acquired the Seaver Co., the only lasting machine manufacturer then outside the combination. United also purchased the McKay Shoe Machinery Co., which produced 70 per cent of the country's heeling machines and 80 per cent of the country's metallic fastening machines. Consolidated already owned the Davey Pegging Machine Co. Within a few weeks of its organization United acquired the only remaining strong competitor, the Eppler Welt Machine Co., and its international subsidiary. In 1901 it

poration's president: "After the formation of the United Company it was manufacturing *every single lasting machine* that was being put out in the United States except the Seaver machine; and in 1900 we acquired the Seaver Company." [83] When Judge Wyzanski made his decision, however, the legality of the original combination was no longer in question, it having been upheld by the Supreme Court in 1918. [84]

Judge Wyzanski acknowledged the superiority of United's products and services, but he did not find that United had "achieved spectacular results at amazing rates of speed, nor has it proved that comparable research results and comparable economies of production, distribution, and service could not be achieved as well by, say, three important shoe machinery firms, as by one." [85] Moreover, the court observed,

> United's control does not rest solely on its original constitution, its ability, its research, or its economies of scale. There are other barriers

---

acquired the remaining welt machine company, the Globe. Justice Clarke quoted Winslow as saying: "Immediately after the organization of the company our welting, outsole stitching and lasting machines were doing about all the welting, outsole stitching and lasting that was being done in the United States." United States v. United Shoe Mach. Co., 247 U.S. 32, 82 (1918). On March 1, 1899, United purchased control of Goddu Co., a manufacturer of metallic fastening machines, under a contract binding the six inventors who had owned the stock to transfer to United all shoe machinery inventions they might make or acquire any interest in for a period of ten years. In 1910 United purchased for $6,000,000 the shoe machinery line that the Thomas G. Plant Co., a shoe manufacturer, had developed as a means of freeing shoe manufacturers from total dependence on United. The record showed fifty-seven purchases by United ranging from $250 for a patent application to the $6,000,000 purchase just described. Winslow and others were indicted for conspiring to restrain trade, but the Supreme Court ruled that the indictment did not charge a Sherman Act offense because the shoe machines combined were not in competition with each other (despite evidence in the record to the contrary). United States v. Winslow, 227 U.S. 202 (1913). Five years later the Supreme Court by a four-to-three vote (Justices McReynolds and Brandeis did not participate) held that the civil suit to dissolve the combination was properly dismissed for the same reason. United States v. United Shoe Mach. Co., *supra.* It also ruled that the alleged abuses of United's leasing system were but the lawful exercise of its patent rights. By 1917 the present United Shoe Machinery Corp., organized in 1905, had merged with and become the successor of the United Shoe Machinery Co.

83. Quoted by Justice Clarke in dissenting from United States v. United Shoe Mach. Co., *supra* note 82, at 81. (Emphasis added.)

84. United States v. United Shoe Mach. Co., *supra* note 82. The majority opinion in finding for United summed up its views in these words: "The company, indeed, has magnitude, but it is at once the result and cause of efficiency, and the charge that it has been oppressively used is not sustained." *Id.* at 56.

85. United States v. United Shoe Mach. Corp., 110 F. Supp. 295, 345 (D. Mass. 1953), aff'd, 347 U.S. 521 (1954).

to competition, and these barriers were erected by United's own business policies. Much of United's market power is traceable to the magnetic ties inherent in its system of leasing, and not selling, its more important machines.[86]

In stating the law on monopolization Judge Wyzanski elucidated the principles laid down in the *Aluminum* case, an opinion he recognized as a turning point in the interpretation of section 2 of the Sherman Act. In doing so he referred to the Supreme Court's opinions in the *Griffith*,[87] *Schine*,[88] *Paramount*,[89] and *Columbia Steel*[90] cases and noted that in the second *American Tobacco* case the Court had "expressly approved" Judge Hand's technique and language. In these cases Judge Wyzanski saw three different but related approaches: (1) "An enterprise has monopolized in violation of section 2 of the Sherman Act if it has acquired or maintained a power to exclude others as a result of using an unreasonable 'restraint of trade' in violation of section 1 of the Sherman Act." [91] (2) It has "monopolized in violation of section 2 if it (a) has the power to exclude competition, and (b) has exercised it, or has the purpose to exercise it." [92] (3) A concern that has acquired an overwhelming share of the market "monopolizes" in violation of section 2 whenever it does business, provided its monopoly is not solely the result of "superior skill, superior products, natural advantages, (including accessibility to raw materials or markets), economic or technological efficiency, (including scientific research), low margins of profit maintained permanently and without discrimination, or licenses conferred by, and used within, the limits of law, (including patents on one's own inventions, or franchises granted directly to the enterprise by a public authority)." [93]

Judge Wyzanski apparently thought that the facts in the case before him satisfied each of these approaches but felt precluded from adopting the first because the Supreme Court had cleared United's lease pro-

---

86. *Id.* at 344.
87. United States v. Griffith, 334 U.S. 100 (1948).
88. Schine Chain Theatres, Inc. v. United States, 334 U.S. 110 (1948).
89. United States v. Paramount Pictures, Inc., 334 U.S. 131 (1948).
90. United States v. Columbia Steel Co., 334 U.S. 495 (1948).
91. United States v. United Shoe Mach. Corp., 110 F. Supp. 295, 342 (D. Mass. 1953), *aff'd*, 347 U.S. 521 (1954).
92. *Ibid.*
93. *Ibid.*

visions under the Sherman Act in the 1918 *Shoe Machinery* case.[94] He found it unnecessary to choose between the second and the third approaches.

> For, taken as a whole, the evidence satisfies the tests laid down in both *Griffith* and *Aluminum*. The facts show that (1) defendant has, and exercises, such overwhelming strength in the shoe machinery market that it controls that market, (2) this strength excludes some potential, and limits some actual, competition, and (3) this strength is not attributable solely to defendant's ability, economies of scale, research, natural advantages, and adaptation to inevitable economic laws.[95]

In short, a business firm monopolizes within the meaning of section 2 of the Sherman Act if it achieves or maintains market power by practices which though not predatory or illegal in themselves are unnecessary to the efficient conduct of business.

Judge Wyzanski is to be congratulated for having clarified and extended the doctrine laid down by Judge Hand. His interpretation of the law (as distinguished from his application of it in formulating remedies) reflects boldness and logic and should do much to relieve the uncertainty created by Judge Hand's somewhat vague concept of monopoly's being thrust upon a firm.

When it came to remedies, Judge Wyzanski was no longer bold, although he was equally logical. He realized that the society in which he lived was satisfied with the contemporary business environment and would not tolerate judgments requiring significant changes in it. So long as the methods by which business grew big were not flagrantly predatory and even though the size achieved was larger than need be for efficiency, the public identified big business with success and would not support the necessary surgery to reconstruct it into more competitive units. As Judge Wyzanski stated the matter,

> To many champions of the anti-trust laws these cases indicate judicial timidity, economic innocence, lack of conviction, or paralysis of resolution. Yet there is another way of interpreting this judical history. In

---

94. See note 82 *supra*. The Court later condemned the leasing practices under section 3 of the Clayton Act. United Shoe Mach. Corp. v. United States, 258 U.S. 451 (1922), and United thereupon softened some of the more onerous provisions.

95. United States v. United Shoe Mach. Corp., 110 F. Supp. 295, 343 (D. Mass. 1953), aff'd, 347 U.S. 521 (1954). (Emphasis added.)

the anti-trust field the courts have been accorded, by common consent, an authority they have in no other branch of enacted law. Indeed, the only comparable examples of the power of judges is [*sic*] the economic role they formerly exercised under the Fourteenth Amendment, and the role they now exercise in the area of civil liberties. They would not have been given, or allowed to keep, such authority in the anti-trust field, and they would not so freely have altered from time to time the interpretation of its substantive provisions, if courts were in the habit of proceeding with the surgical ruthlessness that might commend itself to those seeking absolute assurance that there will be workable competition, and to those aiming at immediate realization of the social, political, and economic advantages of dispersal of power.[96]

Thus did Judge Wyzanski adjust his decision to the temper of the times. He did not order dissolution of the United Shoe Machinery Corporation into three independent companies, as asked by the Government, because it was impractical to do so. He did not order United to discontinue the leasing of machines and sell them outright, a policy recommended by his economic adviser,[97] but left United with the alternative of selling or leasing them (under less restrictive terms than United had imposed) at the option of the user. He concluded that to prohibit leasing altogether would be "undesirable at least until milder remedies have been tried." [98] He did not carry divestiture as far as his economic counsellor thought desirable,[99] being content with merely ordering divestiture of United's business in nails, tacks, and eyelets—

---

96. *Id.* at 348.

97. Carl Kaysen, associate professor of economics at Harvard University, served for two years as economic assistant to Judge Wyzanski while the *Shoe Machinery* case was being tried. He completed his original memorandum for the court in October 1952 and published it with additions in book form in 1956. For his recommendations on putting an end to leasing see UNITED STATES V. UNITED SHOE MACHINERY CORPORATION 275-89 (1956).

98. United States v. United Shoe Mach. Corp., 110 F. Supp. 295, 349 (D. Mass. 1953), *aff'd*, 347 U.S. 521 (1954).

99. Kaysen thought a new shoe machinery and shoe factory supply manufacturer could be created by "divesting United of B. B. Chemical Corporation, its own Cement Shoe department, its two eyelet manufacturing branches, S. O. and O. C. Co. and J. C. Rhodes, and its Eyeletting department," and setting them up with suitable administrative branches as a corporation independent of United. This would be "a step in the direction of recreating conditions similar to those which prevailed before the original mergers which created United's predecessor company." KAYSEN, UNITED STATES V. UNITED SHOE MACHINERY CORPORATION, *supra* note 97, at 289.

"this is the kind of dissolution which can be carried out practically"[100] —and of its distributorship of shoe factory supplies made by companies not a part of United's organization.[101] The court did not order compulsory licensing of United's patents on a royalty-free basis, but the milder remedy of compulsory licensing at reasonable royalties.[102]

Although Judge Wyzanski rendered an opinion admirable for its logic and clarity, he refrained from such bold remedies as would satisfy those "aiming at immediate realization of the social, political, and economic advantages of dispersal of power." He chose milder ones more in keeping with the spirit of the times, with the preconceptions and prejudices of those who regard big business as one of the noblest achievements of this era. His decision is likely to find approval by all reasonable men who have made peace with their environment.

---

100. United States v. United Shoe Mach. Corp., 110 F. Supp. 295, 351 (D. Mass. 1953), *aff'd*, 347 U.S. 521 (1954).

101. Concerning the latter the court said, "And United ought not to be allowed to continue these distributorships because they flowed to United partly, at any rate, as an indirect consequence of United's prohibited monopolization of shoe machinery. To be sure, other advantages flowed to United from its monopolization; but the particular advantages inherent in the large scale distribution of supplies are . . . *easily* severable." *Ibid.* (Emphasis added.)

102. According to KAYSEN, *op. cit. supra* note 97, at 285, the government sought royalty-free licensing, but "the reason for not requiring . . . [it] is simply that the significance of United's patents in maintaining its market position is not so great as to warrant such a drastic remedy." Perhaps the court was guided more by legal precedent than by the patents' lack of significance to United. It found that of the 3,915 patents United held on December 15, 1947, roughly 95 per cent were the result of its own research; the remainder were acquired and served to buttress United's market power even though their economic purposes could have been fulfilled equally well by obtaining nonexclusive licenses. And "the aggregation of patents does to some extent block potential competition" by inducing inventors to offer their ideas to United and enabling it to hedge against "unforeseen competitive developments." United States v. United Shoe Mach. Corp., 110 F. Supp. 295, 339 (D. Mass. 1953), *aff'd*, 347 U.S. 521 (1954). The court ordered compulsory patent licensing on a reasonable royalty basis as "in effect a partial dissolution, on a nonconfiscatory basis." *Id.* at 351.

The remedy is in line with the law's development on compulsory patent licensing in antitrust cases. Besser Mfg. Co. v. United States, 343 U.S. 444, 447 (1952); United States v. United States Gypsum Co., 340 U.S. 76, 94 (1950); United States v. National Lead Co., 332 U.S. 319, 338 (1947). The Supreme Court has refused to order royalty-free licensing on the ground that it would amount to a forfeiture of the patents, a remedy not appropriate to a Sherman Act violation having nothing to do with their validity. Hartford-Empire Co. v. United States, 323 U.S. 386, 414-15 (1945). The Court had earlier denied the right to sue for infringement to a patentee found to have used his patent to monopolize an unpatented article, Morton Salt Co. v. G. S. Suppiger Co., 314 U.S. 488 (1942); B. B. Chemical Co. v. Ellis, 314 U.S. 495 (1942), but it declared that denial of this property right in such circumstances was not a precedent for antitrust remedies that were confiscatory. Hartford-Empire Co. v. United States, *supra*, at 415.

THE CELLOPHANE CASE

The doctrine of workable competition has provided an institutional basis for a lax administration of the antitrust laws. It has afforded a logical reconciliation between a law that condemns in a sweeping manner all combinations in restraint of trade and all monopolizing and attempts to monopolize, and an economic, cultural, and technological environment conducive to vast aggregations of capital in firms so large that they necessarily have power over the market. As a standard in antitrust judgments it has encouraged a rationalization of the status quo. As previously pointed out, the standards by which economists would judge the workability of any arrangement in which sellers vie with one another for the trade of their customers are the structure of an industry, the conduct of firms which comprise it, and their economic performance. The relative weight attached to these several criteria depends on individual judgments. Some economists and a larger number of lawyers attach little importance to structure, holding that competition may be effective with only a few firms in a market, even with only one if the market be narrowly defined.[103] Those who hold this point of view look to interindustry competition to protect the consumer from exploitation.[104] Others hold that the structure of an industry may determine the conduct of the firms that comprise it.[105] This point of view is well expressed by Chief Justice Warren in his dissent in the *Cellophane* case: "The conduct of du Pont and Sylvania [Sylvania Industrial Corporation of America, the only other producer during the period covered by the case] illustrates that a few sellers tend to act like one and that an industry which does not have a competitive structure will not have competitive behavior." [106] Some economists, and lawyers too, who attach relatively great importance to conduct as evidence of monopoly look for discriminatory and predatory practices as the key element in

---

103. Adelman, *Effective Competition and the Antitrust Laws*, 61 HARV. L. REV. 1289 (1948); B. Smith, *Effective Competition: Hypothesis for Modernizing the Antitrust Laws*, 26 N.Y.U.L. REV. 405 (1951); Sunderland, *Changing Legal Concepts in the Antitrust Field*, 3 SYRACUSE L. REV. 60 (1951).

104. Robertson, *On the Changing Apparatus of Competition*, 44 AM. ECON. REV. (Proceedings of the American Economic Ass'n) 61 (1954).

105. Adams, *Dissolution, Divorcement, Divestiture: The Pyrrhic Victories of Antitrust*, 27 IND. L.J. 1 (1951); Lewis, *The Effectiveness of the Federal Antitrust Laws: A Symposium*, (ed. Keezer), 39 AM. ECON. REV. 689, 703 (1949); Rostov, *The New Sherman Act: A Positive Instrument of Progress*, 14 U. CHI. L. REV. 567 (1947).

106. United States v. E. I. du Pont de Nemours & Co., 351 U.S. 377, 426 (1956). In 1946 Sylvania merged with The American Viscose Corporation.

antitrust violations.[107] Others examine the broad strategy of a firm, as did Judge Wyzanski in the *Shoe Machinery* case. And finally some economists and lawyers attach primary importance to an industry's performance as evidence of the workability of competition.[108] Those who do may be concerned less about the existence of power than the manner in which power is exercised. When an industry is characterized by rapid technological advances, when cost and prices show a consistent downward trend, when the product is continuously improved—in short, when the industry's performance appears to be consistent with the general welfare—those attaching primary importance to performance may consider questions about market power merely academic. With the experts disagreeing on the relative importance of structure, conduct, and performance to the workability of competition, the judges must find standards of their own. The standards of the business community are apt to count for more with them than the standards of the academicians.

Seen in this light the district court's decision in the *Cellophane* case[109] should surprise no one. In handing down his decision (which runs through 192 printed pages and presents a detailed but superficial analysis of the evidence), Judge Leahy pointed out that the charge against du Pont of having monopolized cellophane involved two questions: "1. does du Pont possess monopoly powers; and 2., if so has it achieved such powers by 'monopolizing' within the meaning of the Act and under United States v. Aluminum Company of America"?[110] He concluded that "unless the first is decided against defendant, the second is not reached." [111] Judge Leahy did not need to reach the second question, for he found the defendant not guilty. He concluded his opinion with these significant remarks:

> The facts destroy the charges here made. There has been no monopolization or conspiracy or combination or attempt to monopolize shown. The record reflects not the dead hand of monopoly but rapidly declining prices, expanding production, intense competition stimulated by creative research, the development of new products and uses and other

---

107. *E.g.*, Dirlam and Kahn, Fair Competition: The Law and Economics of Antitrust Policy (1954).

108. Griffin, An Economic Approach to Antitrust Problems, American Enterprise Association (1951); Griffin, *Needed: A Realistic Antitrust Policy*, Harv. Bus. Rev., Nov.-Dec. 1956, p. 76; B. Smith, *Effective Competition: Hypothesis for Modernizing the Antitrust Laws*, 26 N.Y.U.L. Rev. 405 (1951).

109. United States v. E. I. du Pont de Nemours & Co., 118 F. Supp. 41 (D. Del. 1953).

110. *Id.* at 54.

111. *Ibid.*

benefits of a free economy. [Neither] DuPont nor any other American company similarly situated should be punished for its success. Nothing warrants intervention of this court of equity. The complaint should be dismissed.[112]

The Supreme Court by a vote of four to three affirmed this judgment.

The Relevant Market for Cellophane

Judge Leahy in reaching his decision considered many supplementary issues, but the decision rests primarily on the single question, what is the relevant market in which du Pont sells cellophane? Is cellophane a differentiated product with characteristics peculiar to itself which isolate it from the competition of other products, or is it merely one of many flexible wrapping materials that possess varied characteristics but on the whole are so much alike that one may readily substitute for another and the producers of all compete vigorously for consumers' preference? The Supreme Court accepted the issue as Judge Leahy defined it. In considering this issue Judge Leahy concluded that

> cellophane is not a unique flexible packaging material in any functional or economic sense. In terms of uses for which cellophane is sold, and the qualities it brings to each use as a wrapping material, cellophane is interchangeable and *in fact* continually interchanged with many flexible packaging materials.[113]

Judge Leahy classified sixteen flexible wrapping materials according to eleven characteristics considered by industrial buyers in gauging their relative merits, and he discussed at length the characteristics of eleven—including aluminum foil, certain films, waxed and greaseproof paper, and glassine—which he regarded as interchangeable with cellophane. He noted that several hundred firms compete in their production and sale and that du Pont in 1949 accounted for only 17.9 per cent of their total square yardage of domestic output and imports.[114]

Purchasers of flexible wrapping materials are primarily makers and distributors of the consumers' goods they package. They are cost- and profit-conscious and carefully compare the qualities and prices of available wrapping materials. They endeavor to choose the material

---

112. *Id.* at 233.
113. *Id.* at 63. (Emphasis in original.)
114. *Id.* at 111.

which will win consumer preference and which, cost considered, will yield the highest profit on the goods they market.[115] Such wrapping materials fall into four main categories: (1) opaque nonmoistureproof wrapping *paper* designed primarily for convenience and protection in handling packages; (2) moistureproof *films* of varying degrees of transparency designed primarily either to protect, or to display and protect, the products they encompass; (3) nonmoistureproof transparent *films* designed primarily to display and to some extent protect, but which obviously do a poor protecting job where exclusion or retention of moisture is important; and (4) moistureproof *materials* other than films of varying degrees of transparency (foils and paper products) designed to protect and display.

Kraft paper is the leading opaque nonmoistureproof wrapping paper. It is relatively cheap, strong, and pliable and gives adequate protection. It does not meet the competition of other wrapping materials for the purposes for which it is primarily designed—the convenient wrapping of packages. At less than one cent per thousand square inches, kraft paper sells for less than cellophane costs. Although Judge Leahy did not specifically recognize the fact, clearly kraft paper does not fall into the relevant market for cellophane.

In 1949, 80 per cent of du Pont's cellophane sales were for packaging food products, and for this use cellophane encounters the vigorous rivalry of vegetable parchment, greaseproof paper, glassine, waxed paper, aluminum foil, pliofilm, Saran, and other films. Judge Leahy analyzed in some detail the nature and extent of rivalry among these materials for wrapping a large number of specific products: white bread, specialty breads, cake and sweet goods, meat, candy, crackers and biscuits, frozen foods, potato chips, popcorn and snacks, cereals, fresh produce, paper goods and textiles, butter, cheese, fish, oleomargarine, chewing gum, other food products, and cigarettes and other tobacco products. Only in the wrapping of cigarettes did cellophane supply as much as 50 per cent of the total quantity (in square inches) of wrapping materials used.[116] It sold only 6.8 per cent of the wrapping

---

115. "Manufacturer of packageable products has a choice of materials from which to choose. Purchase price, cost of application, service available, and functional qualities of each material are factors which control choice, and control volume of material that can be sold in competition with others." *Id*. at 88.

116. In the outer wrapping of packaged cigarettes cellophane has no effective rival. Du Pont cellophane wraps 75 to 80 per cent of the cigarettes sold in the United States. *Id*. at 114. Ordinarily it is only when they can't get it that cigarette makers use any other material, e.g. during a cellophane shortage in the mid-forties. Brown and Williamson

materials used for packaging bakery products. Only as a wrapper for fresh produce did it top the list, and in this field it supplied only 47.2 per cent of the total wrapping materials used. This to the district court did not look like market domination. After examining the shifts among the various materials in their several uses (particularly in the wrapping of candy), after hearing the testimony of flexible wrapping material converters and users, after receiving the results of a market survey prepared by du Pont, after examining the reports of du Pont salesmen, after taking judicial notice of trade publications and writings, and after a personal visit to the 1952 Annual Packaging Show in Atlantic City to see at first hand the manner in which such materials were offered for sale to the trade, Judge Leahy concluded that "duPont cellophane is sold under such intense competitive conditions [that] acquisition of market control or monopoly power is a practical impossibility." [117] By making a detailed examination of the economic factors at work in the relevant market for cellophane as he defined that market, Judge Leahy wrote an opinion that won the approval of the proponents of workable competition. But, as will be shown later, an analysis of economic factors is no better than the analyst's understanding of each factor.

Although its reasoning is more formal and technical than Judge Leahy's, the Supreme Court did not do much better. It accepted as the main issue in the case the relevant market for cellophane, and it gave the term "relevant market" a new definition: "In considering what is the relevant market for determining the control of price and competition, no more definite rule can be declared than that commodities *reasonably* interchangeable by consumers for the same purposes make up that 'part of the trade or commerce,' monopolization of which may be illegal." [118]

The Concept of Cross-Elasticity of Demand

To determine "reasonable" interchangeability the Court introduced the concept of cross-elasticity, saying:

An element for consideration as to cross-elasticity of demand between

---

Tobacco Co. once experimented with selling Kools and Raleighs in a one-piece foil package. *Id.* at 108.

117. *Id.* at 197-98.

118. United States v. E. I. du Pont de Nemours & Co., 351 U.S. 377, 395 (1956). (Emphasis added.)

products is the responsiveness of the sales of one product to price changes of the other. If a slight decrease in the price of cellophane causes a considerable number of customers of other flexible wrappings to switch to cellophane, it would be an indication that a high cross-elasticity of demand exists between them; that the products compete in the same market.[119]

But without testing the facts by correct application of the principle the Court accepted Judge Leahy's findings that the " 'great sensitivity of customers in the flexible packaging markets to price or quality changes' prevented du Pont from possessing monopoly control over price." [120] The Court concluded that "cellophane's interchangeability with the other materials mentioned suffices to make it a part of this flexible packaging material market." [121]

Cross-elasticity is a technical economic concept. By incorporating it into its reasoning the Court ostensibly gave the law a method by which to measure more realistically the workability of competition. In the hands of experts supplied with detailed data on cost changes, price, and shifts in demands, the concept should prove useful in determining the extent to which substitute products can prevent the exploitation of consumers by would-be monopolists. In the hands of judges in antitrust cases the concept is probably not of much use. It may prove a positive deterrent to the effective administration of the Sherman Act. The Supreme Court correctly conceived cross-elasticity as defining the extent to which a change in the price of commodity A affects the sales of commodity B. But to recognize this is to state the problem, not to solve it. If a decrease in A's price diminishes B's sales, cross-elasticity is positive. All this says is that a significant number of consumers, after considering the relative merits of the two products and their prices, have substituted a product whose price has been lowered for one whose price remains unchanged. If a given decrease in the price of one commodity results in a relatively large decrease in the sales of the other, cross-elasticity is said to be high.

On the ratio of cross-elasticity between cellophane and any other wrapping material both Judge Leahy and the Supreme Court are necessarily silent. To determine it business rivals would have had to disclose confidential information which the *Cellophane* case does not reveal. But even if the du Pont record had disclosed the relevant confidential

119. *Id.* at 400.
120. *Ibid.*
121. *Ibid.*

data on changes in sales and prices, and a high positive cross-elasticity between cellophane and a substitute wrapping paper had been shown, this would not warrant the conclusion that the seller of either product was not a monopolist. To determine whether either firm possesses monopoly power it would be necessary to examine the price response of the firm losing business and the cost-price relationships of both products. To recapture business lost or to prevent further losses to product A the firm making product B must lower its price. If price decreases in product A do not bring a decrease in the price of B, a lack of competition between them is indicated. Either the loss of business is too slight to matter—that is, cross-elasticity is low—or the producer of product A has a monopoly advantage which the producer of product B does not have. If product B was already selling at a competitive price, i.e. marginal cost, its producer could not afford to reduce the price, and if he continued to lose business it would have no alternative in the long run but to cease operations. That the producer of product A could afford to reduce its price suggests that it was already getting a monopoly profit, a profit which it hopes to enlarge by selling more at lower prices.

So much for the logic. What are the facts in the *Cellophane* case? Between 1924 and 1938 du Pont reduced the price of cellophane every year, presumably in an effort to increase profits by increasing volume, for a total reduction of over 80 per cent.[122] During this same period the price of glassine and from 1933 the price of waxed paper (prices for earlier years are not available), the two largest selling wrapping papers, remained virtually unchanged. From 1938 to 1940 the price of cellophane declined by 8.6 per cent. During the same years the prices of waxed paper and glassine actually increased. This indicates a low cross-elasticity of demand. Apparently du Pont could ignore the prices of rival papers in setting its own prices. From 1924 to 1950 the price of the principal type of moistureproof cellophane was at all times for which figures are available from two to seven times that of 25# bleached glassine and from two to four and one-half times that of 30# waxed paper, despite a reduction in the average price of cellophane from $2.51 to 49 cents a pound.[123] To the economically sophisti-

---

122. Table of annual average prices from 1924 to 1950, United States v. E. I. du Pont de Nemours & Co., 118 F. Supp. 41, 82 (D. Del. 1953).

123. Defendant's Brief on the Facts and the Law, Appendix A (graph based on prices per 1,000 sq. in.), United States v. E. I. du Pont de Nemours & Co., 118 F. Supp. 41 (D. Del. 1953).

cated this is sufficient evidence that cellophane is a unique product. As the Supreme Court dissenting opinion put it:

> We cannot believe that . . . practical businessmen would have bought cellophane in increasing amounts over a quarter of a century if close substitutes were available at from one-seventh to one-half cellophane's price. That they did so is testimony to cellophane's distinctiveness.[124]

As these price changes took place, cost-conscious buyers (candy manufacturers were a conspicuous example) were constantly revising their judgment as to the relative merits of cellophane, glassine, and waxed paper at the prices at which they could be bought, and some buyers switched from one product to the other. But this is a deceptive interchangeability. Rational buyers will revise their judgment of the relative value of several products that serve roughly the same purpose whenever the price of one or the other changes, and they will not be deterred from doing so merely because the seller of one product is a monopolist. In a general sense all products compete for the consumer's dollar, and a wise monopolist will so adjust cost-price relationships as to obtain the highest return on his investment. He may do so by selling much at a low profit per unit or little at a high profit per unit. That he chooses one policy in preference to the other does not mean that he has surrendered his monopoly. He is merely exploiting it wisely.

Du Pont's Price Policy and Earnings on Cellophane and Rayon

Du Pont officials thought that du Pont could make more money by reducing prices and selling more cellophane. President Yerkes of the Du Pont Cellophane Company expressed his views in this way:

> I am in favor of lowering the price. . . . [I] think it will undoubtedly increase sales and widen distribution. . . . Our price I think is too high based purely on manufacturing cost and too high in comparison with other wrapping papers on the market, and while we cannot approach the price of glassine or other oil papers, if we make a substantial reduction we will in some cases get somewhere near there.[125]

---

124. United States v. E. I. du Pont de Nemours & Co., 351 U.S. 377, 417 (1956).

125. Memorandum of some remarks made at a meeting of the board of directors, Du Pont Cellophane Co., Dec. 11, 1924, Defendant's Exhibit 337, p. 643, United States v. E. I. du Pont de Nemours & Co., 118 F. Supp. 41 (D. Del. 1953). (Hereinafter the references to the exhibits and testimony in this case will not repeat the case citation.)

Walter S. Carpenter, Jr., du Pont's board chairman, stated the du Pont cellophane policy as follows:

> . . . the purpose of reducing our price and also improving our quality was to broaden our market. . . . As a general philosophy I was always in favor of the reduction of the price as we were able to do so by the reduced costs, and I think that I consistently urged that on the management.[126]

Du Pont's policy paid off. During the years from 1924 to 1950 du Pont's cellophane earnings before taxes ranged from 18 per cent to 62.4 per cent on operating investment. They averaged 34.4 per cent.[127] Du Pont's general policy was to increase profits by lowering cost and increasing volume, but its managers did not hesitate to reverse this policy when they thought it would pay to do so. In 1947 earnings had fallen to 19.1 per cent before taxes. Not satisfied with this rate du Pont raised the average price of cellophane from 41.9 cents a pound to 46 cents. The result was an increase in earnings to a 31 per cent rate. At that time its division manager suggested that "if operative earnings of 31 per cent is [sic] considered inadequate, then an upward revision in prices will be necessary to improve the return." [128] He proposed a schedule of prices designed to yield about 40 per cent. This was put into effect in August 1948. Earnings responded quickly, yielding 35.2 per cent in 1949 and 45.3 per cent in 1950. In raising prices du Pont officials apparently were more concerned about the unfavorable publicity this might give them and the effect it might have on the case then pending before Judge Leahy than they were about the relation of cellophane prices to the prices of other wrapping materials. A du Pont division manager put it this way:

> What effect, if any, will a price increase have on our case when it is heard before the Federal Judge? I have not covered this with our Legal Department but in view of the position they took last July and August, prior to the October increase, I am inclined to think they should be brought in for a discussion on this matter.
> The Du Pont Company may get some undesirable publicity from

---

126. Transcript of Testimony 6278-79.
127. Du Pont's Operating Investment, Operating Earnings, and Net Earnings on Cellophane, 1925-1950, Table III, in Stocking and Mueller, *The Cellophane Case and the New Competition*, 45 AM. ECON. REV. 29, 59 (1955).
128. Government's Exhibit 591, p. 7539.

the press. A price increase on Cellophane could be looked upon as added fuel to the present recent spurt in the inflationary spiral and add to the present pressure for an increase in wages. This question is currently a live one at several of our cellophane plants. Probably it would be in order to discuss this with Mr. Brayman.[129]

Only after weighing such factors as these did du Pont officials decide on the price increase.

That du Pont's earnings on cellophane reflected monopoly power is indicated not only by their absolute heights but by comparison with its earnings on its rayon investment. There is a basic similarity between these two products and, up to a certain point, between the ways in which they were developed. Both are derived from the same basic raw material. Both were radical innovations. Du Pont obtained its production rights to both from French producers; both were produced under the same business management and presumably with common business aims; both products have reasonably close substitutes; both experienced a phenomenal increase in production and consumption; both were characterized by rapidly developing technology and a rapid decline in price; and both yielded a high rate of return in their early years, du Pont's earnings on its rayon investment ranging from a high of 38.9 per cent to a low of 15.2 per cent during the period 1922-1929.[130] At the outset both were produced under conditions of monopoly or near monopoly. Here the similarity ends. Du Pont was the sole producer of cellophane until 1930 and thereafter du Pont and Sylvania were the sole producers until 1951, when a third company with du Pont's aid began production.[131] The American Viscose Corporation was the sole producer of rayon at the outset, soon followed by du Pont, but by 1930 the structure of the rayon industry had markedly changed and

129. *Id.* at 7540. Mr. Brayman was the director of du Pont's public relations department.

130. Federal Trade Commission, Investments, Profits, and Rates of Return for Selected Industries (a special report prepared for the Temporary National Economic Committee, 76th Cong., 3d Sess.), 1941, pp. 17988, 17990, 17998. Comparable data on total rayon investment and earnings are not available after 1938. The district court found that du Pont's "price policy for rayon was the same as for cellophane." 118 F. Supp. at 86.

131. In June 1951 Olin Industries, Inc. (in 1954 this company merged with Mathieson Chemical Industries, Inc. to become Olin Mathieson Chemical Corp.) began the production of cellophane at Pisgah Forest, North Carolina. Testimony of Fred Olsen, Olin vice president, Transcript of Testimony 6829. In 1948 du Pont began making its technology available to Olin. Report on "the evidence in support of entry by Olin Industries into the Cellophane business, based on the purchase of patent license 'know-how' from du Pont," Dec. 15, 1948, Government's Exhibit 566, p. 7575.

du Pont was meeting the rivalry of eighteen producers.[132]   This intensification of competition resulted in a sharp decline in the rate of earnings. Du Pont operated its rayon division at a loss in 1930 and averaged only 7.5 per cent in the period from 1930 to 1938.[133]   During this same period the rate of return on cellophane ranged from 18 to 39.9 per cent. [134]

The Strategy of a Monopolist

Not only did its rate of cellophane earnings reflect monopoly power, but du Pont acted with respect to Sylvania as though it believed it had a valuable monopoly that it wanted to protect.[135]   It originally obtained the exclusive right to make and sell cellophane in the American market under patents and with technical knowledge from La Cellophane, Société Anonyme, a French affiliate of the Comptoir des Textiles Artificiels, a French corporation from which it had previously obtained similar rights for rayon manufacture. After entering the agreement with du Pont for the exploitation of the American market La Cellophane made a similar agreement with Kalle & Company for the exploitation of the German market—and ultimately the markets of Austria, Hungary, Czechoslovakia, Yugoslavia, Poland, Russia, Romania, China, Denmark, Sweden, Norway, and Finland[136]—and licensed British Cellophane, Ltd. for the exploitation of British markets. Du Pont thereafter entered into patent exchange agreements with Kalle and British Cellophane which had the practical effect of dividing world markets for exclusive exploitation by the several companies. Du Pont representatives attended an international cartel conference at Paris in February 1930 as guests and observers, and although they did not sign the official cartel agreement, the agreement recognized the North American market as belonging to du Pont and Sylvania.[137]   When the Belgian company Société Industrielle de la Cellulose (SIDAC), which had obtained La Cellophane's trade secrets through two former employees of La Cellophane, began to

---

132. MARKHAM, COMPETITION IN THE RAYON INDUSTRY 47 (1952).

133. Federal Trade Commission, *op. cit. supra* note 130, *ibid*.

134. Stocking and Mueller, *supra* note 127, *ibid*.

135. For a more detailed discussion of the significance of strategy to monopoly see *id*. at 31-44. The statements of fact which follow in the text are based on the district court's findings unless otherwise documented.

136. Letter of Oct. 30, 1929 from C. M. Albright, Du Pont Cellophane vice president, to the company's Buffalo Office, Government's Exhibit 1091, p. 1195.

137. "Official report" of February 11-12, 1930 international cellophone cartel agreement, Paris, Government's Exhibit 1414, pp. 1841-44.

export cellophane to the American market, du Pont sought and obtained additional tariff protection through a reclassification of cellophane. This raised the duty from 25 per cent to 60 per cent ad valorem, a rate high enough to prevent price cutting by importers.[138] A reduction of cellophane prices as du Pont achieved quantity production and lower costs, together with a 45 per cent ad valorem tariff in the Tariff Act of 1930, was enough to virtually eliminate foreign cellophane from the American market. In no year between 1930 and 1947 did imports amount to 1 per cent of domestic cellophane consumption.

Shut out by the tariff from the rich American market, SIDAC established an American subsidiary, Sylvania Industrial Corporation of America, for the manufacture and sale of cellophane in competition with du Pont. Du Pont inaugurated a series of negotiations with Sylvania regarding patent rights and eventually filed a patent infringement suit which was finally settled out of court.[139] The settlement involved an interchange of patent rights and a limitation of Sylvania's production. Sylvania agreed to restrict its production to 20 per cent of total sales of moistureproof cellophane in 1933, this percentage to be increased by 1 per cent annually until it reached 29 per cent in 1942 and the agreement to be enforced by prohibitive royalties for exceeding the amount specified. Sylvania not only geared its production to du Pont's but followed du Pont's pricing practices. Meanwhile, as a bulwark against competition from any other source, du Pont was carrying forward a vigorous program to cover by patents all alternative methods of moistureproofing cellophane.[140]

---

138. Du Pont's quarterly competitive report, second quarter 1929, Government's Exhibit 432, p. 5690.

139. Du Pont's patent attorney gave his impressions of Sylvania's reasons for settling the infringement suit as follows: "During the conference Mr. Menken [Sylvania's general counsel] stated that in his opinion the case should be settled. He said that they were very fearful of what the result would be to their company in the event they succeeded in having the claims of the patents which are involved in the litigation held invalid. He seemed to realize the old adage that the defendant can never win. . . . If the Du Pont Cellophane Company succeeds and the patents are held to be infringed, Sylvania Industrial Corporation will be under injunction and will be obliged to stop manufacturing moistureproof wrapping tissue. On the other hand, if they succeed in having the broad claims of the patents held invalid they will throw the art open, as far as the broad claims are concerned, to anyone and therefore will have additional competition. Sylvania . . . has plenty of ready cash but are [*sic*] hesitant about enlarging their plant facilities pending the litigation since, if successful, they will only invite further competition." Letter dated Aug. 4, 1932, Government's Exhibit 2811, pp. 6073-74.

140. President Yerkes of Du Pont Cellophane Co. in reporting on the success of this project in 1934 said: "This work was undertaken as a defensive program in connection

Du Pont by these several moves clearly recognized cellophane as a unique product which it was determined to produce on a monopoly basis. Du Pont's own executives from time to time specifically acknowledged the ineffectiveness of the competition of rival products. Its Development Department concluded as early as 1923 that glassine, sheet gelatin, and tin foil, at that time cellophane's closest rival products, offered no serious competition because of price and quality differences. Du Pont's 1948 market analysis report evaluated the rival films that had since come on the market in these words:

> The principal markets for non-viscose films have been competitive with Cellophane only to a very minor degree up to this time. Some are used very little or not at all in the packaging field—others are employed principally for specialty uses where Cellophane is not well adapted—none have been successfully introduced into any of Cellophane's main markets due to their inherent shortcomings.[141]

While du Pont was negotiating with Olin Industries, Inc., prior to Olin's becoming the third domestic cellophane producer,[142] Olin Industries reported, "According to du Pont, Cellophane is considered the only all purpose film, and any product to be *truly competitive* with Cellophane must have the following attributes: (1) low cost, (2) transparency, (3) operate with a high efficiency on mechanical equipment, (4) print well both as to speed and appearance." [143] Olin concluded:

> There are no films currently marketed which are potentially competitive to any substantial degree in Cellophane's major markets when measured by the above attributes necessary for wide usage. Other transparent films will find their place for those low volume uses which

with protecting broadly by patents the field of moistureproofing agents other than waxes which was the only class of material disclosed in our original Cellophane moistureproofing patents.

"The investigations on this subject did, in fact, lead to the discovery of a number of classes of materials which could serve equally well for moistureproofing agents. . . . Each of these classes has been made the subject of a patent. . . . Altogether, 13 patent applications are being written as a result of the work done under this project, all in view of strengthening our Moistureproof Cellophane patent situation." Dec. 1933 report to Du Pont Cellophane's board of directors, Jan. 22, 1934, Government's Exhibit 488, p. 6478.

141. Government's Exhibit 595, p. 1147.
142. See note 131 *supra*.
143. Government's Exhibit 566, p. 7575.

can absorb the additional cost of the film and which necessitate certain physical properties not possessed by Cellophane.[144]

Significance of the Cellophane Case

Judging by the structure of the cellophane industry between 1923 and 1951 (with only two producers and with Sylvania's output and pricing policy geared to du Pont's), by the strategy du Pont followed in protecting itself against the competition of rival producers, and by the industry's performance in terms of profit margins, I conclude that cellophane has been sold in American markets under the protection of private monopoly. The basic issue in the *Cellophane* case is clear. I have stated it elsewhere as follows:

> The basic issue in the *Cellophane* case really boils down to this: Would freedom of entry have brought in a larger number of cellophane producers and ultimately lower prices and earnings than have prevailed? I believe it would have. Moreover, if the rivalry of substitute packaging materials, particularly glassine and waxed paper, had in fact forced competitive pricing on du Pont, as the court concluded, du Pont should have been indifferent to the entry of rival cellophane producers. Competition from either cellophane or waxed paper would have resulted in precisely the same cost-price ratios in selling cellophane. As judged by structure, conduct, and performance, Judge Leahy erred in giving a negative answer to his first question: Does du Pont have a monopoly in making and selling cellophane?[145]

And the Supreme Court compounded Judge Leahy's error. If the Supreme Court's conception of cross-elasticity of demand should apply in future antitrust causes, the dissenters are probably right in declaring that the Court has emasculated section 2 of the Sherman Act. If cellophane is merely a flexible wrapping material, the courts might as readily conclude that airlines, railways, bus lines, and river steamers are merely transportation facilities; that aluminum, copper, brass, and steel are merely metals; and that cotton rugs, linen rugs, nylon rugs, braided rugs, linoleum, and similar substitutes are merely floor coverings. Monopolization of one such item need not violate the Sherman Act. To deny the existence of monopoly the courts need only ascertain that

---

144. *Ibid.*

145. Stocking, *Economic Tests of Monopoly and the Concept of the Relevant Market,* *Illinois State Bar Ass'n Antitrust Section Symposium,* Nov. 29, 1956, 2 ANTITRUST BULLETIN 479, 492-93 (1957).

people choose among products serving similar functions in trying to get their money's worth.

Technological progress has increased the variety of products which will serve a particular need. Customers nearly always have a choice between rival products with different specific qualities and different prices. This is the interindustry competition which some economists and laymen think is a substitute for the competition of rival sellers selling the same product. Many believe it makes the contemporary economy workably competitive regardless of a given industry's structure. "Interindustry competition" is a concept by which "reasonable" men may judge a situation without meticulous attention to the relevant economic logic. It enables judges as well as economists to make peace with their environment. Justice Frankfurter in a concurring opinion in the *Cellophane* case put it this way:

> . . . the so-called issues of fact and law that call for adjudication in this legal territory are united, and intrinsically so, with factors that entail social and economic judgment. Any consideration of 'monopoly' under the Sherman law can hardly escape judgment, even if only implied, on social and economic issues.[146]

THE DU PONT-GENERAL MOTORS CASE IN THE DISTRICT COURT

On June 30, 1949, the Antitrust Division of the Department of Justice filed a complaint against du Pont Company and the General Motors Company, alleging that since 1915 these companies had engaged in a combination to restrain trade in the products of the companies and to monopolize a substantial part of that trade in violation of sections 1 and 2 of the Sherman Act. The complaint also alleged violation of section 7 of the Clayton Act. The primary issue in the case was whether the du Pont Company through stock acquisitions had obtained control of General Motors, and if so whether it exercised that control to insure it a protected market for such of its products as were necessary to the business of General Motors and to give it control over the chemical products and processes that General Motors might develop. The district court in finding for the defendants did not rely specifically on the doctrine of workable competition. In a hundred-page decision[147]

146. United States v. E. I. du Pont de Nemours & Co., 351 U.S. 377, 414 (1956).

147. United States v. E. I. du Pont de Nemours and Co., 126 F. Supp. 235 (N.D. Ill. 1954), *rev'd*, 353 U.S. 586 (1957).

Judge LaBuy did not even mention the concept nor did he cite a single legal precedent for his decision. He concluded that the facts did

> not establish that du Pont has been the controlling force in the direction of General Motors affairs, or has been in a position to act as if it owned a majority of General Motors stock. The record shows consultation and conference, but not domination.[148]

Judge LaBuy may have appropriately exercised his judicial perogative in so holding, but it is fairly clear that a district court with different preconceptions sitting in an environment less friendly to big business might just as readily have found that du Pont controlled General Motors.

The more relevant facts on this issue may be briefly stated. Pierre S. du Pont, president of the du Pont Company, and Irenee du Pont as individuals had bought substantial amounts of stock in the General Motors Corporation as early as 1915. In December 1917 the du Pont executive and finance committees authorized the du Pont Company to purchase $25,000,000 of General Motors common stock. John J. Raskob, treasurer of the du Pont Company, in urging the company to make this purchase, said:

> With Mr. Durant we will have joint control of the companies.
>
> . . . .
>
> Perhaps it is not made clear that the directorates of the motor companies will be chosen by Du Pont and Durant. Mr. Durant should be continued as President of the Company. Mr. P. S. du Pont will be continued as Chairman of the Board, the Finance Committee will be ours and we will have such representation on the Executive Committee as we desire. . . .[149]

By 1921 the du Pont Company had increased its investment in General Motors to $79,500,000, representing 38 per cent of the company's outstanding stock. About this transaction Raskob stated, "This gave the du Pont Company approximately 38% of the total common stock of the General Motors Corporation which is practical control and made it necessary to assume complete responsibility for the management." [150]

---

148. *Id.* at 250-51.

149. Government's Trial Exhibit (hereinafter GTX) 124, Record (hereinafter R.) 664, 5230, United States v. E. I. du Pont de Nemours & Co., 353 U.S. 586 (1957). See also the district court's opinion, 126 F. Supp. at 241-42.

150. GTX 235, p. 3, R. 483, 3496.

By 1938 du Pont had reduced its holdings to 23 per cent by a transfer of stock to the Managers Securities Company and through the Securities Company to select executives of General Motors under a stock bonus plan. Du Pont's holdings have since remained at 23 per cent. In 1947 this represented 10,000,000 shares, which in 1950 were split to 20,000,000 shares[151] and by 1957 had increased to 63,000,000 shares.[152] In 1947, 436,510 stockholders held the remaining shares. Of these, 92 per cent owned no more than 100 shares each and 60 per cent owned no more than 25 shares each.[153] At stockholders' meetings in the years 1928-1949 du Pont voted from 30 to over 52 per cent of the stock voted.[154] A proxy committee set up by management friendly to du Pont presumably voted much of the remainder.

The record is replete with evidence that du Pont tried to use its control to get General Motors to buy its products rather than those of its competitors, and that it was in part successful. There is an abundance of evidence indicating that du Pont tried to get a general agreement with General Motors whereby General Motors would turn over to du Pont for exploitation the chemical processes and products which it developed in its own research laboratories; and that du Pont eventually obtained a monopoly in the manufacture of tetraethyl lead, first discovered in the laboratories of General Motors, and a monopoly in the exploitation of freon (an organic fluorine compound) and its derivatives, likewise a General Motors discovery.[155]

Counsel for defendants contended that these several transactions were arm's length transactions involving no coercion, and the district court agreed. But a different court with different preconceptions might just as readily have concluded, as an earlier court in a different case had done, that "domination may spring as readily from subtle and unexercised power as from arbitrary imposition of command." [156]

CONCLUSIONS

This study has developed the thesis that cultural environment——the

---

151. 126 F. Supp. at 244.

152. Wall Street Journal, June 4, 1957, p. 2, col. 2. The *Journal* placed the market value of the stock at $2.5 billion.

153. 126 F. Supp. at 244.

154. GTX 1307, R. 664, 5230.

155. For a detailed analysis of the evidence supporting this view of the case see Stocking, *The du Pont-General Motors Case and the Sherman Act*, 44 VA. L. REV. 1 (1958).

156. North American Co. v. SEC, 327 U.S. 686, 693 (1946).

economic and social milieu——determines the attitudes of the courts in antitrust decisions; and that economists who, like judges, have responded to the same influences, have afforded in the concept of workable competition a logical basis for a lax administration of the Sherman Act. The Supreme Court's reversal of the district court in the *du Pont-General Motors* case[157] would seem to cast doubt on this thesis. Always there are some judges, doughty individualists, who do not drift with the current. That fact might offer a sufficient explanation for the Supreme Court's having overruled the district court. Justices Brennan, Black, and Douglas and Chief Justice Warren constituted the majority in this case. Justices Black and Douglas have made clear in many decisions their belief that a concentration of economic power constitutes a threat to the American way of life. Justice Brennan and Chief Justice Warren appear to be like-minded. Some lawyers have expressed the opinion that had Justices Clark, Whittaker, and Harlan participated in the *du Pont-General Motors* case the decision might have been five to four in favor of the defendants.[158] This is, of course, conjecture, though perhaps reasonable conjecture.

But the majority of the Court in reversing Judge LaBuy may not have been merely manifesting their own predilections. The flow of environmental factors has been generally in one direction, but always there have been countercurrents of varying force. Although the war-engendered prosperity gave the leaders of industry a new confidence in big business and its contribution to the social welfare ("What is good for the country is good for General Motors and vice versa"),[159] postwar developments have made the going tough for many small and moderate-size firms. They have frequently found it expedient to sell out to their rivals, and many that have not done so have fallen by the wayside. The survival of little business in recent years has become a national concern. It has prompted direct federal aid to little business and has resulted in a modification of section 7 of the Clayton Act[160] designed to stay the forces of industrial concentration. It may be that the judges who constituted the Supreme Court majority in the *du Pont-General Motors* case reflected not merely their own predilections but a countercurrent in the flow of social forces.

---

157. United States v. E. I. du Pont de Nemours & Co., 353 U.S. 586 (1957).

158. Rogers, *U. S. v. du Pont—A Judicial Revision of Section 7*, 2 ANTITRUST BULLETIN 577, 581 (1957).

159. Former Secretary of Defense Charles E. Wilson at his final news conference before his resignation, New York Times, Oct. 3, 1957, p. 14, col. 4.

160. 15 U.S.C § 18 (1952).

The Roots of Decline: Business-Government Relations in the American Steel Industry, 1945–1960

PAUL A. TIFFANY

Recent problems in the performance of the American steel industry have prompted a number of calls for an "industrial policy" for this sector. Before any such programs of public intervention can be considered, however, it would behoove public policymakers to examine why the industry fell into its present state of decline. This paper, an abstract of a longer study, analyzes the relations of business and government in American steel from 1945 to 1960, and concludes that public policies had as much to do with subsequent industry decline as did other factors previously delineated by scholars.

THE American steel industry (the larger integrated steel firms) today suffers from serious problems. Growth has lagged, imports have risen, and profits have declined. As one consequence, numerous sources have called for formulation of a "national industrial policy" to arrest these trends. Presumably some form of public intervention would attend to this. Yet before such action can be considered, let alone undertaken, it seems prudent to attempt to understand why the industry entered into its present state of decline. Although several theories have been advanced to explain steel's demise (most of which focus on managerial inadequacies), relatively little attention has been paid to the role of the federal government in abetting this development.[1] The present paper will examine briefly the interaction of government and the steel industry in the years 1945–1960, and will advance the thesis that certain public policies adopted during this period contributed as much to the subsequent decline of the industry as did factors ascribed by previous researchers. As such, it will be concluded that an industrial policy for steel is an ahistorical rationalization that would probably fail, given the idiosyncratic nature of public policymaking in America.

Journal of Economic History, Vol. XLIV, No. 2 (June 1984). © The Economic History Association. All rights reserved. ISSN 0022–0507.

The author is an Assistant Professor in the Department of Management, The Wharton School, University of Pennsylvania, Philadelphia, Pennsylvania 19104.

[1] See W. Adams and J. B. Dirlam, "Big Steel, Invention, and Innovation," *Quarterly Journal of Economics*, 80 (1966), 167–89; G. C. Means, *Pricing Power and the Public Interest* (New York, 1962); Lloyd Ulman, "The Union and Wages in Basic Steel: A Comment," *American Economic Review*, 48 (1958), 408–26; and R. B. Mancke, "The American Iron Ore and Steel Industries: Two Essays" (unpublished doctoral dissertation, Massachusetts Institute of Technology, 1968).

TRUMAN AND THE STEEL CAPACITY DEBATE

The conclusion of World War II found domestic steelmakers in a quandary. War–induced demand had given them their first continuous period of profits since 1929, but most industry leaders feared an imminent return to Depression–era levels of output.[2] The Truman Administration, however, pushed for capacity expansion in steel; without it, public officials feared, the economy would not be able to sustain the recovery.[3] In the international arena, the questionable future of European steel production posed many uncertainties for global trade and its potential effects on American markets. Indeed, the problems of domestic steel capacity and international steel trade were tightly linked. Yet the failure of public policymakers to appreciate fully these linkages, combined with traditional industry reluctance to develop closer state ties, would lead to a series of events in capacity expansion that would eventually prove debilitating for domestic producers.

The problems facing the industry must also be observed against the background of a rapidly changing international role for America. The end of World War II removed any doubts about U.S. dominance in the free world. With the initiation and escalation of Cold War tensions, the nation's leaders were moved fundamentally to reconstruct and reshape American foreign policy to fit with its new global responsibilities. This would not be an easy task, especially in view of traditions of political isolationism and economic protectionism that long had characterized national interests. Yet perhaps surprisingly, America turned to foreign aid and liberalized free trade to support its ideological friends (or to sway wavering nations into its ideological camp). Consequently, the government generally ignored pleas for domestic assistance from those commercial sectors affected by the nation's emerging post-war foreign policies; leaders from both political parties proved reluctant to jeopardize larger national objectives for the sake of internal industrial problems, which usually were perceived to be only of short–term duration. Also, since steel was often the single most important sector in the economic development plans of nearly all nations that received U.S. foreign aid, domestic American steel producers often found their own needs subordinated to these broader political considerations.

Capacity expansion was the issue that initially divided steel industry

---

[2] See Paul A. Tiffany, "The Roots of Decline: Business–Government Interaction in the American Steel Industry, 1945–1960" (unpublished doctoral dissertation, University of California, Berkeley, 1983), pp. 79–118.

[3] See U.S. Senate, Subcommittee on Surplus Property of the Committee on Military Affairs and Industrial Reorganization Subcommittee of the Special Committee on Postwar Economic Policy and Planning, 79th Congress, 1st Session, Joint Hearings, *War Plants Disposal—Iron and Steel Plants* (Washington, D.C., 1946).

leaders from public policymakers. As early as 1943, government planners had begun to turn their attention to "reconversion" problems; a basic objective, they concluded, was implementation of a "full employment economy" to prevent repetition of the mass unemployment of the 1930s.[4] Since steel was a basic commodity necessary to economic growth—and since it was presumed to exert both bottleneck and leverage effects over the economy—public planners called for an expansion of at least 10 million tons of capacity by 1950 to meet expected demand (see Table 1). Industry strategists, however, were dubious. True, they might have agreed that temporary pent–up demand would follow the war's end, but such "abnormal" conditions did not justify the massive investment called for by government.

Yet consistent shortages in the availability of steel soon produced political reaction. Smaller users in particular felt the effects of inadequate supply, and by 1947 their frequent complaints to a receptive Congress resulted in formation of a Senate committee to study the problem.[5] The committee began two years of hearings and analysis that soon elevated the steel shortage—and industry reluctance to expand—to front page headlines. Extrapolating from per–capita production in 1911–1940, industry spokesmen insisted before Congress that steel ingot demand would be only 76.4 million tons by 1950, and 78.5 million tons by 1955 (compared to output of 66.6 million tons in 1946).[6] Government planners, however, made a different forecast. Utilizing projections necessary to sustain full employment in the post–1945 years, it was stated that "total production would need to be 100,000,000 tons or more. . . ."[7] Although the capacity debate generated widespread public controversy, it only masked more fundamental questions: How would domestic expansion be affected by emerging plans to rebuild European mills, and how would the expansion be financed? Neither of these questions received much public attention, and on both counts the government offered little help to the industry.

Steelmakers had legitimate reasons to consider plans for foreign reconstruction. Prior to World War II, the International Steel Cartel coordinated output and prices for most of the world's suppliers (includ-

[4] See Oral History Interview with Louis H. Bean, p. 47, in Oral History Files, Harry S. Truman Presidential Library, Independence, Missouri.

[5] See U.S. Senate, Special Committee to Study Problems of American Small Business, 80th Congress, 1st Session, Hearings, *Problems of American Small Business*, 4 vols. (Washington, D.C., 1947), pp. 587–701.

[6] Ibid., pp. 988–94. Also see Wilfred Sykes, "The Future of the Steel Industry," in American Iron and Steel Institute, *1947 Yearbook* (New York, 1947), pp. 68–83. Sykes, president of Inland Steel Corporation, was the industry's principal spokesman before the Senate committee, and in his AISI paper he developed his arguments more fully regarding steel consumption.

[7] Drawn from Louis Bean's testimony before the Senators; see U.S. Senate, *Problems of American Small Business*, p. 1001.

TABLE 1
STEEL CAPACITY AND PRODUCTION, 1940–1960

Year	Net Capacity[a] (thousand net tons)	Total Production[a] (thousand net tons)	Capacity Utilization (percent)
1940	81,619	66,983	82.1
1941	85,158	82,839	97.3
1942	88,887	86,032	96.8
1943	90,589	88,837	98.1
1944	93,854	89,642	95.5
1945	95,505	79,702	83.5
1946	91,891	66,603	72.5
1947	91,241	84,894	93.0
1948	94,233	88,640	94.1
1949	96,121	77,978	81.1
1950	99,983	96,836	96.9
1951	104,230	105,200	100.9
1952	108,588	93,168	85.8
1953	117,547	111,610	94.9
1954	124,330	88,312	71.0
1955	125,828	117,036	93.0
1956	128,363	115,216	89.9
1957	133,459	112,715	84.5
1958	140,743	85,255	60.6
1959	147,634	93,446	63.3
1960	148,571	99,282	66.8

[a] Ingots and steel for castings.
Source: American Iron and Steel Institute, *Annual Statistical Report* (various years).

ing steel imported into and exported out of the United States).[8] The group's demise in 1939, however, cast doubts over future relations in this internationally traded commodity. If both domestic and foreign producers rebuilt independently in the late 1940s, would there be sufficient demand to satisfy everyone? If not, would American producers again be vulnerable to imports—and European dumping, a problem for local steelmakers throughout the past forty years? More importantly, would such action threaten the industry's recent return to financial respectability after so many years of distress? These were questions of highest priority to the American firms, and they needed further clarification before capacity expansion could be undertaken.

Financing of new capacity was also of major concern to producers. Since new steel plant construction costs generally were estimated at $250 per ton, approximately $2.5 billion would be required to build an additional 10 million tons capacity (compared to total industry equity of $3.9 billion in 1947 when some 91 million tons of capacity were in place). The industry claimed it could not afford to undertake a new round of

[8] See E. Hexner, "American Participation in the International Steel Cartel," *Southern Economic Journal*, 8 (1941), 54–79, and R. Lauderbaugh, "Business, Labor, and Foreign Policy: U.S. Steel, the International Steel Cartel, and Recognition of the Steel Workers Organizing Committee," *Politics and Society*, 6 (1979), 433–57.

capacity investment, given prevailing steel prices, while the Truman Administration insisted that current industry profits were sufficient to finance the recommended additions (see Table 2 for performance data).[9] Through at least the late 1940s steel appears to have been underpriced (see Table 3), and as a result, producers conceivably could have encountered difficulties in financing expansion. From 1947 to 1952 (the Truman years), after–tax profits per ton of steel shipped averaged only $8.55; assuming a per–ton investment cost of $250 and a capacity utilization rate of 92 percent, the after–tax ROI for new capacity would have averaged only 3.1 percent.[10] Yet whenever the industry attempted to raise prices to generate additional investment funds, both the administration and Congress objected loudly, usually forcing restraint by the producers.[11] If steel output were as important to national economic growth as government officials claimed and capital markets would not independently support such expansion, then perhaps some form of public assistance was justified. Yet up until 1950 (discounting occasional threats to nationalize the mills[12]), the administration consistently opposed any special steel benefit programs, declaring that the firms should be able to undertake the task privately.

Meanwhile, foreign governments began to work closely and cooperatively with their own steel firms to plan for post–war reconstruction. In Europe, England, Japan, and the developing nations, business–government cooperation in steel was the rule not the exception.[13] Moreover, significant assistance toward this end also came from America: between 1945 and 1960, direct American aid to foreign steelmakers would total nearly $1.5 billion and indirect assistance added many millions more. "We are industrializing the whole world," complained the president of Bethlehem Steel in 1949, "and deindustrializing the United States."[14]

[9] For examples of the Administration position, see Council of Economic Advisers, "Interagency Report on Steel and Essential Steelmaking Materials" (CEA, March 15, 1949), mimeo, in Council of Economic Advisers Papers, Box 22, Steel Folder, Dwight D. Eisenhower Presidential Library, Abilene, Kansas.

[10] Data used in these calculations are drawn from American Iron and Steel Institute, *Annual Statistical Report* (New York, various years).

[11] See, for example, T. E. Mullaney, "US Steel's Prices Increased $4 a Ton; An Inquiry Is Slated," *New York Times* (December 16, 1949), p. 1, and U.S. Congress, Joint Committee on the Economic Report, 81st Congress, 2nd Session, Hearings, *December 1949 Steel Price Increases* (Washington, D.C., 1950). This was hardly an isolated example; see Tiffany, "Roots of Decline," pp. 119–65.

[12] Perhaps the most noteworthy occasion on which this occurred was President Truman's 1949 State of the Union address, when he said that "if action by private industry fails to meet our needs" in steel production, he would authorize construction of federally owned mills. See *Congressional Record*, Vol. 95, Pt. 1, 81st Congress, 1st Session (January 5, 1949), p. 75.

[13] See Tiffany, "Roots of Decline," pp. 166–209.

[14] Data on the extent of U.S. aid to foreign steelmakers can be found in U.S. Senate, Committee on Finance, 90th Congress, 1st Session, *Steel Exports* (Washington, D.C., 1967), 31–62, 299–304. Aid to foreign steel represented 1.9 percent of total U.S. foreign aid over this span. For the comment by Bethlehem's president, see "Grace Calls Subsidy of Shipping Vital," *New York Times* (October 28, 1949), p. 47.

America's strained steel–state relations temporarily improved with the onset of war in Korea in the summer of 1950. Congress hastily authorized a program of investment support for defense–related industries, and by the end of January 1951 some 15.7 million tons of new steel capacity had been authorized, with $1.4 billion in funding eligible for accelerated depreciation benefits.[15] This appeared to ease the supply issue for the time being. Moreover, industrywide price hikes announced in December 1950 went unchallenged by the government for the first time in the post–war era. This harmony was not to last long. Labor relations in the industry, historically poor, reached a new impasse over contract negotiations early in 1952. With a strike imminent, and with the military counseling that no break in steel output be allowed, Truman seized the mills in April. This provoked one of the more important Constitutional crises of the century, which ultimately resulted in a profound defeat for the President when the producers sued for and won before the Supreme Court a reversal of his action.[16] As Truman's time in office limped to an end, relations between the steelmakers and government seemed as unsettled as ever. Although foreign steel production improved over these years, the U.S. experience was characterized by suspicion and conflict at nearly every turn.

EISENHOWER, THE STEELMAKERS, AND THE ROOTS OF INDUSTRIAL DECLINE

The election of the Eisenhower Administration late in 1952 appeared to bode well for the steel industry. With a "friendly" administration now sitting in Washington, the time appeared ripe for a basic reformulation of industry strategy that would reconstruct domestic governmental relations and reassert American international hegemony in the steel trade. Unfortunately for both the producers and the nation, that strategy would be found wanting. Not only would it fail to reverse the long–term trend of weakening industrial performance, but after a few years it actually hastened the plunge into decline. And perhaps most surprisingly, a major contributor to this eventual outcome would be the very administration that the producers had so enthusiastically welcomed into office.

Through either the commission or omission of various public policies in both the domestic arena and abroad, the new Republican president often displayed an insensitivity to the long–term structural needs of the

---

[15] See "Industry Gets 5–Year Write–Offs," *Iron Age*, 166 (October 19, 1950), 95; "Wilson Puts the Brakes on Granting Certificates of Necessity for Expansion of Steel Industry," *Iron Age*, 167 (March 8, 1951), 110–11; and U.S. Department of Commerce, National Production Authority, Historical Reports on Defense Production, Report No. 28, *Iron and Steel* (Washington, D.C., 1953).

[16] See M. Marcus, *Truman and the Steel Seizure Case* (New York, 1977).

American economy. Even though the steelmakers several times sought to institutionalize a more favorable regime of business-government relations for their affairs, these efforts were rebuffed by the administration. With Washington continuing to pursue a global buildup of defenses against Communist expansionism, public policymakers deemed aid and assistance to foreign steelmakers a higher priority than helping domestic producers. For the latter, government officials declared, the traditional forces of a free enterprise economy unencumbered by public intervention should be enough to ensure success.

After 1952, industry strategists at first focused on an increase in prices, designed to improve cash flows that could be channelled into plant modernization. In addition, cost reductions would be pursued where possible—or in the case of labor costs, consistently accounting for 35 to 40 percent of total industry costs, increases would be moderated. But if these labor cost increases could not be held in check, the strategy called for passing them on to consumers in the form of higher prices. Under the more tolerant economic regime of a Republican administration, it was believed, such a plan would meet little governmental resistance. In general, this premise proved correct, at least in the first term of Eisenhower's presidency. From 1953 to 1956, the index of finished steel prices rose 18.4 percent, whereas the national WPI was up only 3.8 percent (see Table 3). Profits improved as well, allowing for a significant increase in plant modernization and expansion projects (see Table 2).

The fundamental basis for this modernization strategy was the conviction of industry leaders that foreign steel producers, especially those in Europe, were making significant strides in their own postwar growth plans, and that these firms might eventually achieve comparative advantage over the domestic American industry if the latter did not respond forcefully to the challenge.[17] These fears were exacerbated in May 1950 when the French foreign minister shocked the world by announcing a plan to integrate the major Continental producers' coal and steel operations (and by early 1952 these nations were cooperating in a program to fix export prices and allocate export market shares).[18]

To alleviate the potential consequences of this threat, as well as steel rebuilding efforts in other parts of the globe, domestic producers called upon the U.S. administration to develop a revised foreign policy that would—while still addressing the political realities of the postwar world—accommodate the particular needs of domestic industry. The American Iron and Steel Institute, steel's trade association, stated that "it is possible to create new instruments that will permit us to proceed

---

[17] Tiffany, "Roots of Decline," pp. 259–312.

[18] See W. Diebold, Jr., *The Schuman Plan* (New York, 1959), and M. J. Rosen, "The Brussels Entente: Export Combination in the World Steel Market," *University of Pennsylvania Law Review*, 106 (1958), 1079–1116.

TABLE 2

AMERICAN STEEL INDUSTRY FINANCIAL DATA, 1945–1960

(millions)

Year	Revenue	Before-Tax Earnings	After-Tax Earnings	Divi-dends	Depre-ciation	Retained Earnings	New[a] In-vestment	Long–Term Debt	Stockholder Equity	D/E Ratio
1945	$5,921	$303	$184	$138	$339	$46	$115	$485	$3,620	13.4%
1946	4,812	396	265	147	169	117	365	544	3,712	14.7
1947	6,705	694	412	184	239	228	554	605	3,927	15.4
1948	8,119	929	540	205	302	335	642	649	4,566	14.2
1949	7,436	910	533	222	278	306	483	681	4,885	13.9
1950	9,535	1,544	767	312	327	455	505	763	5,458	14.0
1951	11,845	1,961	682	312	374	371	1,051	1,030	6,038	17.1
1952	10,858	1,024	541	316	450	225	1,298	1,447	6,373	22.7
1953	13,156	1,732	735	324	614	411	988	1,327	6,781	19.6
1954	10,593	1,230	637	343	670	294	609	1,486	7,140	20.8
1955	14,049	2,204	1,099	436	737	662	714	1,547	7,920	19.5
1956	15,272	2,159	1,113	508	748	606	1,311	1,568	8,665	18.1
1957	15,592	2,213	1,132	566	766	566	1,723	1,802	9,466	19.0
1958	12,551	1,523	788	540	673	247	1,137	2,145	9,898	21.7
1959	14,233	1,637	831	553	665	277	934	2,303	10,249	22.5
1960	14,221	1,583	811	564	692	240	1,505	2,488	10,545	23.6

[a] New Investment = new investment in plant and equipment.

Source: American Iron and Steel Institute, *Annual Statistical Report* (Washington, D.C., various years).

TABLE 3
STEEL PRICES, WHOLESALE PRICES, AND CONSUMER PRICES (1940–1960)
(Indexes: 1940 = 100)

Year	Basic Steel Prices	WPI[a] (All Commodities)	WPI[a] (All But Farm & Food Commodities)	CPI[b] (All Items)	CPI[b] (All Items But Food)
1940	100.0	100.0	100.0	100.0	100.0
1941	100.4	111.2	107.2	105.0	102.9
1942	100.6	125.6	115.0	116.4	110.1
1943	100.7	131.1	116.7	123.5	113.1
1944	100.7	132.3	118.5	125.5	117.4
1945	103.1	134.6	120.0	128.4	120.2
1946	112.1	154.0	131.8	139.2	125.4
1947	131.4	188.6	160.4	159.4	137.0
1948	150.0	204.3	174.1	171.6	146.8
1949	162.6	194.1	170.5	169.9	148.4
1950	171.2	201.8	176.8	171.6	150.1
1951	184.6	224.7	195.1	185.3	159.7
1952	188.6	218.4	190.6	189.5	163.5
1953	203.6	215.5	191.9	191.0	166.7
1954	212.7	215.9	192.8	191.7	167.7
1955	222.9	216.6	197.0	191.2	168.2
1956	241.4	223.7	205.7	194.0	171.2
1957	264.6	230.1	211.4	200.7	176.9
1958	273.8	233.3	212.1	206.2	180.8
1959	278.4	233.9	215.8	208.0	184.3
1960	278.0	234.1	216.0	211.2	187.3

[a] Wholesale price index.
[b] Consumer price index.
Source: Bureau of Labor Statistics (reproduced in U.S. Congress, Joint Economic Committee, 88th Congress, 1st Session, Hearings, *Steel Prices, Unit Costs, Profits, and Foreign Competition* (Washington, D.C., 1963), p. 123.

in the direction of developing a coordinated foreign economic policy which will have sufficient scope, flexibility and continuity of action to serve the best interests of the country.''[19] Noting the rapid development of steel interests abroad, the Institute went on to promote the reorganization of American international trade relations under a new ''Foreign Trade Commission,'' thus institutionalizing the currently fragmented responsibilities in a single agency that could formulate, coordinate, and implement national trade policies.

On the domestic front, top steel company leaders worked with the Commerce Department to draft a plan to improve relations with the government. An ''Iron and Steel Council'' was proposed, providing a high level public–private forum to coordinate steel industry activities

[19] American Iron and Steel Institute, ''Statement of the American Iron and Steel Institute before the Commission on Foreign Economic Policy'' (Washington, D.C., December 2, 1953); a copy is located in CFEP: Records, 1953–1954 File, Box 19, Hearings–Presentations, AISI Folder, Eisenhower Presidential Library.

affecting the national interest. These would include issues in production, marketing, distribution, capacity, and defense mobilization, among others. Through such a mechanism, it was stated, much of the business–government hostility endemic to the industry since 1945 might be avoided.[20]

Yet the Eisenhower Administration did not react favorably to either of these recommendations. The proposal for a Foreign Trade Commission, submitted to the President's new Commission on Foreign Economic Policy, was simply filed and forgotten; the Commerce Department plan was opposed by the Justice Department on antitrust grounds.[21] As in the past, the steelmakers would be left to themselves to fashion a plan for survival. This placed domestic firms in a position that contrasted sharply with that of firms abroad whose conditions were more generally identified by strong state support for company programs.

The industry strategy for renewal through cost pass-throughs and price hikes fared no better in the long run than did plans for improved governmental ties. Labor relations between the producers and the United Steelworkers temporarily mended after 1952 when a new president was installed at the USW, but by 1955 conditions had reverted to their historical posture of divisiveness.[22] Also, in 1956 Congress began to react sharply to rising steel prices, blaming them for the general inflation that began to infect the American economy in the latter half of the decade. A long congressional investigation into "administered pricing" focused principally on the industry, and resulted in highly unfavorable publicity for the producers.[23] Finally, the basic end to which the price hike strategy was directed—that is, the modernization of plant—also ran into serious problems.

A major difficulty lay in the type of plant expansion pursued by domestic firms. The industry opted for a "rounding–out" approach, in which piecemeal facilities were added to existing mill sites. Although this approach added capacity in a relatively short time, it was usually at the cost of efficiency, since already–cluttered conditions in old mills now would be further congested. The alternative expansion choice, "greenfield" mills designed and built new from the ground up as

[20] See G. H. Baker, "Industry: Cooperates With Capitol," *Iron Age*, 171 (June 18, 1953), 93, and M. D. Reagan, "The Business and Defense Services Administration, 1953–1957," *Western Political Quarterly*, 14 (1961), 576–78.

[21] For broader comment on Eisenhower's foreign economic policies, see B. I. Kaufman, *Trade & Aid—Eisenhower's Foreign Economic Policy, 1953–1961* (Baltimore, 1982). On the Commerce Department proposal, see C. E. Egan, "Sheaffer Resigns as Commerce Aide; Reputed Astin Foe," *New York Times* (September 19, 1953), pp. 1, 6, and U.S. House, Antitrust Subcommittee, Committee on the Judiciary, 84th Congress, 1st Session, Hearings, *WOC's and Government Advisory Groups* (Washington, D.C., 1955), p. 596.

[22] See Tiffany, "Roots of Decline," 313–64.

[23] See U.S. Senate, Subcommittee on Antitrust and Monopoly, Committee on the Judiciary, 85th Congress, 1st Session, Hearings, *Administered Prices*, Parts 2, 3, and 4 (Washington, D.C., 1957). These were the "Kefauver Committee" hearings.

integrated units, generally was not favored—only two such mills were opened in the United States after 1945. Much of the foreign steel expansion, however, was through this method. The question that must be asked, of course, is why did not American firms opt for the more efficient greenfield construction during the strong growth spurt of the 1950s? The primary reason was cost. Rounding–out capacity could be obtained for approximately $80 to $100 per additional ton, whereas greenfield mills cost on the order of $300 to $400 per ton. From 1953 to 1960, after–tax profits per ton of steel shipments averaged $12.08 for the industry; assuming an investment cost of $350 per ton and a 90 percent utilization rate, returns would have averaged only 3.1 percent for greenfield mill output. On the other hand, a rounding–out investment of only $90 per ton and a 90 percent utilization rate would have yielded a 12.1 percent after–tax return.[24] Given these alternatives, the productivity benefits derived from a greenfield mill would have had to be substantial to overcome the short–term financial attractiveness of rounding–out; company decisionmakers obviously did not believe they could do so. "Rounding–out," one contemporary analyst noted,

is popular because it costs only about $100 a ton of capacity, but it is obviously no long–term solution to the production of steel. Eventually, in those [rounded–out] steel plants, something has to give.[25]

What gave, of course, was efficiency and long–term competitiveness—at just the time when many of the industry's foreign rivals were formulating plans for completely new greenfield mills utilizing the latest technology.

Again, a liberalized public policy toward steel plant subsidization might have substantially aided the interests of both the industry and the nation. In fact, steel leaders continuously petitioned the government to extend the Korean War programs of accelerated depreciation for steel plant investment, but this was to no avail. Such a course, concluded Eisenhower's Secretary of the Treasury, would be unwarranted public meddling into the workings of a free market economy.

It must also be noted here that domestic producers chose the standard open–hearth furnace technology for their expansion efforts during the 1950s, whereas foreign mills began to employ a revolutionary new "basic oxygen furnace" (BOF) technology that yielded substantial cost savings and productivity benefits. Indeed, some observers have blamed the post–1960 decline of steel primarily on this decision, citing conditions in which the larger domestic firms were able to ignore technological change stemming from alleged monopoly power in the national

---

[24] Data used in the calculations are drawn from AISI, *Annual Statistical Report*, various years.
[25] *Steel, Story of a Shortage* (1952, no author or publisher shown); a copy is located in the Vertical File, Steel Industry and Trade Section, Truman Presidential Library.

market.[26] Although U.S. firms were slow to adopt the new technology, however, what seems best to account for this phenomenon is the routine of internal decisionmaking prevailing in most steel firms. It was far easier for managers to deny the efficacy of BOF than recommend it: the process had never been tested on large–scale plants comparable to those in the United States; there were no ready sources of bulk oxygen commercially available; the process emitted unacceptable amounts of pollutants into the atmosphere; the prospect for productivity improvements through ongoing research in open–hearth oxygenation was encouraging; total BOF costs were uncertain; the rush to expand, especially for national defense purposes, favored known and reliable procedures; and so on. The combination of these factors appears to provide sufficient explanation of why BOF was not immediately adopted by most American steelmakers. Although this obviously does not excuse the firms' collective failure to innovate, it nevertheless does point to circumstances that go beyond simple monopoly power arguments. To suggest that antimonopoly remedies were the only answer to steel's problems—which most industry critics did—reveals a strikingly bare arsenal of public policies to meet critical national industrial priorities. Unfortunately, the Eisenhower Administration as well as the critics had little else to recommend.[27]

Meanwhile, the industry strategy of raising prices to fund modernization began to unravel after 1956. By that time, company planners increasingly began to fear the speed of the foreign buildup in steel, and as a consequence they stepped up efforts to mitigate labor costs in the industry. The result was a long strike by the USW in mid–1956. Yet the outcome was not favorable to the producers because behind–the–scenes intervention by the White House in this election year ultimately resulted in generous wage and benefit hikes to the steelworkers.[28] When the firms attempted to pass these new costs along to consumers, the Democrat-controlled Congress initiated an aggressive challenge to the action; this eventually worked to chill the cost pass–through practice.[29] In 1959 another strike ensued (the longest in steel history), which proved to be the symbolic breaking point in the industry's failing struggle to maintain international hegemony in the steel trade. Covert administration action again was a consequential factor in bringing about a contract settlement generally unpropitious to management.[30] For the

[26] Adams and Dirlam, "Big Steel, Invention, and Innovation."

[27] Industry arguments opposing early adoption of BOF are best summarized in D. R. Dilley and D. L. McBride, "Oxygen Steelmaking—Fact vs. Folklore," *Iron and Steel Engineer*, 44 (Oct. 1967), 131–52.

[28] See U.S. Department of Labor, *Collective Bargaining in the Basic Steel Industry* (Washington, D.C., 1961), and R. W. Nagle, "Collective Bargaining in Basic Steel and the Federal Government, 1945–1960" (unpublished doctoral dissertation, Pennsylvania State University, 1978).

[29] See Tiffany, "Roots of Decline," pp. 365–427.

[30] U.S. Department of Labor, *Collective Bargaining*, pp. 300–397.

first year in the twentieth century, America in 1959 imported more steel than it exported. This began a trend that has yet to be reversed.

CONCLUSIONS

The post–war history of business–government relations in steel appears to hold few positive lessons for the formation of an American "industrial policy." Although foreign steelmakers were able to fashion cooperative relations with their own governments resulting in the post–war reconstruction of the international steel industry along lines favorable to themselves, American producers were constantly engaged in governmental relations characterized by suspicion, doubt, and hostility. As we have noted, the eventual outcome of this scenario proved disastrous to domestic interests.

Much of the fault, of course, must be borne by the steel managers themselves. Their errors in expansion planning, neglect of technological innovation, arrogance toward labor, and abusive attitudes toward pricing were all instrumental to the problems suffered by the industry during the 1945–1960 period (and beyond). While not denying that managerial inefficiency did exist, one still must acknowledge that a number of American public policies also had critical effects on the post–war structure of the industry and its subsequent decline relative to foreign competitors. The decision of both the Truman and Eisenhower administrations to assist foreign steelmakers while denying aid to domestic producers—despite the latter's pleas for help—was bound to impinge negatively upon industry competitiveness. A fair proportion of the problems that currently plague domestic producers, I assert, have their roots in these earlier policy choices made by public officials.

Today there are frequent calls for establishment of an industrial policy at the national level to resuscitate the fortunes of the steel industry. Although legitimate arguments on both sides of this issue can be marshalled, most proposals to date generally have failed to address the complex historical framework of institutional relations that exists in this arena. Absent such a perspective, I assert, it will be difficult—if not impossible—to implement these plans. If the steel case is any guide, industrial policy may well be incompatible with American political experience.

Business Perspectives on the Full Employment Bill of 1945 and Passage of the Employment Act of 1946

Don Yalung-Mathews
Georgia State University

ABSTRACT

This paper examines the perspectives of the business community on the proposed Full Employment Bill of 1945 and the effect of the business voice in transforming the Full Employment Bill to the Employment Act of 1946. Evidence collected from Congressional hearings and business publications supports the view that business was generally opposed to the Full Employment Bill of 1945. The evidence also suggests that business interests played the most significant role in the "watering down" of the Full Employment Bill. However, the business voice was less successful in affecting the course of U.S. macroeconomic policy.

On January 22, 1945, Senator James A. Murray of Montana introduced a bill in the Senate referred to as the Full Employment Bill of 1945. Essentially, the Full Employment Bill did the following: (1) declared that full employment was a national goal for which the federal government was directly responsible, and (2) specified an apparatus through which the federal government could achieve that goal. After a year of congressional and public debate, a revised version of the bill, the Employment Act of 1946, was signed into law by President Harry S. Truman on February 20, 1946.

This episode in American economic policy has been deemed significant by economic historians for a number of reasons. To many, the Employment Act of 1946 represents a new dimension in the role of government in the American economy. Jonathan R.T. Hughes states that the Employment Act of 1946 "marked a fundamental shift in the notion of government responsibility" [Hughes 1977, p. 148]. In addition, many

331

assert that the Employment Act of 1946 is a vastly different piece of legislation than its precursor, the Full Employment Bill of 1945. Herbert Stein argues that "the failure to pass a 'Full Employment Act' is as significant as the decision to pass the "Employment Act" [Stein 1969, p. 197]. Finally, the Employment Act of 1946, more than any other legislation, has defined the focus of American macroeconomic policy.

Much insight concerning these matters can be gained by examining business perspectives on the Full Employment Bill of 1945. With the exception of the bill's congressional proponents, business was the most significant voice in the debate over the Full Employment Bill. The business community took a very active role in the congressional and public debates over the bill and to a large extent determined the content of those debates. More important, evidence suggests that business was instrumental in the transformation of the Full Employment Bill to the Employment Act of 1946. However, my investigation reveals that the significance of the Employment Act of 1946, and thus the business voice in shaping macroeconomic policy, is much less certain.

Macroeconomic Goals and Policy as Proposed by the Full Employment Bill of 1945

The Full Employment Bill of 1945 introduced by Senator Murray was a document of approximately 2,000 words and eight sections which declared "full" employment as a national policy goal and described specific policy measures to be taken by the federal government to attain this goal. The bulk of the bill was devoted to specifying the agencies responsible for assuring full employment, as well as the macroeconomic course of action itself. Thus, the Full Employment Bill consisted of three key components: (1) a statement of purpose, (2) a specification of the agencies responsible for implementing macroeconomic policy for the purpose of maintaining full employment and (3) a specification of macroeconomic policy to assure full employment.

The stated purpose of the bill was: "To establish a national policy and program for assuring continuing full employment in a free competitive economy..." Full employment is declared essential to the prosperity and well-being of the nation. The bill also contained an important element of Franklin D. Roosevelt's 1944 Economic Bill of Rights: namely, that full-time employment was the right of all Americans. Further, the bill charged the federal government, in conjunction with business, labor and state and local governments, with the responsibility for maintaining full employment.

In specifying the apparatus for maintaining full employment, the Full Employment Bill of 1945 was clear and precise. The federal government agency primarily responsible for maintaining full employment was the executive branch. The President was to submit to Congress a "National Production and Employment Budget" at the beginning of each regular session. The National Budget was to contain an analysis of current and

332

projected economic conditions for the ensuing fiscal year with particular emphasis on: (1) the size of the labor force, (2) the volume of aggregate investment, both private and government, necessary to fully employ the labor force and (3) the volume of aggregate investment, private and government, that was projected to occur. In addition, the President was charged with the responsibility of specifying whatever programs might be necessary to maintain full employment in the National Budget.

The President's National Budget was to be reviewed by the Joint Committee on the National Budget, an agency consisting of a number of specified members of Congress. The Joint Committee was to report the results of its review and recommendations for appropriate legislation to Congress.

The specification of macroeconomic policy was one of the more remarkable elements of the Full Employment Bill. The bill was most precise in defining the type and extent of macroeconomic policy to be implemented.

The primary policy instrument to be used to assure full employment, as put forth by the Full Employment Bill, was federal government expenditures. The extent to which federal spending programs were to be implemented was determined by the gap between the estimated volume of private and government investment necessary to maintian full employment and the estimated volume of private and government investment actually forthcoming in the ensuing fiscal year. Should a gap be predicted, the federal government was to first promote private investment to fill the gap and then provide whatever direct federal expenditure was necessary to eliminate any shortfall. In a case in which actual aggregate investment was predicted to exceed the level of investment necessary to sustain full employment, programs which reduced either private investment or federal government expenditures were to be implemented to prevent inflation.

While the Full Employment Bill mentioned a number of policy options available to the federal government, it gave paramount attention to the instrument of compensatory spending. Taxation was mentioned only in a list of possible policy areas which the federal government might address--along with monopoly and competition, wages and working conditions, and social security to name a few. No mention was made of monetary policy. And even though the bill stated that the federal government should first implement programs encouraging private investment to correct any estimated investment deficiency, the vast bulk of the bill dealing with macroeconomic policy exclusively addressed federal compensatory spending.

Several other aspects of the Full Employment Bill of 1945 should be noted. A persistent problem throughout the process of drafting the bill, and indeed from the first discussions on postwar economic policy to the present day, was exactly how to define "full employment." The bill never specifically defined full employment. It can be inferred from the document that full employment is a condition characterized by: "the existence at

333

all times of sufficient employment opportunities to enable all Americans ... to freely exercise [their] right ... to useful, remunerative, regular, and full-time employment..." Even this statement, if it does represent the drafters' notion of full employment, is rather vague.

In addition, the Full Employment Bill did not provide any specifics with regard to the federal spending programs. Though seemingly implied, public works projects were mentioned only in a statement declaring that expenditures on public works were to supplement, not displace, private investment. Thus, the bill made clear that federal spending constituted the primary macroeconomic instrument to maintain full employment, but left the specifics of the spending programs to the discretion of the executive branch and Congress.

Thus, the major elements of the Full Employment Bill of 1945 were: (1) the assertation that full-time employment is the right of all Americans, (2) the assertion that the federal government is responsible for assuring full employment, (3) the emphasis on compensatory spending as the primary instrument of macro-economic policy and (4) the proposed apparatus for determining and implementing macroeconomic policy.

Business Perspectives on the Full Employment Bill of 1945

General statements about business perspectives on any issue are difficult for a variety of reasons. The business community consists of many individuals, no two of which share exactly the same view. In addition, the sources of information pertaining to business views are great in number. This study examines a number of important sources. The testimony and letters of business representatives recorded in Congressional hearings constitutes the primary source of information for the study. The views expressed during the Congressional hearings are important because these views directly addressed the contents of the Full Employment Bill and were influential in affecting its outcome. In addition, many business publications were examined for views on the Full Employment Bill in particular and post-war employment in general. These sources provide information from which legitimate conclusions concerning business perspectives on the Full Employment Bill of 1945 can be drawn.

Evidence collected from these sources supports the assertion that business was generally opposed to the Full Employment Bill of 1945. Opposition was by no means unanimous, however, and views varied in both focus and intesity.

With almost no exceptions, business interests strongly concurred with the national goal, however vaguely defined, of full employment. As early as 1942, *Fortune* magazine proposed that full employment was essential to the welfare of the nation and the responsibility of the federal government to assure its attainment [*Fortune*, December 1942]. The Republican party adopted this position in 1944 when, in accepting the nomination for President, Thomas Dewey stated: "We Republicans are agreed that full employment shall be a first objective of national policy"

334,

[Bailey 1980, p. 42]. Business publications and Congressional testimony shows additional agreement.

However, much of the business community was opposed to the Full Employment Bill. In particular, business opposition to the Full Employment Bill was virtually united in its negative view of federal compensatory spending. Though many arguments against the Full Employment Bill were expressed, three surfaced repeatedly.

Perhaps the most spirited objection to the Full Employment Bill was that it represented a clear threat to the autonomy of entrepreneurship. Many felt that extending the responsibilities of the federal government to employment conditions would require the subjugation of autonomous business decision-making to the commands of the federal government. Such an approach to economic stabilization thus spelled a reduction of economic and political freedom for the entrepreneur and business manager. In his testimony before the Senate Committee on Banking and Currency, James L. Donnelly of the Illinois Manufacturers' Association stated:

> Efforts to provide full employment through governmental machinery would eventually and inevitably involve controls over spending, distribution and consumption, which is in effect totalitarian government. [Senate Committee on Banking and Currency; Sept. 18, 1945]

William L. Klietz, Vice-President of the Guaranty Trust Company of New York, expressed the same view:

> Responsibility for full employment should not be assumed by the Federal government, because the implementation of such a policy would inevitably lead to the exercise of powers which would inevitably destroy the free enterprise system. [Senate Hearings on S.380, p. 667]

The same concern is evident from an article in the June 1945 issue of *Nation's Business* titled: "How Free Will Free Enterprise Be?"

Many business opponents of the Full Employment Bill also argued that the pervasive use of compensatory spending would result in greater unemployment by creating an environment less conducive to business growth. These individuals argued that the proper role of the government in economic affairs was to provide regulatory stability and flexibility, which increased spending would undermine. The President of the National Association of Manufacturers, Ira Mosher, testified that the role of the federal government was not to provide a plan to mitigate the problems of unemployment, but to foster conditions which would greatly reduce the likelihood of unemployment [Senate Hearings on S.380, p.

335

405

462]. These conditions included balanced budgets, low taxes, and a regulatory framework which enhanced rather than reduced competition.

Other business members stated that public works projects were by no means a certain cure for unemployment. One of the more articulate individuals to come before the House hearings on the Full Employment Bill was George Terborgh of the Machinery and Allied Products Institute. Terborgh testified: "There is no determinate and predictable relation in practice between a given increase in government spending, whether for public works or otherwise, and the reaction of the economy to it" [House Hearings on H.R. 2202, p. 605].

By resorting to spending policies, Terborgh continued, "we could very well find ourselves financing an inflation instead of full employment [House Hearings on H.R. 2202, p. 605]. A Chamber of Commerce pamphlet also expressed doubt about the efficacy of expenditure programs: "In spite of all the planning for jobs during [the Depression] decade, the results were largely unsatisfactory" [Chamber of Commerce, 1945]. Still others believed that the spending provision of the bill would result in higher taxes, budget deficits, and direct competition with private enterprise and would thus undermine business confidence.

Finally, many business interests opposed to the Full Employment Bill asserted that, even if compensatory spending could eliminate unemployment, the successful implementation of such a policy in practice required inordinate skill in forecasting both the correct timing and magnitude of expenditures in order to maintain full employment without generating inflation. Thus, compensatory spending was not a feasible macroeconomic policy. This view was poignantly stated by Ohio Senator Robert A. Taft during the Senate hearings: "Let us suppose that in May of 1929 someone had asked what would happen during the fall of that year. I dare say that answer would not have come anywhere near what did actually happen" [Senate Hearings on S.380, p. 673].

Thus, while the views of business opposition to the Full Employment Bill of 1945 varied in both content and vigor, the most frequently expressed arguments against the bill concerned: (1) the encroachment of the federal government on entrepreneurial freedom, (2) the increased economic instability resulting from compensatory spending and (3) the preclusion of successful implementation of spending programs due to the extreme difficulty in correctly forecasting the timing and extent of expenditures to maintain full employment.

Not all business interests were opposed to the Full Employment Bill. Also, as in the case of opposing views of the bill, many different views in support of the Full Employment Bill were expressed by members of the business community. Three supporting views were frequently asserted.

Many of those in favor of the Full Employment Bill strongly endorsed the "right to work" clause in the bill. The bill stated: "All Americans able to work and seeking work have the right to useful, remunerative, regular and full-time employment..." The testimony during the Senate hearings by Clarence Avildsen, Chairman of the Board of Republic Drill and Tool

336

Company, is an example of business support for this declaration. Avildsen said that the recognition of the right to work was the basis for any federal government employment policy.

Another prominent view in support of the bill was that the federal government was not only responsible for full employment, but was the only institution capable of assuring it as well. If the right to work was considered a legal right, only the federal government could enforce that right; herein lay its responsibility. This view was expressed in testimony and letters of several business members in the congressional hearings.

Associated with this perspective was the view that business was not and could not be held responsible for full employment. Business expressed unanimous agreement with this position in the congressional hearings and business press. Those in support of the Full Employment Bill believed this was further justification for federal employment policies. F.R. von Windegger, President of the Plaza Bank of St. Louis, expressed this viewpoint well during his Senate testimony:

> The most enlightened business leaders today acknowledge that business alone cannot furnish full employment to all those seeking work. In fact, it is recognized that that is not the main purpose of business. Its main purpose is to make a profit. The furnishing of employment is incidental to the main purpose and dependent on profit. Therefore, full employment being necessary to the continued existence of our economic and political system, and necessary for the general welfare, it becomes incumbent upon the government to take whatever steps are necessary to fill the gap left by private enterprise. [Senate Hearings on S.380, p. 417]

A final point advanced in support of the Full Employment Bill was that the bill would prove beneficial to business. The proponents of this view thus did not consider the bill a threat to their autonomy. Harry W. Schacter, President of the Kentucky Merchants Association, said: "Of all the groups in this country, it seems to me that business has the greatest stake in full employment" [Senate Hearings on S.380, p. 401]. He added later: "It is clearly recognized that from the standpoint of enlightened self-interest, business has most to gain, profitwise, in having full employment in an expanding economy" [Senate Hearings on S.380, p. 402]. Senator Murray and his cohorts stressed that government would embark on expenditure programs only when necessary and as a last resort. Supporters of the Full Employment Bill interpreted the document in this way, and thus believed that in providing full employment, the government would in turn be providing much needed stability to the economy.

Thus, those in business who supported the Full Employment Bill of 1945 asserted that the bill recognized the federal government's responsi-

337

bility to enforce the "right to work" and thus maintain full employment and that passage of the bill was in the best interests of business.

Macroeconomic Goals and Policy as Proposed by the Employment Act of 1946

As a result of the lengthy debate in the congressional hearings and some involved negotiation among legislators, the Full Employment Bill was transformed into the Employment Act of 1946. The Employment Act of 1946 was passed easily in both the House and Senate and signed into law by President Truman on February 20, 1946.

The Employment Act of 1946 is a very different document than the Full Employment Bill of 1945. While the Full Employment Bill consisted of a bold statement of purpose which included the "right to work" clause, relatively detailed rules concerning macroeconomic policy which clearly embraced compensatory spending and detailed sections on the agencies charged with executing macroeconomic policy, the Employment Act was much less ambitious.

The Employment Act contained no "right to work" clause and no specific statements about macroeconomic policy. The technical rules concerning compensatory expenditure programs so conspicuous in the Full Employment Bill were absent. Indeed, the Employment Act of 1946 makes no reference to any specific macroeconomic policy instrument, including government expenditure. Further, the Employment Act mentioned several goals of macroeconomic policy, of which employment was given no special emphasis outside of the title of the bill.

The macroeconomic goals and policy "rules" are presented entirely in Section 2 of the Employment Act:

> The Congress hereby declares that it is the continuing policy and responsibility of the Federal Government to use all practicable means consistent with its needs and obligations and other essential considerations of national policy, with the assistance and cooperation of industry, agriculture, labor, and state and local governments, to coordinate and utilize all its plans, functions and resources for the purpose of creating and maintaining, in a manner calculated to foster and promote free competitive enterprise and the general welfare, conditions under which there will be afforded useful employment opportunities, including self-employment, for those able, willing, and seeking to work, and to promote maximum employment, production, and purchasing power.

The remainder of the Employment Act established the Economic Report of the President, the Council of Economic Advisors (CEA) and the Joint Committee on the Economic Report as elements of the economic

338

policy-making process. The President, the CEA and the Joint Committee were charged with the responsibility of monitoring the economy and keeping the Congress informed of its general direction, as well as any prospective policy initiatives.

The Employment Act of 1946 was thus a weaker document that its precursor, the Full Employment Bill of 1945. Though the Employment Act did not rule out compensatory spending, it placed no more emphasis on that particular policy option than any other policy option. In addition, full employment was not the primary goal of macroeconomic policy, according to the Employment Act, but rather one of several goals.

Effects of the Business Voice on Macroeconomic Policy

From its introduction to Congress, the Full Employment Bill of 1945 was controversial. It was vigorously debated by a number of individuals and interests. We have seen that business, in general, was opposed to the bill. In addition, the Full Employment Bill was substantially revised over the course of the legislative process, with several of its most significant features eliminated. It was not the Full Employment Bill which became law, but a much less powerful Employment Act of 1946.

This study now turns to two questions: (1) how significant was the business voice in the transformation of the Full Employment Bill of 1945 to the Employment Act of 1946 and (2) if the business voice played a significant role in this transformation, did it play a significant role in affecting the course of U.S. macro-economic policy.

Determining the relative significance of the business voice in the transformation of the Full Employment Bill is a subtle and difficult task, for business was not alone in its dissent. In addition, members of Congress, though constrained by the sentiments of their constituents, exercise views shaped by their own personal perspectives of the world. However, evidence suggests that business had a significant impact on the transformation of the Full Employment Bill.

Public opinion did not play a large role in the debate over the Full Employment Bill. While several public opinion polls indicated that a significant majority of people favored the notion of federal government assurance of full employment, they also indicate little awareness that such legislation was the subject of debate in Congress [Bailey 1980, p. 180]. A poll taken in the second congressional district in Illinois during July 1945 indicated that eight percent of the respondents had heard of the Full Employment Bill and knew what it was [Bailey 1980, p. 181]. Appeals by President Truman and other members of Congress generated little response [Bailey, p. 181]. Thus, public opinion appears to have been a neutral element in the debate over the Full Employment Bill.

Of the interests opposed to the bill, evidence suggests that the business voice was the most vigorous. The vast majority of individuals testifying in opposition to the bill during the congressional hearings were affiliated with business interests. The same is true of letters appended to

339

the Senate hearings document. In light of Bailey's assertion that many in business declined to testify publicly due to Senator Murray's aggressive treatment of those opposed to the bill, the business voice is all the more significant [Bailey 1980, p. 105].

A number of business organizations conducted substantial lobbying efforts to defeat the Full Employment Bill as well. Two of the most active of these organizations were the National Association of Manufacturers and the Chamber of Commerce of the U.S. Both organizations published several pamphlets denouncing government policy initiatives proposed by the bill. Letters plus newspaper and radio advertisements were used extensively.

Perhaps most significant, however, is the fact that the revisions made to the Full Employment Bill were those most desired by business. Business strongly objected to government infringement upon entrepreneurial autonomy and was very skeptical of the efficacy of compensatory spending and the ability of individuals or agencies to forecast economic conditions. They also argued that a high level of employment was only one of several important national economic goals. These were the primary areas in which the Employment Act of 1946 contained no "right to work" clause. Nor did it place any special emphasis on compensatory spending as a macroeconomic policy tool; rules concerning the mechanics of conducting compensatory expenditure programs, of which forecasting plays such an important part, were absent from the Employment Act. In addition, Employment Act of 1946 listed several national economic goals other than "maximum employment."

Business opposition to the Full Employment Bill was not completely successful, of course: an employment bill was enacted into law, after all. However, the strength of the business voice and how the bill was revised suggest that business significantly affected the transformation.

Since the Employment Act of 1946 is considered by many to be the "Magna Carta of the American economy" [Stein 1969, p. 199], such a conclusion would seem to indicate that the business voice thereby significantly affected the course of U.S. macroeconomic policy. This latter assertion is not at all obvious, however.

An extensive investigation of the course of government involvement in the U.S. economy is far beyond the scope of this paper. However, much evidence suggests to this author that the Employment Act of 1946 was consistent with the evolution of the federal government's role in the macroeconomy over the 75 years prior to the enactment of the bill. From "Munn v. Illinois" to the New Deal, the federal government's involvement in the economy grew from a regulatory nature to a much more active participation. Nonmarket, bureaucratic decision-making and organization had been tested in World War I, the Great Depression, and World War II.

The advent of Keynesian economics gave further momentum to this evolution. Keynesian economics provided theoretical justification for active government intervention in the economy. By the end of World War

340

II, many U.S. economists and policy-makers had become advocates of the Keynesian approach.

The primary significance of the Employment Act of 1946 is generally thought to be its explicit statement that the federal government was henceforth responsible for the state of the economy. Yet by 1946 the federal government had already assumed responsibility for much economic life. Thus, the Employment Act of 1946 does not represent a new direction in national economic policy, but rather the progression of a well-established trend.

Had the Full Employment Bill of 1945, as introduced, became law, national economic policy may well have taken a new direction. Herein lies the influence of business interests on U.S. macroeconomic policy. However, the Employment Act of 1946 did not by any means rule out activist macroeconomic policy.

In fact, during the first recessions after World War II, the federal government implemented activist countercylical policies. During the mild recession of 1948-49, a tax reduction bill, the Revenue Act of 1948, became law over President Truman's veto. Truman vetoed the bill due to concern over inflation. Significantly, the conflict between the President and Congress was not about activist policy, but whether inflation or recession was the more pressing problem. The macroeconomic policy of the Eisenhower administration during the recession beginning in 1953 is a more graphic example of activist government. The Republican President responded to this economic contraction with accelerated federal expenditures, including public works [Lewis 1962, p. 168].

Thus, while business was instrumental in the process of transforming the Full Employment Bill into a much less ambitious Employment Act of 1946, it was not able to halt the trend of an increasingly active role of the federal government in the economy.

NOTES

1. Bailey, Stephen K. *Congress Makes A Law*. Westport, CT: Greenwood Press, 1980 (reprint).
2. Chamber of Commerce of the United States of America. "A Program for Sustaining Employment." Wash., D.C.; 1945.
3. House of Representatives Committee on Expenditures in the Executive Departments. Full Employment Act of 1945: Hearings on H.R. 2202. 79th Cong., 1st Sess., 1945.
4. Hughes, Jonathon R.T. *The Governmental Habit*. New York: Basic Books, Inc., 1977.
5. Lewis, Wilfred. *Federal Fiscal Policy in the Postwar Recessions*. Washington: The Brookings Institution, 1962.
6. *Nation's Business*: "How Free Will Free Enterprise Be?" June 1945.

341

7. Senate Committee on Banking and Currency. "Assuring Full Employment in a Free Competitive Economy." Senate Subcommittee Print. 79th Cong., 1st Sess.; Sept. 18, 1945.

8. Senate Committee on Banking and Currency. Full Employment Act of 1945: Hearings on S.380. 79th Cong., 1st Sess., 1945; p. 667.

9. Stein, Herbert. *The Fiscal Revolution in America*. Chicago: University of Chicago Press, 1969.

10. U.S. Congress Bill. S.380: Full Employment Act of 1945.

342

ACKNOWLEDGMENTS

Arnold, Thurman W. "The Emperor's Old Clothes: III. The Folklore of Capitalism Revisited." *Yale Review* 52 (1962): 188–204. Courtesy of Yale University Law Library.

Bishop, John C. "Delivering the Goods by Air: The United States Air-Cargo Industry, 1945–1955." *Essays in Economic and Business History* 8 (1990): 40–45. Reprinted with the permission of the University of Southern California, Department of History. Courtesy of the University of Southern California, Department of History.

Brune, Lester H. "Guns and Butter: The Pre-Korean War Dispute over Budget Allocations." *American Journal of Economics and Sociology* 48 (1989): 357–71. Reprinted with the permission of the *American Journal of Economics and Sociology*. Courtesy of Yale University Sterling Memorial Library.

Freitag, Peter J. "The Myth of Corporate Capture: Regulatory Commissions in the United States." *Social Problems* 30 (1983): 480–91. Reprinted with the permission of the University of California Press. Copyright 1983 by the Society for the Study of Social Problems. Courtesy of Yale University Sterling Memorial Library.

Freyer, Tony. "The American Revival of Antitrust: Theories of Efficiency Versus Republican Values, 1948–1968." In *Regulating Big Business: Antitrust in Great Britain and America, 1880–1990* (New York, NY: Cambridge University Press, 1992): 298–310. Reprinted with the permission of Cambridge University Press. Courtesy of Yale University Sterling Memorial Library.

Hofstadter, Richard. "What Happened to the Antitrust Movement? Notes on the Evolution of an American Creed." In Earl F. Cheit, ed., *The Business Establishment* (New York: Wiley, 1964): 113–51. Reprinted with the permission of the copyright holder. Courtesy of Yale University Cross Campus Library.

Kaufman, Burton I. "Oil and Antitrust: The Oil Cartel Case and the Cold War." *Business History Review* 51 (1977): 35–56.

Reprinted with the permission of the Harvard Business School. Courtesy of Yale University Sterling Memorial Library.

Kovaleff, Theodore P. "The Antitrust Record of the Eisenhower Administration." *Antitrust Bulletin* 21 (1976): 589–610. Reprinted with the permission of Federal Legal Publications, Inc. Courtesy of Yale University Law Library.

McFadyen, Richard E. "The FDA's Regulation and Control of Antibiotics in the 1950s: The Henry Welch Scandal, Félix Martí Ibáñez, and Charles Pfizer & Co." *Bulletin of the History of Medicine* 53 (1979): 159–69. Reprinted with the permission of Johns Hopkins University Press. Courtesy of Johns Hopkins University Press.

Mazuzan, George T. "Conflict of Interest: Promoting and Regulating the Infant Nuclear Power Industry, 1954–1956." *Historian* 44 (1981): 1–14. Reprinted with the permission of the International Honor Society in History. Courtesy of Yale University Sterling Memorial Library.

Nelson, James C. "A Critique of Governmental Intervention in Transport." In John W. Fuller, ed., *Regulation and Competition in Transportation: Selected Works of James C. Nelson* (Vancouver: The Centre for Transportation Studies, University of British Columbia, 1983): 371–404. Reprinted with the permission of the Rand Corporation. Courtesy of Yale University Law Library.

Nelson, James C. "Improving the Efficiency of the Transportation and Utilities Systems: Effects of Public Regulation on Railroad Performance." *American Economic Review* 50 (1960): 495–505. Courtesy of Yale University Law Library.

Newmark, Craig M. "Does Horizontal Price Fixing Raise Price? A Look at the Bakers of Washington Case." *Journal of Law and Economics* 31 (1988): 469–84. Reprinted with the permission of the University of Chicago Press. Courtesy of Yale University Law Library.

Pratt, Joseph A. "Growth or a Clean Environment? Responses to Petroleum-Related Pollution in the Gulf Coast Refining Region." *Business History Review* 52 (1978): 1–29. Reprinted with the permission of the Harvard Business School. Courtesy of Yale University Sterling Memorial Library.

Prindle, David F. "The Texas Railroad Commission and the Elimination of the Flaring of Natural Gas, 1930–1949." *Southwestern Historical Quarterly* 84 (1981): 293–308. Reprinted with the permission of The Texas State Historical Association. Courtesy of The Texas State Historical Association.

Saletan, Elma M. "Administrative Trustification." *Western Political Quarterly* 11 (1958): 857–74. Courtesy of Yale University Sterling Memorial Library.

Simpson, Sally S. "Cycles of Illegality: Antitrust Violations in Corporate America." *Social Forces* 65 (1987): 943–63. Reprinted from *Social Forces*. Copyright The University of North Carolina Press. Courtesy of *Social Forces*.

Songer, Donald R. "The Impact of the Supreme Court on Trends in Economic Policy Making in the United States Courts of Appeals." *Journal of Politics* 49 (1987): 830–41. Reprinted from the *Journal of Politics*, by permission of the author and the University of Texas Press. Courtesy of Yale University Sterling Memorial Library.

Stocking, George W. "Economic Change and the Sherman Act: Some Reflections on 'Workable Competition.'" *Virginia Law Review* 44 (1958): 537–82. Courtesy of Yale University Law Library.

Tiffany, Paul A. "The Roots of Decline: Business-Government Relations in the American Steel Industry, 1945–1960." *Journal of Economic History* 44 (1984): 407–19. Reprinted with the permission of Cambridge University Press. Courtesy of Yale University Sterling Memorial Library.

Yalung-Mathews, Don. "Business Perspectives on the Full Employment Bill of 1945 and Passage of the Employment Act of 1946." *Essays in Economic and Business History* 8 (1990): 331–42. Reprinted with the permission of the University of Southern California, Department of History. Courtesy of the University of Southern California, Department of History.